PRACTICAL
DATA DESIGN

PRACTICAL
DATA DESIGN

Michael H. Brackett

PRENTICE HALL, Englewood Cliffs, New Jersey 07632

Library of Congress Cataloging-in-Publication Data

Brackett, Michael H.
    Practical data design / Michael H. Brackett.
        p.   cm.
    Bibliography: p.
    Includes index.
    ISBN 0-13-690827-6
    1. Data base design.   I. Title.
QA76.9.D26B73   1990
005.74--dc20   89-15938
                                                CIP

Editorial/production supervision
  and interior design: **Brendan M. Stewart**
Cover design: **Wanda Lubelska**
Manufacturing buyer: **Mary Ann Gloriande**

©1990 by Prentice-Hall, Inc.
A Division of Simon & Schuster
Englewood Cliffs, New Jersey 07632

This book can be made available to businesses
and organizations at a special discount when
ordered in large quantities. For more information
contact:

Prentice-Hall, Inc.
Special Sales and Markets
College Division
Englewood Cliffs, N.J. 07632

Printed in the United States of America

10 9 8 7 6 5 4 3 2 1

ISBN 0-13-690827-6

Prentice-Hall International (UK) Limited, *London*
Prentice-Hall of Australia Pty. Limited, *Sydney*
Prentice-Hall Canada Inc., *Toronto*
Prentice-Hall Hispanoamericana, S.A., *Mexico*
Prentice-Hall of India Private Limited, *New Delhi*
Prentice-Hall of Japan, Inc., *Tokyo*
Simon & Schuster Asia Pte. Ltd., *Singapore*
Editora Prentice-Hall do Brasil, Ltda., *Rio de Janeiro*

To my mother

Contents

CHAPTER TEN   **Data Attributes and Values**   **185**

CHAPTER ELEVEN   **Data Structures**   **204**

CHAPTER TWELVE   **Data Integrity**   **230**

Foreword

We can effectively use only that which we understand. Most executives of corporations have not understood computing, data processing, or information processing whatever it may be called in their organizations. Thus they do not consider it a useful, much less a strategic tool. On the contrary it is frequently treated as a necessary evil, tolerated but not utilized. In many enterprises data processing is an isolated cult-like organization surrounded with myth and mystery, promising the moon in future capability but rarely delivering on the basics today. Executives feel a need to place blind trust in data technology because they are led to believe they could never understand its complexity. The time has come to take the myth and mystery out of data processing.

This book, *Practical Data Design,* does just that. The book illustrates over and over again the need to understand and manage a corporation's data. The book is written from the enterprise's point of view; its organization, management and business entities. All have a natural interdependence on one another and a significant dependence on data. More importantly this book provides a framework for technicians and lay persons alike to address issues related to how data are organized and used in an enterprise. Thus the problem is not only eloquently described but the solution is clearly presented.

Many enterprises today attempt to overlay new technologies on old tired organizations totally ignoring the biblical admonition against putting new wine into old wineskins. The pressing need for quick solutions lead many executives to accept new technologies without careful planning. The result all too often is that inefficiencies are automated, problems compounded and the state of data confusion increased. Chaos is a word frequently used in this book to describe the current state of many corporations.

The process described in this book attempts to correct this severely flawed procedure with a straightforward methodology that integrates the enterprise, its people and business entities with its data. It is a process that all can participate in and understand. No longer do we need to depend on the blind trust of the past. The emphasis is on the data not the applications. The basic premise is that if the data of an enterprise are properly organized to support the business activities of the enterprise then applications can flow quite naturally and moreover can be readily changed to meet the changing needs of the enterprise.

We have done just that at Washington State University with dramatic results. The practical data design techniques are used for all applications development and the corporate database. The end users are directly involved. They participate in the design and development process, not only providing insight and information but truly making decisions on design from a position of knowledge and understanding. Nothing is lost in the translation of requirements from the user to the technician because no translation is necessary. Everyone speaks the same language.

The users at Washington State University who have been involved with this process for some time understand the methodology so well that they apply it to their operations and thus revise many of their business practices to achieve new efficiencies. They become so comfortable with the techniques that they use them to communicate with other departments about proposed changes to business procedures unrelated to data processing. It is an exciting phenomena to watch as former frightened and timid users become enthusiastic practitioners of the new technology.

Practical Data Design and other Computer-Assisted Software Engineering (CASE) tools have allowed data processing professionals at Washington State University to constantly exceed the expectation of users and management, a vast improvement over the previous situation of promise upon promise, and schedule revision after schedule revision as a result of constant overselling of the technology to the user with the concomitant lack of understanding.

We have seen similar success stories in large corporations. We all know the classic and much cited examples of corporations which have achieved a competitive edge with the strategic application of information technology. Corporations such as American Hospital Supply (now Baxter Healthcare Corporation), Federal Express, and American Airlines immediately come to mind. We can readily assume that other corporations will quickly follow the example set by these companies in order to compete on an equal basis. Those that do not surely face problems of continued viability.

From a futuristic point of view the ideas developed by Professor Gareth Morgan in his book *Images of Organization* clearly indicate that the future will demand greater reliance on data and information technology. Professor Morgan draws on research of the brain as an information processor to project how organizations might be formed and self-reorganized in the future. Mr. Brackett's constant emphasis on a well structured database as the foundation for an organization that is going to be readily adaptable to change runs very close to professor Morgan's observations on the possibilities of self-reorganization. Artificial intelligence and expert systems applied to the corporate database are just the beginning.

Practical Data Design is a tool to lead us into the future. Its beauty is in the fact that it is indeed practical. It is not an abstract idea or the product of basic research, but a process that has worked in practice. *Practical Data Design* is not a quick fix that will solve all problems with bad data or organization over night. It is indeed a long process but a very fruitful one with many unexpected payoffs. The key is that this technology can be understood by managers and executives so that these individuals can make knowledgeable decisions and commitments. In all the examples cited above top management commitment was key to success. The results will surprise you and very large benefits can be realized quite early in the process.

Dr. Thomas J. Mueller, Director
Systems & Computing
Washington State University

Preface

Can data be designed?

The answer is a resounding yes. Data can be designed the same as buildings, cars, airplanes, and most anything else we encounter, are designed. Some designs are better than others and some designs are more useful than others, but, generally, things that are designed are better than things that are not designed. This applies to data, and data that are designed are better than data that are not designed.

Design is both a verb and a noun. As a verb, *design* means to conceive and plan out in the mind, to devise for a specific function, to draw plans, create, fashion, and construct something according to a plan, to conceive a plan, a preliminary sketch, or an outline showing the main features of something to be constructed, and to deliberately plan with a purpose. As a noun, *design* refers to the plan, to an underlying scheme that governs the functioning of something, and to the arrangement of elements in something. In this case the something that is designed and constructed is a data resource for an enterprise.

The problems with conventional data are that they are not well designed. Conventional data were designed by concepts in effect at the time they were designed. However, those concepts have changed and conventional data are not well designed by today's concepts. The structure of conventional data is oriented to the structure of applications processing those data and there is a close relationship between applications and their application files. There is a high degree of data ownership and very little sharing of data between applications. In addition, most data are not well named or defined and are not properly documented. Documentation that does exist is not always readily accessible or easily interpreted. Data integrity is low because data edits are incomplete and inconsistently applied by a variety of applications.

The impact of these problems is substantial. There is limited availability of data because the data needed can not be easily identified or accessed. Data redundancy is high and these redundant data often have conflicting values. The variety of different data structures and the existence of redundant data make access to conventional data very difficult and prevents data being readily shared. There is a loss of credibility that leads people to create their own databases which further magnifies the problem. The ultimate impact is poor decisions, wrong actions, and loss of productivity.

To resolve these problems a totally different approach must be taken. Data must be managed as a separate and distinct resource of the enterprise. The data resource must be structured separate from the structure of business activities and separate from the organizational structure of the enterprise. The data resource must be enterprise-wide and structured by data subject-based on entities being managed by the enterprise. Each data unit must be formally named, comprehensively described, and formally documented in a location that is readily accessible by anyone in the enterprise. Comprehensive data integrity rules must be defined and consistently enforced on all data in the data resource.

The benefits of an enterprise-wide subject data resource are substantial. Data are easily identified and readily accessed, and are shared by many applications. The data have high integrity and credibility and the data resource improves. Good decisions are made, the correct actions are taken, and productivity is increased. Most of all, the enterprise can become more responsive to changing needs for information in a rapidly changing business environment.

The change from conventional data to an enterprise data resource is not easy to make, but it is not impossible. It requires a conceptual and cultural change by people in the enterprise and a commitment by everyone in the enterprise to make that change. Most enterprises have a critical need for high quality data to support their business activities in a very dynamic business environment. The only way to meet this need is to design an enterprise-wide subject data resource and convert conventional data to that data resource.

This design effort requires careful planning and coordination and involvement of everyone in the enterprise. Practical design techniques must be available that are easy to understand, but those techniques must be sound and must produce a structurally stable data resource that is flexible enough to the changing information needs of the enterprise. That's what this book is all about.

The book begins with an explanation of the need to design data and the importance of managing data as a resource of the enterprise. Information technology as a discipline for the information age is explained and the relationship between the data resource component and other components of information technology is described. Basic data design concepts are presented for designing an enterprise-wide data resource. The four-schema concept is introduced and management of data and business activity objects is described. The dynamic business environment and the use of business design models to model that environment are presented, followed by presentation of models for designing the data resource.

With this foundation, the process of formally naming and comprehensively defining both basic and abstract data units is explained. The identification and use of data keys is presented, followed by an explanation of data relations and the use of data keys and data relations to enter and navigate through the data resource to store and retrieve data. The processes of normalizing, optimizing, and denormalizing data to support the four-schema concept are described. These techniques are used to identify and define the basic data units that form the framework of the enterprise's data resource. Data structures are presented as the working tool for defining data needs and designing the data resource to meet those needs.

The procedure for defining a comprehensive set of data integrity rules is presented to assure high quality data. Techniques for maintaining current, accurate documentation of all components of the data resource are provided. Emphasis is placed on making this documentation available to anyone in the enterprise that is interested in the data resource. The importance of readily available data is explained and techniques for decentralizing data to improve data availability are described.

Techniques are introduced for converting conventional data to the enterprise's data resource without impacting business operations. Finally, all of these techniques are combined into a method for developing an enterprise-wide data resource. The method includes strategic, retrofit, project, and ad hoc data resource modeling that provides a solid framework for the data resource and allows it to evolve in a consistent manner to meet the enterprise's information needs. The method emphasizes design before construction and design techniques emphasize modeling. Design models are integrated to provide a continuum through the entire sequence from business environment modeling to database implementation.

Design techniques are explained in each chapter and are summarized at the end of each chapter. Basic principles and techniques are highlighted to emphasize their importance. Numerous examples are provided to illustrate use of the techniques and bad practices to avoid. Design techniques are based on theory, but are presented in practical terms that make them easy to apply by data processing personnel and users alike. Direct involvement of users in design of an enterprise-wide data resource is encouraged to assure that data resource meets the business needs of the enterprise.

The design techniques are oriented to design of the data resource. Business environment modeling and design of business activities is not within the scope of this book. However, enough business modeling techniques are presented to show how the business environment and the needs of the enterprise drive development of the enterprise's data resource. There is no derivation of mathematical theory, nor is there any discussion of database management systems or operating environments. There is no discussion of management or organizational issues regarding the data resource or information technology. The design techniques are oriented toward taking the mystery out of designing a data resource for the enterprise.

The book could have been titled *Practical Information Design, Practical Knowledge Design,* or *Practical Database Design,* but data are the problem. If data are properly designed, the physical database, and information and knowledge that are derived from data, will be properly designed. The book could have been titled *Practical Database Modeling* or *Practical Database Development,* but it is not the design of physical databases that is critical. It is design of an enterprise-wide data resource that is critical. The book could have been oriented toward concept or theory, but it is the practical techniques based on those concepts and theories that are used to design the data resource.

These practical data design techniques encourage development and management of an enterprise-wide data resource for the benefit of the enterprise. They ease the cultural change to a new concept by providing a practical view of the new concepts. They produce short term results with long term benefits. They reduce the formidable task of designing a data resource to a task that is achievable. The result is a stable data resource that provides an early return on the investment and supports the enterprise in a dynamic business environment.

Yes, data can be designed.

Acknowledgments

The author thanks Mike Stein and Jon Daisey for their constant emphasis on the importance of a formal physical database design following the logical database design and their thoughts on the physical design of databases. The author thanks Jim Littlefield for his continued emphasis on current documentation and the use of information resource directories for the storage and retrieval of documentation. The author also thanks Dave Brandes and Gordon Abshire for their profound interest in data design and their continued encouragement to complete the book.

Thanks also go to Dave Gibney for constantly looking deeper into data design to find better solutions, to Lavon Frasier for her insight and intuition into the retro-documentation process and development of retrofit data models, to Gunjun Sinha for identifying real-world problems with data design and suggesting solutions to those problems, to Darrell Davenport for his insight into fourth gencration languages and database access, and to Jon D'Aleo for his practical philosophy and perception in the face of adversity. Thanks is extended to Leon Stucki of Future Tech, Inc., for the use of Envisions to develop many of the initial diagrams for this book.

Special thanks go to Tom Crawford for his constructive criticisms and suggestions about the process of designing data to meet the needs of an enterprise. Special thanks also go to Dr. Tom Mueller for his constant emphasis on the social and business side of data design and his emphasis on awareness training and involvement of users in managing their own data.

chapter one

The Need To Design Data

Data must be designed so they can be managed as a resource to support the enterprise's goals in a dynamic business environment.

Why design data?

This is the most frequently asked question regarding data. Data **can** be designed, but **why** should data be designed? What will a good data design do for the enterprise? How will the enterprise benefit from well designed data? The answer is that well designed data form a stable base for an enterprise to effectively manage change and be competitive in a changing business environment.

Change is an inherent and inevitable characteristic of society. Nearly all segments of society are constantly undergoing change and the interactions resulting from change stagger the imagination. Some changes are more rapid than others, some are more irregular, some are of greater magnitude, and some cause a greater impact. But, they all contribute to a constantly changing society. The business environment is one of the most rapidly changing segments of society. It is extremely dynamic and the rate of change is increasing at an alarming rate. Each new wave of change is of greater magnitude and has a greater impact on the enterprise than the previous wave.

There are two basic modes of change in society. Evolutionary changes are those that occur gradually and make nonviolent modifications. Revolutionary changes usually occur very quickly, are very complete and often radical, are accomplished by forceful means, and usually involve changes in government. The changes in the business environment occur rapidly, result in nearly complete change, but are not accomplished by forceful means, and do not involve changes in government. The term **mevolution** is used for defining change that is midway between evolution and revolution. Mevolution is what most enterprises are facing today. They must prepare for change, manage change to their advantage, and plan for survival in the face of change.

INFORMATION TECHNOLOGY TRENDS

Information technology has changed from the first days when data processing became popular to today's environment of artificial intelligence. The emergence of data processing initiated the first wave of the information age with automated transaction processing. It produced numerous changes in technology that had profound impacts on society and the business environment. That wave has been followed by a second wave of artificial intelligence that promises to be even more dynamic.

In the 1950s and early 1960s data processing supported the corporate level of the enterprise and was oriented toward transaction processing of central business functions. Since computers were relatively expensive and people were relatively inexpensive, the computer was reserved for business functions that were critical to the enterprise. There were minimal networks for transmitting data, data were stored in a central location, and security was implied by batch processing.

Data formed relatively finite and distinct sets and each set belonged to one critical business function. Data were stored in application files that were closely tied to applications supporting critical business functions and access to those files was hard coded in each application. The data files were structured according to the application's need and the user "owned" the data simply by owning the application that maintained and used data files. There was minimal, if any, sharing of data between applications and users.

In this environment users knew little or nothing about the design of applications or data files. Data processing personnel were the technical wizards that seemed to come through at the eleventh hour or make clever technical excuses why they couldn't. However, this situation was tolerated because people were relatively inexpensive compared to hardware and computer literacy was relatively low.

In the 1960s and early 1970s data processing migrated to the department level and supported more business activities. Additional business applications were developed in relative isolation and only became semi-integrated through feeds and bridges between applications. Business applications became larger and more detailed, hardware became less expensive, people became more expensive, and computer literacy increased.

Data sets supporting these new applications were not as finite or distinct. Data were becoming common between two or more applications, largely through the process of extracting data from existing files, sorting them into the desired order, and merging them into new files. Accesses to data files were still hard coded in applications and ownership of the data was still maintained by the owner of the application. However, large amounts of redundant data were being created.

Maintenance of redundant data required either feeds between applications or replicated data capture, editing, and storage. Regardless of the method used and the level of control, the data in different application files did not coincide and represented multiple versions of reality. This situation was the beginning of many database problems that plague managers and users today.

Development of application files through the extract, sort, and merge process, began to show the benefits of data views. Each application file was actually a data view of the enterprise's data even though there was no formal enterprise data model. However, data redundancy problems overshadowed the benefits of sharing enterprise data through data views. The data ownership controversy became intense in some enterprises as each user of data claimed to be owner of that data and wanted to be the one that controlled the capture, entry, and updating of the data they used.

In the early 1970s database management systems emerged to resolve the data redundancy and hard coded access problems. They provided a central database, reduced redundant data by storing each piece of data in one place, reduced maintenance by moving the data file access logic from applications to the database management system, and provided unique data views for each application. The concept of data independence was established where the structure of data in the database was independent of the structure of the application using the data. Either structure could change with minimal impact on the other.

In the 1980s information systems include business strategies for a competitive business environment. Critical success factors are identified for an enterprise and innovative and creative information systems are being developed to maintain a competitive edge. The explosion of personal computers, user friendly applications, inexpensive hardware, and computer literacy have carried the computer to each employee for support of their business activities. Users can now have their data and processing done when they need it, where they need it, at a reasonable cost. However, along with these benefits, there is an increased chance of misinterpreted data, high maintenance load, orphan systems, redundantly developed applications, and additional redundant data.

Communication networks are prominent and data now exist at many locations in many different databases. Decentralized processing and databases are becoming common and file servers are being used to move data from a database to a workstation for processing. Database servers are emerging to manipulate data from the database and send the results to a workstation and ad hoc inquiry is becoming routine. Computer literacy is widespread and information technology is supporting all levels of the enterprise.

Artificial intelligence is emerging as expert systems, robotics for locomotion and manipulatory skills, natural language processing, image processing, and the ability to think and learn at least as fast as people do. Expert systems are the most advanced part of artificial intelligence and show the most promise for immediate support of business needs in an enterprise. Robotics is the next most advanced part, but at present robots are largely fancy machines compared to their ultimate potential. With the addition of good expert systems, robotics will become a major asset to an enterprise. Natural language processing includes both speech recognition and response and is currently facing the problems inherent in natural languages. Image processing includes the ability to have vision and to recognize images, which presently requires tremendous processing capability and extremely large databases. The ability to think and learn at least as fast as people is the most controversial aspect of artificial intelligence.

Expert systems require large amounts of data and extensive processing of that data. Data must be represented, stored, and accessed similar to the way people store, access, and use data. This requires a model of the knowledge base showing the decisions to be made, the expertise to make those decisions, and the data required to support that expertise. The problem with developing good expert systems is not the expert system itself, but the acquisition of data that are more complex than the data in conventional applications. Business and technical rules need to be determined to form a good knowledge base. These rules must be obtained from experts in the field, including business managers and technical personnel.

THE CURRENT DATA ENVIRONMENT

Information technology has provided many benefits to society and will continue to provide benefits. However, it has created problems that still exist today and these problems limit the future benefits of information technology if they are not resolved. One of the major problems that must be resolved is the structure and organization of an enterprise's data. These data problems must be corrected to allow information technology to be used to its full advantage.

One major data problem is application files that are structured by an application's need for data not by data subject. Applications are designed to process business transactions and those transactions contain data from several data subjects. Since the same data subject appears in many different business transactions, a data subject is fragmented and stored in many different application files. This multiple storage of the same data is the origin of data redundancy.

> Applications span data subjects causing fragmentation of data and data redundancy.

A related problem is the variety of dissimilar data structures that exist in application files. Since data are stored according to an application's need and applications are structured differently, the data in different application files are structured differently. These dissimilar data structures create data interfaces that are difficult to manage. Any attempt to change application data files to subject data files temporarily increases the number of data interfaces that impact business operations. The data interfaces will ultimately be resolved and subject data files will be developed, but the magnitude of the problem prevents many enterprises from attempting to restructure their data.

Data integrity is another major data problem. Redundant data and inconsistent updating of redundant data result in data that do not coincide with reality. Data edits are incomplete and scattered through a variety of applications, and are inconsistently applied to the same data in different application files which further magnifies the problem. The result is a loss of credibility of the data.

> Data edits are incomplete, fragmented between applications, and inconsistently applied to all data.

Most data lack good naming conventions and good definitions. Many definitions that do exist are not properly documented or readily available. Undefined data that exist in many redundant forms, scattered throughout many application files in many locations, in many dissimilar data structures, are not readily available. Any attempt to select useful data from this environment results in different people selecting different data, making the wrong decisions, and taking the wrong actions.

> Data are poorly named, defined, and documented.

Maintenance of applications that have hard-coded data accesses to application files is a major problem. Any change in the structure of a data file, such as new data elements, results in changes to all applications accessing that file. This maintenance load contributes substantially to the backlog that is common today.

Another problem is the lack of knowledge about the business activities of the enterprise. Many people do not thoroughly know or understand business activities and business rules. The business activities and business rules must be formally defined and consistently applied for the business activities to be correctly performed. Automating unclear business activities based on undefined business rules magnifies the data problems.

End users are facing the same types of change that the information processing staff has been facing for a long time. End user computing leads to improved productivity in the short term but ultimately leads to a backlog of software and hardware maintenance. Changing technology and the changing business environment create the same backlogs in the user area that were created in information processing departments. They also lead to undocumented and orphan applications which will be "dumped" back to the information processing staff.

Rapid solutions to these problems only create additional problems. Fast-track modeling, rapid requirements definition, rapid prototyping, and CASE tools appear to quickly solve problems. However, a quick solution without a method or a plan only creates additional problems faster than conventional methods. These techniques have their place when the proper method has been set, but they can be severely abused without a good method and sound plans.

MANAGING DATA AS A RESOURCE

The basic problem with the current environment is that data are not managed as a separate and distinct resource of the enterprise. The critical nature of data has not been recognized by many enterprises. Data have been treated as pieces of applications that are manipulated to meet application needs and have not been managed as a resource to support enterprise goals. The result is redundant data, incorrect data, unnecessary processing to correct the data or access the proper data, and a general unavailability of data to make correct decisions and take proper actions. In many situations good applications are being build on very bad data.

> The basic problem is that data are not managed as a resource and asset of the enterprise.

The basic problem can be resolved by recognizing data as a separate and distinct resource of the enterprise and managing the data resource with the same intensity that other enterprise resources are managed. An enterprise-wide data resource must be defined where data subjects are identified and all data characterizing a subject are put in one place. Conversion to a subject data resource eliminates dissimilar data structures and data needed by an application are available in the form of data views.

> The basic problem can be resolved by recognizing data as a resource and managing it with the same intensity as other resources of the enterprise.

A database management system is an excellent place to store data subjects because it manages accesses to data and provides data views to applications based on their needs. Applications are free of file management tasks and are more flexible to changing business needs of the enterprise. Data redundancy is reduced and changes in data needs are met quicker. Data integrity is improved and the credibility of data increases.

Comprehensive data definitions are developed for each data unit in the data resource and placed in a data dictionary or directory for ready reference. Comprehensive data integrity rules are defined for each data subject and uniformly enforced for all data in the data resource. Data availability is increased because accurate data can be readily identified and quickly located. The correct decisions can be made and the correct actions can be taken.

As these problems are solved, people can concentrate on learning more about the business. Business activities and business rules can be defined and business models can be developed. A sound knowledge base and useful expert systems can be developed for the enterprise. The enterprise can become more responsive to the changing business environment through quick adjustment of its business activities.

The end user problems are reduced by allowing access to the data resource and by managing decentralization of the data. A data resource structured by subject can be easily decentralized to meet the needs of all people in the enterprise without loss of control over the data. Enterprise-level, department-level, and personal-level applications and databases can be defined and integrated to meet the needs of the enterprise. Computer literacy is increased so professionals and para professionals can work together to manage data and applications to support the enterprise's goals.

A formal development method can be implemented that integrates development of business applications and subject data based on the business needs of the enterprise. The data and applications are structured differently and their development is driven by the business needs. Productivity tools can be used to support the development method and productivity increases without creating additional problems.

The change to management of data as a resource results in reduced data redundancy, improved data integrity, reduced application maintenance, better data availability, better response to changing business needs and correct and consistent decisions and actions. People can concentrate on improving business activities and databases can be decentralized throughout the enterprise to support all employees. The enterprise has a more stable base to manage a changing business environment.

Even though it is difficult to change management of data as a resource, the current environment can not be allowed to continue forever. The increased demand for data will be met, either with the existing environment or with a new environment. Using the existing environment increases the problems that already exist and requires a monumental effort to convert to a subject data resource. Converting to a subject data resource provides a structurally stable database that will be flexible to changing business needs. The longer an enterprise waits the more difficult it will be to convert.

There is no way to automatically reorganize the data and adjust all applications using the data. There are no applications or hardware that will take the existing application files, convert them into a subject database, and adjust the applications accordingly. It takes people, planning, thought, and analysis to design and implement an enterprise-wide subject data resource and restructure applications to use that resource.

The database can not be reorganized overnight. It requires an extended period of time to plan a conversion that will not impact the business operations. An enterprise can not cease operations, reorganize their database, adjust their applications to that database, and then begin operations again. The reorganization must be done *on the fly* without impacting business operations. It can be done, but it requires careful planning and a good understanding of the concepts and techniques of managing the data as a resource.

> Reorganizing data takes careful planning and analysis to create an enterprise subject data resource without impacting business operations.

The objective of an enterprise data resource is to get the right data to right people, in the right place, at the right time, in the right form, at the right cost, so they can make the right decision and take the right action. It means putting data in the hands of every person in the enterprise that needs data to perform their business activities. This objective requires that the data, the people, and the business activities be managed as separate resources and integrated to meet the goals of the enterprise.

Enterprises are beginning to view information technology as an investment center rather than a cost center. They are using information technology to strategic advantage to gain or maintain a competitive advantage and as leverage to gain control in the marketplace. Information technology is supporting the mission, goals, and objectives of the enterprise and is critical to the success of the enterprise. This use of information technology requires that data be managed as a resource and an asset of the enterprise.

SUMMARY

Change is a fact of life. An enterprise must learn to accept change, to manage change to its advantage, and to prosper in the face of change. Managing change means organizing the enterprise to meet the demands of unknown change. Changes may not be predictable, but they can be anticipated, and the response to change can be anticipated. Managing change requires careful planning and management of the data as a resource to support anticipated change. It is not easy, but it is not impossible.

Managing data as a resource requires designing an enterprise-wide subject data resource and restructuring existing data according to that design. This subject data resource provides a stable base for an enterprise to manage change. Restructuring applications and application data files to meet changing needs is only a temporary fix and will not provide long-term stability. Designing a subject data resource provides structurally stable data that can be used to manage change.

A properly designed data resource results in increased productivity and creativity, and innovative uses of information technology to exploit human capability. It results in improved performance and excellence and a professional attitude toward performing business activities to meet an enterprise's goals. It produces a structurally stable data resource yet provides the flexibility needed to manage change. It provides credible data that people can use with confidence, resulting in successful people and a successful enterprise.

Designing an enterprise data resource does not happen by accident. It requires hard thinking, some visionary logic, careful planning, and a real commitment to data resource management by the entire enterprise. It requires a technological and a cultural change to view data as a separate and distinct resource that is managed like other resources. It requires an understanding of the dynamics of the business environment, the goals of the enterprise, and how the data resource can support those goals.

STUDY QUESTIONS

The following questions are provided as a review of data problems and the need to design a subject data resource, and to stimulate thought about the need to design an enterprise subject data resource.

1. Why is change necessary?
2. How are enterprises impacted by change?
3. How are information technology trends helping enterprises?
4. What are the differences between the first and second waves of the information age?
5. How did application files of fragmented data subjects get started?

6. Why have these application files lasted so long?
7. What are the problems with the current application file environment.?
8. How can these problems be resolved?
9. How does a subject data resource differ from application files?
10. What will happen if an enterprise fails to create a subject data resource?
11. What are the benefits of an enterprise-wide subject data resource?
12. Why should data be managed as a separate and distinct resource?

chapter two

Data Resource Concepts

Proper management of the data resource begins with an understanding of basic data design concepts.

How do you design data?

Next to the question "Why design data?", this is the most frequently asked question about data. Whether a person has always believed in designing data or whether they have just become a believer, there is always the question about **how** to start designing a subject data resource that will support the enterprise. Many people want to design data and have an urgent desire to design data properly, but just don't know **how** to get started. They don't know how to tackle the apparent immensity of the problem. They don't know how to go about changing existing application files to a enterprise-wide subject data resource.

The answer is surprisingly simple. You start with the basic concepts about the data resource and build on those concepts with techniques to design and manage data as a resource. Once the techniques are known they can be practiced until a skill is developed for designing and managing the data resource. The approach is no different than learning any other discipline, whether it is theoretical physics or automobile maintenance.

One of the problems with learning concepts about the data resource is the many confusing and sometimes contradictory concepts and terms in use today. The prominent concepts in use today are defined and explained in this chapter and will be used consistently throughout the book. Terms have been selected that avoid confusion and are meaningful and easy to understand without excessive thought or reference. This simplified approach allows people to concentrate on the practical design of an enterprise's data resource and not on the meaning of concepts and terms.

This chapter begins with an explanation of information technology as a discipline for the information age and the relationship of the data resource to that information technology. The components of the data resource are defined and explained and the importance of designing an enterprise-wide data resource is emphasized. The basic concepts for designing the data resource are explained to provide a foundation for the models and design techniques presented in the next two chapters.

INFORMATION TECHNOLOGY DISCIPLINE

The data processing that emerged in the 1950s has evolved to an information technology discipline for the information age. The primary goal of information technology in any enterprise is to get the right data, to the right people, in the right place, at the right time, in the right form, at the right cost, so they can make the right decisions and take the right actions. The data resource of the enterprise must be available to everyone in the enterprise that needs data to perform their business activities. A failure to achieve any part of this primary goal is a failure of information technology to support the enterprise.

> The primary goal of information technology is to get the right data, to the right people, in the right place, at the right time, in the right form, at the right cost, so they can make the right decisions and take the right actions.

Information Technology Structure

In order to achieve this goal an enterprise must have the three-level information technology structure shown in Figure 2.1. The **management** base supports information technology by

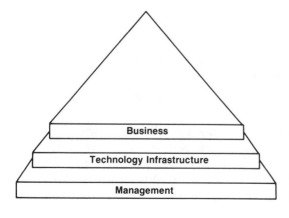

Figure 2.1 Information technology discipline.

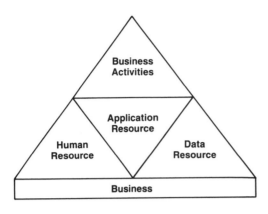

Figure 2.2   Business level components.

emphasizing that all levels of enterprise management are collectively responsible for the management of information technology to support the enterprise's mission and goals. The **technology infrastructure** rests on this management base and represents the processing platform consisting of the hardware and system software that process, store, and move data to support the enterprise's mission and goals. The **business** level represents the business of the enterprise.

The business level of information technology consists of the four components shown in Figure 2.2. The **business activities** component represents all the activities performed by the enterprise. The **data resource** component represents the data needed to support those business activities. The **human resource** component represents the enterprise's workforce that performs the business activities. The **application resource** component integrates the human resource, the data resource, and the business activities into automated applications.

A major problem with management of the data resource has been a lack of awareness of the structural independence of the business level components. They must be structurally independent and data must be managed as a separate and distinct resource of the enterprise. In the information technology discipline **data independence** refers to the separation of the data structure from the structure of the other components. Similarly, **organization independence** is the separation of the human resource structure from the other structures and **business independence** is the separation of the business activity structure from the other structures.

> The business activities, human resource, and data resource components of the business are structurally independent.

The human resource structure generally matches the business activity structure at the higher levels. However, a single business activity can be performed by many people throughout the enterprise, and a person can perform many business activities, so these two structures do not match at the lower levels. The data resource structure does not match either the human resource or the business activity structure. The application resource structure is an integration of the business activity structure, the human resource structure, and the data resource structure.

The data ownership controversy arose because structural independence was not well understood. As long as there were finite sets of data that belonged to finite business activities owned by a finite set of users there was no ownership problem. However, when business activities began sharing data and multiple users claimed responsibility for the control of data that supported those activities there was a data ownership controversy. Management of data as a resource emphasizes that the enterprise owns the data and that all people using the data share responsibility for managing the data resource.

> The enterprise owns the data and all people in the enterprise that use the data share responsibility for managing the data resource.

A related ownership problem that has not yet surfaced in many enterprises is the ownership of applications. Application ownership has not been a problem because applications support business activities owned by one user. However, as individual applications begin to support a wider variety of business activities there could be an application ownership controversy similar to the data ownership controversy. This problem can be avoided by managing the application resource like the data resource. The enterprise owns the applications and all people that use an application share responsibility for managing the application resource.

> The enterprise owns the applications and all people in the enterprise that use applications share responsibility for managing the application resource.

The Data Resource

The data resource component of the business level consists of the three tiers shown in Figure 2.3. The bottom tier represents management of the data resource, the second tier represents the architecture of the data resource, and the top tier represents availability of the

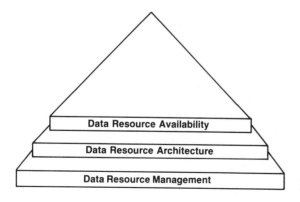

Figure 2.3 Data resource levels.

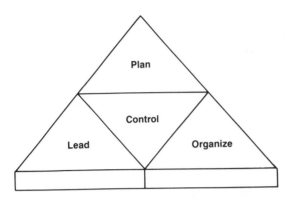

Figure 2.4 Data resource management components.

data resource. The goal of the data resource component is *the cooperative management of an enterprise-wide data architecture that assures readily available data to support the enterprise goals.*

> The data resource goal is cooperative management of an enterprise-wide data architecture that assures readily available data to support enterprise goals.

The components of the data resource management tier are shown in Figure 2.4 The goal of data resource management is *development of a formal plan to organize the data that will lead an enterprise toward control of its data resource.* These components are common components of the management discipline. The data resource is managed by the same principles that all other resources in the enterprise are managed.

> The data resource is managed by the same principles that other resources in the enterprise are managed.

The components of the data resource architecture tier are shown in Figure 2.5. The goal of a data resource architecture is *to develop an enterprise-wide structure of well*

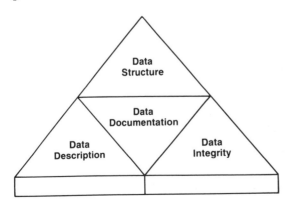

Figure 2.5 Data resource architecture components.

described data, with high integrity, that is properly documented. Data resource architecture is the cornerstone of data resource management and is the component where data resource design begins. The concepts and techniques presented in the book pertain to design of the data resource architecture.

> Data resource design begins with an enterprise-wide structure of well described data, with high integrity, that is properly documented.

The **data structure** component represents the arrangement and relationship of the data units that comprise an enterprise-wide subject data resource. The **data description** component represents the formal naming and comprehensive definition of each data unit in the data resource. The **data integrity** component represents a set of rules for maintaining the quality of each data unit in a complete and correct state under all conditions. The **data documentation** component represents the formal documentation of all information about the data resource in a location that is readily accessible by anyone in the enterprise.

The components of the data resource availability tier are shown in Figure 2.6. The goal of data resource availability is *to provide easily accessible data that is properly protected, adequately secured, and effectively and efficiently used.* Data availability is the ultimate goal of information technology. The **data access** component represents the ability to readily access the database and navigate through it to store and retrieve data necessary to support business activities. The **data security** component represents the protection of data from unauthorized access, alteration, or destruction, and adequate backup and recovery procedures. The **data privacy** component represents the safeguards for assuring the privacy and confidentiality of data. The **data use** component represents the proper and ethical use of data to support business activities.

> Data availability is the ultimate goal of information technology.

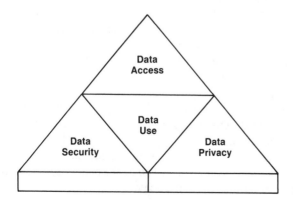

Figure 2.6 Data resource availability components.

DATA DESIGN CONCEPTS

Now that the structure of the information technology discipline and the components of the data resource are understood, the concepts supporting data design can be described. These concepts include business driven data design, the four-schema concept for designing data, the object management concept for managing data and applications, definition of a subject data resource, the concept of time relational data, and the relationship of information and knowledge to data. These concepts support the data design techniques.

Business Driven Design

Design of the enterprise's business activities, data resource, and application resource is driven by the business needs of the enterprise. An enterprise establishes a mission and goals for doing business in a dynamic business environment. Business activities are defined for achieving those goals, an organizational structure of people is defined to perform the activities, and a data resource is defined to support those activities. Finally, applications are developed to integrate the people, the business activities, and the data.

Design of the business activities, the data resource, and applications must be driven by the business needs of the enterprise.

To perform its business activities an enterprise must manage a variety of entities in the business world, such as *customers, vehicles, competitors, employees, products, supplies*, etc. To properly manage these entities an enterprise establishes a set of business rules that are based on laws, ethics, and its own goals. To properly apply these rules to the management of entities, all the situations that could occur for each entity are defined and the actions to be taken for each situation are developed from the business rules. The business activities contain these situations and actions.

Data support the management of entities by providing information about the status, history, and trends of each entity. Each situation that can occur is identified by data available to the enterprise, either from its data resource or from the business environment. The actions that are taken to resolve a situation may result in changes to the data resource and in data being released to the business environment. Since data support the management of entities, the data resource is structured according to those entities.

An enterprise must properly manage entities to achieve its goals. Proper management requires properly structured business activities, properly structured data, and properly structured applications. Therefore, design of the business activities, the data resource, and the application resource is driven by the business needs of the enterprise. They are structured according to the entities that are being managed by the enterprise. This business driven design is a basic concept of information technology.

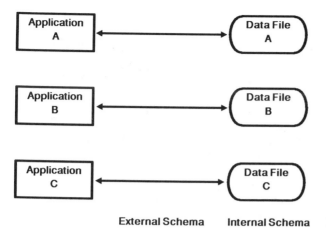

External Schema   Internal Schema   **Figure 2.7** The two-schema concept.

Four-Schema Concept

A **schema** is a diagrammatic representation of the structure of data and represents any set of data that is being captured, manipulated, stored, retrieved, transmitted, or displayed. Initial data resource design was based on the **two-schema concept** consisting of an internal and an external schema, as shown in Figure 2.7. The **internal schema** represent the structure of data in physical files which is relatively fixed and inflexible. The **external schema** represent the structure of data used by applications which is relatively dynamic due to changing business needs.

The problem with the two-schema concept is that external schema do not match the internal schema. If the structures did match, the external schema could be easily obtained from the internal schema. However, a variety of different external schema were needed to meet application needs and these external schema can not be easily obtained from the internal schema. This situation resulted in a conflict between the need for many dynamic external schema and the relatively inflexible internal schema.

In this situation there were only two ways to operate. One way was to perform excessive processing to assemble the external schema needed by each application from the inflexible internal schema. This approach contradicted the objective of efficient processing on expensive computers. The other way was to store data in many internal schema that were close to the applications needs. This approach was usually chosen for faster processing but greatly increased the amount of redundant data.

As more applications were developed under the two-schema concept, more physical files were created and more redundant data were stored. These redundant data were created by the extract, sort, merge process where the data needed by new applications were extracted from existing files, sorted in the proper order, and merged with new data to form new files. Even though processing for a single application was faster, the storage of redundant data became a problem.

The only way to resolve the two-schema conflict was to add a third schema, as shown in Figure 2.8. The new **conceptual schema** became the common denominator between the external schema and the internal schema and the foundation for database management

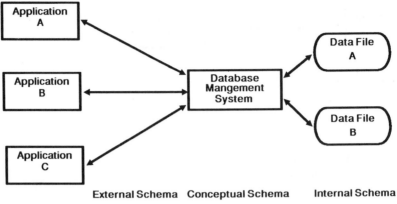

External Schema   Conceptual Schema   Internal Schema

Figure 2.8   The three-schema concept.

systems. The external schema still represent data needed by applications and the internal schema still represent the physical storage of the data. The conceptual schema is the common schema that provide independence between the use of data and the storage of data.

However, as design of an enterprise data resource became more formalized, the principle of business driven design became prominent, and users became more involved in the design process, the three-schema concept became confusing. The problem was in determining what drove definition of the external schema. Typically, applications were developed and the data they needed from the database became the external schema. These external schema were combined to form the conceptual schema which were then used to define the internal schema.

The problem with the three-schema concept is that external schema are developed from the perspective of the database, not from the perspective of the business environment. The external schema represent data external to the database that are needed by the application, with very little concern about why the application needed the data or what the application did with the data. This perspective is incomplete when the business environment is considered. The data needed to manage entities in the business world drives the definition of data needed from the database.

> The three-schema concept does not support business driven design.

The four-schema concept includes a **business schema** which represents data used to manage entities in the business world, as shown in Figure 2.9. These business schema represent data used in the business environment and appear on the business side of an application. External schema still represent data needed by applications from the database and appear on the database side of an application. The four-schema concept allows design of an enterprise-wide data resource from the perspective of the business performed by the enterprise and supports business driven design.

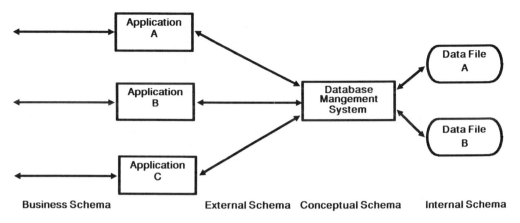

Business Schema   **External Schema**   **Conceptual Schema**   **Internal Schema**

Figure 2.9 The four-schema concept.

> The four-schema concept adds a business schema to support the business driven design concept.

Object Management Concept

Under the two-schema concept an application performed all the tasks necessary to store, retrieve, and process data. These tasks included file management, data edits, and business activities, as shown in Figure 2.10. This was a heavy responsibility for an application and resulted in high maintenance when changes occurred to either data files, data edits, or business activities. However, it was the only way to operate under the two-schema concept.

When the three-schema concept and database management systems emerged the file management tasks were moved from the applications to the database management system, as shown in Figure 2.11. This change of responsibility for file management resulted in less application maintenance because the database management system performed file management tasks. The application responsibility was reduced to business actions and data edits.

Figure 2.10 Conventional application responsibilities.

Figure 2.11 Change in file access management.

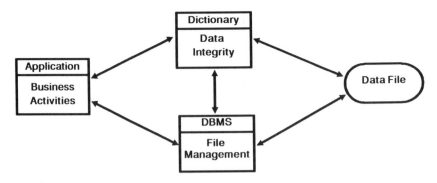

Figure 2.12 Separation of business activities and data integrity.

Data redundancy was reduced by the three-schema concept and the use of database management systems, but data edits are often incomplete and are still performed inconsistently and redundantly by a variety of applications. Also, business activities are often performed redundantly and inconsistently in many different applications.

A concept that is emerging is separation of the data edit and business activity responsibilities, as shown in Figure 2.12. Business activities are performed by business applications and data edits are performed by a data applications, such as an active data dictionary or a database management system. This separation of responsibility allows a comprehensive set of data integrity rules to be defined for each data subject and applied consistently to data entering the database independent of the application updating the database. It also reduces maintenance of business applications and allows them to be oriented toward performance of business activities independent of data integrity.

Separation of the responsibility for business activities and data integrity provides a foundation for resolving the redundancy and inconsistency in performing business activities and for resolving the incomplete and inconsistent enforcement of data integrity rules. Business applications are objects that are completely defined only once and are used in any information system that performs that business activity. Data subjects are objects that have rules for maintenance of their integrity. These rules are completely defined only once and are placed with each data subject to control its integrity. This **object management** concept assures that business actions and data integrity rules are managed as separate objects, are completely defined, and are consistently applied.

> Object management requires the separation of business activities and data integrity rules into objects that are completely defined and consistently applied.

The object management concept requires separation of business rules from data rules. A **business rule** describes how situations relating to entities are managed by the enterprise. A **data rule** describes how data integrity is maintained. The confusion between separation of business rules and data rules comes from the current environment where these rules are intermixed in existing applications and are often defined together when an application is designed. In addition, if the rules are separated, existing applications would still enforce both the business rules and the data rules. Separating the business rules and data rules requires a change in thinking about the way business objects and data objects are managed.

Subject Data Resource Concept

The data resource of an enterprise is structured by data subjects. All the characteristics about one data subject are located with that subject, as shown in Figure 2.13, and any application needing data about a subject goes to that subject to obtain the data. Data characteristics are defined only once and are stored with the subject to reduce redundant data. This **subject data resource** concept is supported by the four-schema concept and the object management concept and provides the foundation for designing the enterprise's data resource.

One of the problems encountered in designing a subject data resource is how data subjects are identified and defined. The data subjects, such as the *customers, vehicles, employees, competitors, products,* and *supplies* mentioned above, are identified from the entities in the business world that are managed by the enterprise. But, the question is how are data subjects identified and defined.

The relational model provides a method of defining and structuring data that reflects the business world. The structural part of the model defines relations of data and the associations between those relations. The integrity part of the model defines rules for maintaining integrity of the data. The manipulative part of the model defines operators for processing the data. The structural and integrity parts of the relational model are used to design the enterprise's data resource.

A relation in the relational model is a two dimensional table consisting of rows and columns that represent a data subject, such as *Employee* shown in Figure 2.14. A row, or tuple, represents a single existence of that data subject, such as *Employee John J. Jones.* A column represents a characteristic about that data subject, such as *Birth Date*. Each cell in the table contains a value of a characteristic for an existence of a subject, such as *Employee John J. Jones Birth Date 8/12/1954.* The rows can be rearranged without affecting the table. The columns can also be rearranged as long as the characteristic name stays with the

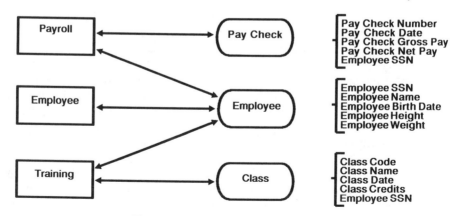

Figure 2.13 The subject data resource concept.

Employee				
SSN	Name	Birth Date	Height	Weight
123-45-6789	John J. Jones	2/28/45	72	145
456-78-9012	Sally M. Smith	1/16/56	64	121

Figure 2.14 A relation represents the employee subject.

column. Tables can be joined by common characteristics, such as *Employee SSN* in *Employee* and *Pay Check*. New tables can be created by extracting rows or columns from an existing table and forming a new table, such as *employees with over 20 years of service.*

The relational model is easy to understand and nearly anyone in an enterprise can understand a database designed with the relational model. The problem is that mention of the relational model implies a database management system and whether or not that system contains all the features of the relational model. It implies the design of physical files directly from the business needs of the enterprise. It does not readily imply design of an enterprise-wide data resource. To resolve this problem, the term **subject data resource** is used rather than **relational model**. The data resource for an enterprise is structured by data subjects based on the relational model. In addition, the logical design of the data resource can be physically implemented into any database management system, whether it is relational, network, or hierarchical.

> Design of the data resource is based on the relational model where data subjects are defined by an enterprise's perception of entities it manages in the business world.

Time Relational Concept

Time creates an interesting twist to data resource design. Time can be used as a subject, as a characteristic, as an indication of frequency or duration, as a trigger to initiate or terminate actions, and to define the time period that data represent. For all practical purposes time forms a sequence from century, down through decade, year, quarter, month, day, hour, minute, and seconds to fractions of a second. All data are valid for some period of time in this sequence. For example, budget data have a valid range of years, quarters, and months, but certainly not seconds or centuries. On the other hand, patient data during heart surgery have a valid range of seconds, but certainly not days or months.

The time period that data represent is known as the **data instance** and that time period may be small, such as a fraction of a second or a few seconds, or large, such as years or longer. The data instance indicates how close data are to reality and how valid data are at representing reality. The data instance is useful for determining what data to use to manage entities. It is also useful to determine the duration of data and when data should be created or destroyed. It is useful with decentralized data, with the backup and recovery of data, with audit trails, and with historical trends and projections. It can also be used to determine the volatility of the data and the probability or frequency of data change. The data instance must be known to properly manage the data resource.

> All data have an instance of time for which they are valid and that instance must be known for proper management of the data resource.

A date-time stamp is often placed in a record to indicate when that record was created or changed. Although this was a help, it was only an indication of when the record was created or when something in the record was changed, but not the change itself. Since before and after images of data were the exception rather than the rule, it was not always possible to determine what data had been changed and what the previous value had been. This situation made it difficult to identify the data instance and to develop trends and projections. Since the business environment is constantly changing, data about that environment is also changing. In addition, enterprises are retaining more data about entities in that environment. In order to properly manage and use this data the instance of the data must be known.

A chronology stamp is used to indicate the data instance. That chronology stamp must be significant to the degree needed by the data. For example, the budget for *3rd quarter 1988*, or the accident occurred at *10:45 PM December 12, 1987*. Every time the data change a chronology stamp must be applied to that data.

The data instance is used to extend the relational model to a **time relational model** which incorporates comprehensive time processing capabilities into the relational model. The time relational model provides the ability to access the time dimension of data and provide views of the database at different points in time. Ideally, these views include the data values, data structure, data integrity rules, and source of the data. Unfortunately, there are no time relational database management systems available to provide this capability. However, the concept can still be implemented.

In most databases data are effective when they are entered and cease to be effective when they are removed. No distinction is made between when data are entered and what time period they represent. During the time data are in the database they are effective and can be used by any application. For example, a new salary table goes into effect on *January 1*. At midnight on *December 31* the old salary table is replaced with the new salary table. If the old table remains too long or the new table is inserted too early any inquiry into salary will be incorrect.

The time relational model establishes the **time independence** concept where the time data enter the database is independent of the time period for which the data are valid. Time independence provides the capability for retroactive updates where the effectiveness of the data takes place in the past, and for proactive updates where the effectiveness of the data takes place in the future. For example, a new employee record could be put in the database in *January* to be effective on *March 1*. Payrolls between *January* and *March 1* would not consider that employee, but payrolls after *March 1* would consider that employee. The reverse is also possible. An employee termination record could be put in the file in *January* to be effective *February 15*. That employee would be paid up through *February 15*, but would not be paid after that time.

> The time relational model provides time independence that allows retroactive and proactive updating of the database.

The true time relational model retains only data changes and a chronology stamp. The database management system aggregates the data for the time frame desired. However, without a time relational database management system, each application must aggregate the data resulting in extensive coding, maintenance, and processing. To avoid these problems, the existing record is duplicated, the appropriate data are changed, and a new chronology stamp is added. These **time occurrences** make it easier for an application to find all the effective data at a point in time and to develop an audit trail of data changes. The disadvantage is the redundant data that are created.

Today's databases typically contain only one record for each existence of an entity. For example, a student will be represented by one student record that contains all the current data about that student. When data about the student change the data in that record are changed so that the record remains current.

In the time relational model there may be multiple time occurrence records for a student, as shown in Figure 2.15. Each of these records represents a time slice for a student. These time slices do not represent another data subject but an extension of the student data subject. Each time occurrence has a chronology stamp showing when the data are effective. Any change to a student's data causes another time occurrence to be entered with a chronology stamp showing when those data are effective. The old time occurrence remains in the file to provide a record of changes for the student. Any data for each term that student attends school follows the same process. All student term records for any student refer to the set of time occurrences for that student.

Is application processing of time relational data feasible today? The answer is yes, in certain situations. If there is a need to track changes to data, there is a high frequency of data changes, and there is a need to access different time slices of data, then time relational is a good approach. If there is only a need for current data and no need to track changes or access time slices of data then time relational is not a good approach. The time relational model will answer some of today's problems, but it requires extra effort and creates redundant data. If the extra effort is justified and the redundant data are properly managed, then time relational data is possible.

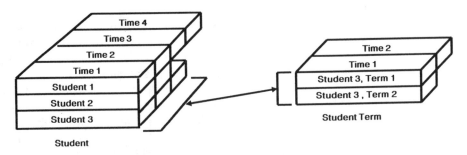

Figure 2.15 The time relational concept.

Information And Knowledge

Data can be aggregated to form information about a subject. This aggregation can be multiple pieces of data at a point in time, a single piece of data at multiple points in time, or multiple pieces of data at multiple points in time. For example, a person's weight today is data, but a person's weight on their birthday every year for the past 10 years is information about that person. A person's weight, height, ethnic origin, hair color, and eye color today is information about that person. All five characteristics on ones birthday for the last 10 years is also information about that person.

Information can also be interpreted data, trends, and projections, not just a collection of individual data values. For example, a sex of male, a weight of 280 pounds, an age of 75 years, and a height of 5 feet 8 inches is information about a person. That information can also be interpreted to represent a short, heavy set, older, man. Similarly, the charges, payments, balance, interest, penalties, and balance on a customers account are information about that account. Interpretation of those data might indicate the customer always pays on time but not the full amount, or always pays late but with the full amount.

When information is retained it becomes knowledge. In the example above, the retention of the five characteristics for a person for the past 10 years becomes knowledge about that person. But, knowledge also pertains to the meaning of data. For example, if the person in the same example above lost 100 pounds, he would be considered to be normal weight. When this knowledge is stored it becomes a knowledge base that contains rules about how things respond or react in the real world. A knowledge base can be used to support expert systems and decision support systems. As these systems evolve, the data and information stored in databases will become an integral part of the knowledge base.

> Information and knowledge are derived from data and proper design of data will result in good information and knowledge.

Since information and knowledge are derived from data, the proper design of data will result in the proper design of information and knowledge. The proper design of today's data will support tomorrow's knowledge bases and expert systems. Therefore, proper design of the data resource will result in good information and good knowledge.

DESIGN MODEL CONCEPTS

A model is a representation of the arrangement and relationship of elements in a system. It is used to visualize and design a system and to plan construction of that system. In the present context, a system is the business environment and the business activities of the enterprise in that environment. Models are used to represent that business environment and to design the business activities, the data resource, the human resource, and applications.

The problem is that design models are not rich enough to capture the full and often diverse meanings of the business environment and the enterprise's activities. There has not been a consistent set of symbols and syntax rules that are used across all models which causes confusion as different modeling techniques are used. Also, design models have not been integrated to provide a continuum throughout the design and development of the business activities, the data resource, and applications.

> Design models can be improved by using a consistent set of symbols and integrating the models into a development method.

Design models can be enriched by improving the syntax, providing consistent rules and symbols, and by integrating the models to provide a continuum through the design and development process. In many cases design models can be enriched by reducing the complexity of the model and simplifying the syntax rules. The approach taken in this book is to provide an integrated set of practical design models that provide continuity through the design and development process. These design models are based on the concepts explained below.

Data Structure Concept

A schema, as explained above, is the diagrammatic representation of data. A **data structure** is the format used to represent a schema and to represent subject data in a relational model. The data structure used in this book is an adjustment of set theory notation to allow the use of long data names and still maintain an understanding of the data structure. It is the basic format for designing the data resource.

> A data structure is the format for a schema based on set theory notation.

When a set F contains the elements a, b, c, d, and e, it is typically shown in the following notation:

$$F = \{a, b, c, d, e\}$$

This notation means that the set F consists of the five elements shown inside the brackets, or that the set F is characterized by the elements a, b, c, d, and e. This notation can be used to represent anything, including data.

In database design, a set represents a subject of data and the elements of that set are characteristics describing that subject. For example, this notation can be used to show the characteristics describing *Vehicles*. Specifically, *year, make, model, color*, and *horsepower* are used to describe each *vehicle*.

$$vehicle = \{year, make, model, color, horsepower\}$$

However, as the number of data attributes gets larger and the names of those data attributes get longer, this notation becomes more difficult to understand. To resolve this problem and maintain an understanding of the structure the format is changed to list the characteristics vertically, as shown in Figure 2.16.

Figure 2.16   Vertical notation for set theory.

The format can be further modified to improve clarity by removing the commas, right bracket, and equal sign. This allows the data names to be lengthened without reducing the understanding, as shown in Figure 2.17.

```
                --
               |    Vehicle Year Manufactured
               |    Vehicle Make
   Vehicle    <<    Vehicle Model Number
               |    Vehicle Color
               |    Vehicle Horsepower
                --
```

Figure 2.17   Modified notation for set theory.

Several data subjects and their respective characteristics can be nested in a similar manner. For example, a vehicle can have many maintenance actions performed. These maintenance actions are nested within the vehicle set, as shown in Figure 2.18. Nesting the maintenance set within the vehicle set means that the maintenance performed on a vehicle describes that vehicle the same as year, make, and model.

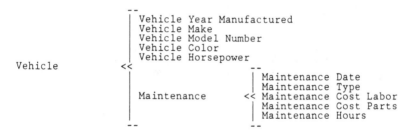

Figure 2.18   Nested sets in modified set theory notation.

Since these data structures represent set theory format they can be manipulated according to standard set theory rules. The intersection, union, compliment, etc., of sets can be easily performed by following the standard set theory rules with the modified format.

Semiotic Modeling Concept

Semiotics is the general theory of signs and symbols and their use in expression and communication. **Semiotic theory** consists of syntactics, semantics, and pragmatics. **Syntatics** deals with the relation between signs and symbols and their interpretation, specifically the rules of syntax for using signs and symbols. **Semantics** deals with the relation between signs and symbols and what they represent, specifically their meaning. **Pragmat-**

ics deals with the relations between signs and symbols and their users, specifically their usefulness.

A design model is a set of signs and symbols that expresses and communicates the design of a system. It is, therefore, part of semiotics and should include all three parts of semiotic theory. Each design model should have specific rules for syntax, an explicit meaning, and a practical value. If it is lacking in any of these components it will be a poor design model and could result in development of a poor system.

> A good design model must have specific rules of syntax, an explicit meaning, and a practical value.

The design models presented in this book have specific rules of syntax, an explicit meaning, and a practical use. Each model has a specific purpose and the models are integrated to provide continuity and consistency from design to construction of business activities, the data resource, the human resource, and applications. Each design model contains several simplified submodels that contribute toward a comprehensive model.

A prominent term today is semantic modeling that is oriented toward the enrichment of design models. Increasing the semantics does increase the meaning of the design models. But, syntax and practical use are just as important. The term **semiotic modeling** provides equal emphasis on syntax, meaning, and practical use and the integration of all design models through the development process. The result is a richer set of models and better design.

> Semantic modeling provides equal emphasis on syntax, meaning, and practical use, and the integration of design models.

Graph Theory

Graph theory provides a base for the diagrams used in design models. Nodes define the points on a graph and edges define the connections between those points. To make the design models easier to develop and understand, specific symbols are used at the nodes of a graph and specific lines are used to connect those symbols. The symbol shape and the line type have unique meaning that is consistent across all design models. Unique names are placed in the symbols and on many of the lines to provide additional meaning.

The state transition diagram is a specific type of graph that shows the states that an object can occupy and the paths that an object can take to move between states. The diagram represents a total system with all possible states and all possible transitions between states. Any input into the system results in the transition of an object to the same state or to another state depending on the conditions of the input and the state the object occupies. This type of diagram is useful for modeling dynamic systems like the business environment.

Graph theory and state transition diagrams support semiotic theory by providing a format for design model diagrams. Each design model contains a submodel that is a diagram showing the arrangement and relationship of elements in the system being modeled. These diagrams add to the practical design of a system.

SUMMARY

Data must be managed as a separate and distinct resource of an enterprise and design of that resource must be integrated with management of the business activities, and the human resource. Design of the data resource is driven by the business needs of the enterprise. The four-schema concept provides a business schema that supports this business driven concept. The object management concept supports the four-schema concept by separating the business rules and the data rules. Business rules are placed with the business activities and data rules are placed with the data.

The data resource is designed based on subjects of data that are defined from the entities being managed by the enterprise. The relational model supports design of a subject data resource through its structural and integrity features. The time relational concept provides additional time processing capabilities to enhance use of a subject data resource.

Design techniques are improved with enriched design models based on semiotic theory that places equal emphasis on syntax, semantics, and pragmatics. The practical development and use of design models is a major objective of this book. Graph theory supports semiotic theory to provide a base for developing an integrated set of design models that are consistent throughout the design and development process. The result is a practical way to design data that can be followed by anyone in the enterprise to develop an enterprise data resource.

Adopting these new concepts and design techniques is as much a cultural change as a technical change. It requires a change in the way people think about the data resource. It requires a reorientation to the dynamic business environment and the data an enterprise needs to be successful in that environment. It requires a reorientation to the management of the data resource to support the enterprise's management of change and recognition of information technology as a discipline for the information age. Management of the data resource must be shared by anyone using that data resource. An enterprise must be proactive in shared management of the data resource to avoid any impacts resulting from a changing environment.

How to design data is a common question. Like any other topic, the design of data begins with an understanding of the basic concepts supporting data design. Specific design techniques are based on those concepts and the techniques are practiced until a person becomes skilled at designing data. The result is a well designed data resource. Designing data is relatively easy when a practical approach is taken based on concepts and techniques that can be understood by anyone in the enterprise. These same concepts and techniques also make use of the data relatively easy. The concepts presented in this chapter begin to answer the **how** of designing an enterprise data resource.

STUDY QUESTIONS

The following questions are provided as a review of data design concepts and to stimulate thought about designing an enterprise data resource within the context of an information technology discipline.

1. How do you start designing the data resource for an enterprise?
2. What is the goal for information technology in an enterprise?
3. What is the structure of information technology and where does the data resource fit into this structure?
4. Why must data be managed as a separate and distinct resource?
5. Why must management of the data resource be shared by everyone using the data?
6. Why must design of the data resource be driven by the business needs of the enterprise.
7. What could happen if design of the data resource were not driven by the business needs of the enterprise?
8. How does the four-schema concept differ from the three-schema concept?
9. How does the four-schema concept support design of the data resource?
10. What is the concept of object management?
11. How does the object management concept support design of the data resource?
12. What is a subject data resource?
13. How does the relational model support a subject data resource?
14. How does the time relational concept enhance a subject data resource?
15. When should time relational data be considered?
16. How can the proper design of data help design of knowledge bases and expert systems?
17. What are the problems with current data design models?
18. How does semiotic modeling help resolve these problems?
19. How does graph theory support design models?
20. Why is the change to these new design concepts as much a cultural issue as a technological issue?

chapter three

Business Design Models

> Design of a data resource to support an enterprise is driven by the business needs of that enterprise.

What do you design first?

Once the basic concepts about designing the data resource are understood the design process can begin. But, where do you start designing and what do you design first? How do you begin the design process?

The best place to start designing the data resource is by modeling the business environment where the enterprise is operating. Since design of the data resource is driven by the business needs of the enterprise and those business needs are based on the interaction between the enterprise and the business environment, the dynamic business environment must be understood to adequately design the business needs. Therefore, design of the data resource begins with an understanding of the nature of the dynamic business environment.

This chapter begins with an explanation of the dynamic nature of the business environment, the behavior of entities in that environment, and management of those entities by the enterprise. The entity life cycle model is presented as a way to model management of those entities to meet the enterprise's goals. Next, the business unit model showing the organizational structure of the enterprise is presented followed by the business information model showing the business transactions that flow between business entities and the enterprise.

Once the business environment and organization of the enterprise are understood the business process models are presented. The business activity model shows the processes performed by the enterprise. The system architecture models show the logical and physical architecture of an information system. The relationships between models is explained after each model is presented. The content, meaning, and use of each of these models is explained and examples are used to illustrate how the models are developed. The explanation and examples are not extensive because business modeling is not the topic of this book. Only an awareness of business models is needed to understand how design of the data resource is driven by the business needs of the enterprise.

THE DYNAMIC BUSINESS ENVIRONMENT

By now it should be realized that the business environment is not in a steady state, but is constantly changing and the enterprise goals are achieved through management of a variety of entities in the business world. These entities, such as *customers*, *vehicles*, *competitors*, *employees*, *products*, and *supplies*, exhibit different types of behavior depending on how they are managed by the enterprise and any external events that might occur and are called **behavioral entities.**

Behavior is not limited to entities representing people. Non-people entities can act, function, and perform the same as people entities. For example, *vehicles* respond differently depending on how they are operated and how they are maintained. If they are not operated properly or serviced regularly they will perform differently than if they were operated properly and serviced regularly. Therefore, behavior can be exhibited by things other than people and it is these behavioral entities that are managed by the enterprise.

Management of behavioral entities begins by understanding the dynamics of the business environment and interactions between the enterprise and these entities. A schematic diagram of the dynamic business environment is shown in Figure 3.1. The management cycle of behavioral entities is shown by the bold arrows in the center of the diagram. A behavioral entity exhibits some type of behavior which creates a business situation. That business situation is resolved with a business action which is an attempt by the enterprise to manage the behavior of that entity.

Entity behavior can be initiated through an external event, through the enterprises attempt to manage it, through interactions with other business entities, or through its own desires. For example, a building may be damaged by a storm which is an external event creating a situation that must be resolved. A vehicle may be improperly painted causing the paint to peel creating a situation that must be resolved. A person may decide to pay only part of a bill that is owed creating a situation that must be resolved.

A business situation is identified by the specific behavior that is exhibited, by data on a business transaction from that entity or another business entity, and data in the enterprise's database. Time can also create a situation, such as 30 days elapsed with no payment received. A business action updates data in the enterprise's database and produces a transaction to the behavioral entity or another business entity in an attempt to change

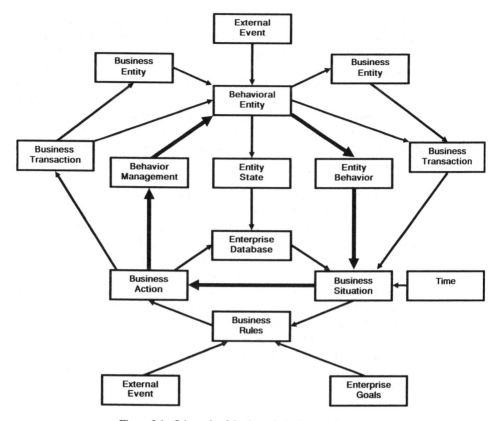

Figure 3.1 Schematic of the dynamic business environment.

behavior. The particular state that a behavioral entity occupies is indicated by the data in the enterprise database.

To properly manage behavioral entities an enterprise establishes a set of business rules and applies those rules to the situations that can occur for each behavioral entity. These rules are developed from an analysis of the business situations that arise, the goals of the enterprise, and any external events. For example, if an enterprise reduces preventive and routine maintenance on vehicles more serious problems will arise that require more expensive repair. If the business rules are adjusted to provide more frequent preventive and routine maintenance then expensive repair will be less. The enterprise may adjust its goals or a law may change the way an enterprise does business which results in an adjustment of the business rules. The process is a constant adjustment of the business rules to manage the behavior of entities, which respond to those rules, which results in further adjustment of the rules.

> Management of behavioral entities is a cycle of adjusting the business rules to control the behavior of entities in the business world.

Each behavioral entity goes through a life cycle consisting of a number of different states. The movement of entities between states occurs through formal transitions resulting from the action taken by an enterprise. The movement of an entity between states provides a pattern of **entity behavior**. All entities, whether people or nonpeople entities, exhibit a pattern of behavior. For example, employees apply for jobs, decline jobs, retire, and resign. Vehicles are operable, have operation problems, are repaired, and are sold. Buildings are constructed, modified, maintained, and destroyed. Some employees are stable and some employees change jobs frequently. Some vehicles are maintenance free and other vehicles need constant maintenance. Some buildings last for years and others are only temporary. These patterns of behavior are useful for adjusting the business rules that manage those entities.

The states and behavior of entities is reflected in data that are received about the entity and stored in the database. However, it is entity behavior that is being modeled, not data behavior. The data do not behave; they only reflect entity behavior. The behavior of entities affects the business rules of an enterprise, and the business rules affect the behavior of the entities. The objective of entity behavior modeling is to adjust the business rules to effectively manage those entities to meet the enterprise's goals.

Modeling entity behavior is beyond the scope of this book. However, the beginning of any behavior modeling is dependent on a good definition of business rules and the separation of business rules from data rules. Both sets of rules must be complete and correct for entity behavior modeling to occur. A weakness of either set of rules will result in a weakness of the entity behavior model. When business rules and data rules are complete and correct, entity behavior can be properly modeled and expert systems and other artificial intelligent applications can be used to provide additional support to the enterprise.

BUSINESS ENVIRONMENT MODELS

Modeling the dynamic business environment begins with development of entity life cycle models and business information models. These **business environment models** show the life cycle of behavioral entities and the business transactions that are necessary to exchange information about those entities. These models are based on semiotic modeling and graph theory and are easy to develop. It is the effort that goes into the analysis of the business environment that is difficult and these practical design models allow that effort to be spent on analysis not on the models themselves.

Even though each model is useful as a model, it is the integration of models that adds value to the design process. Each model drives development of the next model to form a process that constantly refines design of the data resource. A failure at one step in this process will be propagated through all models and will result in a poorly designed database.

Entity Life Cycle Model

Each behavioral entity resides in one entity state at any point in time. The state an entity occupies is a result of the actions taken by an enterprise to control the behavior of that entity. An **entity life cycle model** shows the states that a behavioral entity can occupy and the transitions that can be made between those states. It is used to model the business environment and plan the management of behavioral entities.

> An entity life cycle models shows the states that an entity can occupy and the transitions between those states and is used to plan the management of behavioral entities to achieve enterprise goals.

An **entity state** is a specific state that a behavioral entity can occupy as a result of its behavior and the enterprise's business rules. It represents the status of that entity at a point in time. For example, vehicles could have several states, such as *new*, *active service*, *repair*, *surplus*, and *sold*. An **initial state** represents the status of a behavioral entity when it first encounters the enterprise. For example, when a *vehicle* first encounters an enterprise its status is *new*. A **final state** represents the status of a behavioral entity when it leaves the enterprise. For example, a *vehicle* leaves the enterprise when it is *sold*.

An **entity state transition** is the movement of a behavioral entity from one entity state to another state, or to the same state, as a result of a business action. Each entity transition is the result of an action taken in response to a situation and results in a transition to the same state or to another state. In other words, there is an entity transition for each situation that has been identified. For example, a vehicle that has been damaged moves from the *active service* state to the *repair* state. When it has been repaired it moves back to the *active service* state.

An **entity transition diagram** shows all possible states a behavioral entity can occupy and all the possible transitions for a behavioral entity to move between states during its encounter with the enterprise. The absence of a transition between two states means that such a transition is not possible. A behavioral entity need not pass through every state during its life with the enterprise, and it may pass through the same state many times.

The entity life cycle model consists of the entity transition diagram, a description of each state a behavioral entity can occupy, and a description of each transition that can occur. Each state must have a comprehensive definition explaining the status of an entity in that state. For example, the definition of the vehicle status of *new* might be defined as *any vehicle acquired by the enterprise, whether it has been previously used or not, and has not been prepared for use by the enterprise*. Each entity transition must have a comprehensive definition to explain the requirements or constraints for an entity to make that transition. For example, a *vehicle* moving from the *new* state to the *active service* state must be painted, have an emblem placed on the door, and pass a safety check.

> An entity life cycle model consists of an entity transition diagram and a definition of each entity state and each entity state transition.

These definitions help define the business rules and the actions taken to manage an entity during its encounter with the enterprise. If the entity states and the requirements to move between states are not formally identified and defined the proper actions cannot be taken, and there can not be efficient or effective management of behavioral entities.

An entity life cycle model is easy to develop using only two symbols. An entity state is represented by a circle. The name of the entity state is placed inside the circle, must be singular, and must be unique within the enterprise. An entity transition is represented by a solid line with an arrow on one end indicating the direction of the transition. A transition can flow in only one direction, never in both directions. Each transition must leave a state and arrive at a state, whether it is the same state or a different state. Transitions can not converge or diverge between states. A transition can not originate from nowhere or go nowhere. The name of the transition is placed on the line, must indicate an action, and must be unique within the enterprise.

The entity transition diagram for recruiting employees is shown in Figure 3.2. The initial state is *Person* which is the status of a person that is not associated with an employer in any way. By applying for a position a person can move from the *Person* state to the *Applicant* state. If the application is accepted that person remains an *Applicant*, but if the application is rejected that person returns to the *Person* state. If that applicant successfully passes a test they move to the *Qualified Applicant* state, but if they fail they return to the *Person* state. An *Applicant* can also withdraw and return to the *Person* state.

Once a person becomes a *Qualified Applicant* they can become a *Candidate* by being eligible for a position, they can withdraw and return to the *Person* state, or they can exceed the time limit for qualification and return to the *Person* state. The remainder of the chart can be read in a similar manner. Once the person becomes a *Permanent Employee* they would move to another entity life cycle model representing *Employees*.

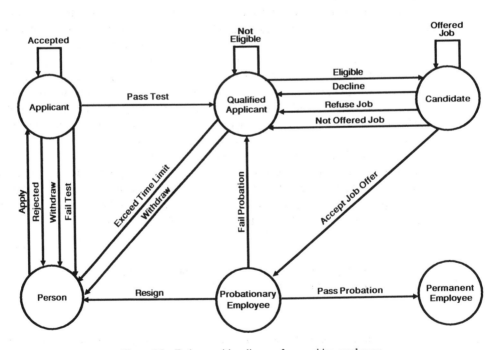

Figure 3.2 Entity transition diagram for recruiting employees.

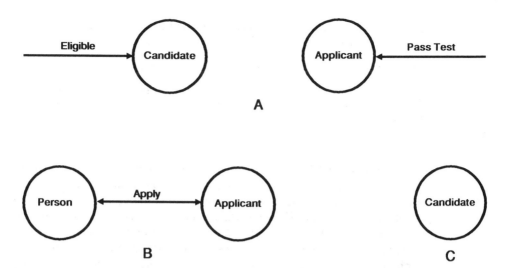

Figure 3.3 Examples of entity life cycle diagram errors.

Some common mistakes with entity transition diagrams are shown in Figure 3.3. Example **A** shows transitions that do not originate from an entity state and do not go to an entity state. Each transition must leave a state and arrive at a state, whether it is the same state or a different state. Example **B** shows a transition that moves in both directions. Since an action can only move an entity in one direction a transition can only move in one direction. Example **C** shows a state with no transitions which means that an entity can never occupy that state. Each of these situations must be corrected to have a useful entity transition diagram.

An entity life cycle model must be developed for each set of behavioral entities that is being managed by the enterprise. For example, if *Customers* are being managed, an entity life cycle model is developed for customers. If *Vehicles* and *Employees* are being managed, entity life cycle models are developed for each of these behavioral entities. Development of entity life cycle models begins the process of defining the business environment and the data resource.

> Development of entity life cycle models begins definition of the business environment and the data resource.

BUSINESS INFORMATION MODEL

The business world operates on business transactions that carry information between business entities. A **business information model** shows those business entities and the transactions that flow between them. It identifies business entities that the enterprise interacts with while conducting business and the transactions necessary for conducting that business. The data on these business transactions begin the definition of data needed to support the enterprise.

> A business information model shows the business transactions that flow between business entities and begins the definition of data to support the enterprise.

A **business entity** is an organizational unit within or outside the enterprise that receives or initiates business transactions of interest to the enterprise. That organizational unit consists of one or more people that take action on business transactions, either by receiving incoming transactions or initiating outgoing transactions. Some business entities may also be behavioral entities, such as a *Customer* because the enterprise is attempting to manage the customer and they are exchanging business transactions with that customer. Other business entities are not behavioral entities because the enterprise is not attempting to control their behavior, such as the reporting of wages earned to the government. The enterprise is only exchanging information with these business entities. Some behavioral entities, such as vehicles, are not business entities because business transactions are not exchanged with them.

A **business transaction** represents a flow of information between business entities. Each business transaction contains data about behavioral entities that are being managed by the enterprise. Generally, only formal business transactions such as reports and documents are shown on the business information diagram because those transactions have a specific format and purpose. However, informal transactions that represent ad hoc communications may also be shown, such as *Employee Counseling, Registration Questions*, if they are useful to the enterprise. These informal transactions may be useful to define data that are needed to respond to the ad hoc communication.

Business transactions and business entities that initiate or receive those transactions are shown on a **business information diagram**. A business information diagram is easy to develop with only two symbols. A hexagon represents a business entity and a solid line with a single arrow represents a business transaction between business entities. The name of the business entity is placed inside the hexagon, must be singular, and must be unique within the enterprise. A solid line with an arrow on one end represents a business transaction. The name of the business transaction is placed on the line, must be singular, and must be unique within the enterprise. The name can include a number to designate the sequence of a set of business transactions, but that number must not be used in lieu of a name.

Business transactions must connect two business entities. A transaction can not appear from nowhere or go nowhere. They must flow from one business entity to another business entity. Business transactions can not converge or diverge between business entities. A convergence or divergence of business transactions shows that some type of processing occurs and, since processing can occur only inside a business entity, transactions cannot converge or diverge outside a business entity.

Business transactions are recursive when the same business entity is the source and destination of the transaction. For example, if the business entity is a *Department*, of which there are many in an enterprise, and a transaction goes from one department to another department, then the transaction is recursive to the *Department* business entity. A recursive business transaction indicates a generic business entity, in this case *Department*. The business information diagram could show each department in the enterprise as a separate business entity with the same transaction flowing between all departments. However, to keep the business information diagram simple those business entities can be shown generically and the transaction becomes recursive to that generic business entity.

When generic business entities appear on a business information model it indicates that secondary responsibilities are performed. For example, the business information diagram might show *Purchase Requisitions* flowing from *Department* to *Purchasing*. The *Department* business entity is a generic business entity representing all departments in the enterprise. Since all departments can submit *Purchase Requisitions* then that submission is a responsibility of all departments. *Purchasing* has the primary responsibility for *Purchase Requisitions* and *Departments* have a secondary responsibility.

The business information diagram is a network and top, bottom, right, and left have little meaning. The movement of the business transactions between business entities have meaning. The placement of business entities is done in a manner to reduce the length of lines representing business transactions and to avoid crossing those lines. Lines that are excessively long or frequently cross add confusion to the model and result in a loss of meaning.

The business information diagram for recruiting employees is shown in Figure 3.4. A *Person* submits and *Application* to the *Recruiting Division* and receives an *Application Response* that tells them whether they were accepted or rejected. That *Person* takes a *Qualification Test* and receives *Qualification Test Results* stating whether they passed or failed the test. That *Person* may also *Withdraw* by notifying the *Recruiting Division*. The

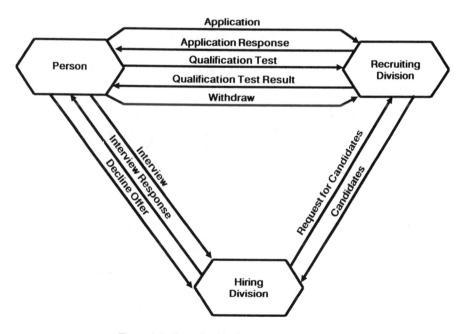

Figure 3.4 Example of business information diagram.

Hiring Division requests *Candidates* and conducts an *Interview* with those *Candidates*. Each *Candidate* receives an *Interview Response* which might include a job offer and the *Candidate* may *Accept* or *Refuse* that offer.

Some common mistakes with business entity diagrams are shown in Figure 3.5. A nonperson business entity is shown in example **A**. Since a business entity is a person or group of people that take action on business transactions, a business entity must represent such a person or group of people. Example **B** shows converging and diverging business transactions. Business transactions cannot converge or diverge outside a business entity because only a business entity can take action on business transactions. Example **C** shows business transactions that do not connect two business entities. Each business transaction must connect two business entities because it represents a movement of business information from one business entity to another business entity. Each of these situations must be corrected to provide a useful business information diagram.

Another common mistake is for a business information diagram to migrate into the data flow diagram described later. A data flow diagram shows the processing that occurs on business transactions. Processing is not a feature of the business information model and inclusion of any processing on the business information diagram detracts from the usefulness and purpose of the diagram. Therefore, whenever a business information diagram

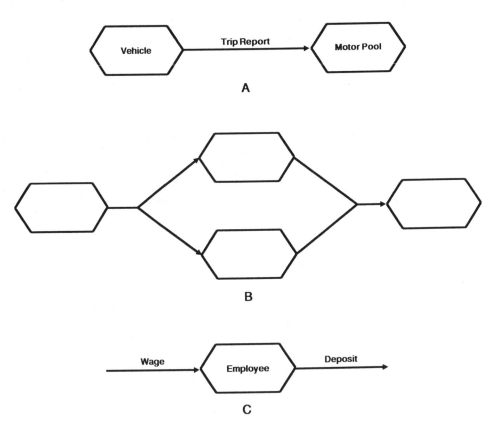

Figure 3.5 Example of business information diagram errors.

begins to show processing rather than just business entities and transactions an adjustment needs to be made.

There can be many business information diagrams for an enterprise and the same business entity or transaction can appear on more than one business information diagram. For example, *Contracts Office* may appear on several different business information diagrams with different business transactions. Collectively, the business transactions on those different diagrams define the total set of business transactions for the *Contracts Office*. Similarly, the same business transaction may appear on more than one diagram to improve understanding of the business environment, although this is less common than the same business entity appearing on different diagrams.

A business entity with many transactions connected to it can be split into subordinate business entities that exist within the parent business entity. For example, a diagram may begin with a business entity for *Federal Government*. As the diagram evolves many transactions are connected with the *Federal Government*. The *Federal Government* business entity can be split into *Internal Revenue Service*, *Department of Education*, and so on, with business transactions to the respective business entities within the *Federal Government*.

A business information diagram may be developed to show the detail within one business entity. For example, business transactions are shown connected with the *Vendor* representing transactions that flow into and out of a *Vendor*, but there is no indication of what goes on inside the vendor. A diagram can be prepared showing the transactions that occur between the business entities inside the *Vendor*. To be complete and correct, this vendor business information diagram must include the transactions flowing into and out of *Vendor* as well as the transactions flowing within *Vendor*.

A **business information model** consists of the business information diagram and a description of each business entity and each business transactions on that diagram. Each business transaction needs to be completely described with a definition of the transaction, the format of the transaction, the data contained in the transaction, its source and destination, frequency, and any other information that is useful to the enterprise. This information is used to develop plans for receiving or preparing the transactions.

> A business information model consists of a business information diagram and a definition of each business entity and business transaction on that diagram.

Development of a business information model is driven by the knowledge of people in the enterprise and once they learn the technique they become involved very quickly. In fact, one of the pleasant problems with business information modeling is that people become so involved they go beyond the scope of the project very quickly. This situation is easily solved by either expanding the scope of the project, or constraining development of the model to the scope of the project.

A business information model can help identify and document business rules, or to identify obscure or nonexistent business rules. These business issues can, and must, be resolved and stated as business rules so that processing may be complete and accurate.

Business Information Relationships

The entity life cycle model and the business information model are often developed together. This process keeps the two models synchronized to define the business environment. In the example above, *Person* is the business entity and that person can be an *Applicant, Qualified Applicant, Candidate,* or *Probationary Employee.* By submitting an *Application* to the *Recruiting Division* they become an *Applicant.* If that *Application* is *Accepted* they remain an *Applicant,* but if that *Application* is *Rejected* they return the *Person* state. The *Person* takes a *Qualification Test* and if they *Pass Test* they become a *Qualified Applicant,* but if they *Fail Test* they return to the *Person* state.

The remainder of the two diagrams are balanced in a similar manner. Each business transaction creates a situation that must be resolved. When that situation is resolved another business transaction may be produced and the behavioral entity may change states or may remain in the same state. Each business transaction results in a transition and each transition results from a business transaction. The result is two business environment models that show how entity behavior is managed by the enterprise. This process is summarized below.

Identify behavioral entities managed by the enterprise

Develop an entity life cycle model for each behavioral entity

Identify and define each state those entities could occupy

Identify and define each possible transition between those states

Identify and define the business entities involved in any way with the behavioral entities

Identify and define the business transactions between those business entities

Develop a business information model

Balance the two models by assuring that each transition results from a business transaction and each business transaction results in a transition

Business Unit Model

An enterprise contains a variety of business units that are structured in some manner to support the enterprise. A **business unit model** shows that organizational structure and is used to identify the business units that receive and initiate business transactions and are responsible for performing business activities. The model begins the definition of business activities and the responsibility for performing those activities.

> A business unit model shows the organizational structure of the people in an enterprise and identifies responsibility for performing business activities.

A **business unit** is an organizational unit within the enterprise consisting of one or more people. It is a business entity within the enterprise that can receive and initiate business transactions and take action on those transactions the same as external business entities. It is also a behavioral entity since it is managed in some manner by the enterprise.

Business units form a hierarchy from the chief executive officer down through each unit in the enterprise based on reporting relationships. This hierarchy is called the **organizational structure** of the enterprise and the model of that structure is called an **organization chart**. The actual names of the units, such as division, department, office, section, etc., may vary from one organization to another, but the hierarchy still exists.

Each business unit must have a formal description of its duties, responsibilities, and reporting relationships. The basic duties and responsibilities of a business unit are inherited from its parent business entity and can not go beyond the scope of the duties and responsibilities of the parent business unit. The definition of the duties and responsibilities of all the subordinate business units fully qualify the duties and responsibilities of the parent business unit.

An organization chart is easy to develop using only two symbols. A hexagon represents a business unit, the same as on the business information model, and the name of that unit is placed inside the hexagon and must be unique within the enterprise to avoid any confusion when defining responsibilities. The hexagon differs from the rectangle used on conventional organization charts. This change was made under the concept of semiotic modeling to provide continuity across all models. A rectangle is used to represent business processes and a hexagon is used to represent business units and business entities.

> A business unit model consists of the organization chart and a description of the responsibilities of each business unit.

A solid line represents a formal reporting relationship or line of authority between business units. That line may be branched between business units to show multiple subordinate business units reporting to a parent business unit. Each business unit must have at least one line of authority connected to it otherwise there is no reporting relationship. Each line of authority must connect two or more business units in order to establish a reporting relationship. Lines or authority can not originate from nowhere or go nowhere. A dashed line may be used to represent informal reporting relationships.

A typical organization chart is shown in Figure 3.6. It begins with the president and shows vice presidents and division directors. The chart could continue to the lowest organizational unit in the enterprise and could include each person in the enterprise. The level of detail is up to each enterprise.

Three common mistakes with organization charts are shown in Figure 3.7. Example **A** shows a business unit without a name and two different business units with the same name. Neither of these situations is acceptable because it is unclear what the business units are and which definitions apply to those business units. Example **B** shows lines of authority that appear from nowhere and go nowhere. This situation is not acceptable because it is unclear what the lines of authority represent. Example **C** shows no lines of authority which indicates there are no reporting relationships. Each of these situations must be corrected to provide a useful organization chart.

There is only one organization chart for an enterprise, however that chart may be too large to be shown on one page. The chart may be subdivided in any manner that is meaningful and shown on multiple pages. For example, one vertical portion of the chart

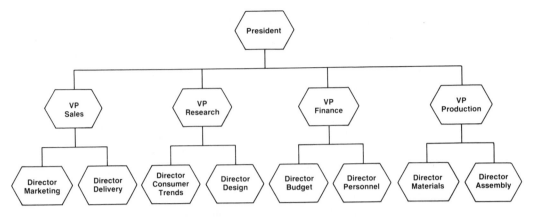

Figure 3.6 Typical enterprise organization chart.

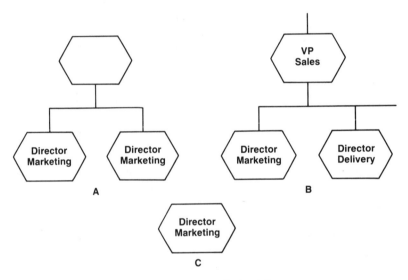

Figure 3.7 Examples of organizational chart errors.

may be placed on a single page to show the lines of authority down through the enterprise. A single page could also show a few levels of the chart, but all business units on those levels. Additional pages would show the next levels for each business unit at the lowest level on the parent diagram.

BUSINESS PROCESS MODELS

When the business environment has been modeled and the behavioral entities, entity states, entity state transitions, business entities, and business transactions, have been identified and described, the business activities and information systems can be modeled. These **business**

process models show the situations that occur, the actions taken for each situation, and the architecture of information systems. The business environment models drive development of the business process models. The two sets of models are closely integrated since the business environment drives definition of the business activities and the data to support those activities.

Business Activity Model

An enterprise performs a variety of business processes to achieve its goals. A **business process** is a unique set of closely related business tasks that form an integrated unit of processing. That processing unit can not be subdivided and still perform its processing. A business process is the basic building block of the business activities performed by an enterprise. For example, a business process might change the number of payroll exemptions for an employee. There are several tasks involved in this process, but those tasks are closely related and inseparable if payroll exemptions are to be changed properly.

Business processes can be grouped into business activities, which can be grouped into business areas, business segments, business functions, etc., to form a hierarchy known as the **business activity diagram**. The grouping of business processes are abstract groupings based on how the enterprise views the organization of its business processes. The names of each level and the number of levels in this hierarchy are not important and may vary from enterprise to enterprise. What is important is that the business processes are grouped in some structure to form a business activity diagram. Since only the processes perform tasks, the abstract grouping of these processes can be changed without changing the processing.

A business activity diagram can be easily developed using two symbols. A rectangle represents each member in the diagram and a solid line without arrows represents the connection of those members in the hierarchy. The lines may be branched between levels to indicate multiple subordinate members. The name of each member is placed inside the rectangle and each name must be unique within the enterprise to avoid any confusion about the function of that member. The process names must begin with a verb to indicate the action that is being taken. The member names in the hierarchy above the processes need not begin with a verb since they do not indicate an action.

A simple business activity diagram is shown in Figure 3.8. The business processes for payroll are shown at the bottom of the diagram. The process names begin with a verb to indicate the action taken. These six payroll processes are grouped into three payroll activities which form the payroll function. All of the processing occurs at the process level and the members in the hierarchy above those processes represent abstract groupings of the basic processes and do not perform any processing.

A variety of errors with business activity diagrams are shown in Figure 3.9. Example A shows a member without a name and members with identical names. Neither of these situations is acceptable because it confuses the meaning and creates difficulty defining and understanding the purpose of each member. Example **B** shows pieces of the hierarchy that are not connected which is not acceptable because it can not be determined what those members represent. Example C shows no lines connecting a member which is not acceptable because the location of that member in the business activity hierarchy can not be determined. These situations must be resolved before the diagram is completed.

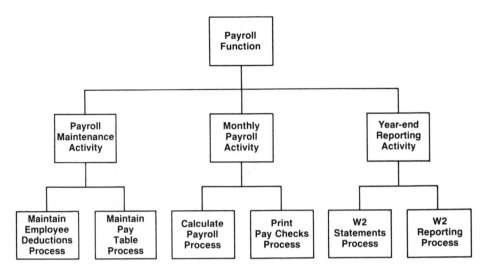

Figure 3.8 Simple business activity diagram.

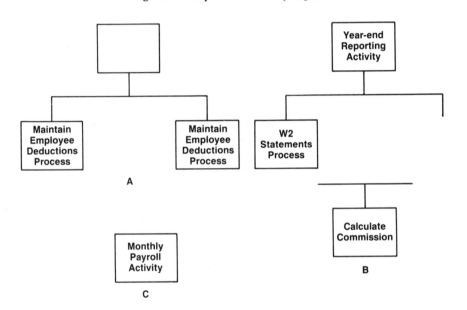

Figure 3.9 Example of business activity diagram errors.

Only one business activity diagram is developed for an enterprise. However, that diagram could be too large to be shown on one page and can be subdivided in any manner that is meaningful and shown on separate pages. Generally, the diagram is divided so that one page shows several levels of the hierarchy. Additional pages show the detail for each member at the lowest level on the parent page.

Each member in the business activity diagram must have a comprehensive definition that includes the scope of activities of its subordinates. The definition of each subordinate must be within the scope of the parent member and must include the scope of its subordinates. If the hierarchy is rearranged, the definitions of the abstract members must be adjusted to represent the activities of subordinates.

The business activity diagram and the description of each member in that diagram form a **business activity model**. A business activity model must be developed for the enterprise before it can adequately manage its business processes. Each member on the model must be properly named and completely defined. The model can then be used to analyze business processes in the enterprise to identify overlapping, competing, or conflicting processes, and gaps where no processes are defined. It can also be used for planning, reorganization, and the addition and deletion of business processes based on the enterprise's goals.

> A business activity model consists of a business activity diagram and the description of each member on that diagram.

Business Process Logic

In the business environment there are situations that occur, conditions that identify those situations, and actions that are taken for each situation. A **business situation** is a specific situation that occurs as the result of time, the arrival of a business transaction, or the actions from a behavioral entity, as explained earlier. Each of these situations is identified by a set of **business conditions** that are the criteria for identifying a business situation. These conditions are determined from data in the enterprise's database, from business transactions, from the actions of a behavioral entity, or from time. **Business actions** are the actions taken in response to each business situation and may result in a change to the database and the release of a business transaction.

> The logic for each business process is defined in sets of situations that contain conditions identifying the situation and actions taken for each situation.

The logic that is performed within each business process can be represented in several ways, such as narrative descriptions, tables, graphs, and structure charts. The structure chart is used here because it completely defines the process logic in an understandable manner that encourages direct user involvement. These **process logic charts** have the same format as data structure charts, with the exception that the sets represent sets of logic, not sets of data.

The situations, conditions, and actions are represented on process logic charts, as shown in Figure 3.10. The set label indicates the situation. The first statements within the set show the conditions that identify the situation. Each condition statement is prefixed with a question mark (?) to indicate it is a condition used to identify that situation. The remaining statements in the set show the actions that are taken to resolve the situation. Each of these actions begin with a verb to indicate that an action is being taken.

```
                       --
                      |   ?Condition(s)
      Situation   <<
                      |    Action(s)
                       --
```

Figure 3.10   Format for process logic.

To illustrate further, the situation might be a loan default as shown in Figure 3.11. A *Loan Default* is identified by the conditions of *No payment on the loan for 60 days, Unable to contact the loan recipient by phone*, and *No response by the loan recipient to a registered letter*. The actions to process this situation are to *Cancel any further credit, File for repossession of collateral property*, and *Refer the loan to a collection agency for collection*.

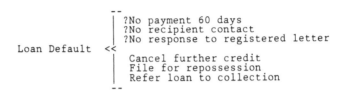

```
                           --
                          |   ?No payment 60 days
                          |   ?No recipient contact
                          |   ?No response to registered letter
      Loan Default   <<
                          |    Cancel further credit
                          |    File for repossession
                          |    Refer loan to collection
                           --
```

Figure 3.11   Process logic for loan default.

All the business situations that can occur must be identified and documented. This exhaustive set of situations defines the process logic for each business process. In other words, a business process contains an exhaustive set of situations that can occur and the actions taken for each situation. If an exhaustive set of situations is not identified the process logic will be incomplete and business situations will not be properly processed.

> Each business process contains an exhaustive set of situations that can occur.

Process logic must be defined for each process in the business activity model including calculation rules. For example, if a loan payment is late there is a penalty and interest is charged against that loan. The calculation of that interest and penalty charge must be documented and used consistently in every process that calculates late payment. One of the problems with conventional information systems is that calculation rules are hidden in programs and are inconsistent between programs. These calculation rules must be identified and documented, just like other business rules, so they can be applied consistently.

The business actions are based on rules developed by the enterprise. A **business rule** is a specific rule stated by an enterprise to manage entity behavior. As explained in the Data Design Concepts chapter, the business rules are placed in the application processes and the data rules are placed with the data. However, if the data rules can not be placed with the data, the processes containing the data rules must be different from the processes containing the business rules. This approach allows all data rules to be placed together and enforced consistently for all data entering the database. These data integrity processes would be placed between the business process and the data subject that is being updated. This procedure allows those rules to be placed with the data when that capability becomes available without impact on business processes.

Business Activity Relationships

The business information model shows the business transactions and the business entities that receive or initiate those transactions. The business unit model shows the structure of the business units in an enterprise. These enterprise business units are a subset of the business entities that process business transactions. The business activity model shows the business processes and the abstract structure of those processes as perceived by the enterprise.

The structure of the business activity model is not like the structure of the business unit model because the structure above the business processes is an abstraction that has no functional purpose while the structure of the business unit model has a functional meaning. The structure of the business activity model may match the structure of the business unit model, particularly near the top because the major functions of an enterprise match the major groupings of business activities. However, since many business units could perform the same business activity, and a business unit could perform many business activities, the structures will generally not match at the lower levels.

Since the structure of business activities is an abstraction of business processes and can be changed without changing the processes, the structure of business activities could be brought into line with the structure of business units. Ideally, the structure of business activities should match the structure of business units for the major areas of responsibility. The primary responsibility for a business process belongs to the business unit that has that functional responsibility. Secondary responsibility for a business process belongs to any other business unit that performs that process.

These responsibilities are shown on a **business process responsibility matrix** that shows the primary and secondary responsibilities for managing business processes in an enterprise. An example of a business process responsibility matrix for recruiting employees is shown in Figure 3.12. The *Applications Unit* in the *Recruiting Division* receives and processes all applications. The *Testing Unit* in the *Recruiting Division* performs all testing.

BUSINESS UNIT

BUSINESS PROCESS	Application Unit	Testing Unit	Certification Unit	Hiring Unit
Application Process	P			S
Conduct Tests		P		S
Certify Candidates			P	S
Select Candidate				P

Figure 3.12   Business process responsibility matrix for recruiting employees.

The *Certification Unit* in the *Recruiting Division* supplies all names to any unit hiring employees. Each of these units has a primary responsibility for these functions. Individual hiring units may also process applications for certain classes of people, so this function is shown as a secondary responsibility for *Hiring Units*.

The responsibilities for business transactions is shown on a **business entity transaction matrix.** All business entities and the transactions that they initiate or receive are shown on this matrix. The business entity transaction matrix for recruiting employees is shown in Figure 3.13. A *Person* initiates an *Application, Qualification Test, Withdrawal, Interview,* and *Decline Offer.* A *Person* receives an *Application Response, Qualification Test Results,* and an *Interview Response.* The same information is shown for the *Recruiting Division* and *Hiring Division.*

		BUSINESS ENTITY	
BUSINESS TRANSACTION	Person	Recruiting Division	Hiring Division
Application	I	R	
Qualification test	I	R	
Withdraw	I	R	
Interview	I		R
Decline offer	I		R
Application response	R	I	
Qualification test	R	I	
Interview response	R		I
Request for candidates		R	I
Candidates		I	R

Figure 3.13   Business entity transaction matrix for recruiting employees.

These two matrices are useful for defining the business environment and how the enterprise operates in that environment. These matrices are developed as the models are developed and used to identify any discrepancies in the way an enterprise operates. When these discrepancies are corrected the enterprise will be flexible to the changing business environment.

SYSTEM ARCHITECTURE MODELS

An information system is a set of processes that receive incoming transactions, produce outgoing transactions, and access data storages to store and retrieve data. The architecture of an information system is represented on a system architecture model similar to the floor plan or blueprint for a building. A blueprint shows how all the components come together to form a complete building. A **system architecture model** shows how the transactions, processes, and data storages come together to form a complete information system.

When a system architecture model is developed it must represent the total information system whether it is automated or manual. One of the most common mistakes is to develop a system architecture model that represents only the automated portions of information systems. This is the same as developing a blueprint for a house but excluding anything that is not made of wood, or the wiring, or the plumbing, from the blueprint. The result is an incomplete model that does not represent the total system and could well result in construction of a system that is incomplete or in error.

A system architecture model represents the total architecture of an information system, including manual and automated components.

System architecture models can represent either the logical or physical construction of the information system. Generally, the logical model is developed first and represents design of an information system. The physical model is developed from the logical model and is used for construction and operation of the system. When an existing information system is being documented the physical system architecture model may be developed first, followed by development of a logical system architecture model.

Logical System Architecture Model

The **logical system architecture model** represents the logical architecture of an information system and is used for the analysis of requirements and design of an information system. It integrates business transactions, business processes, and data into an information system. The model consists of data flow diagrams, a description of each process on the data flow diagrams, and the format of each external data flow.

The logical system architecture model represents the design of an information system to meet the business needs of the enterprise.

A **data flow diagram** consists of data flows, application processes, and data subjects. A **data flow** is a unique set of data flowing into or out of an information system or between application processes and data subjects within an information system. All data flows are shown, whether they are manual or automated. **External data flows** represent business transactions flowing into or out of an information system. **Internal data flows** represent business transactions moving between application processes within an information system.

An **application process** represents either a business process or an internal process and may be either manual or automated. A business process is the same business process defined on the business activity model. An **internal process** is a process used in the information system that is not related to a business process of the enterprise. For example, back up / recovery is an internal process.

A **data subject** represents a single subject of data in the enterprise's data resource and may be manual or automated. For example, *Employee* and *Vehicle* are data subjects that would be shown as data subjects on the data flow diagram. The data for those subjects could be contained in a filing cabinet or in a computer database.

A data flow diagram shows data flows, application processes, and data subjects.

A data flow diagram is developed with three symbols. A rectangle represents an application process, a solid line with an arrow represents a data flow, and a rectangle with convex sides represents a data subject. Data flows must have an arrow on at least one end to show which direction the data is flowing. In some situations a data flow may have an arrow on both ends if the same set of data is flowing in both directions. The name of the data flow is placed on the line and must be unique within the enterprise.

External data flows represent business transactions and have the same name as the business transaction. Internal data flows to and from data subjects do not have names if they represent the movement of the full set of data for that data subject. However, if the data flow represents a data subset, the name of the data flow designates which **data view** is represented. Internal data flows between processes represent an internal transaction and must be appropriately named to designate that transaction. These **internal transaction** names must also be unique within the enterprise and must not conflict with any business transaction or data view names.

A rectangle represents an application process. The name of the process is placed inside the rectangle and begins with a verb indicating action. Each process must have a name and that name must be unique within the enterprise. The business process names must be the same as the names on the business activity model. Internal processes must be appropriately named and that name must be unique within the enterprise and must not conflict with business process names. A rectangle with convex sides represents a data subject and the name of that data subject is placed inside the symbol.

A typical data flow diagram is shown in Figure 3.14. It shows a *License Renewal* process where a *License Application* is received and processed by a *License Edit Update* process. If a *License Application* passes the edit process the data for that application is placed in the *License* data subject. If it fails the edit process the data is placed in the *License Suspense* data subject for correction. A *License Renewal* process sends out *License Renewal Notice* forms based on existing licenses that are nearing expiration.

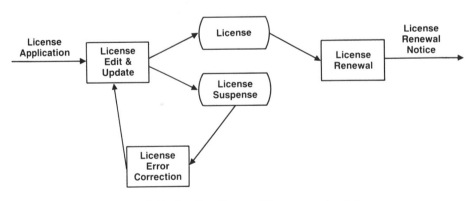

Figure 3.14 Data flow diagram of license renewal system.

Each application process, external data flow, and data subject must have a comprehensive description. If the process is already described for the business activity model that description may be used. If not, a formal description needs to be prepared. If an external data flow is already described as a business transaction that description may be used. If not, a formal description needs to be prepared. Each internal data flow representing a transaction between processes needs to be described. If the data subject is already described that description may be used. If not, a formal description needs to be prepared.

Some logical system architecture models show data subjects as a generic database without specifying the particular data subject. Although these models are useful for defining the processes, and require minimum maintenance to keep data subjects up to date, they are semantically weak for defining data flows and data subjects. Since one objective of the logical system architecture model is to integrate processes and data, they must show the details of those processes, data subjects, and data views.

Logical System Architecture Relationships

The business transactions from the business information model drive development of the logical system architecture model. These business transactions represent the primary requirements of the information system and must drive design of that information system. The processes that receive or prepare these business transactions are added for each business transaction. These business transactions and business processes form the external architecture of an information system. The internal architecture shows how data are processed, stored, and retrieved to meet the needs of the business transactions. Internal processes, data subjects, and data flows are added to support the business transactions. This is where the alternatives for storing, retrieving, and manipulating data to meet business needs are evaluated.

> The business information model drives development of the information system architecture.

The business processes in a logical system architecture model are the same business processes shown on the business activity model. These business processes can be defined by starting with larger business functions or activities and breaking them down until the basic business processes are defined. This process can be done during development of the business activity model or during development of the logical system architecture model. Either method is acceptable as long as the business processes on the business activity model match the business processes on the logical system architecture model.

> The business processes are the same processes shown on the business activity model.

The logical system architecture model represents the design of an information system to support the business of the enterprise. It includes both manual and automated operations and represents all information processing for the enterprise. Therefore, each business transaction must appear on both the business information model and on the logical system architecture model. Also, each business process must appear on the business activity model and on the logical system architecture model. Any discrepancies must be resolved before the models will completely represent the business of the enterprise.

The relationship between business units and business activities is indirectly defined through the system architecture and business information models. The system architecture model shows the business processes that receive an incoming business transaction or initiate an outgoing business transaction. Those same business transactions are shown on the business information model as originating from or terminating at a business unit. Therefore, an indirect connection can be made between business units and business activities. These indirect connections should be reviewed with the responsibilities listed in the **business process responsibility matrix** and any discrepancies should be adjusted.

The business process responsibility matrix for license renewal is shown in Figure 3.15. A *License Application* is shown going into the *License Edit & Update* process on the system architecture model. That same *License Application* would be shown as a business transaction from the *Applicant* to the *Licensing Division* on a business information model. Since the *Application* goes to the *Licensing Division* and to the *License Edit & Update* process, the *Licensing Division* must perform the *Application Review* business process. If *License Edit & Update* is not the responsibility of the *Licensing Division* than some adjustment needs to be made.

BUSINESS PROCESS

BUSINESS TRANSACTION	License Edit & Update	License Renewal
License application	R	
License renewal notice		I

Figure 3.15 Business process transaction matrix for license renewal.

Physical System Architecture Model

The **physical system architecture** model represents the physical construction and operation of an information system. It is developed from the logical system architecture using formal logical to physical conversion criteria for both data and processes. The process logic for each application process is converted to either manual or automated instructions and the automated data subjects are converted to data files by formal rules according to the particular operating environment. The logical to physical conversion criteria are developed by each enterprise based on their physical operating environment. Depending on the results of the logical to physical conversions there could be more or less physical processes than logical processes and there could be more or less data files than data subjects.

> The physical system architecture model represents the physical construction and operation of an information system.

The physical system architecture model consists of a physical flow diagram and a description of each physical process and data file on that diagram. The physical flow diagram is developed using three symbols similar to the data flow diagram. A rectangle with rounded corners designates a physical process, an oval designates a physical data file, and a solid line with an arrow designates a physical data flow. The process and data file names are placed inside their respective symbol and the data flow names are placed on the line.

Figure 3.16 shows the physical system architecture model of the license renewal process shown in Figure 3.14. In this case there was a one-for-one conversion between logical processes and data subjects and their corresponding physical processes and data files.

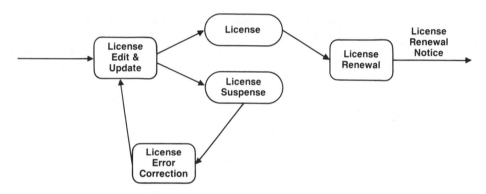

Figure 3.16   Physical system architecture for license renewal.

SUMMARY

The business environment, business process, and system architecture models provide a set of business design models that are very practical for the analysis, discovery, organization, and management of the enterprise and its business activities. They reduce the complexity of the business environment to an understandable level, make the analysis and design time more productive, and reduce development time for information systems. They encourage direct involvement of users in the modeling process because the models represent the environment where the users are operating. They encourage modeling of the business environment, then the logical design of information systems, followed by physical development of those systems.

Under the object management concept, the business processes, business entities, business transactions, and behavioral entities are objects. Managing an enterprise includes

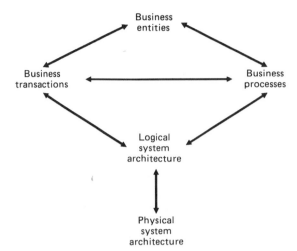

Business
entities

Business
transactions

Business
processes

Logical
system
architecture

Physical
system
architecture

Figure 3.17 Management of business objects.

managing these objects to meet the goals of the enterprise. Behavioral entities are managed through business transactions and business processes that contain situations and actions for each situation. The management of these transactions and processes is shown in Figure 3.17. Business entities initiate and receive transactions and perform processes. Business processes receive and initiate transactions. The logical system architecture manipulates the processes and transactions and defines the physical system architecture.

Each business process performs all the tasks necessary to resolve a situation. There are no bridges or feeds to other information systems. Each process is automated only once and is used in any business activity that requires that process. In other words, the basic business processes are chained together to form business activities independent of the structure of the business activity diagram. This approach, as well as the separation of business rules from data rules, provides the base for management of individual objects with maximum efficiency and effectiveness.

STUDY QUESTIONS

The following questions are provided as a review of business design models and to stimulate thought about the development, meaning, and use of business design models.

1. What is meant by a dynamic business environment?
2. What is a behavioral entity?
3. How are behavioral entities managed?
4. What does an entity life cycle model represent?
5. How are entity states and state transitions identified?
6. What is a business entity?

7. What is a business transaction?
8. What does a business information model represent?
9. How is a business information model developed?
10. What is the relation between a business information model and an entity life cycle model?
11. What does a business unit model represent?
12. What is a business process?
13. What does a business activity model represent?
14. What does business process logic represent?
15. What drives development of process logic?
16. What do system architecture models represent?
17. How do a logical and a physical system architecture model differ?
18. What drives development of a logical system architecture model?
19. What benefits do business design models provide?
20. How is object management related to business design models?

chapter four

Data Resource Model

A comprehensive data resource model is mandatory to properly design and manage the data resource.

What is a data resource model?

This question is always asked when the people in an enterprise start designing and managing data as a separate and distinct resource of the enterprise. What does a data resource model look like? What does it represent? How do you develop one? These questions can be answered with the description of a data resource model.

Models for design of the business activities, the people in an enterprise, and the application resource were presented in the last chapter. These models represent three of the four components of the business level of information technology. The fourth component, the data resource, consists of a data resource management tier, a data architecture tier, and a data availability tier. The data resource architecture is the cornerstone of the data resource and can be modeled with a data resource model.

This chapter presents the data resource model. It begins with a definition of the basic and abstract data units that form the logical and physical structure of the data resource. Next, the components and uses of logical and physical data resource models are explained including the integration of these models with the business design models. The different types of data resource models are described and the criteria for developing a good data resource model are presented. The techniques of how to develop a data resource model begin in the next chapter.

DATA RESOURCE STRUCTURE

Data resource architecture is the cornerstone for designing and managing the data resource. It consists of a data structure, a data description, a data integrity, and a data documentation component. The data resource structure is different from the structures of business activities, people in the enterprise, and applications. It is based on data subjects, the relations between those subjects, and the characteristics of each data subject. The data resource has both a logical structure for design and a physical structure for construction.

> The data resource is structured by data subjects, the relations between those subjects, and characteristics of those subjects.

Logical Structure of Data

The logical structure of the data resource represents the structure of data as perceived by people in the enterprise. It represents their perception of the business environment and the data they need to operate in that environment. It represents the structure of the conceptual schema that is used to define the physical database and to provide data views to the applications to meet the business needs of the enterprise. The logical structure of data consists of basic data units and abstractions of those basic data units.

Basic data units. The **basic data units** define the core of the data resource structure. They form a sequence from the enterprise data resource down to individual data values, as shown in Figure 4.1. The **enterprise data resource** contains all electronic and machine readable data within the enterprise, regardless of the form that data are in or the location where they are stored. It represents the total collection of data residing in all data repositories and is not restricted to just the data in a database management system or just the data on the mainframe computer. In other words, the data in database management systems and the data on mainframe computers are usually subsets of the total data in the enterprise data resource.

Enterprise Data Resource

Data Entity

Data Occurrence

Data Attribute

Data Value

Figure 4.1 Sequence of basic data units.

Data Resource Model

> Basic data units form the core of the enterprise's data resource structure.

The enterprise data resource contains data entities representing subjects of data. A **data subject** is a set of closely related characteristics about objects of interest to the enterprise based on its perception of the business environment. A data subject is a noun that represents a person, place, thing, event, or concept. For example, the topics of interest to an enterprise might be *employees*, *buildings*, *vehicles*, and *customers*. Each of these topics would become a data subject for the enterprise, resulting in *Employee*, *Building*, *Vehicle*, and *Customer* data subjects.

A **data entity** represents a data subject in the enterprise data resource. It contains a collection of facts about a particular data subject. In the example above, *Employee*, *Building*, *Vehicle*, and *Customer* become data entities. A data entity is sometimes referred to as a logical file and in mathematics is referred to as an entity set. However, the term *data entity* will be used throughout this book. Each data entity should represent a single data subject. However, there are situations where a data entity represents more than one data subject or part of a data subject. These situations will be explained later.

> A data entity represents a subject of data about a person, place, thing, event, or concept.

A **data category** is a subset of a data entity, a data subentity, that represents a *can also be* situation. Each data category contains data attributes that characterize that data category as well as the parent data entity. Each data category has one or more companion data categories which are peers of each other and further define the parent data entity. For example, a person exists in the real world and when that person becomes associated with the enterprise they appear as a data occurrence in the *Person* data entity. If that person becomes a customer they appear as a data occurrence in the *Customer* data category. If they become an employee they appear as a data occurrence in the *Employee* data category. If they become a vendor they appear as a data occurrence in the *Vendor* data category. The *can also be* situation for a data category means that a single existence can occur in one or more data categories at the same time. In other words, a *person* can exist as an *employee*, and as a *customer*, and as a *vendor*.

> A data category is a data subentity representing a *can also be* situation.

Data attributes are not duplicated between the parent data entity and data categories. The *Person* data entity in the example above contains data attributes unique to that person as a person. The *Customer* data category contains data attributes unique to that person as a customer. The *Employee* data category contains data unique to that person as an employee. The *Vendor* data category contains data unique to that person as a vendor.

A **data entity type** is a grouping of data occurrences within a data entity or data category that represent a *can only be* situation. The grouping is based on the data values of one or more data attributes. For example, the data occurrences in *Vehicle* might be grouped by *Motor Vehicles* and *Nonmotor Vehicles* based on a *Vehicle-Type Code*, forming two data entity types. The motor vehicles could be further grouped by *Internal Combustion Engine* and *Noninternal Combustion Engine* based on a *Vehicle Engine Code*, forming two additional data entity types. A data entity type is a *can only be* situation because a data occurrence can belong to only one type.

A data entity type is a data subentity representing a *can only be* situation.

A **data entity supertype** is the parent data entity type, and a **data entity subtype** is the subordinate data entity type, when there are two or more levels of entity types. In the example above, *Motor Vehicles* is a data entity supertype of *Internal Combustion Engine* and *Noninternal Combustion Engine*. *Internal Combustion Engine* and *Noninternal Combustion Engine* are data entity subtypes of *Motor Vehicles*. A vehicle *can only be* a *motor vehicle* or a *nonmotor vehicle*, never both. Similarly, a motor vehicle *can only be* an internal combustion engine or a noninternal combustion engine, never both.

An **entity existence** is the real world appearance or manifestation of a data subject. For example, if the enterprise were managing employees and a new employee, *John J. Jones*, were hired, that employee would become an existence of the *Employee* data subject.

A **data occurrence** represents a specific existence of a data entity in the enterprise data resource. For example, *John J. Jones* would become a data occurrence in the *Employee* data entity. A data occurrence is often referred to as a logical data record and in mathematics is referred to as an entity. However, the term *data occurrence* is used in this book because it implies something that occurs in the real world. A data occurrence is sometimes referred to as a data instance, but that term is more appropriately used to designate the time frame that data represent.

A data occurrence represents one existence of a data entity.

Data entities contain data attributes representing characteristics of data. A **data characteristic** is the smallest piece of descriptive information about a data subject that can not be subdivided and still retain any descriptive meaning. It is an adjective that describes a data subject. For example, *Employee SSN* represents a single characteristic that describes the *Employee* data subject. Other data characteristics that describe *Employee* are *Employee Weight, Employee Height,* and so forth.

A **data attribute** represents a data characteristic in the enterprise data resource. Collectively, all of the data attributes in a data entity describe that data entity to the extent needed by the enterprise. A data attribute is sometimes referred to as a data element or a data field. However, the term *data attribute* will be used throughout this book. Each data attribute should represent a single characteristic of data. In the example above, *Employee*

Name, *Employee Weight*, and *Employee Height* are data attributes of the *Employee* data entity. However, there are situations where a single data attribute may represent more than one data characteristic or part of a data characteristic. These situations will be explained later.

A data attribute represents a characteristic of a data entity.

Data attributes contain data values representing properties of data. A **data property** is a quality or trait belonging to a data characteristic. It is a trait that is common to all existences of that data characteristic. It is the basic working unit of data. For example, *Machinist 3* is a single data property of *Employee Job Class* data attribute. Other data properties of *Employee Job Class* might be *Machinist 1*, *Machinist 2*, *Secretary 1*, *Secretary 2*, and so forth.

A **data value** represents a data property in the enterprise data resource. It is the smallest piece of information that is captured stored, retrieved, and manipulated. In the example above, *Machinist 1*, *Machinist 2*, *Machinist 3*, *Secretary 1*, *Secretary 2*, and so forth, are data values of the *Employee Job Class*. Data values should represent single properties of data attributes. However, there are situations where a data value represents multiple data properties. These situations will be explained later.

A data value represents a property of a data characteristic.

Abstract data units.   **Abstract data units** are groupings of basic data units for a particular purpose. These groupings are defined as needed by the enterprise and may change depending on the data needs of the enterprise.

Abstract data units are groupings of the basic data units for a particular purpose.

The enterprise data resource defined above contains all the machine readable data in the enterprise regardless of their location. That term was purposely qualified as the *Enterprise Data Resource* to indicate that it includes all data entities in the enterprise. However, data entities can be grouped according to any topic of interest. For example, the term *Education Database* might be used to refer to all data entities pertaining to education. The term *Registration Database* might refer to all data entities pertaining to registration, which would be a subset of the data entities pertaining to education. The term *Class Database* might refer to all data entities pertaining to classes that were taught, which would be a subset of the data entities pertaining to registration. This particular sequence of abstract databases is shown in Figure 4.2.

Enterprise Data Resource

Education Database

Registration Database

Class Database

Figure 4.2 Abstractions of the enterprise data resource.

Abstractions of data entities may overlap. For example, a *Student Database* might include data entities that are also contained in the *Registration Database*. The purpose of abstract databases is to refer to a grouping of data entities for a specific topic of interest, not to identify rigid groupings of data entities. The boundaries of abstract databases are flexible depending on the topic of interest.

A database is a grouping of data entities for a particular topic of interest.

A **data segment** is a grouping of data entities that are closely related to each other through a high frequency of relationships. There is a low frequency of relationships between data entities in different data segments. For example, *Vehicle*, *Vehicle Use*, *Vehicle Maintenance*, etc., are closely related data entities belonging to the *Property* data segment. *Employee*, *Position*, *Job Class*, and so on, are closely related data entities belonging to the *Personnel* data segment. There is a weak relationship between data entities in the *Property* data segment and the *Personnel* data segment. Unlike the abstract databases described above, data segments define relatively rigid boundaries around groups of data entities based on the frequency of relationships.

A data segment is a grouping of data entities based on an affinity of data relations.

Data segments may overlap slightly. The overlap occurs with the data entities that have a relation between data segments. In the example above, *Employees* are authorized to operate *Vehicles* through a *Vehicle Authorization* data entity. *Vehicle Authorization* would be included in both the *Personnel* data segment and the *Property* data segment. *Employees* and *Vehicles* would be included only in their respective data segment, not in both data segments. In other words, the overlap of these data segments is limited to the *Vehicle Authorization* data entity.

A **data occurrence group** is a set of data occurrences from a single data entity or data subentity that have the same value, or range of values, of one or more data attributes. It represents a set of data occurrences that meet a set of search or selection criteria. For example, all *Motor Vehicle* data occurrences from the *Equipment* data entity that were manufactured by *Ford* form a data occurrence group. Obviously, there are many different data occurrence groups that can be obtained from a data entity based on the selection criteria, making it the most common abstract data unit.

> A data occurrence group is the most common abstract data unit.

A **data attribute group** is a set of two or more data attributes that are closely related and have a high frequency of combined use. For example, data attributes might be defined for *Zip Code Basic* and *Zip Code Extended* which represent single data characteristics. Together these two data attributes form the *Zip Code Complete* data attribute group. Data attribute groups may be stored, retrieved, and manipulated as a single unit, but they represent two or more single characteristics of data.

A **data view** is a set of one or more data attributes selected from a data entity. It can include all or part of the data attributes in a data entity and represents an external schema. For example, the data attributes *Employee Name*, *Employee Birth Date*, and *Employee SSN* might be selected from the *Employee* data entity for a particular application. These data attributes form a data view of the *Employee* data entity.

A data view is also referred to as a user view because it provides a set of data attributes for a user of the database, or an application view because it provides a set of data for an application. The terms logical view, logical user view, and physical view have also be used. Although each of these terms have their own special meaning, the term *data view* will be used in this book because of its broader meaning and independence of the use of the data.

An **application data view** is a set of data attributes that is used by one application. A **combined data view** is a set of data attributes that does not include all the data attributes in a data entity, but contains more data attributes than are used by one application. Several applications can be supported by a combined data view. A **full data view** contains all the data attributes in a data entity and will support all applications accessing a data entity.

Physical Structure of Data

The physical structure of data also forms a sequence that progresses from the enterprise data resource, down through data files and data records, to data items and data values, as shown in Figure 4.3. A **data file** is a set of one or more closely related data records that roughly corresponds to a data entity in the logical structure of data. A **data record** is a record in a physical file that roughly corresponds to a data occurrence in the logical

```
          Enterprise Data Resource
        Data Entity       Data File
     Data Occurrence      Data Record
      Data Attribute       Data Item
             Data Value
```

Figure 4.3 Physical Sequence of data.

structure of data and contains one or more data items. A **data item** is a physical piece of data that corresponds to a data attribute in the logical structure of data. A data item contains the actual data values that are captured, stored, retrieved, and manipulated by applications. These are the same data values shown in the logical structure of data.

The sequence of physical data units and the sequence of the basic logical data units are very similar. It is this similarity that is used to develop the physical database from the logical data resource model. The abstractions of the basic data units can be easily obtained from the physical database if the logical data structure is properly converted to a physical database.

DATA RESOURCE MODEL

The term **data model** is a confusing term to many people. It is used to represent the construct of a database management system, such as network, hierarchical, and relational, and it is used to represent the design of the data resource for an enterprise. To resolve this confusion the term **data resource model** is used in this book to mean the design model for the data resource of an enterprise, not the construct of a database management system.

A complete data resource model for an enterprise consists of a logical data resource model and a physical data resource model. The logical model represents design of the data resource to meet the enterprise's business needs the same as a blueprint or floor plan represents the design of a building to meet the needs of the occupant. The physical model is used to construct the physical database the same as a building is constructed from a blueprint. It is developed from the logical model based on formal conversion criteria according to the physical operating environment. If the design and conversion are done properly the physical database will meet the needs of the enterprise the same as a building will meet the needs of the occupant.

> The data resource model for an enterprise consists of a logical and a physical data resource model.

Both the logical and physical data resource models contain considerable information about the data resource. Placing this information in one model would make that model virtually uninterpretable. Therefore, each logical and physical model consists of a set of submodels that are more understandable and useful and collectively define the total data resource model. The submodels may be diagrams, data structure charts, matrices, or narrative descriptions.

Logical Data Resource Model

The **logical data resource model** is used to analyze and design the enterprise database according to the way the enterprise perceives the business world. The logical data resource model consists of eight submodels: an entity-relationship diagram, an entity type hierarchy diagram, a data control diagram, data attributes, data unit descriptions, data entity keys, data views, and data integrity rules. The logical data model represents the data requirements of the enterprise and is used to design an enterprise data resource to meet those requirements.

> The logical data resource model represents the design of the data resource to meet the business needs of the enterprise.

Entity-relationship diagram. The entity-relationship diagram is one of the most important submodels of the logical data resource model. However, there have been many versions of the entity-relationship diagram and many of these versions have included more than entities and relationships. The entity-relationship attribute, entity-relationship integrity, and entity-relationship processing diagrams are a few examples. Entity behavior has also been included on some entity-relationship diagrams. The inclusion of these features on the same diagram makes it too cluttered to be meaningful and causes confusion. There are also many contradictory symbols between versions of the entity-relationship diagrams and these symbols are not consistent with symbols used in other design models. These inconsistencies add to the confusion.

Another variation in entity-relationship diagrams is how data relations are shown. In some versions data relations can contain data attributes and in other versions they can not contain data attributes. Some versions allow only binary relations and others allow more than two relations between data entities. These variations are confusing to many people attempting to develop entity-relationship diagrams and in some cases have turned people away from data modeling.

The **entity-relationship diagram** used in this book is a submodel of the logical data resource model and contains only data entities and data relations that show associations between those entities. The data relations do not have any data attributes and are not named. Any data relation that has attributes becomes a data entity with a unique name. The types of data entities are contained in their description and are not indicated by separate symbols on the entity-relationship diagram. The entity-relationship diagram uses symbols that have specific meaning and are used consistently across all design models. These standard symbols allow the data resource model to be integrated with the other business design models to form a continuous sequence of design and construction.

> An entity-relationship diagram shows only data entities and the relations between those data entities.

The additional features that have been placed on entity-relationship diagrams are needed for designing the data resource. However, they are placed in the business design models or other submodels of the data resource model. Processing is shown in the business process model and entity behavior is shown on the entity life cycle model. Cardinality is a data integrity rule and is shown on the data integrity submodel. Data attributes are shown in a separate submodel. The result is an entity-relationship diagram that shows only data entities and the relations between those entities. The diagram is easy to develop and easy to understand by anyone in the enterprise.

The entity-relationship diagram shows the structure of the enterprise's data resource. It shows the pathways for navigating through the data resource to store and retrieve data. It provides the basic framework for designing and constructing the data resource.

An entity-relationship diagram is developed with two symbols. A rectangle with convex sides represents a data entity, the same symbol used on the data flow diagrams, and the name of that data entity is placed inside the symbol. Dashed lines between data entities represent the data relations between those data entities and may be nondirectional, monodirectional, or bidirectional. Dashed lines are used to indicate there is only a relation between data entities and not a flow of data. A solid line represents a flow of data, as on the data flow diagrams. Data relations can not appear from nowhere or go nowhere because that situation would not represent any relationship. A data relation has no name since it does not represent any movement of data between data entities. Figure 4.4 shows an example of an entity-relationship diagram.

Entity-type hierarchy diagram. Identification of data entity types form a **data entity-type hierarchy**. This hierarchy can be shown in an **entity-type hierarchy diagram** using a rectangle with convex sides to represent the data entity types, the same symbol used on data flow diagrams and entity-relationship diagrams, and a dashed line without arrows to represent the hierarchy. The lines may be branched to indicate multiple subordinates. For example, employees can be either *classified, exempt,* or *faculty.* A *staff* employee can be either *temporary,* on *probation,* or *permanent.* A *temporary* employee can be either *part time* or *full time.* A *faculty* employee can be either *tenure* or *nontenure* faculty. A *tenure* faculty employee can be on a *tenure track* or could have *achieved tenure.* These situations can be easily shown on an entity type hierarchy diagram as shown in Figure 4.5.

There can be more than one entity-type hierarchy within a data entity. For example, there could also be an entity-type hierarchy of employees that represents their citizenship. Employees could be a U.S. citizen or a citizen of another country. If they are from another country they could be in the U.S. under different visa types and if they are a U.S. citizen they could have gained that citizenship by birth right or by naturalization. Entity-type

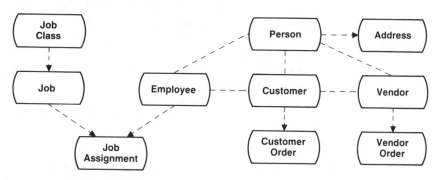

Figure 4.4 Example of an entity-relationship diagram.

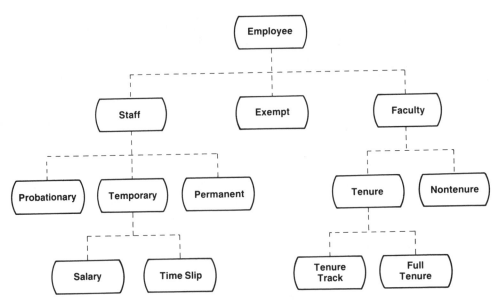

Figure 4.5 Entity-type hierarchy for employees.

hierarchies may be overlapping such as this one for citizenship and the one described above for classified, exempt, and faculty employees.

There can be branches within an entity-type hierarchy diagram. For example, faculty employees could be certified or not certified and certified faculty could be state certified or national certified. This hierarchy would form another hierarchy below faculty similar to the tenure hierarchy.

> An entity-type hierarchy diagram shows the relation between data entity super-types and subtypes.

The entity-type hierarchy diagram is used to define data attributes and data values, to identify data occurrences, to help structure process logic, to define data integrity rules, and structure physical files. Each level on an entity type hierarchy is represented by one or more data attributes that determine which entity type on that level represents the data occurrence. There must be a data value for each entity type and each entity type must be represented by a value. For example, a data attribute represents *classified, exempt,* and *faculty* employees. Another data attribute represents *temporary, probation,* and *permanent* employees. A third data attribute represents *part-time* or *permanent* status, and a fourth data attribute represents *tenured* and *nontenured* faculty employees.

Data control diagram.　A **data control diagram** is a submodel of the logical data resource model and is used to identify updates to data entities and control data integrity. It is used to track the flow of data through information systems to show where data are stored. It is used to identify the source of data, how data are altered, modified, or derived, and the location of data integrity routines. It helps identify redundant or inconsistent processing and redundant or inconsistent data integrity.

A data control diagram looks like a data flow diagram and uses the same symbols as a data flow diagram. Rectangles represent processes, rectangles with convex sides represent data subjects, and solid lines with arrows represent data flows. However, it does not include retrieval of data from the database, such as reports, were the data are not altered or stored. It does not show all uses of the data, just the source of data, data integrity, and the storage of data in the database. It can include information system or enterprise boundaries to show how data move across those boundaries.

> A data control diagram shows the flow of data that updates the enterprise's database.

A data control diagram for employee data is shown in Figure 4.6. Three business processes are shown on the left for *Job Assignment, Employee Update,* and *Training Schedule.* Three data integrity processes are shown in the center for *Job Assignment Integrity, Employee Integrity,* and *Employee Training Integrity.* These data integrity processes assure that any data entering the database meet the data integrity rules. The five subjects of data are shown on the right for *Job, Job Assignment, Employee, Employee Training,* and *Training Class.*

If a *Job Assignment* for an employee is being entered into the *Job Assignment* data entity a check is made to determine if that *Employee* exists and can be assigned to the job, if the *Job* exists, and that the *Job Assignment* does not already exist. If these conditions are met the job assignment is entered. Additional data integrity rules for *Job Assignment* data

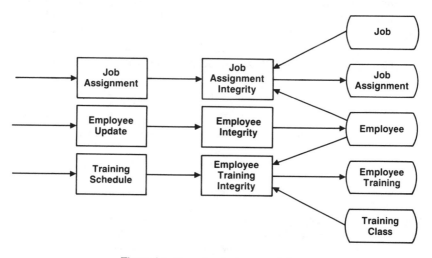

Figure 4.6 Example of a data control diagram.

are checked in the same manner. If there is an error, that error is returned to the business process for correction.

The data control diagram is very useful for separating data rules from business rules and placing those data rules in data integrity processes. It is also useful for identifying the source of data and getting data into the database at the earliest time and for identifying the best procedure for sharing data between separate business entities.

Other logical submodels. The **data attribute submodel** shows all data attributes on a data structure chart for each data subject. For example, the data attributes for a vehicle are shown in Figure 4.7. Each vehicle is characterized by an identification number, a make, a model, a type code, a color, a year of manufacture, and a year of purchase.

```
                    --
                   |  Vehicle Identification Number
                   |  Vehicle Make
                   |  Vehicle Model
        Vehicle    << Vehicle Type Code
                   |  Vehicle Color
                   |  Vehicle Year Manufactured
                   |  Vehicle Year Purchased
                    --
```

Figure 4.7 Data attribute submodel for vehicles.

The **data description submodel** includes the names and definitions for each basic and abstract data unit. The names are based on a formal data naming taxonomy and the definitions are comprehensive definitions of the content of the data, not the use of the data. The naming taxonomy and comprehensive definitions allow each data unit to be uniquely identified and defined, readily located, and properly used.

The **data entity keys submodel** shows primary, foreign, and secondary keys for each data entity. The primary keys uniquely identify each data occurrence in a data entity. The foreign keys identify the parent data occurrence in a parent data entity. The secondary keys identify the access paths into a data entity. The data entity keys are shown on a data structure chart, as shown in Figure 4.8. The *Vehicle Identification Number* is a primary key that uniquely identifies each vehicle. The *Owner Name* is a foreign key to the *Owner* data entity, a parent of the *Vehicle* data entity. The *Vehicle Identification Number* and the *Vehicle Make* and *Vehicle Model* are secondary keys for access into the *Vehicle* data entity.

```
                    --
                   |  #Vehicle Identification Number
                   |
                   |  +Owner Name
        Vehicle    << -Vehicle Identification Number
                   |
                   |  -Vehicle Make
                   |  -Vehicle Model
                    --
```

Figure 4.8 Data entity key submodel for a vehicle.

The **data view submodel** shows the application data views in an information system. Each data view is shown on a data structure chart, as shown in Figure 4.9. The first data view represents a set of *Employee* data used for *payroll*. The second data view represents

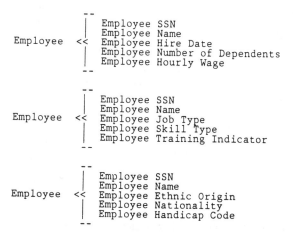

```
                  --
                  |   Employee SSN
                  |   Employee Name
     Employee   <<   Employee Hire Date
                  |   Employee Number of Dependents
                  |   Employee Hourly Wage
                  --


                  --
                  |   Employee SSN
                  |   Employee Name
     Employee   <<   Employee Job Type
                  |   Employee Skill Type
                  |   Employee Training Indicator
                  --


                  --
                  |   Employee SSN
                  |   Employee Name
     Employee   <<   Employee Ethnic Origin
                  |   Employee Nationality
                  |   Employee Handicap Code
                  --
```

Figure 4.9   Data view submodel of the employee data entity.

Employee data used for *training*. The third data view represents *Employee* data used for *minority and handicap employment* statistics.

The **data integrity submodel** shows all the data integrity rules for each data subject. The submodel includes definition of a data domain for each data attribute, definition of the relationship rules between data attributes, data structure and conditional data structural rules, derived data rules, rules for maintaining derived and redundant data, and rules for the retention and destruction of data. These rules are shown in a variety of tables and diagrams.

Physical Data Resource Model

The **physical data resource model** also consists of several submodels that are integrated to form a complete physical model. The physical model includes the file-relationship diagram, the physical data keys for access to a data file, the data items contained in each file, the physical data views that were implemented, and the data integrity constraints for maintaining the quality of the data. The definitions developed for the logical data model apply to the physical data model.

> The physical data resource model represents the physical database that meets the requirements of the logical model and the operating environment.

The physical data resource model is developed from the logical data resource model based on a formal set of criteria for converting the logical model to the physical model. It is used to determine what is in the physical database, how it is constructed, and how it can be accessed. The physical model is used to construct and document the physical database. A physical data resource model may be developed for each logical data model, or if a physical

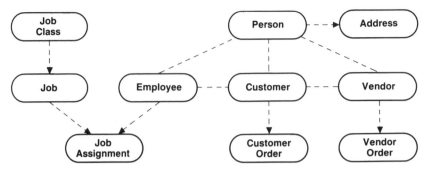

Figure 4.10 Example of a file-relationship diagram.

data model already exists, it is adjusted according to each new or updated logical data resource model.

File-relationship diagram. The **file-relationship diagram** represents the structure of the files in the physical database and the relationships between those files. An oval represents a data file, the same symbol used on the physical system architecture model. The name of the data file is placed inside the oval and represents the name of the physical file. Dashed lines represent data relations between data files, the same as the dashed lines that represented data relations between data entities on the entity-relationship diagram. The dashed lines may be either nondirectional or monodirectional. Bidirectional relations are not allowed on a file-relationship diagram. The data relations between files are not named and may not converge or diverge between data files for the same reasons explained for the entity-relationship diagram. An example of an file-relationship diagram is shown in Figure 4.10. This diagram was developed from a logical to physical conversion of the entity-relationship diagram shown above.

Other physical submodels. The **data item submodel** shows the data items in each data file. The data items in each data file are listed on a data structure chart similar to the way data attributes were listed for each data entity, as shown in Figure 4.11. The submodel is developed from a logical to physical conversion of the data attributes. Data items may be added that were not shown on the logical model and data attributes on the logical model might not be included on the physical model.

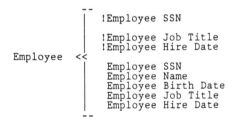

Figure 4.11 Data item submodel for the employee data entity.

Data keys consist of one or more data items that are used to store or retrieve data in the database. The data keys for each data file are shown on the data item submodel similar to the way data entity keys were shown on the logical model. They are the secondary keys that survived the logical to physical conversion and became physical keys in the database.

Physical data views are listed similar to the way they were listed on the logical data model. These data views may be application data views, combined data views, or full data views. Combined and full data views are formed by a combination of application data views during the logical to physical conversion.

Data integrity constraints are shown in the form of process logic that enforces the data integrity rules on all data entering the database. Since the data integrity rules are enforced through data integrity processes the content of those processes are defined by process logic. The data integrity constraints are developed from a logical to physical conversion of the data integrity rules for a particular operating environment. They may be placed in active data dictionaries, database management systems, or in data integrity processes developed by the enterprise.

Data Resource Model Relationships

The data resource model is integrated with business design models much the same as business design models are integrated with each other. The integration of these models provides two matrices that show the interaction between business processes and data, and between business units, and data. These two matrices are used to analyze the business environment and determine which processes should take action on the data and which business units should be responsible for initiating those actions.

A **data management matrix**, often referred to as a CRUD matrix, shows the action taken on each data attribute by each business process that contacts that data attribute. The data attributes are listed on the left and the business processes are listed on the top, as shown in Figure 4.12. The body of the matrix shows the *Create*, *Retrieve*, *Update*, and *Destroy* actions taken on the data by each business process. One or more of the codes may appear in any one cell. For example, a particular business process may retrieve a data

	BUSINESS PROCESS				
DATA	RPKO46	SCN116	CTCO54	KRS421	KRS421
Equipment					
Vehicle					
Equipment license number	C	R,U	R		
Equipment year manufactured	C	R,U	R		
Equipment make	C	R,U	R		
Equipment model	C	R,U	R		
Office					
Equipment type code			R	C	R,U
Equipment serial number			R	C	R,U
Equipment make			R	C	R,U
Equipment model			R	C	R,U

Figure 4.12   Example of a data management matrix.

attribute and then may update that same data attribute. The applications that manipulate any data attribute can be identified by reviewing the row for that data attribute, and all the data manipulated by any process can be identified by reviewing the column for that application.

A data management matrix can be developed for one set of processes, for one data entity, or for a set of data entities. The data attributes are listed within the data entity and the name of the data attribute may include the repository name if it is needed for uniqueness. The business processes at the top of the matrix are structured according to the business activity model. As many levels of that structure as desired are placed on the matrix, but the lowest level must represent the individual business processes that take action on the data. The data attributes on the left of the matrix are structured by data entity.

The data management matrix can also show data occurrence groups. A process may use only certain data occurrence groups and the data occurrence group on the matrix indicates that limited use. Data attributes are listed within each data occurrence group and since a data attribute can appear in more than one data occurrence group it can appear more than once in the data management matrix.

Data values could be added to the data management matrix to indicate which data attributes were used by a process. The addition of data values adds another dimension to the matrix, but it adds considerable value to the matrix. Identification of the data values would assist in determining which data attributes, based on the data values they contained, were managed by a process. The data values are added in an additional column for each process, as shown in Figure 4.13. This matrix indicates that *Equipment Type Codes 1*, *2*, and *3*, are created by process *RPK046* and *Equipment Type Codes 3*, *4*, and *5* are both retrieved and updated by process *SCN116*.

BUSINESS PROCESS

DATA	RPKO46 Value Use	Value	Use	SCN116
Equipment				
Vehicle				
Equipment license number	C			R,U
Equipment year manufactured	C			R,U
Equipment make	C			R,U
Equipment model	C			R,U
Equipment type code	1,2,3 C	3,4,5	R,U	

Figure 4.13 Example of a data management matrix with data values.

A data management matrix shows actions taken on data by business processes.

The data management matrix is derived from an analysis of the business processes and the data flows between those processes and data entities. It is not derived independent of these business models. The data flowing between business processes and data entities is shown on the logical system architecture model. Data flowing into data subjects may create, update, or destroy data. Data flowing out of data subjects represent data retrieved from the database and do not result in any change to the database.

A **data responsibility matrix**, also referred to as a CRUD matrix, shows which business units have responsibility for initiating actions on the data. The data attributes are listed on the left the same as the data management matrix, and the business units are listed on the top, as shown in Figure 4.14. The body of the matrix shows the actions taken on the data by each business units. The business units at the top of the matrix are structured according to the business unit model. As many levels of that structure as desired are placed on the matrix, but the lowest level must represent the business units that take action on the data.

	BUSINESS UNIT			
	Motor Pool		Property Management	
DATA	Maintenance	Reservations	Procurement	Maintenance
Equipment				
Vehicle				
Equipment license number	C	R,U	R	
Equipment year manufactured	C	R,U	R	
Equipment make	C	R,U	R	
Equipment model	C	R,U	R	
Office				
Equipment type code			R	R,U
Equipment serial number			R	R,U
Equipment make			R	R,U
Equipment model			R	R,U

Figure 4.14 Example of a data responsibility matrix.

> A data responsibility matrix shows the business units that perform or initiate actions on the data.

The data responsibility matrix is derived from an analysis of the business units that are authorized to perform each business process. It is not developed independently of these business models. The business units authorized to perform or initiate business processes are shown on the business process responsibility matrix. If a business unit performs or initiates a business process, and that process takes action on the data, then the business unit is responsible for initiating that action.

Data Resource Model Types

A data resource model can be used for several purposes. It can be used for strategic modeling, retrofit modeling of the existing data files, detailed modeling of data needed for each application in a project, data needed for ad hoc applications, and an enterprise model.

A **strategic data resource model** is a model of the major data entities in the enterprise and the data relations between those data entities. It provides the basic architecture for the enterprise's subject data resource by identifying and defining the data entities and data relations between those entities. It provides a broad scope of major data entities for the enterprise, but has minimum detail about each data entity. Its purpose is to set the basic data architecture for the enterprise.

> A strategic data resource model shows data entities representing behavioral entities and the relations between those entities.

A strategic data resource model is developed by people with a knowledge of the business environment and the operation of the enterprise in that environment. It is a top down process that is driven by an analysis of behavioral entities. These behavioral entities become the initial data subjects in the data resource. For example, an enterprise may track *customers*, *vehicles*, *employees*, *buildings*, etc. Each of these behavioral entities results in identification and definition of a data subject. As these subjects are defined the relations between them are also defined.

A **retrofit data resource model** provides additional detail that enhances the structure and content of the strategic data model. The retrofit data resource model includes an entity-relationship diagram, an entity-type hierarchy diagram, data attributes, data entity keys, data views, and data integrity rules that are included in the existing data files. A retrofit data resource model is narrower in scope than the strategic data resource model and is usually developed for one major function of the enterprise, such as *personnel*, *equipment*, or *marketing*.

> A retrofit data resource model enhances the strategic model with data contained in existing data files.

A **project data resource model** provides all the detail necessary to construct physical files that will support the enterprise. It builds on the data architecture provided by the strategic and the retrofit data resource models and contains all the submodels. A project data resource model is developed for each information system project until the structure of the data resource becomes stable. Once the structure and contents become stable the project model is used to determine data that are available in the enterprise's database.

The **ad hoc data resource model** provides additional detail that is needed for ad hoc inquiry into the database. The trend today is toward extensive ad hoc inquiry into the database. Development of the data resource to support major projects frequently does not include the detail necessary for extensive ad hoc processing. Some enhancement is needed, particularly data keys, to support ad hoc processing.

The project and ad hoc data resource models provide all the detail necessary to develop a physical database to support the enterprise.

The **enterprise data resource model** is the cumulative total of all the other data resource models. It represents the current status of the enterprise's data resource, including both application files and subject files and both logical and physical data models. It shows the future plans for that data resource and provides a framework for migrating to an enterprise-wide subject data resource. It is the master model for the enterprise's data resource.

GOOD DATA RESOURCE MODEL

What makes a good data resource model? This question is answered by reviewing some of the problems with existing data resource models and the changes that can occur with an enterprise's data resource. Based on these problems and database changes the criteria for a good data resource model can be defined.

Data Design Problems

The typical approach to database design has been to develop physical files directly from application requirements based largely on the physical operating environment. This approach led to the application files that are prominent today. As the concept of managing data as a separate and distinct resource and formal techniques for designing an enterprise-wide subject data resource based on the business needs of the enterprise emerged, several problems arose. These problems are a result of a conflict between the conventional approach to designing application files and the current approach to designing a subject data resource.

Initial data modeling techniques were incomplete, confusing, fragmented, inconsistent, and poorly understood. People using these techniques encountered difficulty, used the techniques unsuccessfully, and often abandoned them in favor of a more conventional approach. The problem was that these initial techniques were oriented toward logical data modeling with no specific criteria for representing business needs of the enterprise or for developing physical files from the logical model. This lack of a formal process for defining data and converting that definition to physical data files resulted in development of application data files. Database analysts used the logical model as a definition of requirements similar to the use of application requirements. The logical model was just another source of requirements for physical files.

The database analysts also faced the situation of creating a subject database and maintaining existing application files without techniques for managing data between these two different structures. To make this problem worse, there were no techniques for converting application files to a subject database without impacting production applications.

Therefore, database analysts tended to set the logical model aside and develop additional application files to avoid impacting the business operations.

> The major problem with an enterprise's database today is a conflict between the structure of application files and a subject database.

As data resource management techniques emerged, application analysts saw the subject data resource as a chance to reduce their maintenance effort. A reduction of maintenance would allow them to approach the mounting backlog of application requests. When database analysts kept developing application files, the application analysts virtually demanded that a physical subject database be developed like the logical model. However, they did not understand the problems faced by the database analysts. The result was a conflict between the structure of application files and the structure of a subject database that had no apparent resolution.

Data Resource Changes

The dynamic nature of the business environment and the discovery that results from designing a data resource ultimately result in changes to the database. The best design model and the best modeling process will not eliminate all changes to the enterprise's database. These changes are a fact of life and must be accepted. However, there are different types of changes that can occur and some are more severe than others. The impact of these changes can be minimized by being aware of the types of changes that can occur and designing the data resource to minimize the changes.

A **type one change** includes defining new data views and data keys for data that already exist in the database. When data already exist it is easy to create new views of the data and data keys to access data, and it is relatively easy to destroy data views and data keys that are not used. These changes are relatively common and are easy to implement with minimal impact on either the database or applications.

A **type two change** includes creation of new data items in a data file and the rearrangement of existing data items for optimization. Newly defined data items can be placed in an existing data file and data items in the file can be rearranged with minimal impact on the database or applications. These changes are also relatively common and relatively easy to make, although slightly more difficult than creating new data views and data keys from existing data.

A **type three change** includes creation of new data files as a result of the identification of new data subjects. When a new data file is defined it is implemented into the database, populated, and put into production. These changes are relatively common during the early stages of developing a subject database and are relatively easy to implement. As the data resource structure stabilizes these changes will be minimized.

A **type four change** includes splitting data items or data files that already exist, moving data items from one data file to another, or merging data files. This situation occurs when design of the database is incomplete and the rules for designing a subject data resource were not followed. These changes are serious and impact both the structure of the database and the applications using the database.

A **type five change** includes changes to data integrity rules. When data rules are separated from business rules and placed with the data they closely control the integrity of data going into the database. Data entering the database must conform to those rules before they are allowed to enter. Data that enter the database are considered high quality because they passed the data integrity rules. However, any changes to those data integrity rules could seriously impact data already in the database and could result in reediting data.

> Changes to the structure of the subject data resource and the data integrity rules seriously impact data in the database and applications using the database.

The first three changes are normal and easily implemented with a good subject data resource design and a good database management system. They result from a normal evolution of a subject data resource. In time, the addition of new files and attributes becomes minimal and most changes are data keys and data views. The last two types of changes seriously impact the structure of the database and the applications using the database and should be avoided.

A Good Data Resource Model

A good data resource model is the solution to these problems and to minimizing the serious changes to a subject database. That model must be comprehensive and must be integrated with other design models. It must include a logical design of the data resource based on business needs of the enterprise and a physical design based on the logical design and the physical operating environment. In other words, there must be a formal process from business needs to logical design to physical construction. The model must also be easy to develop, understand, and use.

> A good data resource model must meet the business needs of the enterprise and the physical operating environment.

The data resource model described above meets these criteria. It is a complete model that consists of both a logical and physical model. The logical model defines data that meet the business needs of the enterprise and represent the external and conceptual schema as defined by the business schema. The physical model defines data files according to the logical model and the specific operating environment and represents the internal schema.

The logical model helps the application analyst define the data needs of the enterprise. The physical model helps the database analyst construct data files to meet those needs. The formal conversion of the logical to the physical model brings the application analyst and the data analyst together to understand the need for a subject database and the physical capabilities of the operating environment. It provides a smooth transition from design of data requirements that meet business needs to implementation of physical files.

The data resource model makes the structure and meaning of a subject data resource clear to everyone in the enterprise and eliminates any hidden meaning. It provides all the information needed by the user, application analysts, and database analysts. It is dynamic enough to reflect changes to the business environment and the physical operating environment and maintains its integrity over time.

The data resource model produces a structurally stable subject data resource that requires minimum adjustment to correct structural anomalies. However, that database is flexible enough to meet the changing business needs without impacting its basic structure. New data that are not in the database can be easily added with minimum impact on the structure of the database and applications using that database. In other words, the data resource is structurally stable and evolves as the business needs evolve.

A good subject database evolves with the evolving business needs of an enterprise.

The data resource model provides a foundation for defining the existing database environment both as it exists today and as it would exist when restructured into a subject data resource. These two models are used to plan conversion of the existing database with minimum impact on business operations.

SUMMARY

The data resource model provides a practical approach to defining the data required to support the enterprise's business activities and the physical storage of those data. It helps to reduce the complexity of the data resource to a level that is understandable by everyone in the enterprise. It makes the analysis and design time more productive and assures that a physical database is developed that meets the needs of the enterprise and is optimal in a particular operating environment. Like the business design models, it encourages direct involvement of users in design of the data they need.

The data resource model consists of a logical and a physical model. Each of these models contains the submodels shown in Figure 4.15. Each submodel represents one aspect of the data resource and collectively define the logical and physical data resource of an enterprise.

Under the object management concept data are objects just like business processes, business entities, business transactions and behavioral entities. An enhancement of the

```
Data Resource Model
      Logical Model
                  Entity-Relationship Diagram
                  Entity Type Hierarchy Diagram
                  Data Control Diagram
                  Data Attributes
                  Data Descriptions
                  Data Entity Keys
                  Data Views
                  Data Integrity Rules
      Physical Model
                  File-Relationship Diagram
                  Data Items
                  Data Keys
                  Data Views
                  Data Integrity Constraints
```

Figure 4.15   Summary of data resource model components.

diagram shown in Figure 3.17 is shown in Figure 4.16. Data subjects have been added to the right side of the diagram with arrows showing how they are related to business units, business transactions, and the logical system architecture. Business units can perform or initiate actions on the data, business transactions contain data, and the logical system architecture shows the integration of the business processes, the business transactions and the data.

There is no substitute for developing a good data resource model. A *brute force* design of a physical database based solely on physical considerations will just not support the enterprise the way a well designed subject data resource will. Design of the data resource must be a formal process that is business driven and produces a structurally stable database. That process must include a good data resource model and techniques to support development of that model. The result is a well designed subject data resource that will support the enterprise.

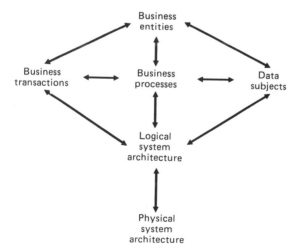

Figure 4.16   Enhanced object management diagram.

STUDY QUESTIONS

The following questions are provided as a review of the data resource model and to stimulate thought about the development, content, and use of data resource models and what constitutes a good data resource model.

1. What does a data resource model represent?
2. What are the basic units of data and why are they termed basic data units?
3. What is the relation between a data subject and a data entity?
4. What is the relation between a data characteristic and a data attribute?
5. What is the relation between a data property and a data value?
6. What are abstract data units?
7. How are abstract data units derived from basic data units?
8. How are a data category and a data entity type related to a data entity?
9. How is the physical structure of data related to the logical structure of data?
10. What does an entity-relationship diagram represent?
11. What has been the problem with some entity-relationship diagrams?
12. What does an entity-type hierarchy diagram represent?
13. What does a data control diagram represent?
14. What are the components of a logical data resource model and what does each represent?
15. What are the components of a physical data resource model and what does each represent?
16. Why are both a logical and a physical model needed?
17. What is the difference between a data management matrix and a data responsibility matrix?
18. How are the data management matrix and the data responsibility matrix developed?
19. What are the types of data resource models and what does each represent?
20. What have been the problems with past data design practices?
21. How can these problems be resolved?
22. What type of changes might occur in an enterprise's database?
23. How can the impact of these changes be minimized?
24. How is the data resource model related to the business design models?
25. What are the benefits of good data resource modeling practices?

chapter five

Data Description

Formal names and comprehensive definitions for each data unit are mandatory for an effective and efficient data resource.

A well designed data resource requires good design techniques and a good process for using those techniques. The first technique to design a data resource is to properly describe data in the data resource. Data description includes formal naming and comprehensive definition of each data unit in the data resource, whether it is a logical or physical data unit and whether it is a basic or an abstract data unit.

Correctly describing each data unit is the most critical step in developing a stable data resource. The data resource can fail to support the enterprise because of something as subtle as inappropriately named or inadequately defined data units. Although other steps in data resource design are certainly important, developing formal names and comprehensive definitions of each data unit is the most important. Correct design of the data resource is based on correctly interpreting and interpreting each data unit which is based on good data unit descriptions.

Describing each data unit in the data resource is the most critical step in designing the data resource.

One of the problems with existing data names is their inconsistency. For example, *birth date*, *date of birth*, *date born*, *birth*, and numerous other variations all represent the birth date of a person. Another problem is that existing data names are frequently meaningless. For example, *status*, *code*, *type*, and *field3* reveal nothing about the contents of the data. The same data name may be used for different data units. For example, *date* may be used to represent *date ordered*, *date shipped*, and *date received*.

In addition to these naming problems, data definitions are generally poor or nonexistent. Data units that are defined are only vaguely defined, such as *Student Name is the name of the student*, or *Customer Code is the status of the customer*. Many data definitions define use of the data not content of the data. The lack of good data unit definitions results in incorrect design of the data resource and incorrect use of the data. The data resource is not structured properly and data can not be readily identified.

This chapter explains techniques for describing data units in an enterprise's data resource. These techniques are integrated with developing the structure of those data units. Identifying data units based on business needs assists the data description process. Similarly, the data descriptions assist identification and structuring of data units. The result is a data resource that is properly structured and well described. People in the enterprise can use that data resource effectively and efficiently to make the right decisions and take the right actions.

DATA NAMES

Naming data units is not always easy, but it is not impossible if the basic principles listed below are followed.

> Each data unit must have a primary data name that is the fully spelled out, real world name of that data unit.
>
> All other variations of that name are considered aliases of the primary name.
>
> The name of each data unit must be unique within the enterprise.
>
> Each data unit name must be meaningful and understandable by everyone in the enterprise.
>
> The data unit name should reflect the structure of the data resource.
>
> The data unit name must represent the contents of that data unit not the use of the data unit.
>
> All data units, including nonelectronic and electronic data, must be formally named.
>
> Basic data units are named first, followed by the naming of abstract data units.

Data Naming Taxonomy

The basic problem with properly naming data units is the lack of a formal data naming taxonomy. Typically, words are used indiscriminately and are not uniformly or consistently sequenced. Most existing data names arose from the use of the data, not the contents of the data unit. These techniques have resulted in the synonyms, homonyms, aliases, and general ambiguity found in data names. The only way to resolve these problems is to establish a formal data naming taxonomy and use that taxonomy faithfully for naming data units.

> A formal data naming taxonomy is required for proper naming of each data unit in the data resource.

The data naming taxonomy presented in this book progresses from the general to the specific, much like the Dewey Decimal System for books, the postal zip code for mail, and names in the animal and plant kingdoms. This general to specific syntax provides a uniform meaning to data and is practical for anyone in the enterprise to use.

A complete data name consists of four parts: the repository name where the data unit is stored, the subject of the data, the characteristic of the data, and a variation of that characteristic. A colon is placed between the data repository and the data subject names, a period is placed between the data subject and data characteristic name, and a comma is placed between the data characteristic name and its variation.

Repository:Subject.Characteristic,Variation

For example, the data name

```
Dallas Tandem Equipment:Vehicle.Vendor ID,Purchase
```

shows the data unit is located in the *Equipment* file on the *Tandem* computer in *Dallas*. *Vendor ID* characterizes the *Vehicle* data subject and represents the *Vendor Name* from whom the vehicle was *Purchased*.

Most of the examples in this book will not contain the data repository name. It is used for identifying the location of decentralized data and for retrodocumenting existing data files. The punctuation has also been left off many of the examples for clarity. However, the punctuation may be used as necessary to make the data name fully explicit.

Data Repository Name

The data repository name uniquely identifies the location of the data and consists of one or more words. The data repository name can be a city, a computer, a file, a room, a combination of these locations, or any other physical location of data. If more than one word is used, they are sequenced from general to specific. For example, if data were located on only one computer the repository name would designate only the physical file, such as *Payroll*. If however, data were located on one of several computers, the data repository name would need to designate the computer, such as *IBM 3090*. If data were spread over several computers and the same file could be located on more than one of those computers, the repository name would include both the computer and the file, such as *IBM 3090 Payroll*. If data were decentralized and the same file could exist on several computers in several cities, the city, computer, and file would need to be identified, such as *Chicago IBM 3090 Payroll*.

> A data repository name identifies the physical location of the data.

The data repository name is used on the physical data resource model to show the location of data. It is particularly useful for showing where data are located in a decentralized environment. It is also useful for retrodocumenting existing data files and for managing data across the interface between application files and a subject database. It is generally not used to design the logical data resource, and will not be shown on most of the design examples.

An enterprise should plan ahead when establishing data repository names. Even though data may initially be centralized or may reside on only a few repositories, the structure of a data repository name should be carefully planned to allow for greater decentralization of data. A data repository naming structure should be chosen that will include possible locations and standard words for those locations. Then, as data are decentralized, the appropriate data repository name can be properly formed. This proactive approach provides meaningful data repository names and reduces the chance of changing data repository names as data become more decentralized.

Data Subject Name

Each data subject must have a unique name that is meaningful and indicates the structure of data. These names can be developed by following a few simple guidelines and naming techniques that overcome most of the problems encountered when naming data subjects.

> A data subject name uniquely identifies a subject of data and indicates the structure of the data resource.

Data subject name guidelines. A data subject name should not be too long or too short. Generally, one to three words is sufficient for most data subject names. If more than three words are used the name becomes a definition and there is increased chance for encountering a physical length restriction. For example, the data subject name *Customer Account Detailed Daily Transaction* is too long and is describing the use of the data not the content. A more appropriate name would be *Customer Account Activity* which is consistent with similar data subjects like *Customer*, *Customer Invoice*, and *Customer Payment* and indicates the structure of data. The definition of a data subject explains its use in more detail.

A single word may be too short and meaningless. For example, a data subject named *Detail* would be meaningless because it is not known what the detail data is about. A better name might be *Account Detail* meaning the detail transactions leading to the current account balance, or *Vehicle Maintenance Detail* meaning the detail about each vehicle maintenance activity. As the data resource evolves and new data subjects are defined other

Detail data subjects may emerge. Providing qualified data subject names will resolve possible conflicts and name changes.

A data subject name should be singular rather than plural because the name represents a single occurrence of an entity, such as *Vehicle* not *Vehicles*. The name should not be possessive, such as *Driver's License* but rather Driver License. If a possessive data subject name needs to be more semantically correct the apostrophe can be dropped, such as *Drivers License*, because many software products do not allow special characters in a data name.

The use of standard words enhances the meaning of data subject names and helps people interpret and understand the data and use it properly. For example, *Activity* can be used to designate all transactions coming into the system that result in changes to stored data. *History* can be used to designate all archival data that is static and stored for future reference. *Suspense* can be used to designate all data that fails an edit process and is awaiting correction.

> Standard words in a data subject name indicate the structure of the data resource.

Validation can be used as a standard word for data subjects that validate or verify codes. For example, the data subject *Account Budget Validation* indicates the valid combinations of *Account* codes and *Budget* codes. *Authorization* can be a standard word to designate authority to perform an activity. For example, *Encumbrance Authorization* can be used to show which employees can encumber money against specified projects. *Detail* can be used to indicate detailed data supporting another data subject, such as *Account* and *Account Detail*.

Using standard words clarifies the meaning of data subjects and indicates the structure of data. For example, *Employee, Employee Activity, Employee History*, and *Employee Suspense* mean current employee data, updates to employee data, archival employee data, and updates in error awaiting correction respectively. *Student, Student Activity, Student History*, and *Student Suspense* have similar meanings for students. These names add meaning to the structure of the data resource.

In some cases there are several words that have equal meaning and either word could be used in the data subject name. For example, *Country, Nation, Dominion, Republic, Kingdom, Empire, Territory*, etc., could all be used with nearly equal meaning. The same applies to *State, Province*, and *District*, to *County, Parish, Precinct*, and *Township*, and to *City, Town, Village, Municipality*, and *Burg*. The most appropriate name should be selected and the other names should be placed in a data subject name thesaurus.

Multiple data subject names can not be used to prefix the data attribute name. Multiple data subject names cause extreme difficulty understanding the true data subject being described. For example, the data subject prefix for wages is *Wage*, not *Employer Wage, Employee Wage*, or even *Employer Employee Wage*. It is simply *Wage*, which is defined as the wage paid by an employer to an employee.

One apparent exception to the multiple data subject names is a fully qualified data characteristic name that looks like a second data subject name. For example, an *Employer* makes many *Tax Payments*, so *Employer* and *Tax Payment* are data subjects. The due date for a tax payment may be different for each employer, and is a data characteristic of each Employer. That data characteristic is named *Tax Payment Due Date* and the data attribute name becomes *Employer Tax Payment Due Date*.

Structural inconsistencies. Data that are not structured by data subject result in inappropriate data subject names. **Synonymous data subject names** occur when the same data subject appears in two or more places with different names. When this happens the true contents of the data subject must be determined and the most appropriate name used as the primary data subject name. The other names can be listed as aliases of the primary name or listed in a data subject name thesaurus. If the same data subject exist in several different data repositories, the same data subject name is used and the repository name is added for uniqueness.

> Structural inconsistencies lead to inappropriate data subject names.

Homonymous data subject names occur when two or more distinctly different data subjects have the same name. When this happens the true contents of each data subject needs to be determined and the most appropriate name for each data subject becomes the primary name. The original names can be listed as aliases or placed in a data subject name thesaurus.

A distinction is made between alias names and synonyms and homonyms. An alias name is simply another name that is used for the same data subject. Generally, aliases are abbreviations or *also known as* names used in different files or programs for the same data subject, such as *Employer*, *Emplr*, and *Emp*. Synonyms and homonyms refer to structural inconsistencies with data subjects and their names. Resolution of these structural inconsistencies and proper naming of data subjects could lead to identification of alias names.

Determining data subject names. A **candidate data subject name** is one that appears to be the best name. As data analysis continues and the data resource model is developed candidate data subject names can be modified based on additional information that becomes available and the evolving definition of a data subject. A good definition of a data subject frequently leads to a good name for that subject. When the data analysis is complete, the data subject name is finalized based on the final definition.

In some situations it becomes very difficult to find a good data subject name for a variety of reasons. When this situation arises, the data analysis process should not cease but should continue without the impact of not having a formal data subject name. Several techniques can be used to allow data analysis to continue and to help determine a formal data subject name. These techniques include defining a data subject without an initial name, developing a data subject with a candidate name, and the use of **Z-words** for an interim name.

A data subject can be identified without a name during the early stages of design. As data structures are developed the set labels are left blank, indicating that a data subject name has been identified. The data attributes listed within that data subject are prefixed with a period indicating there is no data subject name, as shown in Figure 5.1. When the data subject name is determined, it will be added as the set label and as a prefix to each data attribute.

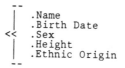

```
     --
    |    .Name
    |    .Birth Date
 << |    .Sex
    |    .Height
    |    .Ethnic Origin
     --
```

Figure 5.1 Data structure with undefined data subject name.

As candidate data subject names are identified they can be used as a set label without changing the data attribute names, as shown in Figure 5.2. This candidate name may be changed without impact on the data attribute names. When the final data subject name is determined it will be added as a prefix to data attribute names.

```
               --
              |    .Name
              |    .Birth Date
 Employee  << |    .Sex
              |    .Height
              |    .Ethnic Origin
               --
```

Figure 5.2 Data structure with candidate data subject name.

Another technique is the use of **Z-words**, like *Zing*, *Zap*, *Zumph*, etc., to indicate a data subject name, as shown in Figure 5.3. These words have absolutely no meaning with respect to data subjects and allow the definition of a data subject to continue without concerns over the most appropriate name. When an appropriate data subject name is determined, the Z-word is replaced with an appropriate data subject name and that name is used to prefix the data characteristic name.

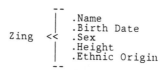

```
            --
           |    .Name
           |    .Birth Date
 Zing   << |    .Sex
           |    .Height
           |    .Ethnic Origin
            --
```

Figure 5.3 Data subject identified with a Z-word.

Z-words are useful when a data subject exists but there is strong disagreement over the name of that subject because of a variety of preconceptions and misconceptions. The use of a Z-word sets that concern aside until the data subject is fully defined and contains most of its ultimate data characteristics. At that time the formal data subject name can be discussed and selected. Generally, when the data characteristics have been identified and defined and the data subject has been defined, the name of that data subject becomes very obvious.

Data category and entity type names. Data categories and entity types are subsets of data subjects and are named the same as data subjects are named. The only possible difference is with entity-type names. Using the example of classified, exempt, and faculty employees, *Classified*, *Exempt*, and *Faculty* are considered data subjects. Since data subjects are defined from the perception of the business environment and different people have different perceptions of that environment, different subjects can be defined. In this case one perception is three subsets of employees and the other perception is three subjects. Regardless of how data subjects, data categories, and entity types are identified, they are named as data subjects.

Summary data and data domain names. A **summary data subject** contains data that are accumulated from one or more data subjects subordinate to the summary data subject. That summary data subject is identified by the data subjects in the hierarchy above the summary data subject, and the name must reflect those subjects. The name for a summary data subject can be too short, such as *Summary*, which provides little indication of what the data subject represents. The name can also be too long, such as *Company Salesman Customer Product Invoice Summary*, which although very descriptive, could easily cause name length problems. The ideal summary data subject name should indicate the subjects being summarized, the standard word *Summary*, and some additional qualifier. For example, *Invoice Summary 1* would be sufficient to indicate that *Invoices* were being summarized and, since several different types of invoice summaries could be developed, a *1* is added as the qualifier. Additional summaries of Invoices would be qualified with a *2*, a *3*, etc. The definition for each summary data subject would explain the data being summarized and the method of summarization.

A **data domain** is a set of values allowed for a data attribute. In reality, a data domain is simply another data subject and is named the same as any other data subject. Traditionally, data domains have been ignored and formal naming of those domains has been nonexistent. However, with the increased interest in integrity of the data resource data domains are becoming common. Consequently, each data domain must be considered part of the data resource and must be formally named.

Data Attribute Name

Each data subject is described by a set of data characteristics. Each of those data characteristics must be formally named the same as data subjects are formally named. If the data characteristic name is not unique, a variation of that characteristic is added as a suffix. This data characteristic name along with the data subject name form the complete name for each data attribute in the data resource.

A data attribute name consists of the data subject name, the data characteristic name, and a data characteristic variation.

Data subject prefix. Each data attribute name must begin with the name of the data subject it describes. If there is no data subject name, it is very difficult, if not impossible, to determine what data subject is being described by the data attribute. For example, *Birth Date* describes the data characteristic but provides no information about the subject it characterizes, such as *Customer*, *Student*, or *Employee*. Lack of a data subject name leads to improper use of the data. Therefore, the data subject name must prefix the data characteristic name, such as *Customer Birth Date*, *Student Birth Date*, and *Employee Birth Date*.

Each data attribute name must be prefixed by one, and only one, data subject name. That data subject name represents the subject of data that the attribute describes, which may not necessarily be the data subject that contains the data attribute. A common mistake in naming data attributes is to assume that the data subject name prefix must be the name of the data subject containing that data attribute. A good example is a foreign key to a parent data subject, as shown in Figure 5.4. Each *Building* is managed by an *Employee* and each *Employee* may manage more than one *Building*, making *Building* subordinate to *Employee*. *Employee SSN* becomes a foreign key in *Building* to identify the employee managing that building.

Building is the data subject which contains four data attributes describing each building and one data attribute referencing the employee managing that building. The four data attributes describing the building contain *Building* as the data subject name. The data attribute that indicates the manager of the building contains the data subject name *Employee* because *SSN* is a characteristic of the *Employee*, not of the *Building*.

```
                 --
                |  #Building ID
                |
                |  +Employee SSN
   Building  << |
                |   Building Name
                |   Building Size
                |   Building Year Built
                |   Employee SSN
                 --
```

Figure 5.4   Data subject prefix to a data attribute name.

If multiple data subject names were allowed, then both *Building* and *Employee* might be used to prefix the employees SSN, giving *Building Employee SSN*. This data attribute name causes confusion because it could indicate that the employee resides in that building, or that buildings have SSN's just like employees. Neither of these situations is correct, and the name is in error. Therefore, only one data subject name is allowed for each data attribute, and that name represents the name of the data subject the data attribute characterizes.

> The data subject prefix indicates the data subject characterized, not necessarily the data subject containing the data attribute.

Data characteristic name.   The data characteristic name follows the data subject name prefix and consists of one or more words that uniquely identify a data characteristic. The name must provide uniqueness within the data subject that characteristic is describing, not between data subjects. Uniqueness between data subjects is provided by the data subject name prefix.

> A data characteristic name uniquely identifies a data characteristic within a data subject.

A data characteristic name should not be too long or too short. If the name is too short it may not be meaningful and if it is too long it becomes a definition rather than a name. An appropriate data characteristic name should be selected that uniquely defines the data characteristic and provides a meaningful name, but does not become a definition of the characteristic.

Prepositions, connectives, and meaningless words should not be used in a data characteristic name. They make the name longer than necessary and add nothing to the meaning. For example, *Date of Birth* can be changed to *Birth Date* or *Date Born*. *Date The Salesman Said The Equipment Would Be Shipped* can certainly be shortened to *Equipment Date Shipped* and have the same meaning.

Data characteristic names can be too general and meaningless, like *Appointment Code 1*, *Appointment Code 2*, and *Appointment Code 3*. These data characteristics could be more appropriately named as *Appointment Pay Rate Code*, *Appointment Work Week Code*, and *Appointment Time Report Code*. These new names add full meaning to each data characteristic and avoid any possible confusion.

Data characteristic names must be fully qualified to be meaningful. For example, *Account Year Total* leaves room for misinterpretation as to which type of year, such as *calendar* year, *state fiscal* year, *federal fiscal* year, or *academic* year. The data characteristic should be specifically named, such as *Account Calendar Year Total* to prevent any confusion or misinterpretation. This qualification allows other yearly account totals to be defined without any impact on existing data attribute names.

The use of standard words in data characteristic names can provide additional meaning and better interpretation. For example, the word *Code* should be used to indicate a data characteristic containing coded values compared to actual values. Use of the word *Code* should also indicate a matching *Description* for that code. For example, the *Employer Class* data subject has both an *Employer Class Code* and an *Employer Class Description*. Use of names like *Employer Class Description Code* or *Employer Class Code Description* are not meaningful because it is unclear if the data characteristic is a code or a description, or both.

If there is no matching description, i.e., the code is self-explanatory, then the word *Code* should not be used. For example, if the values of a data characteristic were *Auto*, *Truck*, *Trailer*, *Motorcycle*, etc., which are self-explanatory and there will be no matching descriptions, the data attribute name should be just *Vehicle Type* rather than *Vehicle Type Code*.

Use of the word *Indicator* designates a binary situation, i.e. , *yes/no*, *true/false*, *0/1*, or *on/off*. An indicator, by definition, can never be more than a binary set of values. An indicator is not considered to be a code and there is no matching description. If there are more than two values, or there could be more than two values, the word *Indicator* should not be used.

A set of standard words should be defined for each enterprise. These standard words might include *date* for all dates, *value*, *amount* or *dollars* for dollar value, *count* or *quantity* for the quantity of items, *description* for a narrative description of an item, *name* for the name of an item, *comment* for narrative comments about an item, *code* for coded values, *indicator* for binary values, *identification* for alpha-numeric identification of an item, *number* for number identification of an item and not a quantity, *type* for the type of item, *status* for the status of an item, and so on. When use of a standard word is appropriate they should be included in the data characteristic name.

Special characters can also be used in data characteristic names if they provide meaning and are allowed by software products. For example, $, +, and % can be used to indicate value in dollars, addition or concatenation, and percentage, respectively. These special characters have a definite meaning and help keep the data characteristic name short. Special characters like # and * should not be used because they have no common meaning and could cause confusion. The *cent sign* should be avoided because it is not readily available on personal computer keyboards. Numbers can also be used to provide meaning and help keep data characteristic names short. For example, *Date6* and *Date8* indicate the formats of two different types of dates, and *Zip5* and *Zip4* indicate the two portions of the current Zip Code.

The term *Class Word* is avoided because it causes a problem with an implied format and implied data subject. For example, the class word *Date* may be defined as date in the format of *DDMMYYYY* and this definition would be standard for all uses of date. However, the word *Description* could be defined as any data characteristic that contained a narrative description, but would have a different format depending on the particular data characteristic. A person using *Job Description* which was 40 characters long might wrongly assume that all other descriptions were also 40 characters long. In extreme cases people have grouped data by class words rather than by data subjects. Therefore, the term *standard words* is used rather than class words.

Data characteristic variation.   Data attribute names must be unique to prevent any confusion. However, there are situations where the same data characteristic exists in several different variations. When a data attribute is defined for each of these variations the uniqueness could be lost. To resolve this problem a data characteristic variation name is added after the data characteristic name to provide a unique data attribute name.

A data characteristic variation name qualifies the variations of a single data characteristic to provide unique data attribute names.

For example, a department has only one name and the data characteristic is *Department Name*. However, that department name can exist in both a complete and an abbreviated form which are two variations of department name, not two separate characteristics. These variations are added after the characteristic name to form *Department Name Complete* and *Department Name Abbreviated*. Naming these two data attributes *Department Name* and *Department Name Abbreviated* leaves some doubt as to the true meaning of the first data attribute and could result in misinterpretation. Therefore, when a variation is required it is added to all variations of that data characteristic.

Another example is people that are currently in one resident hall and are requesting a move to another resident hall. This request must show their current residence hall, and a first and second choice for the move to another resident hall. *Residence Hall ID* is one data characteristic, but there are three variations of this one data characteristic. The variation names *Current*, *First Choice*, and *Second Choice* are added to the end of the data characteristic name to provide unique data attribute names as shown in Figure 5.5.

Data Description

```
                              --
                               |     Resident ID Number
                               |     Resident Name
        Resident Hall Request  <<   Residence Hall ID Current
                               |     Residence Hall ID First Choice
                               |     Residence Hall ID Second Choice
                              --
```

Figure 5.5 Variations for data attribute names.

The use of data characteristic variations is another reason why class words are not used to name data attributes. The class word is typically placed at the end of the name. However, when the data characteristic variation name is used it is placed at the end of the data attribute name to conform to the data naming taxonomy. To prevent a conflict between class words and data characteristic variation names standard words are used anywhere in the name rather than class words at the end of the name.

Data Value Name

Data values are the contents of data attributes and may be either actual values or coded values. Actual data values do not need to be named because the name of the data attribute is sufficient. For example, a person's height is an actual data value and a value of *62 inches* is meaningful. However, coded data values must be named and defined. For example, a grouping of heights in *Employee Height Code* containing the coded values *1, 2,* or *3* does not provide any specific information about a person's height.

Each coded data value must have a formal name that is unique within the enterprise. In the example above, the code values *1, 2,* and *3* might be named *Short, Normal,* and *Tall* which provides additional information about the values. A definition of these names would indicate that *short* is *60 inches and below, normal* is *61 to 72 inches,* and *tall* is *73 inches and taller.* Another example is *Student Admission Code* which contains three values, *1, 2,* and *3.* The names for these codes could be *New Student, Returning Student,* and *Continuing Student* respectively. The definition of each of these names would indicate the specific parameters for determining which coded value is used for each student.

> Each coded data value must have a unique name within the enterprise.

Data values are named the same as data characteristics. The names must be long enough to be unique, but must not be too long or too short. The names must be meaningful and indicate the structure of the data values. Standard words can be defined and used for data values the same as for data characteristics.

Abstract Data Unit Names

The basic data units are data subjects, data occurrences, data characteristics, and data values. Once these basic data units have been properly named, the abstract data unit names can be formed from the basic data unit names. In most situations the abstract data unit names are further qualifications of the basic data unit names.

The abstract data unit names are formed from the basic data units from which the abstractions were derived.

Data attribute group name. A data attribute group name is formed just like a data attribute name except that it is suffixed with the standard word *Group* to indicate that it represents a group of data attributes. This standard word must be used for all data attribute groups. For example, a data attribute group representing the data attributes *Zip Code Standard* and *Zip Code Extended* could be named *Zip Code Group*, and the data attribute group representing the data attributes *Phone Area*, *Phone Exchange*, and *Phone Line* might be named *Phone Number Group*.

The standard word *Group* should be reserved for data attribute groups and not used for other groupings. Other words, such as *class*, *category*, or *type*, should be used rather than *group*. For example, *Vehicle Use Group* should not be allowed for grouping vehicles because it would indicate a data attribute group. A better data attribute name might be *Vehicle Use Class* or *Vehicle Use Category*.

A data attribute group name should not be formed by concatenating the names of the individual attributes. Concatenation produces a name that is too long and frequently causes problems with physical length restrictions. A data attribute group name should be selected that refers to the group of data attributes not all the individual data attributes. Using the phone number example above, a name like *Phone Area Exchange Line Number* would be a poor data attribute group name. It is far better to use a name like *Phone Number Group* because it is shorter and more meaningful. The description of the data characteristic would indicate which data characteristics were contained in the group.

Data occurrence group name. Data occurrence groups represent selections from a data subject and are named by using a qualifier to prefix the data subject name from which those occurrences are extracted. The qualifier indicates the specific selection of data occurrences. For example, if the set of permanent employees were to be extracted from the *Employee* data subject, then the data occurrence group would be named *Permanent Employee*. If employees with *pilot certification* were to be extracted from the *Employee* data subject, then the data occurrence group would be named *Pilot Certified Employee*.

In some situations data occurrence groups are totally variable, such as the results of utility extracts. In these cases the data occurrence group cannot be formally defined because of the variable nature of the group. The data subject should be prefixed with the standard word *Selected* to indicate that the contents of the group depends on the specific selection criteria. For example, *Selected Account* would indicate that the criteria to select data occurrences from the *Account* data subject were variable from one extract to another. Use of the standard word *selected* means the selection criteria are variable from one extract to the next and a precise definition of the extract criteria must accompany the extract.

Data segment and database names. The other two abstract data units are data segments and databases. These data units are named based on the total set of information they contain and are suffixed with either *Data Segment* or *Database* respectively. For example, a data segment that represents all of the employee data, training data, position data, payroll data, and so on, for an enterprise might be called the *Employee Data Segment* or the *Personnel Data Segment*. A database that represents all the data entities used for payroll purposes might be called the *Payroll Database* and a database that is used for the registration of students might be called a *Registration Database*. The words *Segment* and *Database* are standard words.

Generally there is not a problem with the length of names for data segments or databases. The biggest problem is finding a name that includes all of the data contained in the segment or the database. The initial tendency is to use a name that defines the contents. However, like defining data subject names, a good definition of the data segment or the database will produce a meaningful name. The best way to develop a good definition is to paraphrase and combine the definitions of all the major data entities that form the data segment or the database. As this definition is refined an appropriate name almost always emerges.

Business Transaction Names

A business transaction is named uniquely within the enterprise. However, since these business transactions often contain multiple data subjects they are named according to their use in the business environment rather than according to the subjects of data they contain. Although the naming of business transactions has not been a problem in the past, the capability to transmit and store these business transactions electronically creates problems not previously encountered.

For example, a *Quarterly Report on Number of Employees by Salary Class by Ethnic Origin* is a report from an information system that becomes a business transaction. Obviously, this name is too long for most software products, even though it is meaningful. This business transactions needs a shorter name that is still unique and meaningful but meets the length restrictions of software products. A name like *Employee Standards* or *Employee Summary 1* might be appropriate and definition of that business transaction would indicate its contents.

The data attributes within a business transaction are named the same as any other data attributes. Each data attribute characterizes a data subject and just because that data attribute is part of a business transaction does not mean it can go without a formal data attribute name. Even if the data attribute is derived specifically for the business transaction and is not stored on the database, it characterizes a data subject and needs a formal data attribute name. Data attributes that are extracted from the database retain their original name and are not renamed by the business transaction that contains them.

All data in the enterprise's data resource belong to a data subject and must be named and defined whether or not they are stored in the enterprise's database.

A common mistake is to assume that data derived for a business transaction have no data subject and do not need to be formally named. This is a poor practice and leads to data that are improperly defined and used which causes a deteriorating database, particularly in a decentralized environment. Therefore, every data attribute, including those derived for business transactions, must be formally named and defined.

DATA DEFINITIONS

All data units, including logical and physical data units, and basic and abstract data units, must have a good, complete, meaningful definition in addition to a formal name. The formation of a good, complete, meaningful definition for each data unit must proceed in parallel with the naming of that data unit. A properly named data unit with no definition is as useless as a well-defined data unit without a formal name. Both a formal name and a formal definition are needed to provide a complete meaning for each data unit and to assure proper use of the data. An absence or weakness of either a proper name or a proper definition weakens the data resource.

> Every data unit must have a comprehensive definition based on its content not its use.

Inheritance is important in development of data unit definitions. Since a parent encompasses all of its subordinates, and the subordinates comprise the parent, the definition of both the parent and the subordinates must be synchronized with each other. Definition of a parent data unit must encompass the definitions of all of its subordinate data units and the definition of each subordinate data unit must be within the definition of its parent.

Data inheritance means that any level in the hierarchy of data or any level in the abstractions of data inherit the definitions of all levels above it. This applies to data subjects inheriting the properties of parent data subjects, data occurrences inheriting the properties of their data subject, data occurrence groups inheriting the properties of the selection criteria, entity types inheriting the properties of all types in the hierarchy above it, and derived data inheriting the properties of the primitive data from which they were derived. For example, if the definition of *Employee* were *Any person that worked for the enterprise at any time for remuneration in pay or in kind*, then each employee data occurrence would inherit this definition. If the employee were part time, the definition would still be that of an employee, plus the definition of part time.

Definition of data units is a value added process. Definition of subordinates add to the value of the parent, and definition of the parent adds value to the subordinate. Data inheritance is the principle that supports value added data definitions.

> Data unit definition is a value added process.

Existing data unit definitions are generally too short and provide little meaning. For example, data definitions like *Student Name is the name of the student* and *Customer Status is the status of the customer* are frequently seen. These definitions are virtually useless and add little meaning in addition to the data unit name. Data unit definitions need to be fully explicit to a newcomer. No assumptions should be made about the content of the data because assumptions could well result in inappropriate use of the data. A complete data definition should contain a full explanation of the contents of the data unit, the similarity and differences with closely related data units, its format, the source of the data, when and where it is captured, how it is changed, how long it is retained, its historical availability, the units of measurement and precision, and the structural and validity edit criteria.

Data units must be defined based on their content not on where or how they are used. When the true content of the data are known, then the most appropriate use can be made of those data units. Defining the use of a data unit limits the meaning of that data unit and could well limit the use of that data unit in the future, particularly for applications other than the initial application that produced the definition. Since ad hoc processing and decentralized databases are becoming common, a definition that is oriented toward the initial use of the data unit and not the content will limit the full use of that data unit in the future. Therefore, data units must be defined based on their content.

MANAGING DATA DESCRIPTIONS

Proper management of data descriptions includes the identification and avoidance of bad data description practices and the establishment of guidelines to assure the data resource is properly structured and described.

Bad Data Description Practices

There are several bad practices that should be avoided when naming data. These bad naming practices will ultimately lead to a loss of meaning, unnecessary data redundancy, and a deteriorating data resource. These bad practices can be avoided by being aware of the bad practices and by following the data naming techniques explained above.

A poor practice is to number each data subject and not have a formal data subject name, such as *DS001*, *DS002*, etc. Although this appears to avoid naming problems it leads to tremendous difficulty with the identification and meaning of data entities, particularly when there are several hundred data subjects within an enterprise. It also does not provide any indication of the structure of the data. The meaning has been lost by using such a numbering scheme which impacts the interpretability and understandability of the data.

It is also a very poor practice to number each data attribute, such as *DA001*, *DA002*, etc. This approach may appear to avoid naming problems, but it leads to tremendous difficulty with identification and meaning particularly when there may be several thousand data attributes in an enterprise. If a unique number is required for any reason, it can be assigned to each data attribute, but is an alias of the primary name.

Another poor practice is to guess at a data name without determining the definition and the structure of the data. This approach inevitably leads to the wrong names and nonunique names. Data are frequently named by the system or program that uses the data or the physical file where the data are stored. This practice is a result of conventional application file techniques and is wrong in the subject data resource environment. Data must be structured and named by data subject and data characteristic, not by physical storage or use.

The *OF Language*, popular in the 1970s, should not be used. It was originally proposed to bring some order to naming data by forming the data attribute name from the detail to the general, separating each word with the word *of*, such as *Date of Birth of Employee*. It is more meaningful, and produces a shorter name, to follow the taxonomy of a data subject name followed by a data characteristic name progressing from general to specific, such as *Employee Birth Date*.

Meaningless data subject names should be avoided, particularly single word names that could have several interpretations. For example, the words *Transaction*, *Detail*, *Activity*, or *Journal* may have a definite meaning within a project, but may have multiple meanings outside the project. These meaningless words should be avoided in favor of *Budget Transactions*, *Account Detail*, *Customer Activity*, and *Wage Journal*.

Unqualified words, such as *Type*, *Code*, and *Status* should be avoided. For example, *Employer Type*, *Wage Code* and *Student Status* are not fully qualified and are meaningless. It would be better if these data attributes were named *Employer Business Type*, *Wage Payment Code*, and *Student Enrollment Status*. These names are fully qualified and are more meaningful.

A very poor practice is to not have any guidelines for naming data. A lack of guidelines leads to a free-for-all for naming data. The result is synonymous names, redundant data, lack of meaning, and a deteriorating data resource. An enterprise must have explicit data naming guidelines and those guidelines must be followed to assure a sound enterprise data resource.

Developing a data unit definition without a knowledge of the structure of the data is a bad practice. It results in inconsistent definitions that do not truly represent the data unit. The data structure must be understood and the definitions must be consistent within that structure. The best practice is to repeatedly work up and down the structure of data to assure that the definitions are consistent and that there are no gaps or overlaps in the definitions of data units. However, an initial definition of the data unit may help with proper structuring.

Guidelines for Describing Data

Developing data names and descriptions is a cyclic process between naming data, defining data, and structuring data. The data name indicates the structure of the data, but the structure of the data governs the name. The definition helps define the structure and the name, but the structure sets the scope of the definition. None of these techniques drives the process. They must all proceed together to provide data that are properly structured, named, and defined.

Defining data subjects, data characteristics, and data properties is also a cyclic process. Generally, data subjects are identified first, then the data characteristics that describe each subject, and then the data properties for each coded data characteristic. However, this sequence is not always followed. Identification of data subjects sets the scope of its characteristics, but a set of characteristics help identify the data subject. Identification of data characteristics sets the scope of its properties, but a set of properties help identify the data characteristic.

When the basic data units have been identified and described, the abstractions of those data units can be identified and described relatively easy. When the process is completed each data unit in the data resource is properly named and defined.

The responsibility for this process belongs to everyone in the enterprise that uses the data. The primary responsibility may rest with the data administration unit, but that primary responsibility includes facilitating the involvement of everyone that uses the data resource. The data administration unit should establish guidelines for naming and defining data as well as structuring the data resource. The guidelines should apply to all data in the enterprise, whether stored electronically or manually and regardless of where they exist in the enterprise. They should be developed on an enterprise-wide basis with the involvement of anyone that uses the data resource. As soon as the data administration unit becomes too authoritative or abdicates its responsibility, the guidelines will suffer and the data resource will deteriorate.

An enterprise should be proactive in establishing guidelines. Both the existing and future environment must be considered when formulating these guidelines. Neglecting the future environment could lead to extensive adjustment of guidelines and an impact on the data resource as a result of that adjustment. Establishing policies and guidelines that consider the present and the future environment assures that everyone in the enterprise will structure, name, and define data in a consistent manner. This consistency adds to the semantics of the data resource and provides a stable data resource that will support the enterprise.

SUMMARY

The processes of identifying, structuring, and describing data are inseparable. When these processes are successfully integrated a well-structured and well-described data resource will result. Although all of these processes are important, the process of describing data is considered the most important because it is the data unit description that connects the data resource to the user. If this connection is faulty the data resource can not be used effectively or efficiently.

The task of describing data units is not easy, but it is not impossible. The process takes patience, practice, sound techniques, constant analysis and evaluation, and careful thought. A good dictionary or thesaurus are invaluable for assisting with data descriptions. Many times there are arguments and discussions about the data resource, but with a good base of guidelines and techniques, these arguments are about the data resource itself and are productive. Without this base, the arguments are about the process and are nonproductive. The time spent establishing guidelines and techniques is well worth the effort.

The guidelines for describing data units are listed below. These guidelines, along with the techniques explained above, provide an excellent base for describing the data resource.

The description of a data unit consists of a formal data name and a comprehensive data definition.

The formal data naming taxonomy consists of a data repository name, a data subject name, a data characteristic name, and a data characteristic variation name.

The data repository name identifies the location of data.

The data subject name identifies the subject of data being characterized.

Data names progress from general to specific.

Data names must be long enough to be meaningful and short enough to avoid physical length restrictions.

Standard words provide consistent meaning and indicate the structure of data.

Each data unit has one primary name that is the fully spelled out real world name.

Other data unit names are aliases of the primary data name.

Data domains, data categories, and entity types are named the same as data subjects.

Each data attribute has one and only one data subject name prefix.

The data subject prefix indicates the data subject characterized, not necessarily the data subject containing the data attribute.

A data characteristic name identifies a unique characteristic within a data subject.

The data characteristic variation name qualifies versions of the same data characteristic.

Each coded data value must have a formal name that is unique within the enterprise.

Basic data units are named first, followed by naming of abstract data units.

Abstract data unit names are derived from basic data unit names.

All data in the enterprise's data resource belong to a data subject and must be named according to that subject.

All data units must have a comprehensive definition based on the content of that data unit.

Data are defined by content and not by use or storage.

Describing data is a cyclic process between names, definitions, and structure.

Design of the data resource begins with identification and description of the data units. When a formal data naming taxonomy is established and each data unit is named according to that taxonomy and is comprehensively defined the data resource will provide direct support to the enterprise. The data resource will also be structurally stable and will survive changes in the business environment with minimum impact on the support it provides the enterprise. However, it will remain flexible to meet the needs of the enterprise in that changing business environment.

STUDY QUESTIONS

The following questions are provided as a review of data descriptions and to stimulate thought about naming and defining data.

1. What is the most critical step in developing a stable data resource and why?
2. What are the problems with existing data names and definitions?
3. What is the basic problem with data names and definitions?
4. What is the solution to this basic problem?
5. What is the difference between primary names, alias names, and synonyms?

6. What does each part of the formal naming taxonomy represent?
7. What procedure is used to determine a formal data subject name?
8. What can be done when there is difficulty determining data subject names?
9. Under what conditions should data values have names?
10. Why should coded data values have names and definitions?
11. How are abstract data units named?
12. What determines a good data definition?
13. What bad data description practices should be avoided and why?
14. What is the process for structuring and describing data units?
15. Why should enterprise-wide guidelines be established?
16. Who should be involved in forming those guidelines?
17. What could happen when guidelines are formed and enforced unilaterally?
18. How should data names be managed?
19. Are formal data names and definitions really necessary and why?
20. How can lack of data descriptions can cause deterioration of a data resource?

chapter six

Data Keys

Understanding the types and use of data keys is the first step toward designing the structure of the data resource.

Describing data and structuring the data resource are closely related and when done properly produce a well structured, well-documented data resource. Understanding the process of structuring the data resource begins with an understanding of the types and use of data keys. Data keys are data attributes that have a special meaning and use in addition to describing a characteristic of a data subject. Once these data keys are understood they can be combined with data relations and used to enter and navigate through the database to store and retrieve data. Without properly defined data entity keys it would be impossible to navigate through the database or to access data in the database.

This chapter explains the definition and use of data keys. The unqualified term *Key* is often used to mean *Primary Key* and has caused confusion about the use and meaning of primary keys, secondary keys, and foreign keys. Each of these three types of keys have a different meaning and use for designing the data resource. The qualified terms *primary key*, *secondary key*, and *foreign key* will be used in this book to avoid any confusion.

103

PRIMARY KEY

Each data entity must contain a set of one or more data attributes that uniquely identify each data occurrence in that data entity. This set of data attributes is termed a **primary key** and must have a different value for each data occurrence in that data entity. Two or more data occurrences in a data entity can not have the same value in their primary key. If they do, then the primary key does not provide uniqueness and does not form a valid primary key.

A primary key uniquely identifies each data occurrence in a data entity.

Each data entity can have only one **official primary key**. Some data entities may have several sets of data attributes which uniquely identify each data occurrence in that data entity. However, only one of these sets of data attributes can be designated as the official primary key. The other sets are considered **alternate primary keys**.

If a data entity does not have a primary key the data normalization process will not work properly and false data entities can be identified. A common misconception is that a primary key is not required for data entities that have no subordinate data entities. However, if a primary key is not identified for all data entities, including those without subordinates, the data normalization process may not properly verify data entities. Therefore, each data entity must have a primary key.

Each data entity must have one and only one official primary key.

A primary key does not designate access to a data entity. The primary key is used only to uniquely identify each data occurrence in a data entity. Secondary keys are used to identify access to the data as explained in the next section. There are situations where the primary key is never used to access the data, and should never be designated as an access path. If a primary key automatically designated an access path, a physical data key would be developed and maintained and never used which leads to an inefficient database. Therefore, the primary key does not automatically designate an access path to the data.

The data attributes forming a primary key are identified with a **pound sign** (#) in front of the data attribute name, as shown in Figure 6.1. Each individual vehicle in the *Vehicle* data entity is uniquely identified by the *Vehicle License Number* as indicated by the **pound sign** in front of the data attribute name. The same license number value can not be

```
              --
              |   #Vehicle License Number
              |
              |    Vehicle License Number
   Vehicle  <<    Vehicle Make
              |    Vehicle Model
              |    Vehicle Year Manufactured
              |    Vehicle Color
              --
```

Figure 6.1 Primary key for vehicles.

assigned to more than one vehicle and each vehicle must have one and only one license number.

The primary key is placed at the top of the data set and is separated from the set of data attributes that describe *Vehicle*. A data attribute in the primary key is also listed in that set of data attributes that characterize *Vehicle* to form the application data view. Although this procedure creates additional entries it provides a data structure that is more understandable and easier to maintain and modify during the design process. The reason for this procedure will become clearer with the following examples.

Primary Key Types

There are three types of primary keys depending on how many data attributes are included and whether those data attributes are in their home data entity or a foreign data entity. Each of these types of primary keys is explained below.

A data attribute describes a characteristic of a data entity which is considered its **home data entity**. For example, *Vehicle License Number* describes a characteristic of the *Vehicle* data entity which is its home data entity. A data attribute can also be placed in another data entity that it does not describe which is considered a **foreign data entity** and the data attribute is considered a **foreign data attribute**. For example, when *Vehicle License Number* is placed in the *Vehicle Owner* data entity it is a foreign data attribute.

Single primary key.   A **single primary key** consists of a single data attribute that can be in its home or in a foreign data entity. The example in Figure 6.1 is a typical example of a single primary key in its home data entity. *Vehicle License Number* is a single data attribute that characterizes *Vehicle* and uniquely identifies each vehicle.

The example in Figure 6.2 shows a foreign data attribute as a single primary key. For example, *Student History* contains historical data about students. It contains both *Student* data and additional *Student History* data that was not kept about the student when he or she were in school. The primary key for *Student History* is *Student ID Number* which is used to uniquely identify each student in the school, including *Student* and *Student History* data. This situation is also common in entity types where *Employee SSN* is the primary key for *Staff*, *Exempt*, and *Faculty*.

```
                            --
                           | #Student Id Number
                           |
                           |  Student Id Number
        Student History  << |  Student Name
                           |  Student History Graduation Age
                           |  Student History Terms Attended
                           |  Student History Final GPA
                            --
```

Figure 6.2   Foreign data attribute as a single primary key.

Compound primary key.   When a single data attribute can not uniquely identify each data occurrence, additional data attributes are needed. When all of these data attributes are in their home data entity they form a **compound primary key**. For example, the data structure in Figure 6.3 shows *Academic Term* with a primary key composed of three data attributes. Each academic term is uniquely identified by a *Begin Date*, an *End Date*, and a *Type*. All three data attributes are in their home data entity and compose a compound primary key.

```
                              --
                          |   #Academic Term Begin Date
                          |   #Academic Term End Date
                          |   #Academic Term Type
                          |
    Academic Term    <<       Academic Term Begin Date
                          |   Academic Term End Date
                          |   Academic Term Type
                          |   Academic Term Registration Date
                          |   Academic Term Final Grade Date
                              --
```

Figure 6.3 Compound primary key for academic term.

Composite primary key. When several data attributes are needed to uniquely identify each data occurrence, and one or more of those data attributes is a foreign data attribute, they form a **composite primary key**. For example, the data structure in Figure 6.4 shows the hierarchy of *Academic School*, *Academic Field*, and *Academic Course* data entities needed to track all courses taught in a school district. *Academic School* has a single primary key of *Academic School ID*. *Academic Field* has a composite primary key of *Academic School ID* and *Academic Field Code*. *Academic Course* has a composite primary key of *Academic School ID*, *Academic Field Code*, and *Academic Course Number*.

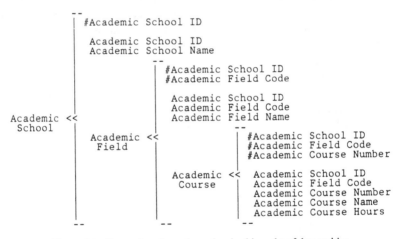

Figure 6.4 Composite primary keys showing hierarchy of data entities.

The data attributes in a composite primary key indicate the hierarchy of parent data entities, as shown above. They can also indicate multiple parents that do not form a hierarchy. The data structure in Figure 6.5 shows the primary key of a data entity representing the appointment of employees to positions. *Employee SSN* identifies *Employee*, which is a parent of *Appointment*. *Position Number* identifies *Position*, which is also a parent of *Appointment*. *Appointment Date* makes each appointment unique since an employee could be appointed to the same position more than once, but not on the same date.

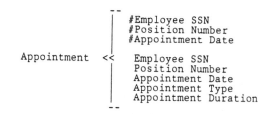

```
                               --
                              |    #Employee SSN
                              |    #Position Number
                              |    #Appointment Date
                              |
         Appointment    <<    |    Employee SSN
                              |    Position Number
                              |    Appointment Date
                              |    Appointment Type
                              |    Appointment Duration
                               --
```

Figure 6.5   Composite primary key showing multiple parents.

Generally, there are very few data entities in an enterprise that have compound primary keys. Whenever several data attributes are needed to form the primary key, those data attributes are usually taken from parent data entities. Therefore, composite primary keys are much more common than compound primary keys. Composite keys are important because they help identify the structure of data subjects while compound keys do not.

Sequence of Data Attributes

The sequence of data attributes in compound and composite primary keys have no meaning as far as uniquely identifying each data occurrence. In other words, they are not **sequence specific**. However, the sequence of data attributes in a primary key should follow the hierarchy of the parent data entities, and the foreign data attributes should be listed before the home data attributes for clarity. Although this sequence is not required for unique identification of a data occurrence, it provides additional information about the structure of the data resource.

> The sequence of data attributes in a primary key indicate the structure of the data resource.

For example, the data structure in Figure 6.4 shows the data attributes in the primary key for *Academic Course* in the same sequence as the hierarchy of parent data entities. The data structure in Figure 6.5 shows the foreign data attributes *Employee SSN* and *Position Number* before the home data attribute *Appointment Date*. These data attributes could have been placed in any sequence. However, placing them in the same sequence as the hierarchy of parent data entities, and showing the foreign data attributes first, increases the semantics of the data model.

Redundant Data in a Primary Key

A primary key must not contain redundant data. No data attribute should be able to be removed without destroying the ability of the primary key to uniquely identify each data occurrence. Therefore, if a data attribute does not contribute to the uniqueness of a primary key it must be removed. If a redundant data attribute is left in a primary key it does not destroy the ability of that primary key to uniquely identify each data occurrence. However, it does result in unnecessary processing and unnecessary data storage.

If each data attribute represents a single data characteristic, then a single primary key can never be redundant. As long as that characteristic uniquely identifies each data occurrence in that data entity it forms a valid primary key. Redundant data in single primary keys can only occur when there are multiple characteristics in a data attribute and one or more of those characteristics represents redundant data.

Redundant data attributes in a primary key must be removed.

Most redundant data in a primary key occurs with compound or composite primary keys. One or more data attributes have been included in the primary key that are not needed to uniquely identify each data occurrence. For example, the primary key in Figure 6.6 consists of *Vehicle License Number* and *Vehicle Year Manufactured*. Since each vehicle can be uniquely identified by the *License Number*, *Vehicle Year Manufactured* is redundant data and could be removed without destroying the ability of the primary key to uniquely identify each vehicle.

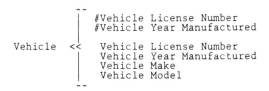

```
                  --
                 |    #Vehicle License Number
                 |    #Vehicle Year Manufactured
                 |
   Vehicle   <<  |    Vehicle License Number
                 |    Vehicle Year Manufactured
                 |    Vehicle Make
                 |    Vehicle Model
                  --
```

Figure 6.6   Redundant data attribute in a primary key.

One reason for listing data attributes that compose a primary key both in the primary key and again in the data attribute list is to prevent losing track of that data attribute during design. If a data attribute were listed only once with the primary key and not with the data attributes, and it was determined that it was redundant data it would be removed from the primary key. If the designer forgot to put it into the data attribute list it would be lost from the data structure which could impact development of the data entity and the availability of that data characteristic. Therefore, the data attributes composing a primary key are listed both in the primary key and in the data attribute list.

Identifying a Primary Key

There are four simple criteria to follow for identifying data attributes that form the primary key. If these criteria are followed, there is a high probability the primary key selected will survive the data normalization process and become a valid primary key.

Any initial primary key is a **candidate primary key**. Each of these candidate primary keys must be proven valid and one of them selected as the official primary key. The candidate primary keys that are invalid are discarded and those that are valid but are not selected as the official primary key become alternate primary keys.

The first, and most important, criteria for identifying a valid primary key is that the data attributes must make each data occurrence in the data entity unique. If the data attributes do not uniquely identify each data occurrence, then it is an invalid primary key. Another candidate primary key should be selected either by adding data attributes to or deleting data attributes from the present candidate or by selecting a totally different candidate primary key.

Second, if several data attributes are needed to define the primary key, none of those data attributes must be redundant with respect to uniquely identifying each data occurrence. If a data attribute does not contribute to the uniqueness of each data occurrence and could be left out of the primary key without destroying its ability to uniquely identify each data occurrence, then there is redundant data in the primary key. The data attribute causing the redundancy must be removed.

Third, if there are several candidate primary keys, then the one that has the fewest data attributes, is the shortest, the most numeric, and the most meaningful should be selected as the official primary key. For example, if there were two candidate primary keys for the customer data entity, one containing *Customer Account Number* and the other containing *Customer Name* and *Customer Address*, the candidate consisting of *Customer Account Number* should be selected as the official primary key because it is the shortest, has the fewest data attributes, and is numeric.

Fourth, when a primary key can not be identified, an implied data attribute might be considered. Frequently, the data attributes that appear on a data structure do not contain all the data attributes necessary to form a valid primary key. Also, the primary key may be a composite primary key requiring data from a parent data entity. When there is difficulty identifying the primary key, these alternatives should be considered.

An alternate primary key may be treated as a primary key, but it should not be relied upon to maintain its uniqueness. Frequently, an alternate primary key will lose its uniqueness because the conditions of a data entity change. For example, if both *Employee SSN* and *Employee Name* were valid candidates for the primary key and *Employee SSN* was picked because it was the shortest and was numeric, then *Employee Name* would become an alternate primary key. However, as the size of an enterprise increases there is the possibility of having two people with the same name and the alternate primary key would cease to be unique. Therefore, alternate primary keys must be used with caution.

Two different data entities may have the same primary key. These data entities usually represent data categories or data subjects. For example, *Person* and *Employee* represent a data entity and a data category respectively and both have a primary key of *SSN*. Similarly, the entity types within Employee, such as *Faculty*, *Staff*, and *Exempt*, may all have a primary key of *SSN*.

Surrogate Keys

Surrogate keys are primary keys that are invisible to the user and are used only by the database management system and database analysts for unique identification of each data occurrence in a data entity. A surrogate key can not be changed by the user or the database analyst and remains the unique identifier of data occurrences regardless of any other changes to the data. A primary key, on the other hand, is visible to the user and can be changed by the user, although that change must be done very carefully. Each enterprise must decide whether surrogate keys are to be used or not depending on their objectives and the capabilities and requirements of their database management system. Only primary keys will be discussed in this book.

SECONDARY KEY

A **secondary key** consists of one or more data attributes that are used to access a data entity to store or retrieve data. A secondary key may identify a single data occurrence, multiple data occurrences, or possibly no data occurrences, based on the value of the key and the data in the database. If a secondary key is used for storing data then it usually identifies a single data occurrence. If it is used to retrieve data occurrences then it may not identify any data occurrences, or it may identify one or more data occurrence.

> Secondary keys provide access to data in the database.

Each data attribute in a secondary key is designated with a **minus sign** (-) in front of the data attribute name. For example, the primary key for each *Building* is *Building ID*, as shown in Figure 6.7. If access to a specific building is needed, a secondary key is defined for *Building ID* as indicated by the **minus sign**. Additional accesses are needed for the type of building and the date the building was constructed as indicated by secondary keys for *Building Type Code* and *Building Date Constructed*.

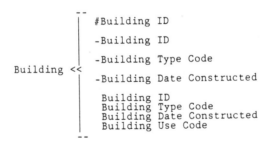

```
                              --
                             |   #Building ID
                             |
                             |   -Building ID
                             |
                             |   -Building Type Code
              Building  <<  <
                             |   -Building Date Constructed
                             |
                             |   Building ID
                             |   Building Type Code
                             |   Building Date Constructed
                             |   Building Use Code
                              --
```

Figure 6.7   Secondary keys for buildings.

Based on the requirements to store and retrieve data, many secondary keys may be identified for a single data entity. These secondary keys are listed below the primary key on a data structure and each secondary key is listed separately. The data attributes in secondary keys are also listed in the set of data attributes that characterize a data entity.

Secondary Key Types

There are four specific types of secondary keys depending on whether the data attributes match the primary key, are only part of the primary key, contain none of the primary key data attributes, or are a mixture of primary key and nonprimary key data attributes. In addition, secondary keys can be used to access data based on a fixed value or a range of values. Each data entity must have at least one secondary key, unless the entire file is read.

Primary key match.   If there is a need to access a unique data occurrence, a secondary key will be identified that contains the same data attributes as the primary key. As explained above, the primary key only indicates uniqueness and does not indicate access to a data entity. A secondary key containing the same data attributes as the primary key needs to be defined for access to a unique data occurrence. For example, the primary key for *Vehicle* in Figure 6.1 consists of only *Vehicle License Number*. If access were to be made for a specific vehicle, the primary key would need to be identified as a secondary key for access as shown in Figure 6.8.

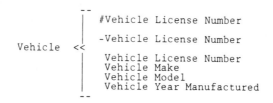

```
            --
           |    #Vehicle License Number
           |
           |    -Vehicle License Number
Vehicle  <<
           |    Vehicle License Number
           |    Vehicle Make
           |    Vehicle Model
           |    Vehicle Year Manufactured
            --
```

Figure 6.8   Secondary key for unique access.

Access to a data entity based on the primary key will yield either one data occurrence if a data occurrence with that value is on the database or nothing if there are no data occurrences with that value in the database. The data attributes in the primary key could also be combined with other data attributes not in the primary key to form a secondary key; however, the result would be identification of either a single data occurrence or no occurrences. For example, the primary key for *Employee* is *Employee SSN* and a secondary key is defined with *Employee SSN* and *Employee Job Title*. If the employee with the SSN specified had the job title specified, then that data occurrence would be obtained. If, however, the employee with the SSN specified did not have the job title specified, no data occurrences would be obtained.

A secondary key that represents an alternate primary key may also be defined. However, since an alternate primary key may not retain its uniqueness, the ability of that secondary key to identify a unique data occurrence may not be maintained. If the alternate primary key loses its uniqueness, then the ability of a secondary key based on the data attributes in that alternate primary key also loses its ability to identify a single data occurrence.

Partial primary key.   Part of a compound or composite primary key can be defined as a secondary key. For example, the primary key for *Academic Course* in Figure

6.4 consists of *Academic School ID*, *Academic Field Name*, and *Academic Course Number*. If all the academic courses for a specific academic field in a specific school were required, *Academic School ID* and *Academic Field Name* would be defined as the secondary key, as shown in Figure 6.9.

```
                          --
                         |    #Academic School ID
                         |    #Academic Field Name
                         |    #Academic Course Number
                         |
                         |    -Academic School ID
      Academic Course  << -Academic Field Name
                         |
                         |     Academic School ID
                         |     Academic Field Name
                         |     Academic Course Number
                         |     Academic Course Name
                          --
```

Figure 6.9 Secondary key representing a partial primary key.

If all academic courses in all the academic fields for any one academic school were also desired, then an additional secondary key containing *Academic School ID* would be needed as shown in Figure 6.10. Additional secondary keys can be added in the same manner until all accesses have been defined.

```
                          --
                         |   #Academic School ID
                         |   #Academic Field Name
                         |   #Academic Course Number
                         |
                         |   -Academic School ID
                         |   -Academic Field Name
      Academic Course  << 
                         |   -Academic School ID
                         |
                         |    Academic School ID
                         |    Academic Field Name
                         |    Academic Course Number
                         |    Academic Course Name
                          --
```

Figure 6.10 Multiple secondary keys.

Nonprimary key. A **pure secondary key** does not contain any data attributes that compose the primary key. *Employee Job Title* has been defined as a secondary key to obtain all employees with a specific job title, as shown in Figure 6.11. For example, if there were 22 data occurrences in *Employee* with a job title of *Master Mechanic*, then 22 data occurrences would be obtained using a secondary key value of *Master Mechanic*.

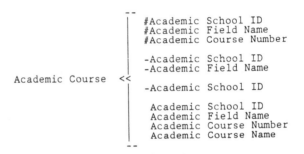

```
                      --
                     |   #Employee SSN
                     |
                     |   -Employee Job Title
                     |
      Employee  <<       Employee SSN
                     |    Employee Name
                     |    Employee Birth Date
                     |    Employee Job Title
                     |    Employee Hire Date
                      --
```

Figure 6.11 Pure secondary key for accessing employee data.

A secondary key consisting of *Employee Job Title* and *Employee Hire Date* is shown in Figure 6.12. If *Master Mechanic* and *June 1980* were the values entered for job title and hire date respectively, then all *Employee* data occurrences containing those values would be obtained.

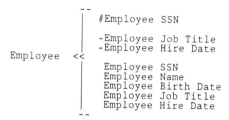

```
                   --
                   |   #Employee SSN
                   |
                   |   -Employee Job Title
                   |   -Employee Hire Date
   Employee    << |
                   |    Employee SSN
                   |    Employee Name
                   |    Employee Birth Date
                   |    Employee Job Title
                   |    Employee Hire Date
                   --
```

Figure 6.12   Secondary key for obtaining hire date and job title.

Mixed primary and nonprimary key.   Data attributes that are not part of the primary key can be added to a partial primary key to form a secondary key. For example, if all 5-hour courses were desired for a specific school and specific academic field, then a secondary key would be defined with *Academic School ID*, *Academic Field Name*, and *Academic Course Hours*, as shown in Figure 6.13.

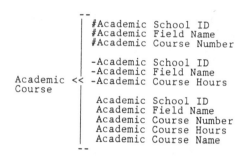

```
                --
                |   #Academic School ID
                |   #Academic Field Name
                |   #Academic Course Number
                |
                |   -Academic School ID
                |   -Academic Field Name
  Academic  << -Academic Course Hours
  Course        |
                |    Academic School ID
                |    Academic Field Name
                |    Academic Course Number
                |    Academic Course Hours
                |    Academic Course Name
                --
```

Figure 6.13   Primary key for obtaining a sequence of academic courses.

Range of Values

The examples so far have shown secondary keys with fixed values, such as a specific SSN or a specific school and course. However, there often is a need to select data based on a range of values. How this need is accomplished, such as retrieving a set of data or initiating a logical read, is not important during design. It is important that a distinction be made between data accesses based on fixed values and those based on a range of values. The decision on how to accomplish that access is made during the logical to physical conversion.

Not all data attributes in a secondary key represent a range of values. There may be a mixture of data attributes that contain a fixed value and data attributes that contain a range of values. A data attribute that is used to access data based on a range of values is indicated by a **percent sign** (%) in front of the data attribute rather than a **minus sign.** For example, if all the four- and five-credit-hour academic courses for a specific school were desired, the secondary key would contain a fixed value for *Academic School ID* and a range of values for *Academic Course Hours* as shown in Figure 6.14.

```
                        --
                      |  #Academic School ID
                      |  #Academic Field Name
                      |  #Academic Course Number
                      |
                      |  -Academic School ID
      Academic  <<    %Academic Course Hours
        Course        |
                      |  Academic School ID
                      |  Academic Field Name
                      |  Academic Course Number
                      |  Academic Course Name
                      |  -Academic Course Hours
                        --
```

Figure 6.14 Secondary key for a range of values.

Sequence of Data Attributes

The data attributes in a secondary key are not sequence specific when fixed values are entered or when there is only one data attribute in the key. However, the data attributes in a secondary key may be **sequence specific** if the sequence of the data attributes will affect the sequence the data is returned. If data attributes are sequence specific, the first data attribute listed for each secondary key is the most major and the last data attribute listed is the most minor.

> The sequence of data attributes in a secondary key may be important for retrieving data.

If there is more than one data attribute in the secondary key and that key is used to initiate a logical read in a database management system, then the sequence of the data attributes determines the sequence the data are obtained from the database. For example, if the secondary key for initiating a logical read were in the order *Employee Birth Date* and *Employee Hire Date*, then all hire dates would be obtained for each birth date. In other words, *birth date* is major and *hire date* is minor. If the two data attributes were reversed, then all birth dates would be obtained for each hire date.

If a secondary key is used for obtaining data occurrences based on a range of values, then the data attributes are also sequence specific. For example, if *Employee Birth Date* and *Employee Hire Date* contained a range of values, then all the hire dates within that range would be obtained within each birth date. This situation is identical to initiating a logical read.

FOREIGN KEY

A **foreign key** is the primary key of a parent data entity placed in a subordinate data entity for the purpose of identifying the parent data entity. Foreign keys are used to identify the parent data occurrence of a specific data occurrence in a subordinate data entity. Without foreign keys there would be no method to navigate between a data occurrence in a subordinate data entity and its parent data occurrence in the parent data entity.

A foreign key identifies the parent data occurrence in a parent data entity.

Each data attribute in a foreign key is designated with a **plus sign** (+) in front of the data attribute name. The foreign keys are listed below the secondary keys on a data structure. The sequence of data attributes in the foreign key must be the same as their sequence in the primary key of the parent data entity. If there is more than one parent data entity, there will be more than one foreign key and each of the foreign keys is listed separately. The data attributes comprising a foreign key are also listed with the data attributes that characterize the data entity.

The data structure for each *Employer* and the *Tax Office* that regulates that employer is shown in Figure 6.15. Each tax office has many employers that it regulates and each employer is regulated by only one tax office. The primary key for *Tax Office* is *Tax Office Number*. Since an employer is regulated by only one tax office, *Tax Office Number* is carried as a foreign key in *Employer*. When any data about the tax office for a specific employer is required, the appropriate tax office data occurrence is accessed and the required data is obtained. Notice that a secondary key for *Tax Office Number* was added for access to *Tax Office*.

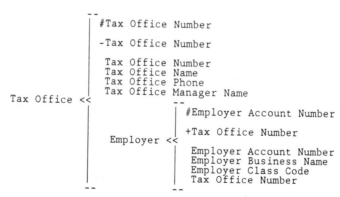

Figure 6.15   Foreign key from employer to tax office.

Types of Foreign Keys

A foreign key is usually stored in the subordinate data entity. When the parent data entity needs to be accessed, that foreign key is used to access that parent data entity and obtain the needed information. However, the foreign key is not stored on the database when it is calculated or derived in some manner just prior to access. This situation usually occurs with time relational data where the specific parent is not known until the time of access.

Since a foreign key to parent data entities is required, the data attributes composing the foreign key must be shown in the data structure. However, since the value for a calculated foreign key is calculated at execution time, the foreign key is not stored on the physical database. To indicate this situation an **at sign** (@) is used rather than a *plus sign* (+) in front of the data attribute name and the data attribute is not shown in the data attribute list.

For example, a table of service fees is maintained with a primary key of *Fee Type* as shown in Figure 6.16. Access to this fee table from *Service* is based on the type of fee, so a foreign key of *Fee Type* would be placed in *Service*. However, the fee type is derived based on the type of service provided, the time the service was provided, such as normal hours or after hours, and the length of time the service took. Since it is derived rather than stored it is identified as a calculated foreign key, but it is not placed in the data attribute list.

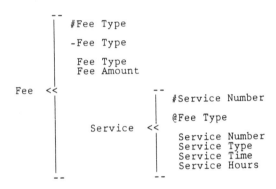

Figure 6.16   Calculated foreign key.

Calculated foreign keys do not occur very often in a subject database. In most cases the data is contained in the database rather than being calculated. However, when the need arises to calculate a foreign key, then that calculated foreign key is indicated as shown above.

SUMMARY

Understanding the different types and uses of data keys is the first step to defining the structure of the data resource. Data keys are used to uniquely identify each data occurrence in a data entity, to provide access to data in the database, and to identify parent data entities. These data keys along with the data relations provide the navigation necessary to enter and navigate through the enterprise's database. The guidelines listed below will help to properly identify the data keys.

Each data entity must have one and only one official primary key.

A primary key provides unique identification of each data occurrence but does not provide access to a data entity.

A data entity may have additional alternate primary keys.

Alternate primary keys may not retain their uniqueness over time.

The sequence of data attributes in a primary key is not important for uniqueness.

The sequence of data attributes in a primary key is important for indicating the structure of data.

Redundant data attributes must be removed from a primary key.

Each data entity must have at least one secondary key for access unless the entire file is read.

A secondary key must show whether fixed values or a range of values is needed.

The sequence of data attributes in a secondary key may be important.

A foreign key is required for each parent data entity.

The sequence of data attributes in a foreign key is the same as their sequence in the primary key of the parent data entity.

A calculated foreign key is not stored in the database.

The sequence of data keys on a data structure is primary keys, secondary keys, foreign keys, and a data attribute list.

All data attributes used in foreign keys are included in the data attribute list, except the data attributes in a calculated foreign key.

STUDY QUESTIONS

The following questions are provided as a review of data keys and to stimulate thought about the importance of data keys in defining the structure of the data resource.

1. What is a primary key and how is it indicated?
2. What is the purpose of a primary key?
3. What are the various types of primary keys?
4. Why must each data entity have a primary key?
5. Is the sequence of data attributes in a primary key important?
6. What problems are caused by redundant data in a primary key?
7. How are these problems resolved?
8. What is a secondary key and how is it indicated?
9. What is the purpose of secondary keys?
10. What are the various types of secondary keys?
11. Why should there be at least one secondary key for each data entity?
12. When might a data entity not have any secondary keys?

13. When is the sequence of data attributes in a secondary key important?
14. What is the difference between a fixed value and a range of values in a secondary key?
15. What is the sequence of listing data keys on a data structure?
16. What is a foreign key and how is it indicated?
17. Why should a foreign key be shown for each parent data entity?
18. Why must the sequence of data attributes in a foreign key match the sequence in the parent's primary key?
19. What is a calculated foreign key?
20. Why are the data attributes in data keys repeated in the data attribute list?

Data Relations and Navigation

Data relations and data keys provide access into and navigation through the data resource to store and retrieve data.

Understanding the types of relations between data subjects and the identification and use of those relations is the next step in defining the structure of the data resource. Once these data relations are identified they are combined with data keys to provide access into the database and navigation through the database to store and retrieve data. When the data keys are properly identified, the data attributes are properly listed, and the data relations are properly identified, the database will provide the data needed by the enterprise.

The entity-relationship and entity-type hierarchy diagrams were explained in the Data Resource Model chapter. They show the data subjects comprising the data resource and the data relations between those data subjects. However, they do not show **how** those data relations are identified or their use. They show only the structure of data subjects and data relations. This chapter explains how data relations are identified from data structures and what use is made of those data relations. It also explains how data keys are combined with data relations to provide access into the database and pathways to navigate between data entities in the database to store and retrieve data.

DATA RELATIONS

A **data relation** represents an association between data occurrences in different data entities or within the same data entity. Associations also occur between data attributes and data values in the same data entities or in different data entities.

> A data relation is an association between data occurrences in different data entities or in the same data entity.

Data relations indicate an association only and contain no data attributes. Anytime a data relation contains data attributes, or appears to contain data attributes, it indicates a data entity that has not been identified. That data entity must be identified and described and the data attributes placed in that entity. Any relations between that data entity and other data entities can then be defined.

> Data relations indicate an association only and have no data attributes.

Data Relations Between Data Entities

There are three basic data relations between data entities. The notation used to represent these types of relations is a concatenation of words with a hyphen. For example, a relation between a single *Employee* and their many *Pay Checks* is a *one-to-many* relation indicating that one *Employee* has many *Pay Checks*. Mathematical symbols are sometimes used, such as *1:M* or *1:N*, but the hyphenated form is preferred for clarity and understandability. Data relations are identified from the arrangement of the data sets in a data structure. Each data set represents a data entity and the arrangement of those sets indicates the type of data relation.

One-to-one data relation. A **one-to-one** data relation means that a data occurrence in one data entity is related to only one data occurrence in the second data entity, and that each data occurrence in the second data entity is related to only one data occurrence in the first data entity. A one-to-one data relation is designated on the entity-relationship diagram by a dashed line between the two data entities with no arrowheads.

A one-to-one data relation is most often used with data categories. For example, a *Person* can be both an *Employee* and a *Customer* of the enterprise. *Employee* and *Customer* are in a one-to-one relation with *Person* as shown in Figure 7.1. Since they are both in a one-to-one relation with the same data entity, they are also in a one-to-one relation with each other.

A one-to-one data relation is indicated on a data structure by placing the two data entities vertically as shown in Figure 7.2. The keyword *-IMAP-* is placed between the two

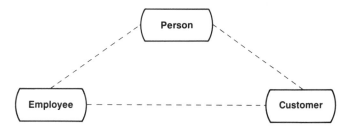

Figure 7.1 One-to-one data relation on an entity-relationship diagram.

data entities indicating an identify mapping of the two data entities. The terms **peer data entity** and **1:1** are also used to indicate a one-to-one data relation.

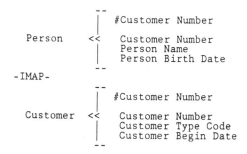

Figure 7.2 One-to-one data relation on a data structure.

One-to-many data relation. A **one-to-many** data relation means that a data occurrence in the first data entity is related to many data occurrences in the second data entity, and each data occurrence in the second data entity is related to only one data occurrence in the first data entity. For example, if there are many *Operators* for one *Boat* to keep the boat operating 24 hours a day, seven days a week, but each *Operator* works on only one *Boat*, there would be a one-to-many data relation *Boat* and *Operator*.

A one-to-many data relation is designated on the entity-relationship diagram by a dashed line with an arrow on one end, as shown in Figure 7.3. The arrow points from the data entity with one occurrence to the data entity with many occurrences. In this situation *Boat* has one data occurrence and *Operator* has many data occurrences so the arrow points from *Boat* to *Operator*. The terms **Parent-Child** and **1:M** are also used to indicate a one-to-many data relation.

Figure 7.3 One-to-many data relation on an entity-relationship diagram.

A one-to-many data relation is shown on a data structure by nesting the data entity with many occurrences in the data entity with one occurrence, as shown in Figure 7.4. The characteristics unique to a boat are listed in the *Boat* set and the characteristics unique to an operator are listed in the *Operator* set.

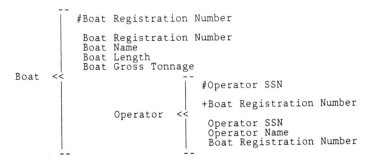

```
      --
      |    #Boat Registration Number
      |
      |    Boat Registration Number
      |    Boat Name
      |    Boat Length
      |    Boat Gross Tonnage
Boat  <<                      --
      |                       |    #Operator SSN
      |                       |
      |                       |    +Boat Registration Number
      |          Operator  <<
      |                       |    Operator SSN
      |                       |    Operator Name
      |                       |    Boat Registration Number
      |                       |
      --                      --
```

Figure 7.4 One-to-many relation on a data structure.

Many-to-many data relation. A **many-to-many data relation** means that a data occurrence in one data entity is related to many data occurrences in a second data entity, and each data occurrence in that second data entity is related to many data occurrences in the first data entity. A many-to-many data relation is the result of two one-to-many data occurrences pointing in opposite directions between the two data entities.

A many-to-many data relation is designated on the entity-relationship diagram by a dashed line between two data entities with an arrowhead on each end. Since a many-to-many data relation is the result of companion one-to-many data relations, it could be shown with two dashed lines with arrowheads pointing in opposite directions. However, for simplicity it is shown as one dashed line with an arrowhead on each end.

For example, if there were many *Pilots* authorized to take a *Boat* into dock, and each of those *Pilots* were authorized to dock many different *Boats*, there would be a many-to-many data relation between *Pilots* and *Boats*, as shown in Figure 7.5. This situation would be identified from two different data structures, one showing many *Pilots* for one *Boat* and the other showing many *Boats* for one *Pilot*. Although these two data structures are correct, the many-to-many situation they create can not be allowed to exist in the physical database and must be resolved by the addition of another data entity.

Figure 7.5 Many-to-many data relation on an entity-relationship diagram.

Inverted Data Relations

An **inverted data relation** shows the relation between one data attribute and its related data attributes in the same data occurrence. One data attribute is designated as a primary data attribute and the other data attributes characterize that primary data attribute. For example, to show all *Boats* by *Gross Tonnage Class* results in the data structure shown in Figure 7.6.

Boat Tonnage Class is the primary data attribute and *Boat* is nested within each *Tonnage Class*.

```
         --
          |   Boat Tonnage Class
          |        --
Tonnage Class <<        |   Boat Registration Number
          |       Boat  <<  Boat Name
          |        |   Boat Length
         --        --
```

Figure 7.6 Inverted data structure for boat by tonnage class.

Since boat data already exist in *Boat*, only the primary key to each boat is needed for each tonnage class. Therefore, the data structure can be reduced to the one shown in Figure 7.7, which is a one-to-many data relation between *Tonnage Class* and *Boat Reference*. *Boat Registration Number* is used to access *Boat* to obtain specific information about each boat.

```
              --
               |   Boat Tonnage Class
Tonnage Class <<     --
               |   Boat Reference  <<  Boat Registration Number
              --     --             --
```

Figure 7.7 Inverted list for tonnage class.

Inverted data relations can be created for any data attribute, or any combination of data attributes, in a data occurrence, giving any data attribute or any set of data attributes the capability of being used as an index to that data occurrence. The result of an access based on an inverted data relation is a set of data occurrences that meets the selection criteria. Secondary keys become inverted data relations, in one form or another, in a database management system and are used to access data.

Implied Data Relations

A valid data relation between two data entities that is shown on the entity-relationship diagram is an **explicit data relation**. A valid data relation between two data entities that is not shown on the entity-relationship diagram is an **implicit data relation**. All valid data relations must be shown explicitly on the entity-relationship diagram to represent the complete structure of the data resource.

> All valid data relations must be shown explicitly on the entity-relationship diagram to show the complete structure of the data resource.

There are three types of implicit data relations that need to be shown explicitly on the entity-relationship diagram. The first is a relation to grandparent data entities, that is data entities that are parents to the parent of a data entity. For example, the data structure for *Academic School*, *Academic Field*, and *Academic Course* in Figure 6.4 shows that *Academic School* is a grandparent of *Academic Course*. However, if the data relations were defined based only on that data structure, the relations between *Academic School* and *Academic Field* and between *Academic Field* and *Academic Course* would be shown explicitly, as shown in Figure 7.8.

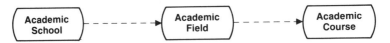

Figure 7.8   Explicit data relations.

The primary key of *Academic Course* contains *Academic School ID* which is the primary key for *Academic School*, the grandparent data entity of *Academic Course*. This indicates a valid data relation between *Academic Course* and *Academic School*. However, there is no explicit data relation between those two data entities. To make this implied data relation an explicit data relation requires drawing a data relation between *Academic School* and *Academic Course*, as shown in Figure 7.9, and identifying a foreign key in *Academic Course* for *Academic School*.

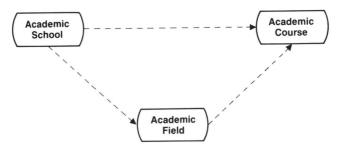

Figure 7.9   Resolution of grandparent implicit data relation.

The second type of implicit data relation is to a data entity that is not part of a composite primary key but is still a parent data entity. For example, the operation of a *Boat* is financed from a specific *Operating Account* which is identified by a primary key of *Operating Account Number*. Since no additional data are required from that *Operating Account*, it does not appear as a foreign key in *Boat* and no data relation is established. However, there is a valid implied data relation between *Boat* and *Operating Account*. Like the implied data relation above, it needs to be shown explicitly to avoid any confusion, as shown in Figure 7.10. *Operating Account Number* becomes a foreign key in *Boat* and a secondary key of *Operating Account Number*.

Figure 7.10   Resolution of nonparent implicit data relation.

The third type of implied data relation exists between two data entities that are in a one-to-one data relation with a common data entity. This situation usually occurs with data categories. For example, if *Customer* is in a one-to-one data relation with *Person* and *Employee* is in a one-to-one data relation with *Person*, then *Customer* and *Employee* are in a one-to-one data relation with each other, as shown in Figure 7.1. This data relation must be shown explicitly to avoid any misunderstanding. The appropriate foreign and secondary keys would be added to each data entities.

Resolution of implicit data relations should not be used to create random invalid data relations when no true data relation exists. Although it may appear proper, creation of **random data relations** results in invalid structures in the data resource. For example, each *Position* belongs to a certain *Job Class* and each *Job Class* belongs to a certain *Job Class Type*. Each *Position* is identified by a *Position Number* with a foreign key for *Job Class ID*. Each *Job Class* is identified by a *Job Class ID* with a foreign key for *Job Class Type Code*. Based on this structure there are data relations between *Job Class Type* and *Job Class* and between *Job Class* and *Position* as shown in Figure 7.11. There is no direct relation between *Job Class Type* and *Position* and a data relation should not be indicated between these two data entities. The only access must be through *Job Class*.

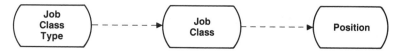

Figure 7.11 Valid data relations.

Data Relations Within a Data Entity

The data relations described so far have been between data occurrences in different data entities. There have been no data relations between the data occurrences within a data entity. For example, individual vehicles are not related to each other in the *Vehicle* data entity. However, there can be data relations between data occurrences within a data entity. For example, there could be paired data occurrences for two employees who are married representing a one-to-one data relation within *Employee*. Each employee data occurrence would point to the spouse employee. The data attribute for pointing to the spouse would be qualified with a variation name to form *Employee SSN Spouse* and each data occurrence would contain the SSN of the spouse.

> Data relations can exist between data occurrences within a data entity.

There can also be one-to-many data relations between data occurrences within the same data entity. For example, a data entity is defined to represent all the organizational units in an enterprise and their reporting relations. Each data occurrence in *Organization*

Unit represents one organizational unit and contains a foreign key identifying its parent organizational unit as shown in Figure 7.12. A foreign key is defined for the parent organizational unit, and is qualified with a variation name to form *Organizational Unit ID Parent*.

```
                              --
                             |    #Organization Unit ID
                             |
                             |    -Organization Unit ID
                             |
                             |    -Organization Unit ID Parent
  Organization Unit <<       |
                             |    +Organization Unit ID Parent
                             |
                             |    Organization Unit ID
                             |    Organization Unit ID Parent
                             |    Organization Unit Name
                             |    Organization Unit Size
                              --
```

Figure 7.12   A one-to-many data relation within organization unit.

A data relation between data occurrences within a data entity are shown as a data entity with a relation to itself. That relation will not have an arrow if it represents a one-to-one data relation and will have an arrow on one end if it represents a one-to-many data relation.

A one-to-one relation between data occurrences within a data entity forms a **closed data relation**. For example, one employee data occurrence points to the spouse data occurrence, which points back to the first data occurrence. The one-to-many relation between data occurrences within a data entity forms an **open data relation** where the relations can be followed to the top or bottom of the hierarchy, but will never return to the starting point.

The relations between data occurrences within a data entity may be optional or mandatory. The one-to-one data relation for spouse is optional because every employee does not have a spouse. However, the data relations for organizational unit are mandatory except at the top of the hierarchy. Every organizational unit must have a parent organizational unit except the highest unit in the organization.

Data occurrences can also form a many-to-many data relation between data occurrences in the same data entity. For example, several parts can be combined into a parent part, and each part may be the component of many parent parts, making a many-to-many data relation between parts. This situation is resolved by defining data entities for *Part* and for *Component* that form a one-to-many data relation, as shown in Figure 7.13. Two foreign keys are defined in *Component* for *Part Number* and *Part Number Component*.

Every part is a data occurrence in *Part* which has a primary key of *Part Number*. Each assembly of parts requires two or more component parts which result in two or more *Component* data occurrences. Each *Component* has a primary key of the part number it goes into, *Part Number*, and its own part number, *Part Number Component*. To determine all components of one part requires finding all *Component* data occurrences for a particular

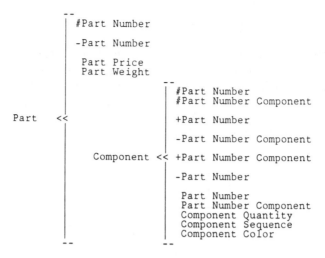

```
     --
    | #Part Number
    |
    | -Part Number
    |
    |  Part Price
    |  Part Weight
    |                  --
    |                 | #Part Number
    |                 | #Part Number Component
Part    <<           |
    |                 | +Part Number
    |                 |
    |                 | -Part Number Component
    |                 |
    |  Component <<   | +Part Number Component
    |                 |
    |                 | -Part Number
    |                 |
    |                 |  Part Number
    |                 |  Part Number Component
    |                 |  Component Quantity
    |                 |  Component Sequence
    |                 |  Component Color
    |                  --
     --
```

Figure 7.13   A many-to-many data relation for parts.

Part Number. To determine all parts that use a particular component requires finding all *Component* data occurrences for a particular *Part Number Component.*

Mutually Exclusive Subordinates

Data entity types are subentities that represent a *can only be* or mutually exclusive situation. Each data entity supertype is related to two or more data entity subtypes that are mutually exclusive. For example, *Customers* may be *Active* or *Inactive* as shown in Figure 7.14. *Customer* is a data category of *Person* and a supertype of *Active Customer* and *Inactive Customer.* The two subtypes are mutually exclusive because a customer can not be both active and inactive.

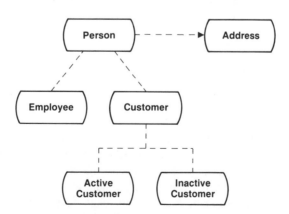

Figure 7.14   Mutually exclusive subordinate data entities.

Mutually Exclusive Parents

Two parent data entities may be mutually exclusive parents of a subordinate data entity. This relationship is shown with a branched data relation between the mutually exclusive parent data entities and the subordinate data entity with an arrow indicating a one-to-many data relation, as shown in Figure 7.15. A vehicle may be owned by either a *Person* or a *Company*, but never both. A *Person* or a *Company* may own more than one vehicle forming a one-to-many relation with *Vehicle*.

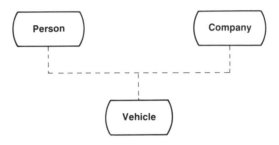

Figure 7.15   Mutually exclusive parent data entities.

Data Attribute and Value Relations

Generally, there are no relations between data attributes other than characterizing a data entity. However, data attributes can be related to each other the same as data occurrences. These **data attribute relations** exist between data attributes within the same data occurrence, between data attributes in different data occurrences in the same data entity, or between data attributes in different data occurrences in different data entities. Data attribute relations and data value relations are important for defining data integrity rules but have little to do with structuring the data resource.

> Data relations can exist between data attributes in the same data entity or different data entities.

A one-to-one data attribute relation means that a data attribute is related to only one other data attribute, and that data attribute is related only to the first data attribute. A one-to-many data attribute relation means that a data attribute is related to two or more other data attributes, but each of those data attributes is related only to the first data attribute. A many-to-many data attribute relation means that one data attribute is related to many other data attributes, and each of those data attributes can be related to two or more other data attributes including the first data attribute.

The values of data attributes may also have a one-to-one, one-to-many, and many-to-many relation. These **data value relations** are similar to the relations between data attributes.

DATA NAVIGATION

Primary keys, foreign keys, and data relations provide the pathways for navigating through a database. Secondary keys provide access into data entities to store and retrieve data. The combination of pathways and accesses provide the **data navigation** necessary to enter the database and move between data entities to store and retrieve data. The database can be entered by accessing any data entity that has a secondary key. Once the database is entered navigation to other data entities is done along the pathways defined by data relations and access is made into any data entity based on secondary keys.

> Data navigation is the process of entering the database and moving between data entities to store and retrieve data.

Once the database has been entered the navigation between data entities can be performed up the data structure to parent data entities or down the data structure to subordinate data entities. In other words, data navigation can be performed in either direction along a data relation. It is not limited to the direction of the arrows on a data relation. The arrows only indicate the type of data relation, not the direction of navigation.

> Data navigation follows data relations and can go in either direction along a data relation.

Navigation along a data relation between data entities is considered **direct navigation**. If navigation needs to go between two data entities that are not directly related that navigation must go by some indirect route through one or more other data entities. This **indirect navigation** may require unnecessary processing and delay if the two data entities have a valid relation that is not shown explicitly. Therefore, all valid data relations must be shown explicitly on an entity-relationship diagram.

> All data relations must be shown explicitly on the entity-relationship diagram for efficient navigation.

Efficient navigation in a database depends on the proper identification of data keys and data relations. This identification is done on data structure charts using the techniques described above. As data structures are developed, the arrangement of data sets and the identification of data keys in each set identify the data relations and data accesses that make data navigation possible.

Access Down the Data Structure

Access down the data structure occurs when navigation is from a parent data entity to a subordinate data entity. In this case, all subordinate data occurrences for a parent data occurrence are obtained. For example, *Room* information is desired for each *Building* as shown in Figure 7.16. Initial entry into the database is to *Building* to obtain data for each building. Once the data for each *Building* have been obtained *Room* will be accessed to obtain the required data for each room in that building.

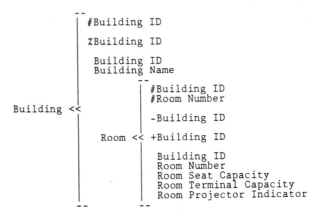

Figure 7.16 Access down the data structure.

Since access is made to all buildings in order of *Building ID*, a secondary key for a range of values is defined, as indicated by the percent sign. Since all rooms in a building are desired, a secondary key is identified for *Building ID* only, excluding *Room Number*. In other words, a secondary key is established for a partial primary key of *Building ID*. The result is access to all rooms with the specified *Building ID*.

> Access down the data structure provides all the subordinate data occurrences for a parent data occurrence.

Another example of access down the data structure is shown in Figure 7.17. An inquiry is made for a specific vehicle and the trip, or trips, that vehicle took on a specific date. Initial entry is made into *Vehicle* based on *Vehicle ID* and the appropriate vehicle data are obtained. Access is then made to *Trip* based on the *Vehicle ID* and the *Trip Start Date*. Any data occurrences matching the values in that secondary key will be obtained.

If no vehicle data were desired there would be no need to access *Vehicle*. Access could be made directly to *Trip* with the secondary key of *Vehicle ID* and *Trip Start Date*. When data occurrences with those values were found the appropriate data could be obtained and processed.

A third example of access down the data structure is shown in Figure 7.18. An inquiry is made for all biology classes taken by a student during the fall of 1982 and the

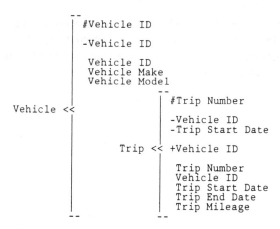

```
        --
       | #Vehicle ID
       |
       | -Vehicle ID
       |
       | Vehicle ID
       | Vehicle Make
       | Vehicle Model
       |              --
       |             | #Trip Number
       |             |
  Vehicle <<         | -Vehicle ID
       |             | -Trip Start Date
       |             |
       |     Trip << +Vehicle ID
       |             |
       |             | Trip Number
       |             | Vehicle ID
       |             | Trip Start Date
       |             | Trip End Date
       |             | Trip Mileage
        --            --
```

Figure 7.17   Access down the data structure with secondary keys.

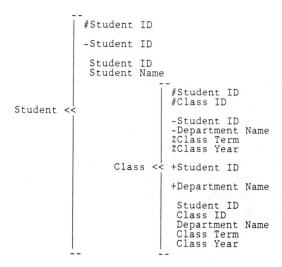

```
        --
       | #Student ID
       |
       | -Student ID
       |
       | Student ID
       | Student Name
       |              --
       |             | #Student ID
       |             | #Class ID
  Student <<         |
       |             | -Student ID
       |             | -Department Name
       |             | %Class Term
       |             | %Class Year
       |             |
       |    Class << +Student ID
       |             |
       |             | +Department Name
       |             |
       |             | Student ID
       |             | Class ID
       |             | Department Name
       |             | Class Term
       |             | Class Year
        --            --
```

Figure 7.18   Access down the data structure with a range of subordinates.

winter of 1983. Initial access is made into *Student* with *Student ID* to obtain the student's name. Access is then made to *Class* based on *Student ID* and *Department Name* as fixed values, and *Class Term* and *Class Year* as a range of values.

Access Up the Data Structure

Access up the data structure occurs when navigation is from a subordinate data entity to the parent data entity. In this case, the parent data occurrence for a subordinate data occurrence is obtained. For example, a company has many budgets uniquely identified by a *Budget ID*, as shown in Figure 7.19. Each budget has many accounts uniquely identified by *Account Number*. Initial access is made to *Account* based on *Account Number* and data are obtained for that account. Access is then made up the data structure to *Budget* using *Budget ID* to obtain the budget data occurrence.

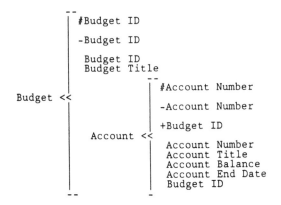

Figure 7.19   Access up the data structure.

Access up the data structure provides the parent data occurrence.

Another example of access up the data structure is shown in Figure 7.20. Each account has many account activities. *Account Title* and *Account Balance* are needed for any accounts that have account activities with a specific *Account Activity Code*. Initial access is made to *Account Activity* based on *Account Activity Code*. When account activities with that code are obtained, access is made to *Account* based on the *Account Number* to obtain the account title and balance.

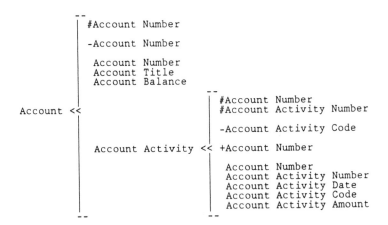

Figure 7.20   Access up the data structure for a fixed value.

A third example of access up the data structure is shown in Figure 7.21. All the account activities that were processed between *March 1* and *March 31* are desired. Initial access is made into *Account Activity* using *Account Activity Date* with a range of values. When an account activity is found between those dates, *Account* is accessed based on *Account Number*.

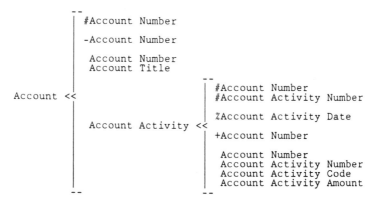

```
        --
       | #Account  Number
       |
       | -Account  Number
       |
       |  Account  Number
       |  Account  Title
       |                      --
       |                     | #Account  Number
Account <<                   | #Account  Activity  Number
       |                     |
       |                     | %Account  Activity  Date
       |  Account Activity <<|
       |                     | +Account  Number
       |                     |
       |                     |  Account  Number
       |                     |  Account  Activity  Number
       |                     |  Account  Activity  Code
       |                     |  Account  Activity  Amount
        --                    --
```

Figure 7.21   Access up the data structure for a range of values.

Multidirectional Access

The examples above show accesses either up or down the data structure. Although many data structures have only accesses down the structure or only accesses up the structure there are many data structures that have accesses both up and down the data structure. **Multidirectional access** is a combination of access up and access down the data structure as needed. There is nothing done differently just because there is multidirectional access.

Multidirectional access is a combination of access up the data structure and access down the data structure.

For example, a company has many divisions as shown in Figure 7.22. Each division has many employees and each employee takes many business trips. A report needs to be made for each employee, showing the division they belong to and all the business trips they made. Initial access is made into *Employee* by reading all the records in whatever order they are stored. Therefore no secondary key is needed. For each employee, access is made to *Division* to obtain *Division Name*, and access is made to *Trip* for each business trip that employee took.

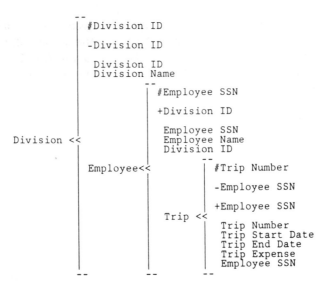

```
                          --
                         |  #Division ID
                         |
                         |  -Division ID
                         |
                         |  Division ID
                         |  Division Name
                         |          --
                         |         |  #Employee SSN
                         |         |
                         |         |  +Division ID
                         |         |
    Division <<          |         |  Employee SSN
                         |         |  Employee Name
                         |         |  Division ID
                         |         |        --
                  Employee<<       |       |  #Trip Number
                         |         |       |
                         |         |       |  -Employee SSN
                         |         |       |
                         |         |       |  +Employee SSN
                         |      Trip <<    |
                         |         |       |  Trip Number
                         |         |       |  Trip Start Date
                         |         |       |  Trip End Date
                         |         |       |  Trip Expense
                         |         |       |  Employee SSN
                         |         |       |
                          --        --      --
```

Figure 7.22   Data structure with multidirectional access.

Access to Multiple Parents

Occasionally, access needs to be made to more than one parent data entity. This type of access usually occurs with code tables or with data entities that resolve a many-to-many relationship between two parent data entities. For example, the data structure in Figure 7.23 shows *Wage* as having two parents: *Employer* and *Employee*. In this case *Wage* resolves the many-to-many data relation between *Employer* and *Employee*. A report is desired showing all the wages for each employee and the employer that paid those wages.

Since access is made to each employee, no secondary key is required in *Employee*. The wages are obtained for each employee from *Wage* based on *Employee SSN*. *Employer* is accessed for each of those wages based on *Employer ID* to obtain employer data. The primary key, secondary key, foreign key, and data attributes are not repeated in the second *Wage* set because it represents navigation to *Employer* and only *Employer ID* is needed as a foreign key.

If the report was to be in order by *Employee SSN* then a secondary key would be added to *Employee* for *Employee SSN* to obtain data in SSN order. If the report was to be in order by *Employee Name* then a secondary key would be added to *Employee* for *Employee Name* to obtain data in name order. Each of these secondary keys is a range of values since more than one employee was to be obtained.

Multiple Accesses to One Parent

Multiple accesses to a single parent can be made from several subordinates data entities. For example, if the same set of data were required from *Job Class* for use by both

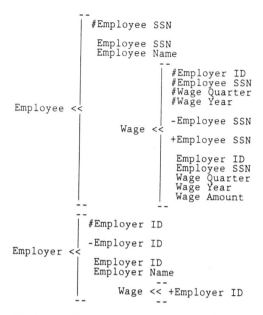

```
             --
            | #Employee SSN
            |
            |  Employee SSN
            |  Employee Name
            |                --
            |               | #Employer ID
            |               | #Employee SSN
            |               | #Wage Quarter
 Employee <<|               | #Wage Year
            |               |
            |               | -Employee SSN
            |    Wage <<    |
            |               | +Employee SSN
            |               |
            |               |  Employer ID
            |               |  Employee SSN
            |               |  Wage Quarter
            |               |  Wage Year
            |               |  Wage Amount
             --              --
             --
            | #Employer ID
            |
            | -Employer ID
 Employer <<|
            |  Employer ID
            |  Employer Name
            |                --
            |    Wage << +Employer ID
             --              --
```

Figure 7.23 Data structure with multiple parent access.

Appointment and *Position*, then both *Appointment* and *Position* would be shown within *Job Class*, as shown in Figure 7.24. The primary keys, secondary keys, and data attributes were left off the *Appointment* and *Position* data entities for simplicity, but would normally be shown.

```
                  --
                 | #Job Class ID
                 |
                 | -Job Class ID
                 |
                 |  Job Class ID
 Job Class <<    |  Job Class Title
                 |                --
                 |    Appointment << +Job Class ID
                 |                --
                 |                --
                 |    Position << +Job Class ID
                  --              --
```

Figure 7.24 Multiple accesses to parent for the same set of data.

If different sets of data were required from *Job Class* by *Appointment* and *Position*, there would need to be two data structures, as shown in Figure 7.25. Each data structure shows a different data view from *Job Class*. In other words, the data view is different for access from *Appointment* and from *Position*. Again, the primary keys, secondary keys, and data attributes were left off *Appointment* and *Position* for simplicity, but would normally be shown.

```
            --
          |  #Job Class ID
          |
          |  -Job Class ID
          |
Job Class << Job Class ID
          |  Job Class Title
          |
          |             --
          |   Appointment << +Job Class ID
            --              --


            --
          |  #Job Class ID
          |
          |  -Job Class ID
          |
          |  Job Class ID
Job Class << Job Class Title
          |  Job Class Description
          |  Job Class Salary Range
          |
          |              --
          |    Position << +Job Class ID
            --             --
```

Figure 7.25 Multiple accesses to a parent for different sets of data.

If a fully qualified foreign key is used to access the parent data entity, it is implied that the foreign key in the subordinate data entity is equivalent to the primary key in the parent data entity. Figure 7.26 shows a foreign key fully qualified with a variation name in *Position* being used to access the parent *Job Class*. *Job Class ID Current* is equivalent to *Job Class ID* and is used to access *Job Class*. This is the reason why the sequence of data attributes in a foreign key must be the same as their sequence in the primary key of the parent data entity.

```
            --
          |  #Job Class ID
          |
          |  -Job Class ID
          |
          |  Job Class ID
Job Class << Job Class Title
          |  Job Class Description
          |  Job Class Salary Range
          |
          |              --
          |    Position << +Job Class ID Current
            --             --
```

Figure 7.26 Use of fully qualified foreign key for accessing a parent.

Access to Mutually Exclusive Subordinates

Access to mutually exclusive subordinates is made with the data attribute used to designate data entity types. For example, if access is made to *Vehicle* to obtain all *Motor Vehicles* the *Vehicle Type Code* would be used to identify those motorized vehicles. A secondary key would be defined for *Vehicle Type Code* and the value for motor vehicles would be used for access. This is one reason why a data attribute is required for each level on a data entity type hierarchy.

Access To Mutually Exclusive Parents

The situation can arise where a data entity has multiple parents, but only one of those parents is valid for a single data occurrence. For example, a *Vehicle* may be owned by either a *Person* or a *Company*. Both *Person* and *Company* are parents to *Vehicle* and *Vehicle* will contain a foreign key to each of those parents, as shown in Figure 7.27. However, only one of those foreign keys will have a value for each data occurrence and the other one will be empty.

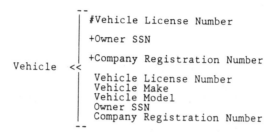

```
                        --
                        |   #Vehicle License Number
                        |
                        |   +Owner SSN
                        |
                        |   +Company Registration Number
            Vehicle  << |
                        |   Vehicle License Number
                        |   Vehicle Make
                        |   Vehicle Model
                        |   Owner SSN
                        |   Company Registration Number
                        --
```

Figure 7.27   Access to an optional parent data entity.

All data attributes in a primary key must have a value for every data occurrence. The primary key for a data entity that has optional parents can not be a composite key because one or more of those data attributes will not have a value. Therefore, data attributes in the primary key of a data entity with optional parents can not be data attributes from the primary key of any of those parents. Another primary key must be identified that does not contain the data attributes of the primary key of either parent data entity.

> The data attributes in a primary key must always have a value.

Access for Verification Only

Access can be made to a parent data entity for verification purposes only. In this case no data are obtained from the parent data entity. If a data occurrence is found the verification is true and if no data occurrence is found the verification is false. This procedure is often used for data editing or for validating authorizations. For example, access to *Vehicle Type* to determine if a certain *Vehicle Type Code* is valid is shown in Figure 7.28. Notice that there are no data attributes, other than *Vehicle Type Code*, listed in the *Vehicle Type* data entity indicating that no data attributes are obtained.

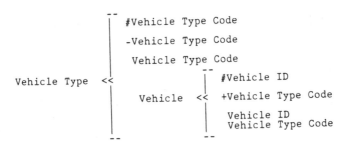

Figure 7.28   Access for validation purposes.

SUMMARY

Primary keys provide unique identification of each data occurrence in a data entity and foreign keys provide identification of parent data occurrences. Secondary keys identify access into a data entity and data relations identify pathways between data entities. Data navigation is the process of entering the database through any data entity that has a secondary key and navigating through the database along the pathways identified by the data relations. Secondary keys provide access into a data entity to store and retrieve data.

Efficient and effective data navigation is possible in a well-structured data resource. A well-structured data resource begins with the definition of data keys and data relations. This definition is done with entity-relationship diagrams, entity-type hierarchy diagrams, and data structures. Data entities, data keys, and data relations are identified on data structures based on the business needs of the enterprise and the data entities and data relations are shown on entity-relationship and entity-type hierarchy diagrams.

Understanding the different types of data relations, the development of data structures, and the relation between data structures and entity-relationship and entity-type hierarchy diagrams helps to define a well-structured data resource. The guidelines listed below help properly develop data structures and define data entities and the relations between those data entities.

A data relation defines an association between data occurrences, between data entities, or within a data entity.

Any data relation that has data attributes must be defined as a data entity.

Data relations are identified by the arrangement of sets in a data structure.

The data entities and data relations identified on data structures are shown on an entity-relationship diagram.

Mutually exclusive subordinates are shown on an entity-type hierarchy diagram.

Entity-relationship and entity-type hierarchy diagrams show data entities and data relations, but no detail within data entities.

Data structures show the data keys and data attributes within data entities.

All valid data relations must be shown explicitly on the entity-relationship diagram.

Random invalid data relations are not allowed.

Data navigation can occur between data entities only along explicit data relations.

Data navigation can occur in either direction along an explicit data relation.

The primary key for a data entity with mutually exclusive parents must not be a composite primary key.

The data attribute list on each data structure represents an application data view.

STUDY QUESTIONS

The following questions are provided as a review of data relations and navigation and to stimulate thought about the importance of data relations in defining the structure of the data resource.

1. What is a data relation and what does it represent?
2. Why do data relations not have any data attributes?
3. How are data relations identified?
4. What is the difference between the three types of data relations?
5. What is an inverted data relation?
6. What is the difference between explicit and implicit data relation?
7. What are the three types of implicit data relations?
8. Why should implicit data relations be shown explicitly on the entity-relationship diagram?
9. What happens when random data relations are defined?
10. What data relations exist between data occurrences within a data entity?
11. What data relations exist between data attributes?
12. What is data navigation?
13. How are data keys involved in navigation?
14. What does access up the data structure provide?
15. What does access down the data structure provide?
16. What is multidirectional data access?
17. How is multiple access to a common parent defined?
18. How is access to multiple parents defined?
19. How is access to mutually exclusive parents different?
20. What is access for verification only?

chapter eight

Data Normalization

Data normalization assures the data resource is properly structured by data subjects based on the business environment.

Data normalization brings the data resource to a normal state that is in conformity with a standard. That standard is a structure of data subjects where all characteristics that describe a data subject are stored together and relations are identified between those data subjects. Data subjects are identified based on the enterprise's perception of the business environment and data normalization verifies those data subjects and assures that data characteristics are properly placed in each data subject. Data normalization also assures that the primary key for each data subject is valid and that foreign keys and data relations are properly identified.

The data normalization process consists of three steps to normalize data into data subjects, to optimize those data subjects into the enterprise's data resource, and to denormalize those data subjects into data files. Data normalization supports the four-schema concept by converting business schema into external schema, optimizing those external schema into a conceptual schema, and denormalizing the conceptual schema into internal schema.

> Data normalization supports the four-schema concept by verifying data subjects, optimizing those subjects, and denormalizing them into data files.

The chapter begins with an explation of data anomalies that can occur and how they impact the structure of the data resource. The four-schema concept is reviewed and the processes of data normalization, data optimization, and data denormalization are explained. The processes are explained in practical terms that are easy to understand and use and are integrated with the data key and data navigation techniques explained earlier.

DATA ANOMALIES

An anomaly is a deviation from the general rule or standard method. A **data anomaly** is a situation where the structure of data deviate from the standard data resource structured by data subject. When data are not structured by data subject the chances for redundant data and lost data are increased resulting in a deteriorating data resource. There are three types of data anomalies that can occur and all three types cause problems with redundancy and completeness of data.

> Data anomalies occur when redundant versions of the same data characteristic are not uniformly and consistently updated.

Update Anomaly

An **update anomaly** occurs when there are redundant versions of the same data characteristic that are not all updated with the same data values at the same time. These **redundant data attributes** represent different versions of the same data characteristic. Anyone accessing these different versions of a data characteristic may get different values and could make the wrong decisions or take the wrong actions based on those values.

Redundant data attributes occur when a data attribute characterizing a parent data entity is included in each data occurrence of a subordinate data entity. When an update to that data attribute is made, that update must be made to each data occurrence in the subordinate data entity rather than to just one data occurrence in the parent data entity. This not only causes unnecessary processing, but data occurrences in the subordinate data entity are frequently missed resulting in different data values for different versions of the same data characteristic.

For example, a data structure with multiple orders for each customer is shown in Figure 8.1. *Customer Phone* is stored both in *Customer* and in each *Order* for that *Customer*. When the *Customer Phone* value changes, the *Customer* data occurrence and all *Order* data occurrences for that customer must be changed. If all data occurrences are not changed at the same time with the same data value there will be multiple versions of the customers phone number and an update anomaly will have occurred.

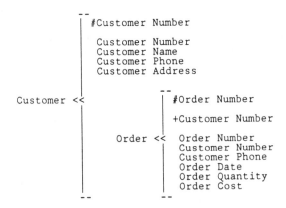

```
                                --
                               | #Customer Number
                               |
                                 Customer  Number
                                 Customer  Name
                                 Customer  Phone
                                 Customer  Address

                                             --
                                            | #Order Number
                                            |
            Customer  <<                     +Customer Number
                          |                 |
                          |                   Order Number
                            Order  <<         Customer Number
                          |                 | Customer Phone
                          |                 | Order Date
                          |                 | Order Quantity
                          |                 | Order Cost
                          |                 |
                                --             --
```

Figure 8.1   Update anomaly for customer phone.

The best way to prevent an update anomaly is to place *Customer Phone* in *Customer* and not in any other data entity. Any updates to *Customer Phone* will be made only to *Customer*. Whenever *Customer Phone* is needed access is made to *Customer* using *Customer Number* to obtain that phone number.

An update anomaly can also occur when redundant data attributes are placed in a data entity that is not directly related to the home data entity. For example, *Customer Address* is stored in *Customer*, where it belongs, and it is also stored in *Catalogue* which is used to send new catalogues to customers. When a customer's address changes, the address must be changed in both *Customer* and *Catalogue*. If not, there is an update anomaly.

Insertion Anomaly

An **insertion anomaly** occurs when a data attribute characterizing a parent data entity exists in each data occurrence of a subordinate data entity, but not in the parent data entity. This is similar to the update anomaly described above, except that the data attribute does not appear in the parent. Data for a new parent can not be completely added when there are no subordinate data occurrences because there is no place to store the parent data that is located in the subordinate data occurrence.

For example, a data structure with multiple trips for a vehicle is shown in Figure 8.2. *Vehicle Year* has been placed in *Trip* and not in *Vehicle*. When a new vehicle is acquired and data about that vehicle are available, but that vehicle has not yet been on its first trip, *Vehicle Year* can not be added to the database because there are no *Trip* data occurrences.

The best way to prevent this loss of data is to place *Vehicle Year* in *Vehicle* and remove it from *Trip*. Then, whenever a new vehicle is added to the database which has not been on any trips the *Vehicle Year* can be added to the *Vehicle* data occurrence.

Deletion Anomaly

A **deletion anomaly** is the reverse of an insertion anomaly. As long as there is at least one subordinate data occurrence, the data can be captured and stored. However, when the last

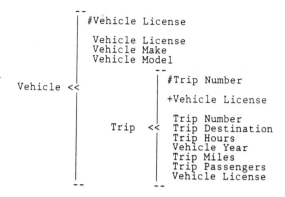

```
        --
       |  #Vehicle License
       |
       |   Vehicle License
       |   Vehicle Make
       |   Vehicle Model
       |            --
       |           |  #Trip Number
Vehicle <<        |
       |           |  +Vehicle License
       |           |
       |    Trip  << Trip Number
       |           |  Trip Destination
       |           |  Trip Hours
       |           |  Vehicle Year
       |           |  Trip Miles
       |           |  Trip Passengers
       |           |  Vehicle License
        --          --
```

Figure 8.2 Insertion and deletion anomalies for vehicle year.

subordinate data occurrence for a specific parent is removed from the database, any data attributes characterizing the parent that are stored only in that subordinate data occurrence are lost. This situation also results in an incomplete database just like an insertion anomaly.

For example, if the *Trip* data shown in Figure 8.2 were periodically deleted and that deletion process removed all *Trip* data occurrences for a *Vehicle*, the data for *Vehicle Year* would be lost causing a deletion anomaly. The best way to prevent a deletion anomaly is to place *Vehicle Year* in *Vehicle* and to remove it from *Trip*, the same as for an insertion anomaly.

Data anomalies can be prevented by assuring that each data attribute is placed in its home data entity, except those data attributes used in composite primary keys and foreign keys. Properly describing data attributes helps to identify data attributes that are not in their home data entity and proper designation of data keys validates the existence of foreign data attributes.

> Data anomalies can be prevented by placing each data attribute in its home data entity, except for data attributes in composite and foreign keys.

NORMALIZING DATA

Normalizing data prevents data anomalies by assuring that data entities represent valid data subjects and that each data attribute is properly placed in those data entities. It also supports the four-schema concept explained in the Data Design Concepts chapter. The relation between the four-schema concept and data normalization is shown in Figure 8.3. External data flows represent business schema that are normalized to produce internal data flows representing external schema. These internal data flows are optimized to form the logical data model that represents the conceptual schema. The logical data model is denormalized to produce the physical data model that represent the internal schema.

Data Normalization

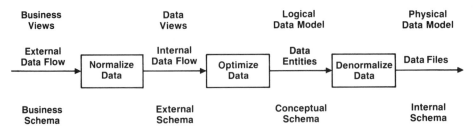

Figure 8.3 Relation between the four schema concept and data normalization.

The business schema are unnormalized data representing business views of data needed by the enterprise. These business schema are normalized into data views of subject data entities that contain data attributes and data keys. These data views are optimized into the conceputal schema representing the logical design of the data resource. The conceptual schema are denormalzied into the internal schema representing physical design of the data resource.

A common misconception about data resource design is that data should be grouped by their use and not by data subject. Grouping data by their use results in application files that contain large amounts of redundant data resulting in the data anomalies described above. Defining data entities that represent single subjects of data and placing data attributes that characterize the subject in that data entity allow data to be stored nonredundantly and shared between applications. Data are retrieved as needed in the form of data views which are manipulated by the application to produce business views. Updates are data views passed through subject data integrity rules and stored in the database. The result is less processing, more accurate data, and a structurally stable data resource.

> Normalizing data assures a structurally stable data resource.

Data Normalization

The data normalization step converts business schema into data views of subject data entities. The objective of data normalization is to identify data entities that represent single subjects of data and place data attributes that characterizing those subjects in the proper data entity. It follows a set of rules based on normalization theory that assure data entities represent single subjects of data as identified by the enterprise's perception of the business environment. The data normalization process is not constrained by the physical operating environment where data will be stored.

Business schema are unnormalized data that are not nicely structured by data subject, but they do represent a legitimate data structure. All business schema are considered unnormalized because they generally contain abstract data units, calculated data, derived, and redundant data attributes, although a few business schema may represent normalized data. That structure differs from the structure of subject data in the enterprise's data resource. Passing all business schema through the data normalization step assures that all data are properly normalized.

Repeating groups.   The data normalization process begins by identifying and removing repeating groups of data and placing those groups in separate data entities. A **repeating group** is a group of data attributes that repeat two or more times for the same value of a primary key. To look at it another way, the primary key does not uniquely identify each data attribute in a repeating group. Removing repeating groups places the data in **first normal form**.

When identifying repeating groups of data attributes, a distinction is made between how often a data attribute occurs and how often it changes. This distinction is made because it is the multiple **occurs** that identify repeating groups, not the multiple **changes**. For example, a *Student* has only one legal name and that name occurs only once for each student. The data attribute would be labeled *Student Name* and characterizes *Student*. A student's name may be legally changed many times, such as through marriages, divorces, or court orders, but there is still only one legal name for a student at any point in time. Since the legal name occurs only once per student it is a characteristic of *Student*. However, if a student takes many classes, then classes occur multiple times for a student and constitute a repeating group. That repeating group of classes is separated from *Student* and placed in a separate *Class* data entity.

Repeating groups are identified by taking each data attribute and determining if it can be uniquely identified by the primary key. If it can be uniquely identified, then it can remain in that data entity. However, if it needs different data attributes for unique identification, then it must be removed and placed in another data entity that has the appropriate primary key. For example, a data structure for a company's profits and sales is shown in Figure 8.4. Data attributes are named *Profit* and *Sales* for *Quarter 1*, *Quarter 2*, *Quarter 3*, and *Quarter 4*.

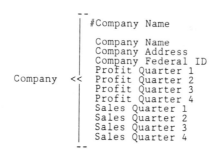

```
                        --
                       | #Company Name
                       |
                       |  Company Name
                       |  Company Address
                       |  Company Federal ID
                       |  Profit Quarter 1
         Company   <<  |  Profit Quarter 2
                       |  Profit Quarter 3
                       |  Profit Quarter 4
                       |  Sales Quarter 1
                       |  Sales Quarter 2
                       |  Sales Quarter 3
                       |  Sales Quarter 4
                        --
```

Figure 8.4   Unnormalized company sales and profit data.

There is a repeating group for quarter within the company because *Quarter* can not be uniquely identified by *Company Name*. This repeating group for quarter must be removed to a *Quarter* data entity which occurs many times within *Company* as shown in Figure 8.5. The profit and sales data attributes are moved to *Quarter* and the names are changed accordingly. *Year ID* and *Quarter ID* are added to identify each *Quarter*.

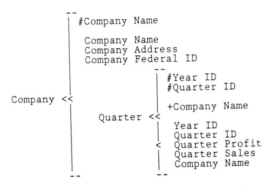

```
            --
           |  #Company Name
           |
           |    Company Name
           |    Company Address
           |    Company Federal ID
           |          --
           |         |  #Year ID
           |         |  #Quarter ID
  Company <<         |
           |         |  +Company Name
           | Quarter <<
           |         |    Year ID
           |         |    Quarter ID
           |         < Quarter Profit
           |         |    Quarter Sales
           |         |    Company Name
           |          --
            --
```

Figure 8.5   First normal form for company sales and profit.

There is only one data attribute each for profit and sales. Since a quarter is repeated multiple time for the company, the profit and sales data need appear only once for each quarter. This also makes the task of data description easier since there are fewer data attributes.

> A data attribute must be uniquely identified by the primary key.

MULTIVALUED DATA ATTRIBUTES

To be a group there must be two or more data attributes and when this group is repeated two or more times it becomes a repeating group. However, if there is only one data attribute that is repeating it can not be considered a repeating group, but is referred to as a **multivalued data attribute** because the same data attribute can have multiple values in the same data entity. In other words, the same data characteristic is repeated several times with different values. Since a multivalued data attribute is not considered a repeating group, it is frequently ignored during the identification of repeating groups.

For example, an employee may belong to many *Social Organizations*. The names of those social organizations may initially be placed in *Employee* as a multivalued attribute, as shown in Figure 8.6. The data attribute names are *Social Organization 1*, *Social Organization 2*, etc., to show that an employee can belong to several social organizations.

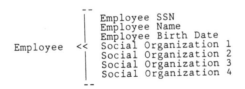

```
               --
              |   Employee SSN
              |   Employee Name
              |   Employee Birth Date
  Employee   << Social Organization 1
              |   Social Organization 2
              |   Social Organization 3
              |   Social Organization 4
               --
```

Figure 8.6   Example of a multivalued data attribute.

Ignoring these multivalued data attributes during identification of repeating groups can result in a data resource that is not properly normalized. The multivalued data attributes would be left in *Employee* rather than being removed and placed in a separate data entity. Moving the multivalued data attributes to a separate data entity results in an additional primary key and secondary key being defined which is often considered unnecessary and time consuming.

> Multivalued data attributes must be considered as repeating groups during data normalization.

However, what can happen is that several different multivalued data attributes can exist in a data entity when these separate multivalued data attributes actually form a repeating group. Since this repeating group is not identified and removed, the data resource is not properly normalized. Therefore, multivalued data attributes must be placed in a separate data entity, as shown in Figure 8.7.

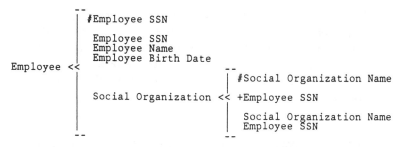

Figure 8.7 Moving multivalued data attributes to separate data entity.

A common misconception is that if multivalued data attributes are defined as a separate data entity, they will just be nested back to the parent during denormalization. This may happen, but additional data attributes could also be identified for that data entity which could prevent nesting during denormalization. Therefore, multivalued data attributes must be placed in a separate data entity during normalization. If they become nested during denormalization they will be legitimately nested.

Partial key dependencies. Each data attribute in a data entity must be dependent on the whole primary key. In other words, each data attribute must be uniquely characterized by every data attribute in the primary key. If a data attribute is not characterized by the entire primary key it constitutes a **partial key dependency** and must be removed and placed in another data entity. The removal of partial key dependencies places data in **second normal form**. Partial key dependencies can only occur with compound or composite primary keys, never with single primary keys.

Partial key dependency is checked by taking each data attribute in a data entity and comparing it to the primary key. If the entire primary key is needed to uniquely define that data attribute, then it belongs in that data entity. If, however, only part of the data attributes in the primary key are needed to define that data attribute, then it must be removed and placed in another data entity. For example, a development project consists of many separate tasks and many personnel can be assigned to each task. The data structure for *Task Assignment* is shown in Figure 8.8. A composite primary key of *Project Number*, *Task Number*, and *Personnel Number* is needed to uniquely identify each *Task Assignment*.

```
                       --
                      | #Project Number
                      | #Task Number
                      | #Personnel Number
                      |
                      | Project Number
         Task         | Task Number
   Assignment  <<     | Personnel Number
                      | Task Assignment Begin Date
                      | Task Assignment End Date
                      | Task Assignment Estimated Hours
                      | Task Assignment Actual Hours
                      | Personnel Name
                       --
```

Figure 8.8 Unresolved partial key dependency.

The four *Task Assignment* data attributes require all three data attributes in the primary key for unique identification and belong in *Task Assignment*. However, *Personnel Name* can be uniquely identified by *Personnel Number* because a person's name does not change with each task assignment. To resolve this partial key dependency, *Personnel Name* must be removed from *Task Assignment* and placed in a data entity with a primary key of *Personnel Number*.

Any data attribute that does not require the entire primary key for unique identification must be removed.

Interattribute dependencies.   A data attribute can not be dependent on another data attribute in the same data entity. If it is dependent on another data attribute, there is an **interattribute dependency**. The dependent data attribute must be removed and placed in another data entity. Resolving interattribute dependencies places data in **third normal form**. To identify interattribute dependencies each data attribute is compared to every other data attribute in the data entity to determine if there is a dependency.

For example, all five data attributes in the data structure shown in Figure 8.9 are uniquely identified by the primary key so the data structure is in second normal form.

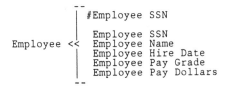

```
                    --
                   | #Employee SSN
                   |
                   | Employee SSN
     Employee  <<  | Employee Name
                   | Employee Hire Date
                   | Employee Pay Grade
                   | Employee Pay Dollars
                    --
```

Figure 8.9 Unresolved interattribute dependency.

To identify partial key dependencies *Employee Name* is compared to *Employee SSN*, then *Employee Hire Date* is compared to *Employee SSN*, then *Employee Pay Grade*, then *Employee Pay Dollars*. None of these data attributes is dependent on *Employee SSN*. The process continues by comparing *Employee Hire Date*, *Employee Pay Grade*, and *Employee Pay Dollars* to *Employee Name*. Then *Employee Pay Grade* and *Employee Pay Dollars* are compared to *Employee Hire Date*. Again there is no dependency. Finally, *Employee Pay Dollars* is compared to *Employee Pay Grade* a dependency is found because the dollars can be identified by pay grade. Therefore, *Employee Pay Dollars* is moved to another data entity named *Employee Pay* where the primary key is *Employee Pay Grade*, as shown in Figure 8.10. *Employee Pay Grade* is inserted as a foreign key in *Employee Pay*.

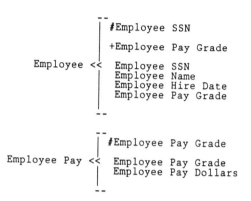

Figure 8.10 Interattribute dependency resolved with another data entity.

When checking for third normal form, interattribute dependencies must be checked on all data attributes, including those in the primary key. If interattribute dependencies are found in the primary key, they must be resolved the same as interattribute dependencies outside the primary key. One of the reasons for repeating the data attributes comprising the primary key in the list of data attributes for a data entity is to assure that interattribute dependencies with the data attributes comprising the primary key are checked. For example, the primary key for automobile *Model* might be identified as *Manufacturer Name* and *Model Name* as shown in Figure 8.11. This data structure is in second normal form since the repeating groups are separated and the data attributes in each data entity belong to the full primary key.

When checking for third normal form, it is determined that *Model Name* uniquely identifies each model and the *Manufacturer* of that model. In other words, no two manufacturers have the same model names. Therefore, there is an interattribute dependency between *Model Name* and *Manufacturer Name*. *Manufacturer Name* is considered redundant data and is removed from the primary key for *Model*, as shown in Figure 8.12.

The reason for an interattribute dependency existing in a primary key is a poor choice of data attributes for the primary key. Had the definition of a model been made before the primary key was designated, the primary key would have contained only *Model Name* and the third normal form would not have identified any interattribute dependencies involving the primary key. Actually, a thorough second normal form analysis would have identified

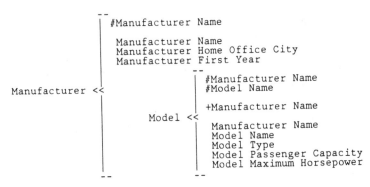

Figure 8.11 Second normal data structure of manufacturer and models.

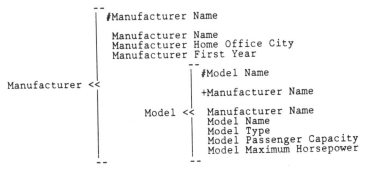

Figure 8.12 Third normal data structure of automobile models.

the interattribute dependency in the primary key if the definition of *model* had been available. None of the data attributes would have required the full primary key and would have been moved out of that data entity to one having *Model Name* as the primary key. Therefore, a good description of a data entity and the proper description of data attributes in a primary key before normalization begins will make the normalization process go faster.

> Any data attribute that is dependent on another data attribute must be removed.

Coded data represent interattribute dependencies that become a separate data entity. If a data entity contains a code and a matching description, the description is dependent on the code and needs to be moved to another data entity and the code becomes the primary key in that data entity. In many cases, the description data attribute is not identified immediately and a separate data entity is not considered. However, considering the importance of data integrity rules and the use of code tables for enforcing data integrity, all codes should be placed in a separate data entity as soon as they are encountered. The standard word **Code** in the data attribute name helps identify these situations.

Interentity dependencies. Interentity dependencies must also be considered when designing a subject data resource. For example, the data structure in Figure 8.13 shows *Students* with many *Abilities*, such as reading, writing, and speaking, and many *Languages*, such as French, German, and English. This data structure indicates that *Ability* is related to *Student* and *Language* is related to *Student*, but there is no relation between *Ability* and *Language*.

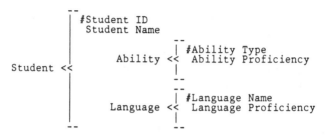

Figure 8.13 Data structure for students with unrelated abilities and languages.

However, if *Ability* and *Language* are related, they can not be separated as shown in Figure 8.13. They must be combined into the same data entity as shown in Figure 8.14. For example, a student actually has many *Skills* which consist of related abilities, such as speaking German fluently, and learning the art of Chinese cooking.

```
        --
       | #Student ID
       |  Student Name
Student <<          --
       |           |  Skill Type
       |  Skill << Skill Country
       |           |  Skill Proficiency
        --          --
```

Figure 8.14 Data structure for students with many skills.

It is best to look for interentity dependencies when defining data entities. When these dependencies are found, the two data entities should be combined into one data entity. Interentity dependency is a situation that is frequently overlooked when data normalization is based only on the primary key. In the situation above, the different primary keys for *Ability* and *Language* would indicate two separate data entities and the data attributes listed belong in those data entities. However, when the dependency is found the two data entities are combined into one true data entity. A good definition of these two data entities from the enterprise's perspective of the business environment would help identify this dependency.

> A good definition of data entities will prevent interentity dependencies.

Derived Data

Any data resource has data that are derived from other data. Pure data normalization emphasizes that no derived data should be stored in the database because they constitute implied redundant data. Any derivable data should be derived at the time they are needed rather than derived and stored in the database. This approach assures that derived data are accurate because they are derived from primitive values at the time they are needed.

However, this approach may result in extensive processing where there are many contributors to derived data and there are many accesses to derived data, such as an online environment. To reduce this extensive processing, data are derived once and stored and access is made to the stored data. However, this approach could lead to derived data that do not coincide with their primitive data. In other words, the primitive data change but there is no rederivation of data.

Practical data resource design emphasizes that derived data should be evaluated to determine if it is best to derive the data once and store them, or to derive the data each time they are needed. The frequency of use, volitility of the data, amount of storage, and derivation time are factors to consider. Maintenance of derived data becomes a data integrity issue rather than a data normalization issue.

> Derived data must be evaluated to determine if they are derived and stored or derived when needed.

Selecting Wrong Primary Key

Before the data normalization process can begin, a primary key must be identified. The data normalization process allows any data attribute, or set of data attributes, to be chosen as a primary key. If the wrong primary key is chosen, no data attributes will be left after the data normalization process and another primary key will have to be identified. The correct primary key will ultimately be found, but only after unnecessary work. It is best to identify a commonsense primary key that has a high probability of surviving the data normalization process.

For example, the data attributes in *Student* are shown in Figure 8.15. If *Student Birth Date* were picked as the candidate primary key, each data attribute would be checked to determine if it were uniquely identified by *Student Birth Date*. *Student ID Number* can not be uniquely identified by *Student Birth Date* since there can be more than one *Student ID Number* for the same birth date. Therefore, *Student ID Number* is moved out of *Student*. *Student Name* can not be uniquely identified by *Student Birth Date* since there can be more than one Student Name for any single birth date, so it is also moved out of *Student*. This

```
Student ID Number
Student Name
Student Birth Date
Student Grade Average
Student Class Standing
```

Figure 8.15 Student data for determining primary key.

process continues until all data attributes have been removed and only *Student Birth Date* is left. This situation indicates that *Student Birth Date* is not an acceptable primary key.

Next, *Student Grade Average* could be selected as the candidate primary key. Through the same process described above, all data attributes would be removed from *Student* because they could not be uniquely identified by *Student Grade Average* and only *Student Grade Average* would be left. The process could continue with *Student Class Standing*, *Student Name*, and any other data attributes that characterize *Student*. Finally, *Student ID Number* would be selected as the candidate primary key. None of the data attributes would be removed because they could all be uniquely identified by *Student ID Number*. Therefore, *Student ID Number* would be verified as the official primary key for *Student*.

> Data normalization will ultimately find the proper primary key, but careful selection will speed the process.

This process can be shortened by reviewing the data attributes in a data entity and determining which would be a good candidate for becoming the primary key. Then each data attribute in that data entity would be reviewed as described above to determine if it could be uniquely identified by the candidate primary key. The process can also be shortened by taking each data attribute that is removed from a data entity and determining what would be the primary key that could uniquely identify it. Once that primary key is determined, it may the primary key being sought for the other data attributes.

When a data attribute is determined not to be an acceptable primary key, such as *Student Birth Date* above, it should no longer remain in the data entity. In other words, since it is the only data attribute remaining in the data entity after all other data attributes have been removed that data entity should not be considered as a valid data entity because the data attribute does not represent a key. It indicates a false data entity and will only confuse the design process if it remains.

If a primary key can not be found, then the data attribute or data attributes that would uniquely identify each data occurrence have not yet been identified. The definition of the data entity should be reviewed to determine what the data entity represents. Then, using this definition, the appropriate characteristics can be identified that uniquely identify each data occurrence. Once these characteristics are identified they can be named and placed in the data entity as the primary key.

Once a primary key is found, the process can continue to determine if there are additional primary keys. Occasionally, additional primary keys are found and the best of those candidate primary keys can be selected as the official primary key. The others will become alternate primary keys.

OPTIMIZING DATA

Data entity optimization is the process of combining data characteristics for the same data entity. The process is important because data normalization is oriented toward creating additional data entities when data attributes need to be removed from a data entity. As different development teams work on different projects and create new data entities it is possible that synonymous data entities will be created. If there were no process to combine these synonymous data entities they would continue to exist and would cause deterioration of the data resource.

> Data optimization assures that there are no synonymous subject data entities in the data resource.

Although the process of combining synonymous data entities sounds simple, the task of identifying synonymous data entities is not quite so simple. Data entities may have different names and may even have different primary keys. They could have the same primary key but the data attributes in the primary key may have different names. The data entities and data attributes could even have different definitions. This is perhaps the most challenging task for the person or group in charge of designing a subject data resoruce.

The first data optimization step is one of prevention. As each data attribute is removed from a data entity during the data normalization process it should not automatically become another data entity. The existing data entities in the enterprise should be reviewed to determine if an appropriate data entity already exists. A good data resource directory and data entity name thesaurus will help the search for an appropriate data entity. If an appropriate data entity is found then the data attributes in that data entity should be reviewed to determined if the candidate data attribute already exists in that data entity. If it already exists it should be used. If not, it can be added.

For example, the *Personnel Name* that appeared in *Task Assignment* needed to be removed because it had a partial key dependency. As it is removed the existence of a data entity for *Personnel Name* should be determined. If *Personnel* exists and does not yet have a data attribute for personnel name then *Personnel Name* would be placed in *Personnel*. If *Personnel Name* already exists in *Personnel* it should be reviewed to determine if it would suffice for the task management project. If so, then the appropriate foreign key would be created for access to *Personnel* to obtain *Personnel Name*. If not, some other resolution needs to be made based on the requirements for task management.

However, if no *Personnel* data entity were found the search should continue for similar data entities, such as *Employee, Worker, Staff*, etc. A good data entity name thesaurus would help determine an appropriate data entity. If a similar data entity were found, such as *Employee*, and *Employee Name* were available and acceptable, then it could be used by the task management project. However, a discrepancy is created because *Personnel Number* is used in the task management project and *Employee SSN* is used for *Employee*. If *Employee* is the established data entity, then the task management project should modify its use to *Employee* rather than create a synonymous *Personnel* data entity.

If a synonymous data entity cannot be found based on the data entity name and definition, then the primary keys of other data entities need to be reviewed. This process is harder because the names of the primary key data attributes may not be the same as those in the candidate data entity. The number of data attributes in the primary key and the names and definitions of those data attributes will help. For example, a data entity may be defined for *Building* with a primary key of *Building ID*. No *Building* data entity is found and no

Building ID data attribute is found. However, further review shows that *Facility* exists with a primary key of *Facility ID*. When the definitions are reviewed it is found that a building is in fact a facility and the data attributes are merged.

If the data attribute names and definitions do not help, the domain of values for the primary key data attributes may help identify synonymous data entities. If the domain of values is the same for data attributes in the primary key, or very close to the same, then there is a chance that the two data entities are the same. For example, a data entity may be established for *Rivers* with a primary key of *River Name*. A candidate data entity appears for *Streams* with a primary key of *Stream Identification*. When reviewing the existing data entities it is not obvious that *Rivers* and *Streams* are the same. However, looking at the values for the two primary keys it is obvious that *Stream Identification* is the name of the stream and *River Name* is the name of the river and that the two data entities are the same.

The similarity of data attributes in two data entities is also a consideration for identifying synonymous data entities. Using the *River* and *Stream* example above, the data attributes for *Streams* are largely identical with the data attributes for *Rivers* according to the data definitions. Therefore, the two data entities could be considered the same.

Alternate primary keys could indicate synonymous data entities. When reviewing the primary key for identifying synonymous data entities, the alternate primary keys should also be considered. It is entirely possible that a data entity already defined has a primary key and one or more alternate primary keys. The candidate data entity may have a primary key that matches the alternate primary key of an established data entity. When this happens the primary key for the candidate data entity can be changed to match the primary key of the data entity already established. Using the *River* and *Stream* example again, *Stream Identification* could have been selected as the primary key and defined as a unique identification number assigned as each stream is identified. *Stream Name* is identified as an alternate primary key. Comparing the alternate primary key of *Stream Name* to the primary key of *River Name* would indicate that the two data entities might be synonymous and could be combined.

The format of data attributes in a data entity can also be reviewed to help determine if the primary keys are the same or if the data attributes are similar. If the data attribute formats are similar, then the definitions should be reviewed to determine if they are, in fact, the same data attributes.

The data optimization process is used to combine data views into a conceptual model of the data resource. Each data view follows the same process described above to assure that it is included in the proper data entity in the enterprise's data resource. If no matching data entity is found by the above process, a new data entity can be created with relative certainty that it is unique.

DENORMALIZING DATA

Conceptual schema are converted to internal schema through a denormalization process following a precise set of rules depending on the physical operating environment. This formal logical to physical conversion process assures that the integrity of the conceptual schema is not compromised and that constraints of the physical operating environment are met. Data denormalization is constrained so that it does not alter the basic structure of the conceptual schema. It only makes adjustments to the basic structure for operational efficiency.

> Data denormalization assures that the integrity of the conceptual schema is maintained while the constraints of the operating environment are met.

Data denormalization is a process that adapts the conceptual schema to the physical operating environment, not a process to unstructure the data. A common misconception about data denormalization is that it results in a return to the unnormalized business schema that began the data normalization process. It is wrongly assumed that if there is a return to unnormalized data, then why not use those unnormalized data to define physical data files. However, this is not the situation. Data denormalization produces denormalized data, not unnormalized data.

Data Entity Denormalization

Each data entity does not automatically become a separate data file in the database. Another common misconception is that each data subject must become a separate data file to have a subject database. This was never the intent of a subject database. The intent was to access the physical database using the formal data entity and data attribute names, not the names of the physical files and physical fields. This intent to use real world names of data has been misinterpreted as meaning that there is always a one-for-one conversion between data entities and data files.

However, data files can not be defined with complete disregard for the structure of subject data entities. Therefore, denormalization of data entities follows the rule that each data entity becomes a data file with the same name and one record type unless one of the exceptions apply. For example, the *Employee* data entity becomes the *Employee* data file with one record type representing each employee data occurrence, unless an exception applies.

> Each data entity is converted to a data file unless an exception applies.

The exceptions fall into two basic categories. The first category is denormalization of first normal form by nesting a repeating group with its parent on the same physical file. The second category is denormalization of third normal form by placing similar data entities on the same physical file.

A data entity may be denormalized to two or more data files when the number of data records that need to be stored exceed the limits of a database management system. Multiple data files are created with all the data attributes in each record. The names of the data files are the names of the data entity prefixed or suffixed by a qualifier that makes the data file name unique. For example, if there were too many *Vehicle* records to be contained on one data file, two data files could be established. The decision on how to split the file is usually based on use of the data so that accesses to both data files by a single application is limited. The separation for *Vehicles* might be based on entity types, such as *Motor Vehicles* and *Nonmotor Vehicles*, and the two data files would be named accordingly.

One data entity may be denormalized into two or more data files when the record size exceeds the limits of a database management system. Either multiple record types could be created on the same data file or multiple data files could be created. This decision depends on the limitations of the particular database management system and use of the data. If multiple data files are created, their names will be the same as the data entity name with a prefix or suffix to make the data file name unique within the enterprise. For example, if data about *Buildings* exceeded the record size of a database management system the data could be split based on *construction and value characteristics* of the building and *contents and use characteristics*. The data file names might be *Building Construction* and *Building Content* to reflect this split.

Multiple data entities may be combined on one data file when there are very few data attributes in a data record or very few data records in a data file. Multiple data record types may be created within the same data file representing the data entities that are stored on that data file. The name of that data file may be the name of the prominent data entity in that data file or, if there is no prominent data entity, a new data file name could be created that indicates the data contained in that data file.

The combination of several code tables onto one physical data file is an excellent example of the combination of multiple data entities on one data file. Frequently, there are many code tables used by one application and the combination of those code tables on one data file makes access to those tables easier. For example, if there were twelve data entities representing code tables for *Customer*, those code tables could be placed in one data file for ease of access. The name of that data file might be *Customer Tables*.

Multiple data entities may also be combined on one data file by nesting those data entities. This situation can only occur when there is only one parent data entity accessing the nested data entity, there is no chance for another parent data entity that will access the nested data entity, the parent and the nested data entities are closely related, and there is a high frequency of combined use of the data in the two data entities. The name of the data file becomes the name of the parent data entity in that data file.

For example, each *Employee* has many *Pay Checks* and each *Pay Check* has many *Deductions* forming three data entities. *Pay Check* is also subordinate to the *Financial Account* where the money is obtained to pay the employee which provides multiple parents to *Pay Check*. Therefore, *Pay Check* can not be nested in *Employee*. However, *Deductions* have only one parent and have a high frequency of use with that parent. Therefore, *Deductions* may be nested with *Pay Check* in the *Pay Check* data file.

Successive nesting of data entities becomes difficult to manage and is not recommended. For example, *Deductions* could not be nested within *Pay Check* and then *Pay Check* nested within *Employee*, assuming there were no other parents to *Pay Check*. This successive nesting makes access to the database extremely difficult and many database management systems do not have the capability for successive nesting.

Generally, a subordinate data entity is nested in one parent data entity only when the conditions described above are met. However, under extreme conditions requiring peak performance, a subordinate data entity may be nested into two or more parent data entities. This situation creates redundant data and those redundant data must be consistently undated or the quality of the database will deteriorate rapidly. This situation is not recommended unless there is an extremely good reason for creating the redundant data.

Closely related data categories may be placed in one record on one data file if there is a high frequency of use of the data between those data categories or there are few data attributes in the data categories. The name of the data file is the name of the parent data entity if it is included. If the data file represents several related data categories excluding the parent data entity, then a unique name should be selected that indicates the contents of the data file.

A data entity might not be defined as a data file when there is no need to access that data entity. This situation usually occurs when the data entity has only a primary key and is not needed for validation or access to another data entity. For example, *Academic Year* is established to substantiate data attributes in the primary key of *Student Year*. However, there are no data attributes in *Academic Year* and there is no need for access. Therefore, a data file is not created for *Academic Year*.

Other data entities may be denormalized for operational efficiency based on these criteria. Frequency of use by applications or concerns over security might be considerations for grouping or splitting data entities. Each situation must be carefully evaluated to assure that the logical model is not compromised and that any redundant data are routinely and consistently updated.

Data Attribute Denormalization

Data attributes are denormalized much the same as data entities are denormalized. Each data attribute becomes a separate data item and the name of the data attribute becomes the name of the data item unless an exception applies. For example, the *Employee Birth Date* data attribute becomes the *Employee Birth Date* data item unless an exception applies.

> Each data attribute is converted to a data item unless an exception applies.

The exceptions are denormalization of second normal form by placing a data item in all the data records of a subordinate data file. Denormalization of partial key dependencies should only be done under extreme conditions requiring peak operational performance because redundant data are created. The redundant data must be thoroughly documented and the update routines must be adjusted to update all occurrences of redundant data in a consistent manner to maintain the quality of the database. Creation of redundant data attributes in subordinate data entities is not recommended unless there is an extreme performance problem that can only be resolved by the creation of redundant data. Each of these cases must be reviewed very carefully to determine if the redundant data are absolutely needed.

Data items that are not defined as data attributes may be added to the data file when they are needed for unique identification of a data record. This situation occurs when two or more data entities are combined on one data file in the form of multiple data records and the primary key does not uniquely identify each data record on that file. One or more data items need to be added to the data file to make each data record unique. For example, several code table data entities are combined onto one data file. Each code table contains a primary key that uniquely identifies each code within the table. However, since code tables could contain the same values of the primary keys an additional data attribute is needed to uniquely identify each record in the data file. The addition of *Table Number* would make each data record unique. This situation can usually be prevented by the addition of *Table Number* in each code table data entity.

A data item can also be created when the number of data items in a data key exceed the capabilities of a database management system. Two or more data attributes can be combined to reduce the size of the data key to meet database management system limitations. The individual data attributes that are combined must also be maintained as separate data items in the data file.

A data attribute would not be converted to a data item when data entities are nested and redundancy is created between data attributes in the primary key of the parent and data attributes in the primary key of the subordinate data entities. This situation can only occur with composite primary keys. Redundant data attributes in the subordinate data entity do not become data items on the data file. For example, *Building* is identified by a *Building ID* and each *Room* is identified by *Building ID* and *Room Number*. If *Room* were nested in *Building* on the same data file the *Building ID* data item for each room would not be needed and could be removed.

The sequence of data items in a data record depends on the particular database management system and the operating environment. The frequency of use of a data attribute indicates how often that data attribute is accessed, such as 5000 times per year. The periodicity of access indicates the time frame that the data attribute is accessed, such as 5000 times evenly throughout the entire year, or 5000 times the last week of the year. The method of access, such as batch during off-shift or online access during prime time indicates response time. The periodicity and frequency of null values indicate possible grouping of null data items. Data attribute groups allow the data attributes in a group to be placed together on the database. The size of a data item and the number of data items in a data record may also be important for the arrangement of data items in a data record. The skills of a capable database analyst should be used to determine the importance and use of these factors.

Several subordinate data entities can be nested into the same parent data entity following the rules defined above. However, there could be a problem with the foreign keys in the nested data entities. Some database management systems do not allow duplicate data item names in the same data file and if the foreign keys in the subordinate data entities have the same names there could be a conflict. The names of the data items in the foreign keys should be qualified with a variation name to make them unique.

Data Access Conversion

Each secondary key on the logical data model becomes a data key on the physical model. For example, if a secondary key of *Employee Birth Date* were identified for access to *Employee* then a data key would be defined consisting of *Employee Birth Date*. Data keys can not be created unless they appear on the logical model. If data keys are randomly generated and there is no justification for existence of those data keys then unnecessary resources are used to maintain that data key.

Secondary keys might not be converted to data keys when part of another secondary key may be used to accomplish the same access. If another secondary key contains the same data attributes, in the same sequence, and the noncommon data attributes could be nulled, then that secondary key could be used and the secondary key under consideration could be dropped. For example, there is one secondary key of *Employee Birth Date* and *Employee Name* and another secondary key of *Employee Birth Date*. The first secondary key could be used for access by entering the value for the birth date desired and nulling the value for the employee's name, if the database management system contained this feature. The secondary key for *Employee Birth Date* could be removed.

Data keys can also be removed from a subordinate data entity when data entities are nested on one data file and the data key in the subordinate data entity is available in the parent data entity. For example, if *Room* were nested within *Building* on the same data file and there was a secondary key in *Building* of *Building ID* and there were also a secondary key in *Room* of *Building ID*, the secondary key in *Room* could be dropped. This situation usually occurs when secondary keys in the subordinate data entity contain the same data attributes as the primary key of the parent data entity.

Data keys can be dropped when the position of the nested data entity will suffice for a key. For example, if quarterly data are nested within a record representing a year and the sequence of the nested data occurrences represent the sequence of quarters in the year, the secondary key for identification of quarters could be dropped. Data keys can also be dropped when a routine external to the database management system will perform the searching, sorting, or selecting of records.

The criteria for converting secondary keys to data keys depends on many factors and requires the knowledge of a capable database analyst to analyze the options and choose the most appropriate option. The frequency and periodicity of use of the data key, the probability of blank or null values, the volatility of the data values of the secondary key, where the search and selection criteria could be performed, and percentage of data records obtained could all be factors for consideration. In addition, depending on the capabilities of the particular database management system, the data keys could be maintained continuously, could be created and destroyed as needed, or could be created each time they were needed. There are tradeoffs to all of these options and the data analyst and database analyst should consider these tradeoffs before deciding on how the access indicated by a secondary key is to be met.

Data View Conversion

The logical data resource model contains data views between data entities and applications. These application data views may be converted to physical application data views or they may be merged into combined or full physical data views. Generally, many related application data views are merged into a combined physical data views.

Physical application data views are used primarily for data that are privileged or secure and their use is limited to a specific application and that application is limited to specific individuals. Physical application data views require minimum maintenance since they are used by very few applications. If the application requires a change in the data view there is very little impact to other applications. However, there could be many data views to document if some constraints are not placed on the use of physical application data views. Therefore, physical application data views should be used only for purposes of security and confidentiality.

A physical combined data view is a set of data attributes that does not contain all the data attributes in a data entity, but more than those used by one application. These data views are the workhorse of data views in a production environment. Most of the applications in an information system will access a physical combined data view even though they do not use all the data items in that data view. Therefore, physical combined data views should be standard unless otherwise designated.

Physical combined data views require more maintenance than physical application data views because there is a greater chance of change from applications using the data view and greater impact of change. For example, if two applications are using the same combined data view and one of those applications requires another data attribute, some type of change needs to be made. Either a new data view can be defined or the existing data view can be changed. If the data view is changed the other applications must be changed. This situation may or may not be a problem depending on the particular database management system.

Physical full data views contain all the data items in a physical file. They should not be defined for every data file and given indiscriminately to every application needing data from that data file. There is a loss of control over data used by each application and there could be unintentional updates to the database. In addition, if a particular database management system does not support a two-stage data view concept the maintenance of physical full data views could also become unmanageable.

Some database management systems support a two-stage data view. The first stage data view includes data items available from the data file and the second stage includes data items actually used by an application. Both of these data views must be documented in the data resource directory to properly identify the data actually used by an application and avoid impacts of data view changes. Some database management systems allow a data view to include data items from two or more data files. When this capability is available it is even more important to keep track of the data actually used by an application. Therefore, the application data view from the logical model and any physical data views that are defined must be documented in the data resource directory.

Integrity Rule Conversion

Each data integrity rule on the logical model is converted to data integrity constraints on the physical model. Enforcement of those data integrity constraints can be done by an active database management system, by a data integrity application, or by data integrity routines accessed by applications. The possibilities for enforcement of data integrity constraints are many and varied and are beyond the scope of this book. The important thing to remember is that data integrity rules defined on the logical model must be enforced to maintain integrity of the database.

SUMMARY

Data normalization is a process that assures data subjects identified by the enterprise's view of the business environment form valid single subject data entities that are unique within the data resource and are properly converted to data files in the database. It is composed of three steps that are based on the four-schema concept and produce a data resource structured by subjects that will meet the business needs of the enterprise. The process is practical and understandable and can be used by anyone in the enterprise that is responsible for managing the data resource.

Data normalization is integrated with the processes of describing the data, defining data keys and data relations, and identifying pathways for navigating through the database. Data normalization confirms the structure of the data and is easier when each data entity and data attribute is properly named and defined. However, the data name depends on the structure of the data. Properly identifying data keys depends on the structure of the data and the structure of the data depends on properly defined data keys. Although this seems like an impossible situation, it is a very useful process for properly structuring the data resource.

The data normalization guidelines listed below help assure that the data resource is properly structured and a database is developed that will support the enterprise. When any difficulty is encountered, it is best to pause and properly describe each data entity and data attribute. If a definition already exists it should be reviewed and enhanced to provide a better definition. As explained in the Data Description chapter, the most critical part of data resource design is proper naming and definition of data. Without good data descriptions the data resource can never be properly designed.

Identify data subjects and data characteristics needed to support the enterprise as business schema.

Describe each data subject and each data characteristic from the enterprise's perspective of the business environment.

Identify a primary key for each data subject that uniquely identifies each data occurrence and contains no redundant data.

Each data subject becomes a candidate data entity until it is verified as unique within the data resource.

Each candidate data entity is compared to every other data entity in the data resource to determine if a data entity with the same primary key exists.
    Review each data entity description for similarity.
    Review data entities with similar names for similarity.
    Review alternate primary keys for similarity.
    Review the data domain for the primary key.
    Review the formats of the primary key data attributes.
    Review data attribute descriptions for similarity.
If no similarity is found, the candidate data entity is probably a unique data entity.

If a data entity is found, the data entities are merged or an alteration is made to make the two data entities unique.

If a dependency is found with another data entity, they should be merged.

If no matching data entity is found, the candidate data entity becomes a unique data entity within the data resource.

Each data characteristic becomes a candidate data attribute until it is verified as unique within the data resource.

If that data characteristic is part of a repeating group that is not uniquely identified by the primary key, it is moved to another data entity that has the appropriate primary key.

If that data characteristic is multivalued, it is moved to another data entity that has the appropriate primary key.

If that data characteristic needs only part of the primary key for unique identification, it is moved to another data entity with the appropriate primary key.

If that data characteristic has a dependency with another data characteristic, the dependent data characteristic is moved to another data entity with the appropriate primary key.

If the data characteristic survives, it becomes a data attribute that describes that data entity.

Data entities are converted to data files unless an exception applies.

Repeating groups may be denormalized if they meet the criteria.

Interattribute dependencies may be denormalized if they meet the criteria.

Data attributes are converted to data items unless an exception applies.

Partial key dependencies may be denormalized if there is sufficient reason to create redundant data and their consistent update is assured.

Secondary keys are converted to data accesses if their conversion is justified.

Application data views are converted to physical application data views or may be combined to physical combined data views or physical full data views.

Data integrity rules are converted to whatever routines are appropriate for enforcing data integrity.

If data are not properly normalized the result will be the propagation of application files that are prominent today. These files contain redundant versions of data characteristics that contain different values. In addition to unnecessary processing, these values can lead to wrong decisions and wrong actions. These impacts can be prevented by designing a data resource structured by data subjects where each characteristic of that subject is stored in one place. The result is a data resource that will support the business needs of the enterprise.

STUDY QUESTIONS

The following questions are provided as a review of data normalization and to stimulate thought about the data normalization process and development of a subject database that supports the enterprise.

1. What does the term *Normalization* mean?
2. How are data normalization and the four-schema concept related?

3. What are data anomalies and why are they a problem?
4. How can data anomalies be prevented?
5. What is the objective of data normalization?
6. What are the common misconceptions about data normalization?
7. How are unique subject data entities maintained?
8. What are repeating groups and how are they normalized?
9. How are multivalued data attributes treated?
10. What are partial key dependencies and how are they normalized?
11. What are interattribute dependencies and how are they resolved?
12. What are interentity dependencies and how are they handled?
13. What are the alternatives for handling derived data?
14. How is data normalization related to naming and defining data?
15. What is the objective of data optimization?
16. How are data optimized?
17. What is the objective of data denormalization?
18. How might data be denormalized?
19. How are primary keys selected?
20. What happens when data are not properly normalized?

Data Entities

A structurally stable data resource depends on identification of true single subject data entities.

Correct identification of basic data units is an important step in properly structuring the data resource. Data entities are one of the basic data units that, along with the relations between those entities, form the basic structure of the data resource. Knowing the types of data entities, how to properly identify data entities, the practices that properly identify data entities, and bad practices to avoid will produce a structurally stable data resource.

A structurally stable data resource depends on identification of data entities that represent single subjects of data. All characteristics that describe a data subject become data attributes in that data entity. Once these basic data units are properly structured the abstract data units can be properly identified and defined. If the basic units are not properly structured the abstract data units will not be properly identified and defined and the data resource will be structurally unstable.

This chapter begins with an explanation of the different types of data entities and their uses. The relation between data subjects and data entities is explained and the definition of true data entities is presented. Next, the techniques for identifying true data entities based on data subjects identified from the business environment and verified by data normalization are explained, followed by poor practices that should be avoided. Knowing these good techniques and bad practices will produce single subject data entities that will form a structurally stable data resource.

TYPES OF DATA ENTITIES

A data subject is a set of closely related characteristics about a person, place, thing, event, or concept of interest to the enterprise based on its perception of the business environment. A data entity ideally represents a single data subject in the enterprise's data resource. However, many data entities do not meet the ideal and contain data that do not represent single subjects of data. Therefore, a data entity is more appropriately defined as a set of related data for a specific purpose.

Using this broader definition of a data entity, an **application data entity** contains a set of data for use by one or more applications and is structured according to the structure of those applications. A **subject data entity** contains a set of data representing a single data subject and is not oriented toward the structure of any application using the data. Applications interact with a subject data entity through data views that contain the data required by an application.

Subject data entities that have been identified based on the business environment and verified through the data normalization process are **true data entities**. They have a name, a definition and a primary key and may have foreign and secondary keys and one or more additional data attributes. A **false data entity** is a data entity that has not been properly identified based on the business environment and verified by the data normalization process. It could have originated from the data normalization process and not been supported by the business environment, or from a perception of the business environment that could not be verified by data normalization.

> The identification and definition of true single subject data entities is mandatory for a stable data resource.

The data normalization process explained in the last chapter verifies the existence of a data subject and assures those data subjects are unique within the enterprise. It assures that all characteristics describing a data subject are placed in the same data entity. However, the data normalization process is not foolproof and will not automatically produce a data resource of true data entities. The process requires an understanding by the people using the process about the nature of data entities and how they are identified and defined. This understanding begins with an awareness of the different types of data entities, how they are identified, and what they represent.

Data Category

A **data category** is a subentity that represents a *can also be* situation. For example, an employee is working and receiving wages. When that employee becomes unemployed they are a claimant seeking unemployment payments based on the wages they earned as an employee. When they become employed again they cease to be a claimant collecting unemployment and are an employee collecting wages. In this case *Person* is the parent data entity and *Employee* and *Claimant* are data categories. Data attributes unique to that person as an employee or as a claimant belong in the respective data categories and data attributes unique to that person as a person belong in *Person*. Data categories represent data subjects and are managed the same as data entities. They have one-to-one data relations with their parent data entity and with each other.

> Data categories represent subentities in a peer relation with their parent data entity and are managed like any other data entity.

Data Entity Types

A **data entity type** is subentity that represents *can only be* situations in a data entity. For example, *Boats* can be either *Passenger* or *Freight* and *Passenger Boats* can be either *Pleasure* or *Commercial*. Identification of data entity types forms an entity-type hierarchy. Data entity types represent data subjects and are managed the same as data entities.

> A data entity type represents a mutually exclusive grouping of data occurrences in a data entity.

Associative Data Entity

An **associative data entity** is a data entity that represents a data relation that has data attributes. Data relations can not have any data attributes and any data relation that has data attributes must be defined as a data entity and managed like any other data entity. However, it is important to know that a data entity represents a relation between other data entities. The term *associative data entity* is used to designate a data entity that forms a relation between other data entities. For example, the relation between an *Employee* and a *Job* is a *Job Assignment*, meaning the assignment of an employee to a job. However, *Job Assignment* has data attributes, such as starting date, ending date, and so on, and can not remain as a data relation. It is defined as an associative data entity that relates *Employee* and *Job*.

> An associative data entity represents a relation between data entities that has data attributes.

Recursive Data Entity

Generally, there are no relations between the data occurrences in a data entity. For example, a vehicle with license number *XYZ 123* has no relation to the vehicle with license number *ABC 789*. However, there are situations where the data occurrences in a data entity can be related to other data occurrences in a one-to-one or a one-to-many relation. A **recursive**

data entity contains data occurrences that are related to other data occurrences in a one-to-one or a one-to-many relation.

> A recursive data entity represents one-to-one and one-to-many data relations between data occurrences in the same data entity.

Data occurrences in a data entity may have a one-to-one relationship. For example, there could be paired data occurrences for two employees who are married. Each employee data occurrence has an internal foreign key that points to the spouse data occurrence. The data attribute for pointing to the spouse might be *Employee SSN Spouse* and each data occurrence would contain the *SSN* of the spouse, if there were a spouse, as shown in Figure 9.1

```
                    --
                   | #Employee SSN
                   |
                   | +Employee SSN Spouse
                   |
   Employee <<       Employee SSN
                   | Employee SSN Spouse
                   | Employee Name
                   | Employee Birth Date
                    --
```

Figure 9.1 A one-to-one data relation for employee.

A recursive data entity with a one-to-one relation is shown on the entity-relationship diagram as a single data entity with a one-to-one data relation to itself, as shown in Figure 9.2. A one-to-one relation between data occurrences forms a **closed data relation**. One employee data occurrence points to the spouse data occurrence, which points back to the first data occurrence.

Figure 9.2 A one-to-one recursive data entity.

The data occurrences in a data entity may have a one-to-many data relation that defines a hierarchy. Using this one-to-many reference, all the subordinates of one parent data occurrence, or the parent data occurrence of one subordinate data occurrence, can be determined. This relationship allows definition of a hierarchy of data occurrences in one data entity rather than establishing multiple data entities to show that hierarchy.

For example, a data entity could be established to represent all organizational units in an enterprise and their reporting relations. Each data occurrence represents one organizational unit and contains a data attribute identifying its parent organizational unit as shown in Figure 9.3. The internal foreign key contains the same data entity name, *Organizational*

Unit, but is fully qualified with the variation name *Parent*. Using this parent organization unit identification allows navigation up or down the organizational structure by moving through data occurrences within *Organizational Unit*.

```
                        -- 
                        | #Organizational Unit ID
                        |
                        | -Organizational Unit ID
                        |
                        | -Organizational Unit ID Parent
Organizational Unit  <<
                        | +Organizational Unit ID Parent
                        |
                        |  Organizational Unit ID
                        |  Organizational Unit Name
                        |  Organizational Unit Size
                        --
```

Figure 9.3   A one-to-many data relation for organizational unit.

A recursive data relation is shown on the entity-relationship diagram as a single data entity with a relation to itself, as shown in Figure 9.4. *Organizational Unit* has a one-to-many data relation to itself indicating that the data occurrences within Organization Unit are related to each other in a one-to-many relationship. The one-to-many relation between data occurrences forms an **open data relation** where the relations can be followed to the end, i.e., the top or bottom of the hierarchy, but will never return to the starting point.

Figure 9.4   A one-to-many recursive data entity.

The relations between data occurrences in a recursive data entity may be optional or mandatory. The one-to-one relation described above for spouse is an **optional data relation** because not every employee has a spouse. However, the relation for the organizational unit recursive data entity is a **mandatory data relation,** except at the top of the hierarchy. Every organizational unit must have a value for the parent organizational unit, except the highest organizational unit in the enterprise.

Another example of a recursive data entity is the definition of geographic areas where each data occurrence represents a particular geographic area. For example, cities, counties, states, countries, etc., form a hierarchical relationship of geographic areas. Since there can be different hierarchies, e.g., the structure of geographic areas in different countries form different hierarchies, it is better to define a recursive data entity than to define many separate data entities representing all possible hierarchies of geographic areas. In the case of geographic areas there is an internal foreign key to the parent geographic area.

Data occurrences in a recursive data entity can contain cumulative information that is derived from subordinate data occurrences. For example, the number of people supervised

Data Entities

could be derived for each organizational unit, or the population and land area could be derived for each geographic area. These data attributes must be maintained when there is a change to the values in one or more of the subordinate data occurrences contributing to the derived data.

Cyclic Data Entities

Data occurrences can also form a many-to-many relation where one data occurrence is related to many other data occurrences, and each of those data occurrences is related to many others, including the first. This many-to-many situation is resolved by defining two data entities that are in a normal one-to-many relation and refer to each other in a cyclic manner. These **cyclic data entities** resolve the many-to-many relation between data occurrences. For example, companies can split and merge in many ways during the course of their existence. To track the splitting and merging of these companies, as well as the data about each company, requires two data entities, as shown in Figure 9.5.

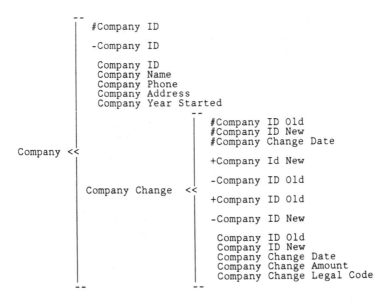

Figure 9.5 Many-to-many data relation showing business splits and merges.

The data attributes characterizing any company are contained in *Company* and those characterizing a change between companies are contained in *Company Change*. *Company Change* would be accessed to find the predecessors of a company using *Company ID Old*. Data about each of those predecessors could be obtained from *Company* using *Company ID New*. The same procedure could be performed for successor companies using *Company ID New* for access to *Company Change* and returning to *Company* with *Company ID Old*. This processing results in a cycling between the two data entities, hence the name cyclic data entities.

Cyclic data entities represent resolution of many-to-many data relation between data occurrences within a data entity.

Cyclic data entities are shown on entity-relationship diagrams as two data entities in a one-to-many relationship, as shown in Figure 9.6. Each data occurrence in *Company* is related to many data occurrences in *Company Change*.

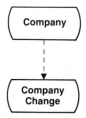

Figure 9.6 Cyclic data entities.

Another example of cyclic data entities is the classic parts assembly or parts explosion situation. Several parts are put together to make another part, which in turn becomes a part that is combined with other parts to make a larger part, and so on. In addition, any part could be used as a component in more than one part, making parts a many-to-many relation with itself. This situation is resolved by defining data entities for *Components* and *Parts* that are in a one-to-many data relation as shown in Figure 9.7.

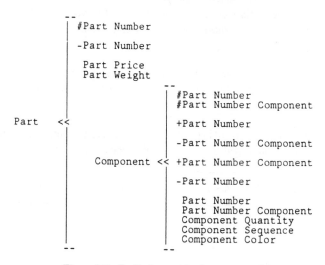

Figure 9.7 Cyclic data entities for parts assembly.

Each part is a data occurrence in *Part* characterized by part number, price, and weight. Each assembly of parts requires two or more component parts which result in two or more *Component* data occurrences. Each component part is characterized by the part number it goes into, *Part Number*, its own part number, *Part Number Component*, the quantity of the component, the sequence components are needed, and the component color. The component part also exists as a data occurrence in *Part*. To determine all component parts used in one part requires accessing all *Component* data occurrences with a particular *Part Number*. To determine all parts that use a particular component requires accessing all *Component* data occurrences for that particular *Part Number Component*.

A similar situation is menu preparation where food components are combined to make other components, which in turn may be combined, and so on until the final product is obtained. Any one food component could be used to prepare several final dishes making food components in a many-to-many data relation with itself. This situation is resolved exactly the same way the part component problem was resolved.

Data can be accumulated for cyclic data entities similar to the way data are accumulated for recursive data entities. For example, calories, salt content, and cholesterol could be accumulated for food dishes, and total price and weight could be accumulated for assembled parts. This accumulation would be done by adding up those values for each component involved in the combination process. When the components contributing to the derived data attribute change values the derived values need to be reaccumulated to represent the true value.

Resolution Data Entity

A **resolution data entity** is an associative data entity established to resolve a many-to-many data relation between data occurrences in two data entities. The resolution data entity is in a many-to-one relation with each data entity involved in the many-to-many data relation. For example, many employees can be authorized to expend money from one account, and one employee can be authorized to expend money from many accounts, putting *Employee* and *Account* in a many-to-many relation.

> A resolution data entity represents the resolution of a many-to-many data relation between data occurrences in different data entities.

Account Authorization is established to resolve this many-to-many relation, as shown in Figure 9.8. It contains the data attributes necessary to authorize an employee to expend

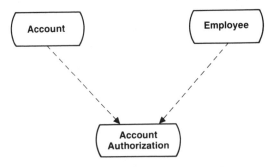

Figure 9.8 Example of a resolution data entity.

money from one account, such as *Employee SSN, Account ID, Account Authorization Begin Date, Account Authorization End Date, Account Authorization Amount,* and so on. Each combination of employee and account constitutes another data occurrence in *Account Authorization.* In other words, *Account Authorization* contains a list of primitive combinations of valid employees and accounts.

Summary Data Entity

A **summary data entity** contains summary or derived data accumulated from detail data contained in one or more data entities that are subordinate to the summary data entity. Summary data entities are unique in that they are dependent on the hierarchy of the data entities involved in the summary. For example, there are several data relations between the *Salesman, Customer, Product,* and *Invoice* data entities in a *Company* as shown in Figure 9.9.

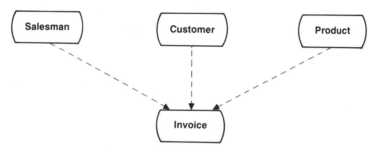

Figure 9.9   Data relations for invoices.

Three separate hierarchies of these data entities could be defined for the summary of invoices by product, as shown in Figure 9.10. In the first hierarchy, *Invoices* are summarized by *Product* within each *Customer,* for each *Salesman.* In the second hierarchy, *Invoices* are summarized for all *Customers* by *Product,* within *Salesman.* In the third hierarchy, *Invoices* are summarized for all *Customers* and *Salesman* by *Product.* Clearly, the *Invoice* summaries by *Product* for each of these three hierarchies will result in different values. For example, the summary of *Invoices* by *Product* within *Customer* and *Salesman,* the first hierarchy, will have a different value than the summary of *Invoices* for all *Customers* by *Product* within *Salesman,* the second hierarchy.

```
Salesman  { Customer  { Product   { Invoice
Salesman  { Product   { Customer  { Invoice
Product   { Salesman  { Customer  { Invoice
```

Figure 9.10   Three hierarchies from Salesman, Customer, and Invoice.

Each of these summaries of *Invoices* by *Product* has a primary key that uniquely identifies that summary data occurrence. The data attributes forming the primary key indicate the hierarchy of the summary. For example, the primary key in the first hierarchy

Data Entities

consists of *Salesman Number, Customer ID*, and *Product Code*. The primary key for the summary of *Invoices* by *Product* in the second hierarchy consists *of Salesman Number* and *Product Code*. The primary key for the third hierarchy *is Product Code*. Since the primary keys are different, there are three different data entities and the invoice summary values will be different for each data entity.

> Summary data entities represent summary of data based on the hierarchy above the summary level.

Changing the sequence of the data entities above the summary does not alter the primary key or the value of the summary. For example, the summary of *Invoices* by *Product* within *Salesman* for each *Customer* provides the same values as the summary of *Invoices* by *Product* within *Customer* for each *Salesman*. The only difference in these two hierarchies is that the two data entities above *Product* were exchanged, as shown in Figure 9.11, but the primary key for the summary data entity remains the same and the summary values are the same.

```
Salesman  { Customer  { Product   { Invoice

Customer  { Salesman  { Product   { Invoice
```

Figure 9.11 Changing hierarchy of data entities above the summary data entity.

In each situation previously described, the summary value is placed in *Product*. However, the data subject representing that summary value is not *Product*, it is an invoice summary data entity. However, it is not the same invoice summary data entity in all situations. To avoid long data entity names, the convention is to name those data entities *Invoice Summary 1, Invoice Summary 2*, etc., as explained in the Data Description chapter.

Summaries could also be derived for data entities other than *Product*. For example, summaries of *Invoices* could be derived for *Customer* or for *Salesman*, Each of these summaries would have hierarchies similar to those for the summary of *Invoices* by *Product*. Each of these summaries would also be an *Invoice Summary* data entity with a qualifying number. Each of these summary data entities must be documented in the data resource directory.

Selecting particular *Invoice* data occurrence groups for the summary, such as *Overdue Invoices* rather than *All Invoices*, does not change the data subject. Since the primary key is the same, the summary data entity is the same. But, the data attribute in that summary data entity has a different value because it represents only *Overdue Invoices* not *All Invoices*. Since different *Invoice* data occurrence groups were used to accumulate the summary values, different data attributes must be used to store those values. Therefore, the data attributes might be named *Invoice Summary 2 Overdue Amount*, and *Invoice Summary 2 Total Amount*.

> Selection of data occurrences below the summary level result in different data attributes, not a new summary data entity.

Data entities above the summary level determine the primary key and define the summary data entity. Different parent data entities form a different primary key and, consequently, define a different summary data entity. Rearranging the same parent data entities does not result in a different summary data entity. Selection of data occurrences below the summary level results in different data attributes to store those values, but those data attributes belong to the same summary data entity.

Phantom Data Entity

A **phantom data entity** justifies existence of a data attribute in the primary key of a subordinate data entity, but does not have any other data attributes or use. For example, *Student* contains data about a student, such as name, birthdate, and gender, and *Student Year* contains data about that student each year they are in school, such as credits taken, grade point average for the year, and financial aid received. The primary key for *Student* is *Student ID Number* and the primary key for *Student Year* is *Student ID Number* and *Academic Year Number*.

> A phantom data entity substantiates the data attributes in the primary key of a subordinate data entity.

The primary key for *Student Year* indicates there should be two parent data entities, *Student* and *Academic Year*. However, only *Student* is identified as a data entity. The question could be asked, "What data entity substantiates *Academic Year Number* as part of the primary key of *Student Year*?" The answer is *Academic Year* which is a phantom data entity because it is used to substantiate the primary key but has no other purpose. Adding a phantom data entity to a data resource model, as shown in Figure 9.12, improves the semantics of the model.

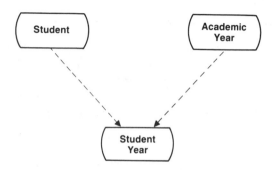

Figure 9.12   A phantom data entity for academic year.

Key-Only Data Entity

A **key-only data entity** has data attributes forming the primary key and no other data attributes. A true key-only data entity exists for a purpose, even if that purpose is to substantiate the data attributes in the primary key of another data entity, as with a phantom data entity. True key-only data entities must be retained on the data resource model. A false key-only data entity has no purpose, such as the key-only data entities identified during the process of determining the primary key for a data entity and should be eliminated from the data resource model.

> A key-only data entity is a true data entity that contains only the data attributes comprising the primary key.

Code Table

There are two basic types of data values: actual values and coded values. **Actual data values** are the actual labels or measurements for entities, such as a person's name, a vehicle manufacture date, or the maximum occupancy of a room in a building. **Coded data values** are codes assigned to characteristics that represent an actual value or a group of values. For example, *New Student*, *Returning Student*, and *Continuing Student* could be coded into values of *1*, *2*, and *3* respectively. Similarly, the ranges in a person's weight could be coded into weight groups of *Under Weight*, *Normal Weight*, and *Over Weight*.

Coded data values require a table that shows what each value represents. For example, when *Employee Weight Code* contains a value of *OW* a description must be supplied with that value. The table of values shows that *OW* means *Over Weight* and provides some parameters for actual weight. A table of coded values and their descriptions is termed a **Code Table** and is a data entity in the data resource. It can be used to either encode or decode data by accessing the table with a description or a value.

> A code table is a data entity representing a set of coded data values and their descriptions.

A code table must be defined for each data attribute that contains coded values. To help identify these data attributes the standard word *Code* is used in the name, as explained in the Data Description chapter. For example, *Employee Status Code* contains coded values and requires a code table of the descriptions of those values. However, *Employee Height* contains the actual height and does not need a supporting code table.

> A code table must be defined for each data attribute containing coded values.

Each code table is a separate data entity that is in a one-to-many data relation with the data entity containing the coded value. For example, *Employee* has a data attribute for *Employee Status Code*. *Employee Status* contains a *Code* and a *Description* for each employee status. Since many employee data occurrences can have the same *Employee Status Code*, but any single employee data occurrence has only one *Employee Status Code*, there is a one-to-many data relation between *Employee Status* and *Employee*.

Data Domain

A **data domain** contains a set of allowable values for a data attribute. A code table is the data domain for a data attribute that contains coded data values. In the example above, the *Employee Status* code table is the data domain for *Employee Status Code*. The value for *Employee Status Code* can be any of the values listed in the *Employee Status* table. Code tables begin the definition of data domains for each data attribute in the data resource. Additional data domains are defined for data attributes containing actual values. Each data attribute must have a supporting data domain.

> A data domain is a set of allowable values for a data attribute.

Data domains are managed like any other data entity. A data domain is used to enforce data integrity. A data domain can also be used for determining the values that can be used for selecting data from the database and for encoding data going into the database.

DATA ENTITY IDENTIFICATION

Proper identification of data subjects is based on the enterprises perception of the business world and data normalization. Each data subject is initially identified from the business environment and is based on identification of behavioral entities, external events, business transactions, and any supporting data subject. However, different people in the enterprise have different perceptions of the business environment which could result in definition of different data subjects. Once these different perceptions are brought together a data subject can be identified. Then each data subject can be verified by the data normalization process and formally accepted as a true subject data entity.

Identifying data subjects is similar to several people inside an old barn looking out through various holes and cracks in the barn wall. Each person sees a different part of the environment outside the barn and will describe that environment based on what they see. For example, one person may see plowed fields, another may see livestock grazing in green pastures, another may see a variety of farm buildings, and so forth. If a single person described the environment based on what that person alone saw, the true environment would be misrepresented. However, if everyone combined their views the true environment would be described.

This is exactly the situation data resource managers face today. Each person in the enterprise has a relatively narrow view of the business environment based on one's involvement in the business. The only way to get a complete perspective of the true business environment is to include a wide variety of people that collectively have a complete perception of that business environment and teach them the concepts and techniques of proper data subject identification. This is one reason why direct involvement of users in design of the data resource is emphasized.

The concept of a data subject is difficult to understand particularly for people that have been closely associated with application data entities. The difficulty is changing the orientation from a data structure supporting applications to a structure of data subjects. Changing this orientation is one of the major difficulties in establishing a procedure to identify subject data entities and convert application data files to a subject data resource.

Several techniques can be used to identify single subjects of data. The first, and most important, is the perception the enterprise has of the business environment and the behavioral entities being tracked during their encounter with the enterprise. The second is the process of data normalization to verify those subjects. Other techniques include reasoning about the data, use of current names and definitions, and a constant review of existing data.

Data Entity Purity

Synonymous data entities occur when a data subject is represented in two or more places with different names. For example, one development team may identify a data entity for *Employee*, while another development team may identify a data entity for *Worker*, and a third team may identify a data entity for *Staff*. All of these data entities represent people employed by the enterprise. Synonymous data entities need to be combined into one true subject data entity that contains all the data characteristics about that subject.

Homonymous data entities occur when two or more different data entities have the same name. For example, a data entity for transactions against a customer's account might be labeled *Activity* by a development team. Another development team might label maintenance tasks for vehicles as *Activity*, and a third team might label changes to student data as *Activity*. Obviously, these three data entities are different and unrelated even though they have the same name. Homonymous data entities need to be resolved by selecting a more explicit name and providing a complete definition for each data entity.

These examples show synonymous and homonymous data entities in their simplest form. The situation becomes more confusing with degrees of synonymous and homonymous data entities. For example, the team defining *Employees* may include only people employed by the enterprise, while the team defining *Workers* may include anyone on the job site whether employed by the enterprise or by a contractor. Similarly, the team identifying activities for students may be including activities for the *students' financial accounts* as well as the *students' academic curriculum*. These situations can only be resolved by good data descriptions and data normalization.

A **multiple subject data entity** contains two or more complete subjects of data. For example, if data about a *Vehicle* and data about each *Owner* of that vehicle are stored in the same data entity that data entity becomes a multiple subject data entity. This situation usually occurs with conventional application files structured by an application's use of data. Since an application generally requires several subjects of data, those subjects were combined into one application data entity.

A **partial subject data entity** contains part of a single subject of data. The remaining part of that data subject may be contained in one or more other data entities. For example, a payroll application data entity may contain employee data relating to paying employees and a training application data entity may contain employee data relating to training employees. Since only part of the employee data characteristics are in each application data entity, and some may be in both, each application data entity is considered a partial subject data entity.

A **complex subject data entity** contains a mixture of multiple and partial data subjects in the same data entity. It could contain several partial subjects of data, several partial and complete subjects, both partial and multiple subjects of data, or partial, multiple, and complete subjects of data. For example, an existing application data entity may contain data about employees that take vehicles from the motor pool, data about those vehicles, the trips those vehicles take, and the maintenance performed on those vehicles. Since there is a mixture of complete subjects of data and partial subjects of data, it is considered a complex subject data entity.

Data Entity Identification Techniques

A data subject is a noun representing a person, place, thing, event, or concept. Data subject identification consists of identifying subjects that are of interest to the enterprise and verifying those data subjects by data normalization. Identifying data subjects can be a difficult and frustrating process even when people are thoroughly familiar with the concept of data subjects and single subject data entities. The identification process can be aided by providing five specific steps for identifying data subjects using the techniques explained in previous chapters.

The first step is to identify behavioral entities that are managed by the enterprise and the data directly supporting those behavioral entities. This step uses the knowledge of people in an enterprise who know the business activities of the enterprise and the business environment. These people can analyze the business environment and identify behavioral entities that are managed to achieve the enterprise's goals. These behavioral entities become the initial data subjects in the enterprise's data resource. For example, an enterprise manages employees, customers, buildings, products, and vehicles. These behavioral entities become data subjects in the data resource.

When behavioral entities are identified, any data subjects that directly support those behavioral entities can be identified relatively easily. For example, employees hold jobs and receive pay checks, customers place orders, buildings have rooms, products have components, and vehicles have maintenance. These data subjects are added to the data resource.

The second step is to analyze business transactions and business events to identify data subjects. For example, the wages paid an employee, a customer's bills and payments, and contracts for building maintenance are business transactions that become data subjects. Business events, such as an automobile accident, issuance of a driver's license, and sales promotion campaigns are business events that become data subjects. Analyzing business transactions and events can identify additional data subjects, such as the people, vehicles, and location of an automobile accident. However, caution should be used because not all business transactions and business events become data subjects some transactions and events may contain multiple data subjects.

The third step is to prepare comprehensive definitions of each data subject, business transaction, business event, and business process to identify data subjects. These definitions are reviewed to locate nouns that indicate data subjects. For example, a business process produces a report of the expenditures from each financial account by development project, indicating data subjects for expenditures, accounts, and projects. If the definition of a data subject contains the word *and* there may be multiple data subjects. For example, the definition of an employee states that it contains employee and payroll deduction data indicating data subjects for employees and deductions.

Data subject definitions can also be compared to identify common data subjects. Any similar definitions or definitions containing the same noun indicates common data subjects. For example, a pay check definition states that a pay check contains information about an employee's pay and deductions from their pay. These deductions could be the same deductions contained in the employee definition above.

The fourth step is to identify a primary key for each data subject and normalize those data subjects to verify them as single subject data entities. Data normalization may identify additional data entities for repeating groups, partial key dependencies, and interattribute dependencies. When a data entity is identified it becomes a candidate data entity that goes through the data optimization process to assure it is unique within the enterprise.

The data attributes in each primary key are reviewed to identify foreign data attributes. There must be a parent data entity to substantiate the existence of each foreign data attribute in a primary key. If a parent data entity does not exist one must be defined, even if it is only a phantom data entity.

The fifth step is to review the data relations between data occurrences within and between data entities. Data relations between data entities are identified as each new data entity is defined. Each data entity must have at least one data relation to another data entity. If a data entity has no data relations it should be reviewed very carefully for validity.

If the data relation is a many-to-many relation, a resolution data entity must be identified and data relations established with the two parent data entities. The initial many-to-many data relation is removed. For example, employees can hold many jobs and each job can have many employees forming a many-to-many data relation between employees and jobs. This relation is resolved with a job assignment data entity that has a many-to-one data relation with employee and job. The original many-to-many data relation between employee and job is removed.

Many-to-many data relations can also be resolved with a business rule rather than with a resolution data entity. For example, there is a many-to-many relation between employees and addresses. However, an enterprise is not interested in all the employees at one address, only in the addresses for an employee. Therefore, a business rule stating this interest resolves the many-to-many data relation into a one-to-many data relation between employees and addresses.

If a data relation has attributes, it must be defined as a data entity and data relations established with associated data entities. For example, a customer buys many products forming a one-to-many data relation between customer and product. However, the purchase of a product may have a date, a price, and other data and must be defined as a data entity. Therefore, a customer makes many purchases and each purchase includes one or more products and data about the purchase.

Data categories can be identified through *can also be* situations and situations where data entities intersect and the same data attribute could legitimately belong to both data entities. For example, customers and employees intersect with a few data attributes, such as name, birth date, and ethnic origin, while each has many additional unique data attributes. Three data entities should be defined for employees, customers, and person. The best criteria to determine if data categories exist is to check for a "can also be" situation. If a person can be a customer and they can also be an employee, data categories should be defined.

Data categories occur most frequently with people data entities. When a data entity is defined for a person, a check should be made for other person data entities in the data resource and the parent data entity should be identified. One-to-one data relations are established between the parent data entity and its data categories.

Mutually exclusive subordinate data subjects indicate data entity types. For example, a customer may be active or inactive, indicating that active customers and inactive customers are data entity subtypes of customer. Each data entity should be reviewed to determine if it is mutually exclusive with any other data entities. If a mutually exclusive situation is identified, the data entities become data entity types of a larger data entity supertype. Similarly, each data entity should be reviewed to determine if it contains mutually exclusive subtypes.

Mutually exclusive parent data entities indicate a mutually exclusive one-to-many relation. For example, a vehicle may be owned by either a person or a company, but never both. These types of relations are not common, but they do exist.

Data occurrences within a data entity normally have no relations to each other. However, one-to-one and one-to-many data relations can occur and indicate a recursive data entity. Many-to-many data relations between data occurrences within a data entity indicate cyclic data entities.

Each data attribute must have a data domain defining the allowable values for that data attribute. If that data domain contains a list of values or other data attributes, such as a code table, it becomes a data entity.

These five steps help identify single subject data entities in the data resource and validate those data subjects as single subject data entities. When the proper people with a knowledge of the business activities of an enterprise are included in the identification process and the process is business driven with technical verification single subject data entities can be readily identified. Once the basic framework of single subject data entities and data relations is established, additional data entities can be easily added without impact on existing data entities or applications.

Bad Data Entity Identification Practices

There are several bad data entity identification practices that should be avoided. Even well-intentioned people that know how to define single subject data entities develop bad practices. Knowing these bad practices, as well as the techniques to follow, help avoid the bad practices and allow people to develop a well-structured subject data resource.

A limit should not be placed on the maximum number of data entities within the enterprise. The total number of data entities is not important during logical data resource design and should not even be considered. What is important, is that data subjects are properly identified and verified as single subject data entities. Limiting the number of data entities forces combination of data attributes into fewer data entities resulting in multiple-subject data entities. If this process is allowed to continue, these multiple subject data entities lead to a deteriorating data resource.

The number of data attributes describing a data subject should not be used as the criteria for combining or creating data entities. The number of data attributes in a data entity is not important during logical data resource design. What is important is that single subject data entities are properly identified and that all data attributes that characterize a data entity are placed in that data entity.

There must be a basis for a data entity to exist and a person should not guess at the existence of a data entity. The inclusion of a data entity in the data resource as a result of pure speculation leads to identification of false data entities and a deteriorating data resource. Each data entity must be based on a valid data subject and verified by data normalization.

Sometimes, key-only data entities are ignored or discarded as useless because they do not have data attributes other than those in the primary key. However, a data entity may be used to justify the existence of a primary key, such as a phantom data entity, or it may be used for validation where the existence of a primary key indicates a valid option. There is also a chance that a data entity is a true data entity for which additional data attributes will be defined at a later date. In these cases the data entity should be retained until proven otherwise. For example, a data entity is identified for *County* and contains only *County Code* as the primary key. There is a high probability that *County* will contain additional data attributes such as *County Name, County Size, County Population*, and so on, so it should be retained as a true data entity.

If a key-only data entity is used for validation, the data entity name should contain the standard word *Validation* to designate it as a true data entity. For example, a data entity is identified with only *Account Code* and *Budget ID*, both of which compose the primary key. This data entity resolves a many-to-many relation between the *Account* and *Budget* data entities and serves to validate the proper use of an *Account Code* and *Budget ID* pair. It should be retained as a true data entity named *Account Budget Validation*.

If a data entity is truly empty other than the primary key, there is no chance of additional data attributes being identified, and it is not used for validation or justifying the existence of a data attribute in a primary key, it can be discarded. However, discarding a data entity must be done only after careful analysis.

The constraints, or capabilities, of a DBMS should not be used as criteria for creating or destroying data entities. There is a tendency to use the number of files available in a DBMS as the criteria for creating data entities, such as many files are available so many data entities can be defined, or only a few files are available so very few data entities should be define. It is better to identify true data entities during logical data resource design and then decide how to denormalize those data entities into physical files during physical design.

Another database management system constraint is the number of I/O's, the access time to obtain the required data, or the number of files that need to be opened for an application. These constraints are usually based on the impact of a billing algorithm rather than on true data entity concerns. However, they are still used to reduce the number of data entities resulting in fewer physical files. If the billing algorithm cannot be adjusted, or the other benefits of a subject database cannot be explained, data denormalization and physical design should include these concerns. They should not be used during logical data resource design when true data entities are being identified.

Identification of data entities based on the use of data by applications should be avoided. This approach produced the multiple, partial, and complex subject data entities that are common today. These nonsubject data entities are making it difficult for an enterprise to convert to a subject data resource. Propagation of these nonsubject data entities only magnifies the problem.

The only sure method to identify true single subject data entities is to use the techniques described above. Anytime identification of data entities goes beyond these techniques and uses unnecessary constraints, false data entities are identified that lead to a deteriorating data resource.

SUMMARY

Correct identification of true single subject data entities is one of the most critical steps in the development of a well-structured data resource. Data entities must be properly identified based on the business environment and verified by data normalization, they must represent single subjects of data, and they must be properly named and defined. Identification of these single subject data entities is relatively easy when the techniques described above are followed. These techniques are summarized in the following guidelines:

Properly identify data subjects based on the business environment.

Validate single subject data entities through data normalization.

Use the knowledge of people in the enterprise to identify subjects of data.

Place all data attributes characterizing a data subject in the same data entity.

Evaluate the validity and use of a key-only data entity before it is retained or discarded.

A data relation containing characteristics becomes a separate data entity.

A data subject resolving a many-to-many relation between two data entities becomes a resolution data entity.

Data subjects in a one-to-one relation with a parent and with each other become data categories.

A data subject representing a mutually exclusive type of a data entity becomes a data entity type.

Code tables and data domains become separate data entities.

A data subject representing summary data becomes a separate data entity.

A data subject representing a one-to-one or one-to-many data relation between data occurrences in the same data entity becomes a recursive data entity.

A data subject representing a many-to-many relation between data occurrences in the same data entity becomes a cyclic data entity.

A data subject that has data attributes substantiating the data attributes in a primary key becomes a phantom data entity.

Do not place a limit on the maximum number of data subjects or data entities in an enterprise.

Do not combine or separate data entities based on the number of data attributes.

Do not define data entities based on perceptions of physical files that may be defined.

Do not guess about the existence of a data entity.

Do not automatically discard all key-only data entities.

Do not define data entities based on the physical limitations of a database management system where the data may reside.

Do not define data entities based on the use of data by an application.

STUDY QUESTIONS

The following questions are provided as a review of the data entities and identification techniques, and to stimulate thought about the process of identifying true subject data entities.

1. What are the critical steps in developing a stable data resource?
2. What is the difference between application and subject data entities?
3. What is a true data entity?
4. What is a data subject?
5. What are the different types of data entities and what does each represent?
6. How do recursive data entities differ from cyclic data entities?
7. How do data entity types differ from data categories?
8. How are summary data entities identified?
9. Why is a phantom data entity necessary?
10. Why must foreign data attributes have a corresponding data entity?
11. Why should code tables and data domains become separate data entities?
12. Why are nonsingle subject data entities a problem?
13. Why is it difficult to identify single subject data entities?
14. What is the difference between synonymous and homonymous data entities?
15. What is the difference between partial, multiple, and complex subject data entities?
16. What steps are used to identify data entities?
17. Why is data subject identification driven by the business environment?
18. Why are data subjects verified by data normalization rather than identified by data normalization?
19. What bad data entity identification techniques should be avoided?
20. What factors can cause deterioration of an enterprise data resource?

Data Attributes and Values

> Single characteristic data attributes and single property data values must be
> defined to support a structurally stable data resource.

    After correct identification of single subject data entities, the correct identification of
data attributes and data values is necessary to support a well-structured data resource.
Knowing the types of data attributes and data values, how to properly identify data
attributes and data values, and bad practices to avoid will produce single characteristic data
attributes and single property data values that support the enterprise's data resource.

    Although identification of data values usually follows identification of data attributes
and identification of data attributes usually follows identification of data entities, the
process can also work the other way. Identification of data values may help identify data
attributes and identification of data attributes may help identify data entities. Although the
process is presented in the sequence of data entities, data attributes, and data values, it can
work in either direction to identify the basic data units in an enterprise's data resource.

    Identification of the basic data units is also closely related to the naming and
definition of those data units. A comprehensive definition and a formal name help identify
data entities, data attributes, and data values and determine their structure. Determining
their structure also provides a formal data name and a comprehensive definition. Therefore,

the processes of naming and defining data are closely related to the process of structuring data and all three processes are used to identify the basic units of data.

This chapter begins with an explanation of the different types of data attributes and data values and their uses. The relations between data characteristics and data attributes and between data properties and data values are explained. Next, the techniques for identifying true data attributes and true data values are explained, followed by bad practices that should be avoided. Knowing these techniques and bad practices produces single characteristic data attributes and single property data values to support the data entities in a data resource.

Data Attributes

A **data attribute** represents a data characteristic in the data resource. In conventional databases data attributes often contain multiple characteristics of data and in some cases these data attributes characterize data in two or more data entities. Multiple characteristic data attributes create **implied redundant data** that make consistent updating extremely difficult if not impossible. In addition, access to data is extremely difficult because the desired characteristics of data can not be readily identified and if more than one data attribute representing the same data characteristic is identified it is difficult to determine which one to use.

Data attributes are initially identified by determining the characteristics of a data subject and the placement of that data attribute in the proper data entity is verified by the data normalization process. However, even though data attributes are placed in the proper data entity by the data normalization process, they may not be properly identified and may contain multiple characteristics of data. Therefore, single characteristics of data must be identified, defined as data attributes, and then placed in the proper data entity.

Data Attribute Types

A **true data attribute** represents a single characteristic of data and is the standard for a subject data resource. A **false data attribute** does not represent a single characteristic of data. There are several types of true data attributes based on the type of characteristics they represent. The definitions of these types of data attributes is useful for identifying and defining single characteristic data attributes.

> A true data attribute represents a single characteristic of a data subject.

Primitive and derived data attributes. A **primitive data attribute** is fundamental to the data subject it characterizes. Its data value is obtained directly from the entity and is not based on any derivation of data values in other data attributes. For example, a person's *name*, *height*, and *weight*, and the *manufacturer* of a vehicle are primitive data attributes about entities.

A **derived data attribute** is one whose value is derived from the data value in one or more contributing data attributes which may be either primitive data attributes or derived data attributes. In other words, there may be several levels of derived data attributes in a database. For example, the designation of a foreign student may depend on the country of citizenship and the visa type. The data attributes in a summary data entity are also derived data attributes because they represent a summary of contributing data attributes. Encrypted data attributes are another form of derived data attributes.

The value of a derived data attribute is based on a derivation algorithm that may use one or more contributing data attributes. Data attributes contributing to a derived data attribute may be in the same data entity or may be in different data entities. Anytime one or more of those contributing data attributes changes the derived data attribute must be rederived in order to keep the database correct. For example, the determination of a customer's account balance, which is stored in *Customer*, is based on the summation of all charge and payment transactions in *Customer Activity*. Anytime a charge or a payment is made the account balance changes.

The data attributes contributing to a derived data attribute may not be exhaustive, e.g., all the values of contributing data attributes may not be used for deriving data attributes. For example, the *Country of Citizenship* is used to indicate a foreign student only when the country is not the *United States*. Therefore, the data value of *United States* in *Country of Citizenship* would never be used to derive the type of a foreign student.

The values of contributing data attributes usually can not be determined from a derived data attribute. For example, when *High School Grade Point Average*, *Precollege Test Score*, and *Aptitude Test Score* are used to determine *Student Admission Eligibility*, those individual contributing data values can not be determined from the resulting *Student Admission Eligibility*. However, in some cases where the derivation algorithm has only one variable, such as changing *dollars* to *yen*, the value of the contributing data attribute can be determined. For example, a person's age is derived from their birth date and the current date. Their birth date could also be determined from their age and the current date.

A derived data attribute may be derived at execution time and appear only on the output, or it may be derived once and stored in the database. That choice depends on the use of the data and the physical operating environment. Generally, the more active derived data attributes are calculated at execution time and the more static data attributes are derived once and stored on the database.

It is relatively easy to explain the concept of single characteristic data attributes for primitive data. The difficulty comes with explaining single characteristic data attributes for derived data. The perception is that if several data attributes contribute to a derived data attribute then that derived data attribute is not representing a single data characteristic, which is not true. There is a difference between single characteristic data attributes and the number of contributing data attributes for derived data. Derived data must represent single characteristics the same as primitive data attributes.

> Derived data attributes must represent single characteristics of data just like primitive data attributes.

As an enterprise's data resource evolves the number of derived data attributes increases, as shown in Figure 10.1. When the data resource is first defined it is composed

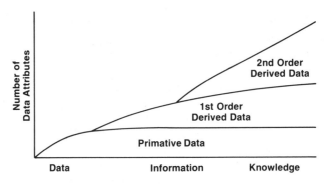

Figure 10.1 Evolution of derived data attributes.

largely of primitive data attributes. As the data resource evolves, the number of primitive data attributes remains relatively static and the number of derived data attributes increases. Initial derived data attributes are **first order derived data attributes** whose contributors are all primitive data attributes. The number of first order derived data attributes continues to increase slightly as the data resource evolves. As the data resource becomes mature and begins supporting knowledge-based applications, **second order derived data attributes** are defined based on both primitive and derived data attributes. The number of second order derived data attributes continues to increase as the data resource evolves. Therefore, primitive data attributes must be properly identified and defined to assure that derived data attributes represent single data characteristics.

> As the enterprise's data resource evolves, the number of derived data attributes increases rapidly.

Derived data attributes can be either active or static. An **active derived data attribute** means the contributing data attributes still exist in the database and their data values can change. The customer's account balance explained above is a good example of an active derived data attribute.

A **static derived data attribute** means the contributing data attributes either no longer exist in the database or have values that can never change. For example, *Quarter Vehicles Serviced* is determined by counting the number of unique vehicles that had one or more maintenance operations performed during the *Quarter*. After the quarter is over and all maintenance records have been processed, the *Quarter Vehicles Serviced* is calculated and the maintenance records are destroyed. *Quarter Vehicles Serviced* becomes a static derived data attribute because the contributing data attributes do not exist and can not be changed.

Inherent and acquired data attributes. An **inherent data attribute** is one that belongs to a data subject regardless of where or how it is used. For example, *Birth Date*, *Name*, and *Gender* are inherent to a person. They characterize that person whether that person is a customer, an employee, a student, or a vendor. Generally, inherent data attributes form a relatively finite set of data attributes for each data subject , and they are usually obvious and easy to identify. Inherent data attributes are also relatively stable data attributes.

Acquired data attributes are assigned to a data entity and are used for a specific purpose. For example, *Social Security Number*, *Customer Account Number*, *Driver License Number*, and so on, are data attributes acquired by a person. Each of these data attributes has a specific purpose for which it was assigned, such as *Customer Account Number* identifying a customer. These acquired data attributes are relatively stable data attributes similar to inherent data attributes. Other acquired data attributes, such as *Customer Account Balance* are acquired but are less stable.

Home and foreign data attribute. A data attribute is at home when it is located in the data entity which it characterizes. For example, *Employee Name* is at home in *Employee*. It is easy to determine when a data attribute is in its **home data entity** when the data entity name prefix is the same as the set label containing the data attribute. Most data attributes in the data resource are in their home data entity.

A data attribute is **foreign data attribute** when it is in a data entity that is not its home data entity. A data attribute may be placed in another data entity because it is a data attribute in a foreign key or a composite primary key, or because the data entity represents a transaction. For example, wage data is being entered, edited, and stored, as shown in Figure 10.2. Data that passes *Wage Edit* goes to *Wage* and data that fails *Wage Edit* goes to *Wage Suspense*.

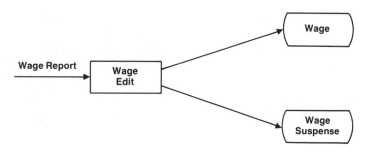

Figure 10.2 Wage data entry, edit, and storage.

The data structure for *Wage* is shown in Figure 10.3. All data attributes except two begin with *Wage* because they characterize a wage. The other two data attributes, *Employer Account Number* and *Employee SSN*, are used to compose the primary key.

Wage Suspense represents an interim storage in the process of obtaining good wage data and has very few home data attributes, as shown in Figure 10.4. Most of the data attributes characterize other data entities, such as *Employee*, *Employer*, and *Wage*. The only data attribute that characterizes *Wage Suspense* is *Wage Suspense Number*. All other data attributes are foreign data attributes because they characterize a data entity other than *Wage Suspense*. *Employee Name* is used to verify *Employee SSN* if there is an error and *Staff ID* is the person entering wage data. These two data attributes are used to correct errors in wage data and do not go into *Wage*.

```
        |‾‾  #Employer Account Number
        |    #Employee SSN
        |    #Wage Quarter
        |
        |    +Employer Account Number
Wage  <<     +Employee SSN
        |
        |    Employer Account Number
        |    Employee SSN
        |    Wage Quarter
        |    Wage Hours
        |    Wage Dollars
        |    Wage Type
        |__
```

Figure 10.3 Wage data entity structure.

```
                       |‾‾  Wage Suspense Number
                       |    Employer Account Number
                       |    Employee SSN
                       |    Employee Name
Wage Suspense   <<     |    Wage Hours
                       |    Wage Dollars
                       |    Wage Type
                       |    Wage Quarter
                       |    Staff ID
                       |__
```

Figure 10.4 Wage suspense data entity structure.

The same situation is true for other data entities, such as extracts for report genera-
tors, incoming activity transactions, and audit trails. It is not proper to name all data
attributes by the data entity in which they reside. This approach creates many synonyms
leading to data redundancy, storage anomalies, and a deteriorating data resource. Data
attributes must be named by the data entity that they characterize regardless of the data
entity where they exist. This is one of the major misconceptions about a subject data
resource and is a source of problems with identifying and naming data attributes.

> Data attributes are named by the data subject they characterize, not the data
> entity where they reside.

Data Attribute Purity

A true data attribute represents a single characteristic of data, as explained above. However,
several things can happen to make data attributes become false data attributes. They can
contain more than one characteristic of data, they can contain variable characteristics of
data, or they can contain part of a data characteristic.

Synonymous data attributes. Data attributes are synonymous when one data
characteristic has two or more data attribute names and is located in two or more places.

Synonymous data attributes may occur within one data entity, but are more common between two or more data entities. The existence of synonymous data attributes leads to data redundancy, update anomalies, and a deteriorating data resource.

> Synonymous data attributes lead to data redundancy, data anomalies, and a deteriorating data resource.

Synonymous data attributes can occur within the same data entity. For example, the birth date for a student might be defined as *Student Birth Date* and as *Student Date Born*. This situation occurs when there are many teams working on a large project, or when the project extends over a long period of time and there is no common source of documentation.

Synonymous data attributes can also occur between data entities. For example, data attributes might be defined for a customer, such as *Customer Name*, *Customer Address*, *Customer Phone*, and so forth. Other data entities might be identified for *Warranty*, *Order*, and *Payment* which are related to *Customer*. Synonyms occur when data attributes are defined for *Warranty Customer Name*, *Order Customer Name*, and *Payment Customer Name*. The true data attribute is *Customer Name* and it should be defined that way. In addition, if *Customer Name* is not the primary key for *Customer*, it should not be stored in the *Warranty*, *Order*, or *Payment*. It should be stored in *Customer* and the appropriate foreign key, such as *Customer Account Number*, should be used to access *Customer*.

The examples above are simple and rather obvious. However, synonyms can be very subtle and difficult to detect. For example, a company may have many employees including auditors, terminal operators, and claim reviewers. Data entities may be identified for *Audit*, *Tax Payment*, and *Claim*. The identification of data attributes for employees involved in each of these data entities is different, such as *Audit Auditor ID*, *Tax Payment Operator Code*, and *Claim Interviewer Number*. On further analysis, each of these data attributes is a six-digit identification code for each employee, commonly referred to as *Staff ID* which is unique to a specific employee in a specific job. These synonyms are resolved by inserting *Staff Id* in *Audit*, *Tax Payment*, and *Claim* in place of *Auditor ID*, *Operator Code*, and *Interviewer Number*.

Some data attributes may appear to be synonyms, but are not true synonyms. For example, data attributes in *Vehicle* may be defined for vendors that sell the vehicle, vendors that carry the loan for the vehicle, and vendors that perform maintenance on the vehicle. These data attributes are named *Vendor Number Manufacturer*, *Vendor Number Loan*, and *Vendor Number Maintenance*. Although the data values stored in each of the data attributes are the vendor number and are used to access data occurrences in *Vendor*, they refer to different data occurrences in *Vendor*. These data attributes are not synonyms but are variations of a single data characteristic qualified with a variation name.

Homonymous data attributes. Data attributes are homonymous when two or more different data attributes have the same name which is the reverse situation of synonymous data attributes. It is a structural problem that is just as serious as synonymous data attributes and must be resolved to prevent a deteriorating data resource.

> Homonymous data attributes are as serious as synonymous data attributes and cause a deteriorating data resource.

Homonymous data attributes usually occur between two or more data entities. For example, *Transaction Code* is identified in *Tax Payment*, *Employer Activity*, and *Wage* implying that *Transaction* is a data entity and the codes are foreign keys to *Transaction*. However, on careful analysis, the code values and meanings are different for the transactions in each of these data entities. Even if they were the same transaction code values initially, the definitions are different and there is a high probability those code values would be different in the future because the processing is different for each transactions. The different processing could mean different transaction codes to meet processing needs.

Homonymous data attributes are resolved by identifying each transaction code within its respective data entity. This identification results in a *Tax Payment Transaction Code*, an *Employer Activity Transaction Code*, and a *Wage Transaction Code*. The values of these codes can be defined and changed based on the requirements of the data entity to which they belong.

Single characteristic data attribute.   A **single characteristic data attribute** is one where only a complete, individual characteristic of a data subject is stored in the data attribute. A single characteristic data attribute is a true data attribute, and is standard for all data attributes in the subject data resource. Any data attribute that does not contain a single data characteristic is a false data attribute and must be corrected.

> Data attributes must represent single characteristics of data to properly support the enterprise's data resource.

All data attributes must be single characteristic data attributes before data normalization can be done properly. If anything other than single characteristic data attributes exist, data normalization may be very difficult if not impossible. For example, if a multiple characteristic data attribute contained data characteristics that belonged in two different data entities, then that data attribute could not be properly normalized and placed in one data entity. The single characteristics must be identified as separate data attributes to be properly placed in their correct data entity.

In addition, single data characteristics must be identified to identify entity types. It is very difficult to develop an accurate entity-type hierarchy and to define identifying data attributes for each level of that hierarchy if the data attributes do not represent single data characteristics. In fact, development of an entity-type hierarchy can help identify and resolve the existence of false data attributes.

Multiple characteristic data attribute.   A **multiple characteristic data attribute** occurs when two or more characteristics are combined into one data attribute. For example, a data attribute might be identified to define a particular quarter of the year and named *Quarter Year*. This data attribute actually contains two data characteristics for the quarter and the year, such as *484* for the *fourth quarter* of *1984*. Each of these characteristics must be defined as a separate data attribute, such as *Quarter Number* and *Year Number*.

> A multiple characteristic data attribute represents two or more data characteristics and must be redefined into single characteristic data attributes.

The multiple characteristic data attribute defined above is a **sequential multiple characteristic attribute** because the two characteristics are sequentially placed in the data attribute. If necessary, they could be substringed out of the multiple characteristic data attribute, but substringing capability in a database management system is not an excuse for defining multiple characteristic data attributes. Each data characteristic must be defined as a separate data attribute. That attribute can then be manipulated, stored, retrieved, updated, or identified as a key independent of every other characteristic for that data entity.

Another example of a sequential multiple characteristic data attribute is monthly hours worked. There is an absolute maximum of 744 hours that could be worked in a month. However, if the hours are reported, they are the actual hours worked. If the hours are calculated by method 1 they are stored as 1000 plus the number of hours, and if calculated by method 2 they are stored as 2000 plus the number of hours. In other words, the first digit indicates how the hours were obtained and the last three digits are the actual hours worked. These two characteristics must be placed in two data attributes for *Hours Indicator* and *Hours Worked*.

Sequential multiple characteristic data attributes can be either fixed or variable. **Fixed sequential multiple characteristic data attributes** means the data characteristics are in the same format in each data occurrence. The quarter and year explained above is a fixed sequential multiple characteristic data attribute because the quarter and the year are always in the same positions. **Variable sequential multiple characteristic data attributes** means the characteristics are not in the same format. For example, a person's name is a variable sequential multiple characteristic data attribute. The first name, middle initial, and last name are in the same sequence but are not always in the same positions in each data occurrence.

A sequential multiple characteristic data attribute should not be confused with a data attribute group. A data attribute group is two or more true data attributes that are closely related and frequently used together. These data attributes are grouped together and given a data attribute group name containing the standard word *Group*. That data attribute group is not a multiple characteristic data attribute. The difference is that each data characteristic is defined separately and placed in a group. For example, a date is a data attribute group consisting of three separate single characteristic data attributes for day, month, and year.

A more complicated type of multiple characteristic data attribute occurs when the data characteristics are intertwined such that each characteristic is not readily identifiable. This **intertwined multiple characteristic data attribute** is disastrous because, unlike the sequential multiple characteristics above, each individual characteristic of the intertwined characteristics can not be readily obtained. For example, gender, hair color, and eye color have been combined into a *Customer Type Code*. The code values are *1* for *female, blond* *hair, blue eyes,* 2 for *male, blond hair, blue eyes,* 3 for *female, brown hair, blue eyes,* and so forth. These three data characteristics must be separated into three data attributes for *Customer Gender Code, Customer Hair Color,* and *Customer Eye Color.*

Occasionally the situation is encountered where an intertwined multiple characteristic data attribute is mandatory. This usually occurs when data are given to an organization outside the enterprise that does not have a true subject data resource. In this case, the data should be stored as single characteristic data attributes in the enterprise's subject data resource and then combined into the intertwined multiple characteristic data attributes required for reporting outside the enterprise. This procedure helps eliminate the implied data redundancy that occurs when giving data to two or more organizations outside the enterprise that require different combinations of single characteristic data attributes. The only other solution is to store several intertwined multiple characteristic data attributes for outside reporting which further aggravates the problem of implied redundancy.

> True data attributes should be combined as necessary for outside reporting rather than storing false data attributes in the enterprise's data resource.

A source of intertwined multiple characteristic data attributes is the physical orientation toward saving space, whether on cards, tape, or disk. Usually, several spaces could be saved by intertwining characteristics into one code. For example, if a one-digit gender code, a one-digit hair color code, and a one-digit eye color code were combined into a two-digit-type code, one digit could be saved. This 33% saving of space was not an insignificant savings in the days of physical orientation when hardware was expensive.

Intertwined multiple characteristic data attributes are frequently not exhaustive, such as when the values do not cover all combinations of the individual code values of the component characteristics. Since these code values are not exhaustive, data can be inadvertently lost because the appropriate code is not available. For example, if there were two gender codes, five hair color codes, and four eye color codes there should be 40 possible customer-type codes. Frequently there are less than 40 codes defined meaning that not all combinations are represented and frequently there are more than 40 codes defined meaning there are overlaps or combined codes. Each data characteristic must be identified as a separate data attribute to avoid these problems.

Valid multiple characteristic data attributes. In certain cases **valid multiple characteristic** data attributes are allowed. Although these data attributes violate the definition of single characteristic data attributes, they are operationally efficient and usually become standard for an enterprise. For example, dates which contain day, month, and year, and a person's name which contains first name, middle initial, and last name may be defined as valid multiple characteristic data attributes. These valid multiple characteristic data attributes are acceptable as long as they are sequential. Intertwined multiple characteristic data attributes are not valid and not allowed. Wherever possible, data attribute groups should be used and the individual data characteristics should be defined as data attributes.

> Sequential multiple characteristic data attributes are valid under certain situations that should be defined for each enterprise.

Another valid sequential multiple characteristic data attribute occurs when a database management system can not handle a primary key with several data attributes. When this constraint is encountered, several characteristics are combined into one data attribute which is used as a combined data key. When a combined data key is created, both the combined data attribute and the individual data attributes must be maintained. One way to avoid defining a combined data key is to define another primary key or use an alternate primary key that has fewer data attributes.

A **data block** is a set of data attributes in one data entity that, if truly normalized, would exist in several data entities with a foreign key referencing those data entities. However, for purposes of formatting, processing efficiency, and ease of maintenance, these data attributes are stored in one data entity as a data block. For example, a recursive data entity might be established for *Geographic Area*. Each data occurrence in that data entity would represent a single geographic area, such as a city, county, state, or country. Addresses contain city, state, and in some cases, country. If address data were fully normalized they would contain a foreign key to *Geographic Area* for city, state, and country. Anytime a full address was needed, foreign keys would be used to obtain the desired city, state, and country names.

This navigation, and subsequent formatting, makes processing of addresses, and editing and updating of addresses, a time consuming and costly process. It is better to store address data as one data block that is properly formatted and edited and move that data block as needed. In this case, the data attribute names would be *Address City Name*, *Address State Name*, and *Address Country Name*. A data block is really a denormalization of data that is accepted as standard for an enterprise.

> A data block represents denormalized data attributes that are accepted as standard for an enterprise.

A similar situation could occur with people's names. For example, the names of people, could be normalized with reference to those names via a foreign key. Anytime a person's name was needed, the foreign keys would be used to retrieve the components of the name. This structure leads to the same problems described above for addresses, and for this reason names are defined as a data block. However, names could be separated into data attributes for first name, middle name, and last name to allow sorting and different sequences for printing.

Variable Characteristic Data Attribute. A **variable characteristic data attribute** has a different characteristic based on the type of data entity containing the data attribute. For example, *Student* might contain prospective students, undergraduate students, and graduate students as data entity types. A data attribute for *Student Status Date* means the date interviewed for a prospective student, the date first enrolled for an undergraduate student, and the date of graduation for a graduate student.

> A variable characteristic data attribute represents a different data characteristic for each data entity type and must be redefined into single characteristic data attributes.

These three data characteristics should be defined as three separate data attributes. If all data characteristics are not valid for a data entity type, the valid situations are defined as data integrity rules. The null feature of a database management system could be used to save storage space. However, that feature should not be preempted with the use of a variable characteristic data attribute.

The use of a variable characteristic data attribute makes selection of data occurrence groups very difficult. The selection requires more logic, or additional data attributes, making the selection more difficult. In the example above, the type of student must be known before the *Student Status Date* becomes meaningful which makes selection particularly difficult for ad hoc processing. In addition, data could be lost when the student status changes and data are not properly updated. Creation of three data attributes for date interviewed, date enrolled, and date graduated provide the correct data.

Complex characteristic data attribute. A **complex characteristic** data attribute is a combination of a multiple characteristic data attribute and a variable characteristic data attribute. For example, there are three types of customers for new, good credit, and poor credit. *Customer Code* carries a combination of income, interests, and potential buying power for new customers, a combination of maximum credit limit and rate of payment for customers with good credit, and a combination of credit rating and probability of collection for customers with poor credit. This *Customer Code* is a complex characteristic data attribute.

> A complex characteristic data attribute is a combination of a multiple and a variable characteristic data attribute and must be redefined as single characteristic data attributes.

Although this situation is relatively rare, it does exist and can be a far more serious problem than either the multiple or variable characteristic data attributes individually. Each of these data characteristics must be defined as a single characteristic data attribute. In the example above, there should be seven data attributes defined for *Customer Income*, *Customer Interests*, *Customer Buying Potential*, *Customer Credit Limit*, *Customer Payment Rate*, *Customer Credit Rating*, and *Customer Collection Probability*.

Mutually exclusive data attribute. **Mutually exclusive** data attributes represent two or more data characteristics that will never have values at the same time in the same occurrence. For example, a product is shipped to a customer in one of several ways, such as parcel post, bus, air freight, etc. A data attribute is defined for each of these modes of shipping and the one used for any particular shipment contains a *Y* and the others contain a *blank*.

> Mutually exclusive data attributes represent a situation where the values of a data attribute were raised to data attribute level.

Another example of mutually exclusive data attributes is a set of data attributes each representing a single value of a code. For example, *Customer Payment Code* might have three values, *1*, *2*, and *3*. A data attribute would be defined for each of these codes, such as *Customer Payment 1*, *Customer Payment 2*, and *Customer Payment 3*. If the payment code was *1*, then *Customer Payment 1* would contain a *1* and the other two would be blank. If the payment code was *2*, then *Customer Payment 2* would contain a *2* and the other two would be blank. Only one data attribute would have a value in a data occurrence.

Mutually exclusive data attributes result from raising the values of a data attribute to the data attribute level. This was usually done for ease of selecting and sorting data occurrences. However, the amount of overhead and logic becomes monumental, particularly when there are many possible values of a code. These values should be placed in their respective single subject data attributes and the selection capabilities of a database management system used to obtain the desired data occurrences.

Data Attribute Identification Techniques

As with data entities, data attributes must be properly identified and structured. If a data attribute represents more than a single characteristic of data, or part of a single characteristic of data, then it is a false data attribute and is not allowed in the subject data resource. Data normalization plays an important part in the placement of data attributes in their proper data entity. However, data attributes can not be successfully normalized unless careful attention is paid to identifying true data attributes. Therefore, the processes of identifying single characteristic data attributes must precede the data normalization process.

> Identification of single characteristic data attributes precedes the data normalization process.

Identification of data attributes is driven by the business needs of the enterprise. All the characteristics needed to identify and manage a data subject must be identified and defined. The best place to start is with the data characteristics necessary to identify each existence of a data subject. Then the data characteristics necessary to characterize each existence are identified, followed by other data characteristics necessary to manage that existence. Business transactions and business activities can be reviewed to identify characteristics that are needed to manage data subjects.

The people in an enterprise that have intimate knowledge of the data should be involved in preparing data definitions and identifying single characteristic data attributes. Most people can be easily trained to identify and define single data characteristics. When this skill is combined with an intimate knowledge of the data, true data attributes will be defined.

A comprehensive definition should be prepared for each data attribute and reviewed for multiple characteristics. For example, a definition that states *the customer type code defines the customers gender, eye color, and hair color* should indicate multiple data characteristics. A definition that identifies a condition might indicate a variable characteristic data attribute. For example, the definition that states *the date represents a graduation date when the student is a graduate student* indicates the existence of a variable characteristic data attribute. Each of these data characteristics should be defined as a separate data attribute.

If there is difficulty with forming a data attribute name or developing a definition, there is a chance that data attribute represents a more than one data characteristic. The data attribute should be carefully analyzed to identify the individual data characteristics. If this approach does not work, a partial characteristic data attribute may exist. Similar data attributes should be reviewed to determine the single data characteristic.

An attempt should be made to break each data attribute into smaller pieces. Sometimes this attempt will identify multiple data characteristics. It might also identify partial characteristic data attributes that can be combined to form a single characteristic data attribute. This approach should not be pursued to absurdity, but can be used to identify individual data characteristics.

Similar data attribute definitions should be reviewed to identify synonymous and homonymous data attributes. For example, definition of an *Employee Gender Code* and a *Customer Gender Code* indicate synonymous data attributes. The data characteristic is *Gender Code* which has a corresponding *Gender Definition* and should be defined as one data attribute in the *Gender* data entity. A good data resource directory and a data attribute name thesaurus help identify these situations.

Closely related data characteristics, such as the characteristics in an address or a person's name, may be defined as data blocks. Other closely related data characteristics, such as the characteristics in a date, may be defined as individual data attributes and as a data attribute group.

Once single characteristic data attributes have been identified and defined they can be normalized. Data normalization assures that data attributes are placed in the proper data entity. This is a relatively minor step in identifying data attributes and is more appropriate for identifying data entities. However, it does help identify data attributes and supply the proper data entity prefix to the data attribute name.

Bad Data Attribute Identification Practices

There are several bad practices that lead to identification of false data attributes. When data attributes are not properly identified, they lead to a loss of meaning, redundancy, and a deteriorating data resource. Most of the bad practices result from not being aware of the types of false data attributes explained above.

Using physical constraints, such as the space available on a database management system, or the speed of search and selection are used as criteria for combining or splitting data characteristics is a bad practice that leads to identification of false data attributes. With the exception of data blocks, the use of physical constraints should occur during data denormalization and not during identification of single characteristic data attributes.

Haste is another bad practice that leads to identification of false data attributes. When people are in a hurry and do not completely define and analyze each data attribute, false data attributes are defined. Tight schedules and limited budgets should not be an excuse for haste in identifying single characteristic data attributes.

Lack of coordination between development teams and lack of a current accurate data resource directory leads to synonymous and homonymous data attributes. Whenever development teams work independently and do not coordinate their efforts directly or through a data resource directory false data entities are defined.

Limited involvement of users that have knowledge of the data needed by business activities leads to incomplete definitions and identification of false data entities. Users with knowledge of business activities must be included in data attribute definition, and in many cases should lead the data definition effort.

The only sure method to identify true single characteristic data attributes is to follow the techniques identified above and avoid the bad practices. The result is identification of true data attributes that contribute to stability of the enterprise's data resource.

DATA VALUES

A **data value** represents a property of a data characteristic. In conventional databases a data value often contained multiple data properties and, in some cases these multiple data properties spanned two or more data characteristics. In extreme cases they spanned two or more data subjects. These multiple property data values created problems with interpretation of data and with access to the data. In many cases these multiple property data values created an implied redundancy very similar to the redundancy in multiple characteristic data attributes.

Data values are initially identified by determining the properties of a data characteristic that need to be captured and stored in the database. These properties are identified through a detailed analysis of the data characteristics that are defined for each data subject. Once the data characteristics are identified, the types of data values that are allowed for those data characteristics are identified.

Data Value Types

There are two basic types of data values in the data resource. **Actual data values** are actual measurements about data entities. For example, a person's name, the color of a vehicle, the size of a room, and the credit hours for a course are actual data values. They have a meaning of their own that needs no further interpretation.

Coded data values are data values that are encoded in one form or another. The actual data is not readily available in a form that has meaning to the user. For example, a *Student Registration Type Code* might contain the values of *1*, *2*, or *3*. These data values have no meaning of their own. In this case the values mean *less than a full course load of*

15 credit hours, a *full course load of 15 to 18 credit hours,* and a *heavy course load of more than 18 credit hours,* respectively. Each of these three groupings is a single property of *Student Registration Type Code.*

Data Value Purity

A coded data value must represent a **single property** of a data characteristic. For example, the values of *Student Registration Type Code* represent single property data values. If, however, there were only two type codes for less than normal credit hours and for normal or greater than normal credit hours, there would be a **multiple property data values** for normal and greater than normal credit hours. This multiple property data value creates problems identifying students that carry a heavy course load from those that carry a normal course load.

> A multiple property data value represents two or more data properties and must be redefined as single data property data values.

The origin of this multiple property data value was an application orientation where the only interest was two groupings of students for less than normal and normal or greater credit hours and two codes met that need. However, as greater use is made of the enterprise's data resource, particularly ad hoc inquiry, the need to distinguish between normal and heavy course loads could emerge. That need can not be met with two code values but it could be easily met with three code values. Therefore, all coded data values must represent single properties of data characteristics.

Multiple property data values are not the same as multiple characteristic data attributes. Multiple characteristic data attributes represent more than one data characteristic in a data attribute. Multiple property data values represent more than one data property in a single value of a data attribute.

Synonymous data values occur when a single data property exists in two or more locations with different names. This situation usually occurs with synonymous data attributes. However, it can also occur with multiple characteristic data attributes. For example, there could be synonymous data attributes for *Students Admission Code.* One set of admission codes have the values *1, 2,* and *3* for new students, students that were there last term, and students that were there before the last term but not the last term. Another set of codes have the values *A, B,* and *C* for the same situation. These two sets of codes are synonymous and need to be combined into one set of codes that is used by the entire enterprise.

Homonymous data values occur when several different data properties have the same values. For example, if *returning student* is defined as being *any student that attended the college anytime in the past* by one application and another application defined returning student as *one that attended in the past but was not in attendance during the last term*, there is homonymous data values. In other words, two different meanings of data values have the same definition. The individual properties must be identified and a unique code must be assigned to each property.

Data Value Identification

Data values are identified by analyzing the contents of each data attribute. When the contents represent actual data, the data values are relatively easy to identify. When the contents represent coded data values, the individual properties being coded need to be determined and a code assigned to each of those properties.

There is a trend away from coding actual data values like height, weight, and so forth. Coding actual values hampers the ability to select data based on actual value, particularly in an ad hoc environment. For example, an ad hoc inquiry may need a range of actual values that includes parts of two different groupings of the actual values. Therefore, only non-quantifiable properties should be coded, such as the admission code described above. Actual values, such as a person's height, should be entered as actual values.

> Actual data values should not be coded in a subject data resource.

If artificial groupings of actual data values are necessary, another data entity should be identified for those groupings. For example, if a person's height were to be coded a *Height Category* code table data entity could be identified with a *Height Category Code* representing the ranges of a person's height and a corresponding *Height Code Description*. This approach allows additional groupings of a person's height to be defined in additional code table data entities while the actual data values remain intact. In other words, a separate code table data entity is defined for each artificial grouping of actual data values.

> Artificial groupings of actual data values should be defined as a separate code table data entity.

Coded data values are identified by the business needs of the enterprise and are best identified by people in the enterprise that are familiar with the business activities. A comprehensive definition should be developed for each coded data value and reviewed to identify multiple property data values. The word *and* frequently indicates existence of multiple property data values. Similar data value definitions should be reviewed to identify synonymous and homonymous data values.

Each code table should be reviewed to assure that each coded data value in that table represents a single property data value. Any multiple property data values must be redefined as single property data values.

SUMMARY

Identification of data attributes and data values follows identification of data entities and supports the structure of a data resource established by definition of data entities and data relations. A thorough understanding of the types of data attributes and data values, the techniques for identifying single characteristic data attributes and single property data values, and the bad practices to be avoided help identify and define data attributes and data values that assure a structurally stable data resource. When these techniques are not followed the data resource begins to deteriorate. The criteria listed below summarize the techniques to use for identifying true data attributes and data values.

Identify and define single characteristic data attributes and single property data values.

Identify and define valid sequential multiple characteristic data attributes when their existence is necessary.

Identify and define data blocks when their use is necessary for operational efficiency.

Identification of true data attributes and data values is driven by the business needs of the enterprise.

Identification of true data attributes and data values should be done by people that are familiar with the business activities of an enterprise.

A comprehensive definition of each data attribute and data value helps identification and prevents synonymous and homonymous data attributes and data values.

Use of a data resource directory and close cooperation between development teams prevents definition of synonymous and homonymous data attributes and data values.

Physical constraints must be avoided when defining true data attributes and data values.

Haste and limited user involvement must be avoided when identifying and true defining true data attributes and data values.

Artificial groupings of actual data values must be defined with a separate code table data entity.

STUDY QUESTIONS

The following questions are provided as a review of data attributes and data values and to stimulate thought about the process of identifying and defining true data attributes and data values.

1. How are identification of data attributes and data values related to identification of data entities?
2. What is the difference between primitive and derived data attributes?
3. What is the difference between active and static derived data attributes?
4. Why is proper definition of derived data attributes important?
5. What is the difference between inherent and acquired data attributes?
6. What is the difference between home and foreign data attributes?
7. What is the difference between synonymous and homonymous data attributes?

Chapter Ten

8. How are false data attributes different from true data attributes?
9. Why should data attributes represent single characteristics of data?
10. What valid multiple characteristic data attributes are allowed in the data resource?
11. What techniques are used to identify single characteristic data attributes?
12. How does data normalization assist with data attribute identification?
13. What bad practices should be avoided when identifying data attributes?
14. What are the basic types of data values?
15. How are single property data values identified?
16. How do false data values differ from true data values?
17. What is the difference between actual and coded data values?
18. Why should users be involved in the identification and definition of true data attributes and data values?
19. Why is a comprehensive definition important in identifying true data attributes and data values?
20. What factors can cause deterioration of a subject data resource?

Data Structures

> Data structures are the working tools for developing and using the enterprise's data resource.

Data structures are the working tools for design, construction, and use of the data resource. They show the data on business transactions, and the data moving into and out of information systems, and between processes and data entities within an information system. They show data subjects, data relations, data attributes, primary and foreign keys, secondary keys, and data views. They show data files, data items, and data keys. They show the business needs and the logical and physical design of the data resource.

The concept of a data structure was presented in the Data Resource Concepts chapter and data structures have been used throughout the book to illustrate various techniques for defining data. However, the actual construction and manipulation of data structures has not been explained. This chapter presents the techniques for developing data structures for business transactions and manipulating those data structures to develop a data resource for the enterprise.

DATA STRUCTURE CONCEPTS

Design and construction of the data resource is based on the four-schema concept presented in the Data Design Concepts chapter and referred to in the Data Normalization chapter.

Figure 8.3 may be reviewed for a better understanding of the four-schema concept. The external data flows going into and out of an information system are business schema that represent business transactions in the business environment. The internal data flows between processes and data entities are data views that represent the external schema. These data views are subsets of data attributes from a data entity used by applications to store and retrieve data. The internal data flows are obtained by normalizing the external data flows.

> The four-schema concept is the foundation for constructing a data resource.

The internal data flows are optimized into conceptual schema that represent data subjects. These data subjects and the relations between them form the logical data resource model that defines the basic structure of the data resource for an enterprise. The logical data resource model contains all the data subjects and all the data characteristics for each data subject. The conceptual schema are denormalized into internal schema that represent data files. These data files and the relations between them form the physical data resource model for an enterprise.

The external data flows are business transactions representing data flowing into or out of an information system, as shown in Figure 11.1. Any data structure representing data flowing into an information system is an **Input Data Structure** and any data structure representing data flowing out of an information system is an **Output Data Structure**. Any data structure representing data flowing between processes within an information system is a **Combined Data Structure** because it represents an output from one process and an input into another process.

The internal data flows are data views representing data flowing between processes and data entities. Any data structure representing a data flow from a process to a data entity is a **Necessary Data Structure** because it represents data necessary to maintain the database. Any data structure representing a data flow from a data entity to a process is a **Required Data Structure** because it represents data required from the database to support a process. The necessary and required data structures are application data views. Input data structures are normalized to produce necessary data structures and the output data structures are normalized to produce required data structures.

This concept can also be viewed from the perspective of a process, as shown in Figure 11.2. A process receives input data from data entities in the form of required data

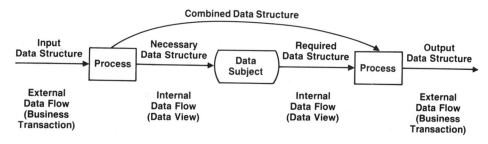

Figure 11.1 Data structures on the system architecture model.

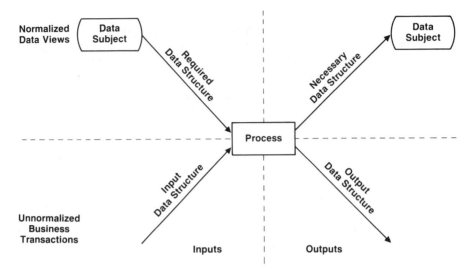

Figure 11.2 Four-schema concept and the process.

structures, data from the business environment in the form of input data structures, and the input side of a combined data structure. A process also produces output data for data entities in the form of necessary data structures, data for the business environment in the form of output data structures, or the output side of a combined data structure.

The function of any process is to take the input data, either from data entities or the business environment, and produce the output data, either for data entities or the business environment. All the data needed to produce the output data must be available through the input data, and all the input data must be needed to produce the output data. If any input data are not available the output data will not be produced properly and unnecessary input data are a waste of resources. Therefore, the input data structures must contain all the data and only the data needed by a process to produce the output data.

> A process takes input data and produces output data.

DATA STRUCTURE FORMATS

Each external data flow represents a business transaction that has a format and a data structure. The format of the external data flow is defined during development of the business design models. Occasionally, external data flows do not appear to have a visible format, such as electronic transmission of business transactions. In these situations the format of the data on the electronic medium is the format of business transaction. A data structure is developed for each external data flow based on the format of the data exactly as it appears in the business transaction. The data structure is considered unnormalized because it is not in the proper form for developing a subject data resource.

The format of a business transaction drives composition of the data structure representing that transaction.

A required data structure is developed for each output data structure. It includes data from data entities that appear on the output and data from data entities that are used to derive data for the output but do not appear on the output. It does not include data that are not stored in data entities. A required data structure may represent more than one internal data flow, as shown in Figure 11.3. Each internal data flow represents a data view from one data entity. If data are required from three data entities there will be three internal data flows.

A necessary data structure is developed for each input data structure. It includes data that appear on the input and are stored in data entities and data that are derived and stored in data entities. It does not include data that are not stored in data entities. A necessary data structure may represent more than one internal data flow, as shown in Figure 11.4. Each internal data flow represents the data view for one data entity. If data are placed in three data entities there will be three data views and three internal data flows.

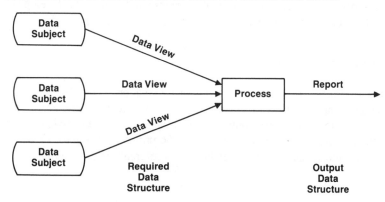

Figure 11.3   Relation between output and required data structures.

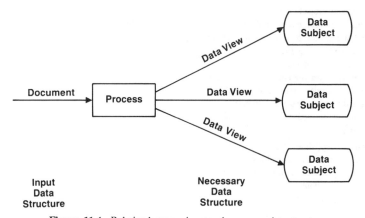

Figure 11.4   Relation between input and necessary data structures.

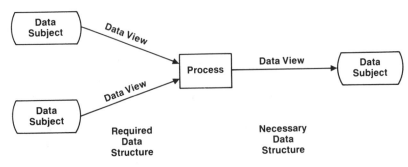

Figure 11.5 Process with only required and necessary data structures.

Occasionally a process may have only required and necessary data structures, such as processes that move data between data entities. In this case the necessary data structure represents the data flowing out of the process and is used to develop the required data structure for data moving into the process, as shown in Figure 11.5.

DATA ATTRIBUTE SYMBOLS

Data attribute symbols are special characters that prefix the data attribute name on a data structure chart. A variety of symbols are used to indicate special uses of the data attributes in addition to their use for containing data values that characterize a data entity. Many of these symbols have already been used in the previous examples. However, each of these data attribute symbols is explained below for reference and are summarized in Figure 11.6.

Symobl Use	ODS	RDS	IDS	NDS
Implied data subject name	.	.	..	
Calculated, output, not in database	@			
Literal or constant, output, not on database		,		
Sorth ascending sequence	/			
Sort decending sequence	\			
Appears on input, not entered into process				<
Appears on input, entered, not in database				>
Required from database, not on output			=	
Not entered, derived, stored in datbase				:
Primary key	#			#
Secondard key, single value	-			-
Secondary key, range of values		%		
Foreign key, stored in databass		+	+	
Foreign key, calculated		&	&	
Questionable attribute	?	?	?	?

Figure 11.6 Summary of data attribute symbols.

Chapter Eleven

Data attribute symbols indicate special use of data attributes.

A **period** (.) is used on any data structure to indicate the data subject name has been omitted from the data attribute name and is the same as the label of the set containing the data attribute. For example, if the data attribute *.Birth Date* were contained in the set labeled *Employee* the complete name of that data attribute is *Employee.Birth Date*. This convention is used when there is difficulty determining the data subject name.

A **question mark** (?) is used on any data structure to indicate a data attribute is questionable. For example, the data attribute *?Vehicle.Color* indicates some feature of vehicle color is in question. That question must be resolved and the question mark removed before the data structure is considered complete and correct.

An **at sign** (@) is used on output data structures to indicate the data attribute appears on the output, but it is calculated or derived in the process and is not obtained from the database. For example, *@Employee.Age* indicates that the employee's age is calculated during processing and is not obtained from the database. If the data attribute was calculated or derived but was obtained from the database, the *at sign* is not used.

A **quote mark** (') is used on output data structures to indicate the data attribute appears on the output and contains a literal or constant that is not obtained from the database but is imbedded in the process. For example, *'Report.Title* indicates the title of the report is stored in the process and is not obtained from the database. If a literal or constant is obtained from the database the *quote mark* would not be used.

Both the *at sign* and the *quote mark* are used during the design process to evaluate where data are obtained. If the data are obtained from the database neither the *at sign* nor the *quote mark* are used. If the data are created in the process the *at sign* is used and if the data are stored in the process, the *quote mark* is used. These symbols can be changed during the design process as various alternatives for creating and storing data are evaluated.

The **forward slash** (/) and **back slash** (\) are used on output data structures to indicate the sort sequence of data on the output. The *forward slash* indicates the data attribute is used to sort in ascending sequence and the *back slash* indicates the data attribute is used to sort in descending sequence. The sequence of data attributes involved in the sort indicate the sequence of sorting. The first data attribute is the most major sort and the last data attribute is the most minor sort. For example, */Employee.Birth Date* and */Employee.Name* indicate that the output will be sorted by birth date in ascending sequence with employees listed within each birth date by employee name in ascending sequence.

A **left caret** (<) is used on input data structures to indicate a data attribute appears on the business transaction but is not entered into the process. Since the data are not entered into the process they can not be stored in the database. For example, *<Applicant.Signature* indicates the applicant's signature appears on the business transaction but is not entered into the process.

A **right caret** (>) is used on input data structures to indicate a data attribute appears on the business transaction, is entered into the process, but is not stored in the database. That data attribute may be used to verify, calculate, or derive other data attributes during processing, but it is not stored in the database. For example, *Applicant.Weight* indicates the applicant's weight is entered into the process but is not stored in the database.

Data Structures

An **equal sign** (=) is used on required data structures to indicate a data attribute is obtained from the database to support preparation of the output, but is not shown on that output. For example, =*Vehicle.Engine Horsepower* indicates the vehicle horsepower is obtained from the database and used by the process but does not appear on the output. If the data attribute is obtained from the database and appears on the output, regardless of how it is used in the process, the *equal sign* is not used.

A **colon** (:) is used on necessary data structures to indicate a data attribute is not entered into the process, but is calculated or derived and stored in the database. For example, :*Employee.Age* indicates the employee's age is not entered into the process but is calculated within the process and stored in the database. If a data attribute is entered into the process and stored on the database, regardless of how it is used in the process, the *colon* is not used.

A **pound sign** (#) is used on required and necessary data structures to indicate a data attribute is used to define a primary key. For example, #*Employee.SSN* indicates the employee's social security number is used to define the primary key.

A **plus sign** (+) is used on required and necessary data structures to indicate a data attribute is used to compose a foreign key to identify the parent data occurrence in the parent data entity. For example, +*Employee.SSN* in *Pay Check* identifies the employee who received that pay check.

An **ampersand** (&) is used on required and necessary data structures to indicate a data attribute is used to compose a foreign key but the value of that foreign key is calculated and is not stored on the database. For example, &*Fee.Type Code* indicates the fee type code value is calculated in the process before access is made to the parent data entity and is not stored in the database.

A **minus sign** (-) is used on required and necessary data structures to indicate a data attribute belongs to a secondary key with a single value. For example, -*Vehicle.License Number* indicates access is made into *Vehicle* using the vehicle license number with a single value. If a data attribute belongs to a secondary key that uses a range of values, the *minus sign* is not used.

A **percent sign** (%) is used on required data structures to indicate a data attribute belongs to a secondary key for access with a range of values. For example, %*Vehicle.Engine Horsepower* indicates access is made into *Vehicle* using the vehicle engines horsepower containing a range of values. A *percent sign* is not used on necessary data structures because access is not made into a data entity to store data using a range of values.

A **blank** ( ) is the default character that prefixes a data attribute and indicates the data attribute has no special use or meaning. A *blank* on input and output data structures indicates the data attribute is input to the process and is stored in the database, or is obtained from the database and appears on the output. A *blank* on necessary and required data structures indicates the data attribute has no special use.

If the primary key is derived by the process and stored in the database, the *pound sign* indicates the data attribute is used to compose the primary key and the *colon* indicates the data attribute is derived by the process. The *pound sign* appears on the data attribute at the top of the data structure where the primary key is identified and the *colon* appears on the data attribute in the list of data attributes at the bottom of the data structure. This is one of the reasons for separating the primary keys, the foreign keys, the secondary keys, and the list of data attributes characterizing the data entity into separate groups within the data structure.

DATA STRUCTURE COMPOSITION

Data structure composition is the process of developing input and output data structures from the formats of the business transactions. A data structure is developed for each external data flow and is used to define the data resource. The correct composition of a data structure for each business transaction is mandatory for development of a correct data resource. The steps described below assure the proper composition of the input and output data structures.

> Business transactions represent business schema that drive development of the enterprise's data resource.

The sets on a data structure for an external data flow represent either data entities or data occurrence groups including data entity types. If the set represents a data entity then all data occurrences in that data entity are considered to be included in that set. If the set represents a data occurrence group then only the data occurrences that meet the selection criteria are included in that set. The name of the set label indicates whether that set represents a data entity or a data occurrence group. For example, *Employee* represents all employees and *Pilot Certified Employee* represents only employees that are certified as pilots, which is a subset of all employees. This is one reason why it is important to name and document each data entity and each data occurrence group.

> Correct composition of external data structures is mandatory for designing a correct data resource.

Each data entity and data occurrence group identified on a business transaction becomes a set on the data structure. The sets are arranged to represent the relations of data entities and data occurrence groups exactly as they appear on the external data flow. All data must be accounted for on the data structure. No adjustments are made to the data structure based on knowledge of the data normalization process or knowledge of the physical database where that data reside. No data are added that do not appear on the business transaction and no data are eliminated. Common omissions are data attributes that appear on input data flows but are not entered into the information system, such as signatures, and data attributes that appear on output data flows but are provided by the process, such as titles and headings.

> Every data attribute must be accounted for during data structure composition.

The highest level set in a data structure must represent a single occurrence data entity. This requirement is necessary to assure that all data entities and data relations on a business transaction are identified. If the highest level set on a data structure is not a single occurrence data entity, then the format and definition of that business transaction must be reviewed until the highest level data entity has been found. Generally, the highest level data entity is the enterprise itself and all other data entities are subordinate to the enterprise.

Each data entity and data occurrence group must be named and defined. No data entity or data occurrence group is exempt from being described. A lack of documentation leads to confusion about the meaning of a set on the data structure and could lead to improper selection of data occurrences if that set represents a data occurrence group. Each data attribute on the data structure must also be named and defined. No data attribute should be exempt from being described. In some situations the assumption is made that the data will not be stored in the database and therefore does not need to be named or defined. This assumption is false because all data are used by the enterprise, whether they are stored in the database or not, and that use dictates the formal naming and comprehensive definition of each data unit.

> Each data entity, data occurrence group, and data attribute must be described and documented.

Each data entity and data occurrence group must represent a single data subject and each data attribute must represent a single data characteristic. Composition of data structures for business transactions is the step where single units of data must be identified and defined. If single units of data are not identified at this step, the errors will be propagated through the entire data resource.

> Each data entity and data occurrence group must represent a single subject and each data attribute must represent a single characteristic.

Data attribute symbols are used as needed to indicate special use or meaning of data attributes. These symbols may be adjusted as the analysis and design process continues and decisions are changed about the use of data attributes. In fact, use of data attribute symbols assists the analysis process by forcing designers to use the appropriate symbol.

Composing Output Data Structures

Output data structures are easily composed by following a few single steps. These steps are similar to the steps for composing input data structures described later. First, the highest level, single occurrence data entity is identified and the highest level set on the output data structure. It is the data entity that includes all other data entities, data occurrence groups, and data attributes, and in most cases is the enterprise itself. For example, if a report is for a company then *Company* is the highest level data set on the data structure.

> An output data structure is developed for every business transaction flowing out of an information system.

Second, the next level on the output data structure is the output itself. For example, if the output is a report, such as *Employee Training Report*, then the second level on the data structure represents that report. This nesting shows that there are, or could be, many employee training reports within the company.

Third, successively lower levels are placed on the data structure representing each repeating group shown on the business transaction. The hierarchy is developed according to the one-to-many data relations as they appear on the business transaction, not as they would be normalized for the data resource. If the business transaction represents a table, data shown vertically are placed at a higher level in the data structure than data shown horizontally.

Fourth, data attributes are placed in the appropriate sets corresponding to where they appear on the format of the business transaction. Again, the data attributes are listed as they appear on the business transaction, not as they would be normalized for the data resource.

Fifth, data attribute symbols are added as necessary to identify special use of the data attributes. *Quote marks* are added for literals or constants that are stored in the process and *at signs* are added for data attributes that are created or derived for the transaction. The algorithm used for calculating or deriving data must be defined and documented.

To illustrate further, a *Vehicle Report* is designed to meet the needs of an enterprise for managing the vehicles in its motor pool, as shown in Figure 11.7. This report lists the miles driven and the job identification for each vehicle and each operator by each division within the company.

```
REPORT RX143A      ACE COMPANY VEHICLE REPORT      June 20, 1982

        Division        Operator        Vehicle     Job  ID    Miles
          Name            Name          License                Driven

Administration        Smith           R 14569      A 432        123
                      Wilson          R 14325      A 602        468
                      Wilson          X 44622      A 602         96
                      Jones           X 54789      A 103        102
                      Jones           P 44938      A 498         84

Administration Total                                            873

Construction          Burke           K 87604      C 606        498
                      Paulson         D 54983      C 406        672

Construction Total                                            1170

Company Total                                                 2043
```

Figure 11.7   Format for the vehicle report.

The output data structure for this vehicle report, shown in Figure 11.8, is composed according to the guidelines described above. The highest level data entity is *Company*, since there is only one company, and there are many vehicle reports within the company. Therefore, *Vehicle Report* is nested within *Company*. The report lists many divisions vertically and each division contains many operators and each operator drives many vehicles. Therefore, the structure of *Division*, *Operator*, and *Vehicle* is nested within *Vehicle Report*. The output data structure represents the structure of the vehicle report.

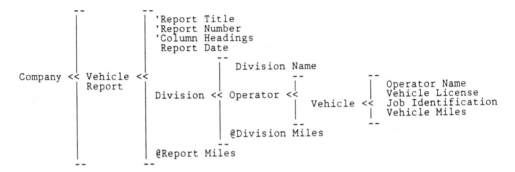

Figure 11.8 Output data structure for vehicle reports.

The data attributes from the vehicle report are placed in the set corresponding to where that data attribute appears on the report. *Report Title*, *Report Number*, *Column Headings*, and *Report Date* are placed in *Vehicle Report*. The first three are prefixed with a *quote mark* indicating they are literals stored in the process. *Division Name* is placed in *Division*. *Operator Name*, *Vehicle License*, *Job Identification*, and *Vehicle Miles* are placed in *Vehicle*. Notice that *Operator Name* is not placed in the *Operator* set because the operator's name appears with each vehicle on the report. *Division Miles* and *Report Miles* are placed in their respective sets and are prefixed with an *at sign* indicating they are calculated.

The statistical report in Figure 11.9 shows a typical table for fish landings with species of fish listed horizontally and fishing boats listed vertically. Totals are shown at the right for each boat and at the bottom for each species. The company total for all boats and all species is shown at the lower right. This report represents the typical cross-footed report common in many enterprises.

```
REPORT 7982          HIGH SEAS FISH COMPANY        June 29, 1979

Boat Name      ---------  Species Pounds  ---------    Total
               Salmon     Tuna    Flounder    Other    Boat

Arianne        1436                                     1436
All Mine                  2968    1628                  4596
Lady Luck                                      4233     4233
Swashbuckler              1982                   941    2923
Sally M        4876                                     4876

Total Species  6312       4950    1628         5174    18064
```

Figure 11.9   Format for a fish landing report.

The required data structure shown in Figure 11.10 was developed following the guidelines described above. *Company* is the single occurrence data entity that contains all other data entities and becomes the highest level set on the output data structure. *Fish Report* is nested within *Company* because it represents the business transaction and there are many fishing reports for the company.

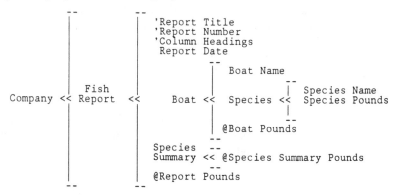

Figure 11.10 Output data structure for the fish report.

The repeating groups on the report are *Boat* and *Species*. However, there are two different repeating groups for species. One repeating group represents the species for each boat and the other repeating group represents the species summary for the report. Since both boat and species summary are repeating groups within the report the third level of the data structure contains two sets, one for *Boat* and one for *Species Summary*. The fourth level contains one set for *Species* within each boat.

Once the basic data structure is completed, the data attributes are placed on that data structure. *Report Title*, *Report Number*, *Column Headings*, and *Report Date* are placed in *Fish Report* and the first three are identified as constants contained within the process. *Boat Name* is placed within *Boat*, and *Species Name* and *Species Pounds* are placed within the detail *Species* set. *Boat Pounds* is placed in *Boat*, *Species Summary Pounds* is placed in *Species Summary*, *Report Pounds* is placed in *Report*, and all three are prefixed with an *at sign* indicating they are calculated.

Composing Input Data Structures

An input data structure is developed for each business transaction entering an information system. All data entities, data occurrence groups, and data attributes that appear on that input must appear on the input data structure. Some of the data attributes may be shown redundantly on the input data structure but they represent the way data appear on the input. External data flows represent the format of data as they are used by the enterprise and are not normalized in any way.

> An input data structure is developed for every business transaction flowing into an information system.

The steps for composing input data structures are very similar to the steps for composing output data structures. The highest level set on the input data structure represents a single occurrence data entity that contains all other data entities and data attributes. The second level on the input data structure represents the input itself, such as a document or a screen. Successively lower levels are created for each repeating group shown on the input. The data attributes are placed within this basic structure corresponding to where they appear on the input. Finally, the data attribute symbols are added to indicate special use or meaning of the data attributes.

All data on a business transaction must be accounted for on the input data structure. No data should be arbitrarily left off the data structure and no data should be arbitrarily added. Generally, input data structures are easier to develop, and are simpler than output data structures.

A *Staff Time Update Document* used by a task management system is shown in Figure 11.11. The document is completed every week by each employee and shows each task that employee worked on during the week and the hours spent on each of those tasks.

```
                        Ringdolph Company
               Task Management Information System

                   Staff Time Update Document

     Employee SSN:                          Week Ending Date:

     Employee Name:

     Task Number            Task Title            Hours Used
```

Figure 11.11   Input document for staff time update.

The input data structure for the *Staff Time Update Document* is shown in Figure 11.12. *Company* is the highest level set in the data structure because it is the single occurrence data entity that contains all other data entities and data attributes. *Calendar Week* is the next level because the documents represent each week the company is in business. *Employee* and *Task* become the next two levels because there are many employees that work on tasks each week and an employee could work on many tasks. Even if several employees worked on the same task, the document shows several tasks for one employee and *Task* is nested within *Employee*.

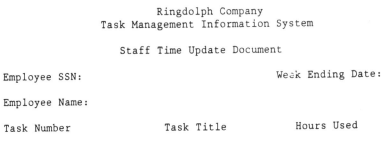

Figure 11.12   Output data structure for staff time update document.

The left carets on *Employee SSN* and *Employee Name* indicate these data attributes are not entered into the information system. They are used only to substantiate the employee listed on the document is assigned to that project. *Calendar Week Ending Date* is entered but is not stored on the database. It is used to calculate the primary key for each task week.

A simple application form for membership into an organization is shown in Figure 11.13. The applicant enters their name, address, age, height, weight, and phone number, and signs the application.

```
                        Membership Application Form
Applicant Name:

Applicant Address:

City:               State                   Zip Code:

Applicant Age:      Applicant Height:       Applicant Weight:

Applicant Phone:

Applicant Signature:
```

Figure 11.13 Membership application form.

The input data structure for this application form is shown in Figure 11.14. The highest level set on the data structure represents the *Club* where the applicant is applying for membership. The next level represents the applicant information that is contained on the form. All data on the form are entered into the information system except the applicant's signature and all data that are entered are stored in the database.

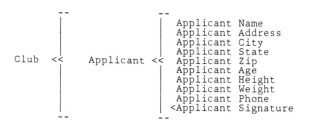

Figure 11.14 Input data structure for application form.

Composing input data structures is relatively simple compared to composing output data structures. However, an input data structure must be prepared for each input to properly identify and name all the data attributes that an enterprise manages and define the database that will store the data.

In todays online environment the use of menus, prompts, and conversations is becoming more common. Menus usually contain a list of functions that can be selected and do not involve access to the database unless those menus are stored on the database. Prompts are used to request certain key data prior to accessing the database. Conversations represent a two-way dialog with the user. Menus, prompts, and conversations involve both an output and an input and normally require both an output data structure and an input data structure. Development of these data structures assure that the data resource is properly defined and that all data are accounted for within a process.

However, in some situations development of both input and output data structures for menus, prompts, and conversations is a repetitive effort that adds nothing to definition of the data resource. In these situations, only the pertinent data structures need to be developed. It is up to the designer to determine which data structures are needed and which data structures can be eliminated.

DATA STRUCTURE NORMALIZATION

When output and input data structures have been composed, they need to be normalized to data views of the data resource. Each output data structure is normalized to a required data structure and each input data structure is normalized to a necessary data structure. The process of normalizing input and output data structures is more difficult than the process of composing those data structures, but it is not impossible if the principles of data normalization are understood and a few guidelines are followed.

Every data attribute must be accounted for during the normalization process. Data attributes on the output data structure can either come from the database, from an input data structure, or from the process. Each data attribute must be reviewed to assure that it is available or that data attributes needed for its creation are available. If the appropriate data attributes are not available some adjustment needs to be made to the data structures to assure that each data attribute on the output data structure is available.

> Every data attribute must be accounted for during the data normalization process.

If a data attribute stored on the database is calculated, the data attributes needed for that calculation must be available either on an input data structure or from the database. If they are not available, some adjustment needs to be made to the data structures to assure that they are available. In addition, every data attribute that is entered into a process must have some use in that process. It must be used to calculate a data attribute, to verify a data attribute, stored in the database, or appear on an output. If there is no use for a data attribute in a process, then there is no reason for that data attribute to be entered into the process.

Data structure normalization often cycles with the data structure composition. This cycling is normal and should continue as long as necessary to assure that both data structures are properly developed.

Developing Required Data Structures

A required data structure is developed for each output data structure. The procedure for developing required data structures is explained below in a series of steps that progress from the output data structure to a fully normalized required data structure. The sequence of these steps can vary slightly according to personal preference as long as the end result is a fully normalized data structure that accounts for all data. Several iterations of refinement may occur on each required data structure until that structure represents a fully normalized data structure that accounts for all data.

A required data structure is developed for every output data structure.

First, an initial required data structure is prepared based on the output data structure. That initial data structure includes all sets and set labels that appear on the output data structure but does not contain any data attributes.

Second, data attributes on the output data structure that are identified as literals or constants are crossed out. These data attributes will not appear on the required data structure because they are stored in the process. The required data structure represents only data retrieved from the database.

Third, data attributes on the output data structure that are calculated or derived are crossed out. However, as each calculated data attribute is crossed out the remaining data attributes on the output data structure are reviewed to determine if all data attributes needed to calculate the derived data attribute are present. If one or more data attributes that are needed for calculation are not present, they must be obtained from the database or from an input data structure. If these data attributes are obtained from the database, they are placed on the required data structure and are prefixed with an *equal sign* to indicate they are required from the database to support processing but do not appear on the output. They are placed in the set representing the subject data entity from which they will be retrieved.

Fourth, data attributes on the output data structure that are not obtained from the database but are obtained through an input data structure are crossed out. The input data structures for that process are reviewed to determine if those data attributes are available on the input data structures. If they are not available on an input data structure, they must be added to the appropriate input data structure.

Fifth, any data attributes remaining on the output data structure that have not been crossed out are moved to the required data structure and placed in the set representing the subject data entity from which they will be retrieved. If a set represents a data occurrence group rather than a data entity, the set label will need to be changed to the data entity name. Each data occurrence group requires a secondary key to obtain the desired records. If a set representing the subject data entity from which the data attribute will be retrieved is not on the required data structure, it is added.

Sixth, the hierarchy of the sets on the required data structure are reviewed and adjusted to show the one-to-many and one-to-one data relations. Any adjustment may result in one or more sets being moved and in several sets being placed in the same level on the required data structure.

Seventh, each set on the required data structure is reviewed to assure that it is completely normalized and that all repeating groups, partial key dependencies, inter-attribute dependencies, and interentity dependencies have been resolved. Any final adjustments to the required data structure are made to assure that it is completely normalized.

Eighth, all sets on the required data structure that do not have any data attributes are removed from the data structure. This house-keeping step removes unnecessary sets.

Ninth, a primary key is identified for each subject data entity on the required data structure and the data attributes composing that primary key are prefixed with a *pound sign* and placed at the top of the set. Occasionally, the data attributes composing the primary key are not on the required data structure and must be added. They are added to both the primary key at the top of the set and to the data attribute list.

Tenth, foreign keys are placed in subordinate data entities on the required data structure. Each data set except the two highest level sets must have a foreign key to its parent. The highest level set has no parent and the second level set needs no foreign key to the highest level set because it has only one data occurrence. All the data attributes necessary to compose the foreign key may not be available and must be added to both the foreign key and to the attribute list.

Eleventh, secondary keys are added to each data entity on the required data structure requiring access. The data entity where access is first made is identified and any secondary keys needed for access are identified. Then the accesses up and down the data structure are identified and the appropriate secondary keys are added to each set. The accesses to select records for a data occurrence group must also be added to the data structure. Occasionally, data attributes need to be added to the required data structure to compose a secondary key. When these data attributes are added, they are placed both in the secondary key and in the data attribute list.

Twelfth, each data attribute and each data entity on the required data structure are reviewed to assure that it has a formal name, a comprehensive definition, and is properly documented.

Required Data Structure Examples

These guidelines can be applied to the output data structures described above to provide required data structures. The output data structure for *Vehicle Report* is shown in Figure 11.8. The first step to normalize that data structure is to develop an initial required data structure that is the same as the output data structure without any data attributes, as shown in Figure 11.15.

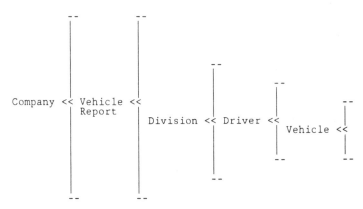

Figure 11.15 Initial required data structure for vehicle reports.

The second step is to cross out *Report Title, Report Number,* and *Column Headings* on the output data structure because they are literals contained in the process. The third step is to cross out *Division Miles* and *Report Miles* because they are calculated. Since *Vehicle Miles* is used to calculate both *Division Miles* and *Report Miles,* no additional data attributes are added. The fourth step is to cross out *Report Date* because it is obtained from an input data structure. The fifth step is to move each remaining data attribute to its appropriate set on the required data structure. The result of these actions is shown in Figure 11.16. Notice that *Operator Name* now appears in *Operator* rather than in *Vehicle.*

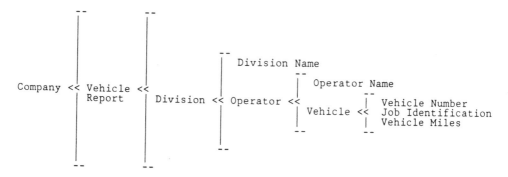

Figure 11.16 Required data structure for vehicle reports after the fifth step.

The sixth step is to adjust the required data structure to show the proper one-to-one and one-to-many data relations. The seventh step is to review the required data structure and assure that it has been properly normalized. No adjustments are necessary for relations or normalization on this required data structure. The eighth step is to remove *Vehicle Report* from the required data structure because it contains no data attributes. The result of these actions is shown in Figure 11.17.

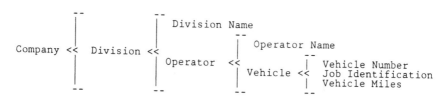

Figure 11.17 Required data structure for vehicle reports after the eighth step.

The ninth step is to add a primary key for each data set on the required data structure. The primary key for *Operator* is *Operator Identification* rather than *Operator Name* so it is added to the primary key and to the data attribute list. The primary key for *Division* is *Division Name* and for *Vehicle* is *Vehicle Number.* The tenth step is to add the foreign key to each subordinate set on the required data structure. *Division Name* is added to *Operator* and *Operator Identification* is added to *Vehicle.* The eleventh step is to add secondary keys for access. Initial access is to *Division* with subsequent access to *Operator* and *Vehicle.* All records in *Division* are read so there is no secondary key for *Division.* The secondary key in *Operator* is *Division Name* and the secondary key in *Vehicle* is *Operator Identification*. The final step is to review all the names and definitions for each data entity and each data attribute and assure they are documented. The final required data structure is shown in Figure 11.18.

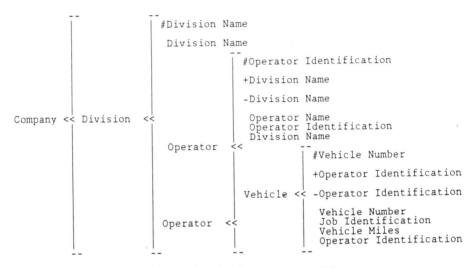

```
     --                    --
      |                     | #Division Name
      |                     Division Name
      |                      --
      |                       | #Operator Identification
      |                       +Division Name
      |                       -Division Name
Company << Division    <<       Operator Name
      |                         Operator Identification
      |                         Division Name
      |                 Operator  <<      --
      |                           |        | #Vehicle Number
      |                           |        +Operator Identification
      |                           Vehicle << -Operator Identification
      |                           |        Vehicle Number
      |                 Operator   <<       Job Identification
      |                           |        Vehicle Miles
      |                           |        Operator Identification
     --            --             --       --
```

Figure 11.18 Final required data structure for vehicle reports.

This example was relatively simple, but it shows the steps that are needed to normalize an output data structure into a required data structure. The same procedure was followed for the output data structure representing the fish report shown in Figure 11.10. The final required data structure is shown in Figure 11.19

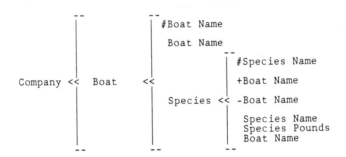

```
        --        --
         |         | #Boat Name
         |         Boat Name
         |          --
         |           | #Species Name
Company << Boat  <<   +Boat Name
         |         Species << -Boat Name
         |           |        Species Name
         |           |        Species Pounds
        --        --          Boat Name
```

Figure 11.19 Final required data structure for the fish report.

Developing Necessary Data Structures

Developing necessary data structures from input data structures is very similar to developing required data structures from output data structures. The same twelve steps are followed, but there are some differences because of the differences between input and output data structures. These differences are explained in the following steps.

A necessary data structure is developed for each input data structure.

First, an initial necessary data structure is prepared based on the input data structure. The initial data structure includes all the sets and the set labels that appear on the input data structure but does not contain any of the data attributes.

Second, data attributes on the input data structure that are identified as appearing on the input but not entered into the information system are crossed out. These data attributes will not appear on the necessary data structure because they are never entered into the process.

Third, data attributes on the input data structure that are entered into the information system but are not stored on the database are crossed out. However, each of these data attributes should be reviewed to determine why they are entered. If no use can be found for these data attributes, then they should not be entered and the *right caret* should be changed to a *left caret*.

Fourth, data attributes that are calculated by the process and placed on the database are identified with a *colon* and placed on the necessary data structure. For each of these calculated data attributes all the data attributes needed for calculation must be available. If they are not available, they must be made available either on an input data structure or on a required data structure.

Fifth, any data attributes remaining on the input data structure that have not been crossed out are moved to the necessary data structure and placed in the set representing the subject data entity where the data will be stored. If a set representing that data entity is not on the necessary data structure, it is added.

Sixth, the hierarchy of sets on the necessary data structure is reviewed and adjusted to show one-to-many and one-to-one data relations. Any adjustment may result in one or more sets being moved and in several sets being placed in the same level on the necessary data structure.

Seventh, each set on the necessary data structure is reviewed to assure that it is completely normalized and that all the repeating groups, partial key dependencies, inter-attribute dependencies, and interentity dependencies have been resolved. Any final adjustments to the necessary data structure are made to assure that it is completely normalized.

Eighth, all sets on the necessary data structure that do not have data attributes are removed from the data structure. This house-keeping step removes unnecessary sets that were left over from the initial necessary data structure.

Ninth, a primary key is identified for each subject data entity on the necessary data structure and the data attributes composing that primary key are prefixed with a *pound sign*. Occasionally, data attributes composing the primary key are not on the necessary data structure and must be added. When data attributes are added they are added both to the primary key and to the data attribute list.

Tenth, foreign keys are placed in subordinate data entities. Each data set except the two highest level sets must have a foreign key to its parent. The data attributes composing the foreign key are prefixed with a plus sign. If data attributes are not available, they are added to both to the foreign key and to the data attribute list.

Eleventh, secondary keys are added to each data entity on the necessary data structure requiring access. Generally, access is made to the database for every set on a necessary data structure and that access is usually done with fixed values. If data attributes need to be added to compose a secondary key, they are added to both the secondary key and the data attribute list.

Twelfth, each data attribute and each data entity must be reviewed to assure that it has a formal name and definition and is properly documented.

Necessary Data Structure Examples

These guidelines can be applied to the input data structures described above to provide necessary data structures. The input data structure for *Staff Time Update Document* is shown in Figure 11.12. The first step to normalizing that data structure is to develop an initial necessary data structure that is the same as the input data structure without any data attributes, as shown in Figure 11.20.

Figure 11.20 Skeleton necessary data structure for staff time update document.

The second step is to cross out *Employee SSN* and *Employee Name* because they are not entered into the information system. The third step is to cross out *Calendar Week Ending Date* because it is not entered into the database. *Calendar Week Ending Date* is used to calculate *Task Week Ending Date*. The fourth step is to identify any calculated or derived data attributes. *Task Week Ending Date* is derived from *Calendar Week Ending Date*. The resulting data structure is shown in Figure 11.21.

Figure 11.21 Necessary data structure for staff time update document after the fourth step.

The fifth step is to move the remaining data attributes from the input data structure to the necessary data structure and place them in the set that represents the data entity where they will be stored. The sixth step is to adjust the hierarchy to show the proper data relations. The seventh step is to verify that the necessary data structure is properly normalized. The eighth step removes any sets from the necessary data structure that have no data attributes. *Calendar Week* and *Employee* are removed. The resulting data structure is shown in Figure 11.22.

```
            --              --
            |               |    Task Number
  Company <<     Task   << :Task Week Ending Date
            |               |    Task Week Hours
            --              --
```

Figure 11.22 Necessary data structure for staff time update document after the eighth step.

The ninth step is to add primary keys to each data entity on the necessary data structure. *Task Number* is added to *Task*. The tenth step is to add foreign keys, however, there are no foreign keys to be added. The eleventh step is to add a secondary key for *Task Number*. The twelfth step is to verify that all data attributes and data entities are properly named, defined, and documented. The final necessary data structure is shown in Figure 11.23.

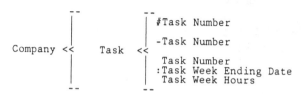

Figure 11.23 Final necessary data structure for staff time update document.

DATA STRUCTURE OPTIMIZATION

Development of a subject data resource is output driven with input verification. The required data structures are used to develop an output data resource model and the necessary data structures are used to develop an input data resource model. Each of these models is compared to the system architecture model, to the enterprise data resource model, and to each other to assure that the models coincide. Any discrepancies are resolved before a complete logical data resource model is developed. The detailed procedure is explained in a previous book (Brackett, 1987), but will be briefly reviewed here.

> Development of the logical data resource model is output driven with input verification.

Definition of a data resource from only the outputs results in an incomplete data resource model. This approach accounts for all data attributes and data accesses required to obtain data from the database. However, it often misses data accesses needed to place data into the database. These data accesses are only identified on the necessary data structures and are frequently different from data accesses shown on required data structures. This approach also misses verification of data attributes that are needed from the database. Just because there is a requirement for data from the database does not mean those data are automatically maintained in the database. Their maintenance must be verified.

Definition of a data resource from only the inputs also results in an incomplete data resource model. This approach accounts for all data attributes and data accesses necessary to store data in the database. However, it misses data access needed to retrieve data from the database. Since many more data accesses are needed for retrieving data from the database than are needed to store data in the database, many data accesses are not identified. In addition, many data attributes are stored that are not used and many data attributes that are needed are not stored.

Definition of a data resource from both the inputs and outputs at the same time does not resolve these problems. It does resolve the problem of identifying all data accesses that are needed, but it does not resolve the problem of storing all the data, and only the data, needed to support the outputs. There is no verification that all the data needed, and only the data needed, are stored in the database.

Therefore, the best approach to developing a logical data resource model is to develop an input data resource model and an output data resource model and compare these models with each other, with the system architecture model, and with the enterprise data resource model. This comparison assures that all the data needed, and only the data needed, are maintained and that all data accesses are defined. Comparison with the system architecture model assures that all data entities identified on the data resource model appear on the system architecture model and that all data entities on the system architecture model appear on the logical data resource model. Comparison with the enterprise data resource model assures that the data entities and data attributes are properly named and defined and that no synonymous or homonymous data are defined. Any discrepancies must be resolved before the input and output data resource models are considered complete and accurate.

Once the input and output data resource models have been developed and compared they can be merged to form a complete logical data resource model. The logical data model is then denormalized to develop the physical data resource model.

Developing the input and output data resource models is performed by decomposing required and necessary data structures into single sets representing individual subject data entities and combining those sets by data entity. To develop an input data resource model all necessary data structures are decomposed into individual sets representing data entities and combined by data entity to form a complete set of data for each data entity. The same procedure is followed for developing the output data resource model from required data structures and for developing the logical data resource model from input and output data resource models.

Each set on a required or necessary data structure represents a subject data entity and contains primary keys, foreign keys, secondary keys, and data attributes. The placement of those sets in the data structure indicates the data relations. When a data structure is decomposed these sets are taken out of the structure and their relations and used to verify or enhance the entity-relationship and entity-type hierarchy diagrams. When all data structures have been decomposed, all sets representing the same data entity are combined to form a complete set of data for that data entity. The combined primary keys, foreign keys, secondary keys, and data attributes are listed for each data entity.

The data attribute list for each data entity represents the data views for that application. These application data views must be documented because they represent the data actually used by the application. If these application data views are merged into combined or full data views during data denormalization, the identification of the actual data used by an application will be lost unless these application data views are documented.

When all sets representing the same data entity have been combined the result is reviewed for accuracy. Primary keys are reviewed to assure that there is only one primary key and that it is reasonable. Foreign keys are reviewed to assure that they are reasonable and represent every parent data entity. Secondary keys are reviewed to assure that they are reasonable and to determined if the number of secondary keys can be reduced. Finally, the data attributes are reviewed to assure they are in the proper data entity and are properly named.

The enterprise data resource model is most helpful for this process. It represents the current status of the enterprise database. Any discrepancies between the logical data resource model and the enterprise data resource model must be evaluated and some adjustment made. If the logical data resource model identifies enhancements to the enterprise data resource model, those enhancements are made. If the logical data resource model contains conflicts with the enterprise data resource model, the source of the conflict must be identified and resolved. The result is a complete and accurate enterprise data resource model and a logical data resource model that is consistent with that enterprise data resource model.

DATA STRUCTURE DENORMALIZATION

The logical data resource model represents the data needed to support the business needs of the enterprise. It is an optimized form of business data that defines a subject data resource containing single units of data. However, this logical data resource model is not always acceptable for building the physical database. The logical model must be adjusted for the physical operating environment before the physical data files are constructed, but the integrity of the logical data resource model must be maintained. The data denormalization process was explained in the Data Normalization chapter.

The result of data structure denormalization is a physical data resource model that maintains the integrity of the logical data resource model but adjusts that model to be operationally efficient in a particular environment. Any changes to that operating environment result in changes to the denormalization rules which can be applied to the logical data resource model to form an adjusted physical data resource model. The physical database is then adjusted accordingly. Production statistics can be used to adjust the physical data resource model to make improvements in operational efficiency.

SUMMARY

Data structures are the working tools for developing a data resource. They are used to define data on business transactions, to normalize those data into data views of subject data entities, to define the logical data resource model based on those data views, and to denormalize the logical data resource model into a physical data resource model that is implemented into a particular operating environment. This procedure is summarized in the following guidelines:

An input data structure is composed for each business transaction flowing into an information system.

An output data structure is composed for each business transaction flowing out of an information system.

Each input data structure is normalized into a necessary data structure.

Each output data structure is normalized into a required data structure.

Necessary data structures are optimized to form an input data resource model.

Required data structures are optimized to form an output data resource model.

Output and input data resource models are compared with each other, with the system architecture model, and with the enterprise data resource model.

Output and input data resource models are optimized to form a logical data resource model.

The logical data resource model is denormalized to form a physical data resource model.

The procedure to compose input and output data structures is summarized in the following steps:

Identify the highest level, single occurrence data entity.

Add the business transaction itself as the second level.

Add successively lower level data sets that represent data entities or data occurrence groups based on identification of repeating groups.

Add data attributes to each set as they appear on the business transaction, not as they would be normalized.

Add data attribute symbols as necessary to identify special use of data attributes.

The procedure to normalize input and output data structures into necessary and required data structures is summarized in the following steps:

Develop an initial normalized data structure containing the sets and set labels, but no data attributes.

Cross out literals and constants on output data structures. Cross out all data attributes that are not entered into the information system on input data structures.

Cross out calculated and derived data attributes on output data structures. Cross out all data attributes entered into the information system but not placed on the database on input data structures.

Cross out data attributes on output data structures that are obtained from input data structures. Identify calculated data attributes and place them on the necessary data structures.

Move remaining data attributes to the initial required or necessary data structure.

Adjust the hierarchy of the initial required or necessary data structure into one-to-one and one-to-many relations.

Review the initial required or necessary data structure to assure it is completely normalized.

Remove any sets that do not contain data attributes.

Identify primary keys for each subject data entity except the highest level.

Identify foreign keys for each subject data entity except those in the top two levels.

Identify secondary keys for access into each subject data entity.

Confirm that each data entity and data attribute is named, defined, and documented.

STUDY QUESTIONS

The following questions are provided as a review of the process for developing data structures and to stimulate thought about the use and importance of data structures for defining and constructing a data resource.

1. What is a subject data resource?
2. How is the four-schema concept involved in creating a subject data resource?
3. Why is a knowledge of data structures important for developing a subject data resource?
4. What are the various types of data structures and how is each used in developing an enterprise subject data resource?
5. What is the basic function of each process in an information system?
6. What is the purpose for the data attribute symbols?
7. What does the process of data structure composition accomplish?
8. How are input and output data structures composed?
9. What happens when input and output data structures are not composed properly?
10. Why are output data structures more difficult to compose than input data structures?
11. What does the process of data structure normalization accomplish?
12. How are input and output data structures normalized?
13. What happens when data structures are not properly normalized?
14. Why is data structure normalization more difficult than data structure composition?
15. Why are necessary data structures usually simpler than required data structures?
16. What does the process of data optimization accomplish?
17. Why are input data resource models and output data resource models developed and compared to the system architecture and the enterprise data resource model?
18. What does the process of data denormalization accomplish?
19. What is wrong with conventional approaches to defining a database?
20. Why is the approach of output driven with input verification a better approach?

Data Integrity

A comprehensive set of data integrity rules assures the existence of high-quality data in the enterprise's data resource.

Once the basic data units have been properly identified, defined, and structured, data integrity rules must be defined to assure those data units remain in a state of high quality. High-quality data are complete and correct at all times under all conditions for the instance of time they represent. High-quality data is maintained through a comprehensive set of data integrity rules that clearly and precisely define the criteria for maintaining high-quality data in the enterprise's data resource.

Data quality is often overlooked or treated lightly resulting in many of the data quality problems found in today's databases. The time required to identify, design, code, and maintain comprehensive data integrity rules is high and adds to the development and maintenance cost of applications. Reduction or elimination of data integrity reduces this cost, but it allows low-quality data to enter the database and allows data already in the database to deteriorate. The result is increased maintenance to raise data quality to an acceptable level.

Conventional data integrity rules have been placed in a variety of applications and each application has enforced only the rules applicable to data it processes. There has been no overall structure or consistency to data integrity rules resulting in conflicts and inconsistencies in the way the rules are applied. Redundant data maintained by separate applications have varying degrees of quality due to different integrity rules being applied by different applications. Most of these data integrity rules are mixed with business rules and have minimum documentation which makes them difficult to understand and maintain. In addition, many applications allow extensive overrides to data integrity rules which often makes it easier to override an error than correct the data.

Most conventional data integrity rules pertain to data values allowed for individual data attributes. A few conventional data integrity rules pertain to relations between data attributes and almost no rules pertain to maintaining the structure of data, derived data, redundant data, or for defining data retention. Some attempts have been made to place structural data integrity rules on entity-relationship and entity-type hierarchy diagrams but these rules are often incomplete.

This chapter explains practical techniques for defining a comprehensive set of data integrity rules. These data integrity rules include data values rules, data structure rules, rules for maintaining derived and redundant data, and rules for retention of data. They are separated from business rules and are placed with the data so that all data entering the database must pass through those rules. The result is an enterprise data resource with consistently high-quality data.

DATA INTEGRITY RULES

Data integrity rules are an integral part of the data resource model and are developed during design of the data resource. They are defined for the basic data units and the relations between those units. These basic data units must represent single units of data, such as single subject data entities, single characteristic data attributes, and single property data values. If the basic data units are not defined as single units of data, the best data integrity rules will not be completely effective.

> Data integrity rules assure that data are complete and correct at all times under all conditions for the instance of time they represent.

Developing good data integrity rules is not always easy, but it is not impossible. It requires an awareness that data integrity rules apply to all data entering the database as well as to data already in the database. It requires an awareness of the structure of the data resource and the types of data integrity rules that need to be defined. Data value rules pertain to the data values allowed for each data attribute and each relation between data attributes. Structural rules pertain to the relations between data occurrences. Derived data rules pertain to the maintenance of derived and redundant data, and data retention rules pertain to how long data are retained and when they are destroyed.

> Data integrity rules are defined for the basic data units and the relations between those units.

Data Value Rules

The first category of data integrity rules includes rules for the integrity of data values. Data value rules are defined for each data attribute and each relation between data attributes. These rules identify the allowable values for each data attribute.

> Data value rules are defined for each data attribute and each relation between data attributes.

Data domains. A data domain represents the set of values allowed for a single data attribute or for a relation between data attributes. Those allowable values may be listed or they may be represented by a rule. A **data value domain** contains the actual values that are allowed in a data attribute and a **data rule domain** contains rules which define the values allowed in a data attribute.

> A data domain represents the values allowed for a single data attribute or a relation between data attributes.

A data value domain can contain a closed set of values, an open set of values, or disjoint sets of values. A **closed set of values**, such as *1, 2, 3, 4, 5*, seldom, if ever, change. An **open set of values** could be *the next sequential number increasing from 1000 with no upper limit*. A **disjoint set of values** could be *1, 2, 5, 7, 12, and 14*, or multiple ranges such as *1 through 10 inclusive, 20 through 39 inclusive, and 50 through 59 inclusive*.

A data rule domain specifies a range, a maximum or minimum limit, or the format of a data attribute and is expressed in the form of a rule rather than a list of individual values. For example, a range might be specified as *greater than or equal to 50 and less than or equal to 100*. A limit is expressed as *less than or equal to 100*, or *greater than 500*. A format is expressed as *numeric with two decimal places, character string right justified*, or *50 free-form characters*.

A single data domain could support more than one data attribute if the range of values for those data attributes were identical. For example, data attributes containing indicators such as *0/1, True/False, On/Off,* or *Yes/No* could be represented by one data domain. However, a data domain supporting several data attributes could result in errors. For example, one data domain could support *Vehicle Value, Equipment Value*, and *Building Value* with a rule of *numeric value less than $10,000 with no cents*. If the value of buildings is increased to *$50,000* but the value of vehicles and equipment remains within *$10,000* a new data domain needs to be established for *Building Value*. If the existing data domain were changed to *$50,000*, the vehicle and equipment values could well be in error. If it were not changed, valid building values would fail the integrity rules. Therefore, a data domain is defined for each data attribute.

> A separate data domain is defined for each data attribute and each relation between data attributes.

Data domain management is the process of identifying and maintaining data domains for the enforcement of data integrity rules. It is an area of data resource management that has been largely ignored in the past. However, with increased emphasis on data integrity and data quality, data domain management is becoming increasingly important. Data domains are subject data entities and are designed and managed the same as any other subject data entity.

> Data domains are data entities and are managed the same as any other subject data entity.

Data attribute values. A data domain is defined for each data attribute to show the values that are allowed for that data attribute. If the data attribute contains coded values, its data domain is the code table for that data attribute. For example, the values allowed for

Vehicle Type Code	Vehicle Type Description
1	Automobile
2	Bus
3	Pickup Truck
4	Tandem Axle Truck
5	Motorcycle
6	Trailer
7	Farm
8	Off Road

Figure 12.1 Data domain for vehicle type code.

Vehicle Type Code and the meaning of each of those coded values are listed in Figure 12.1. Each value of *Vehicle Type Code* must be one of these allowable values.

If a data attribute contains actual values, its data domain can be either a data value domain or a data rule domain. Nine logic operators that can be used to express data integrity rules are shown in Figure 12.2. For example, *Building Unit Area GE 50 AND LE 100*, *Student Credit Hours GT 12*, and *Vehicle Horsepower LT 500* are valid data integrity rules that define the range of allowable values for a data attribute.

```
EQ        Equal to
GT        Greater Than
LT        Less Than
GE        Greater Than or Equal To
LE        Less Than or Equal To
NE        Not Equal To
AND       And situation
OR        Or situation
NOT       Not situation
```

Figure 12.2   Logic operators for data integrity rules.

Conditional data attribute values.   Many data attributes are related to other data attributes and the values that are allowed for each data attribute depend on those relations. A **one-to-one data attribute relation** means that a data attribute is related to only one other data attribute, and that data attribute is related only to the first data attribute. A **one-to-many data attribute relation** means that a data attribute is related to two or more other data attributes, but each of those data attributes is related only to the first data attribute. A **many-to-many data attribute relation** means that one data attribute is related to many other data attributes, and each of those data attributes can be related to two or more other data attributes including the first data attribute. These data attribute relations can exist between data attributes within the same data occurrence, between data attributes in different data occurrences in the same data entity, such as a recursive data entity, or between data attributes in different data occurrences in different data entities.

Three constraints can be applied to the relations between data attributes. A **required constraint** means a certain value in one data attribute requires the existence of a value in another data attribute. For example, each *Vehicle* requires a *Vehicle License Number* and a *Vehicle Type Code*. An **optional constraint** means the existence of a value in one data attribute does not require or prevent the existence of a value in another data attribute. For example, a *Student* may supply their *Birth Date* but it is not required. A **prevented constraint** means the existence of a value in one data attribute prevents the existence of any value in another data attribute. For example, *Engine Horsepower* is prevented for *Non-motorized Vehicles*.

Constraints for the existence of data attribute values can be shown in several ways. *Prevented* means a data attribute that is prevented for a specific combination of data values. *Optional* means an optional value and a data occurrence is valid with or without a value in that data attribute. *Required* means a required value and a value must appear in each data occurrence. The indication of required or optional is usually presented in table form for each data entity. For example, data domains for the constraints in *Vehicle* and *Student* are shown in Figure 12.3. *Vehicle License Number* and *Vehicle Type Code* are required for every vehicle. *Student Name* is required for each student, but *Student Birth Date* is optional.

```
Vehicle
        Vehicle License Number          Required
        Vehicle Type Code               Required

Student
        Student Name                    Required
        Student Birth Date              Optional
```

Figure 12.3   Data domain for constraints in two-data entities.

A data domain is defined for each relation between two or more data attributes.

A separate data domain is established for each relationship between data attributes and contains all combinations of values allowed for that relationship. For example, an *Employee Type Code* might contain the values *1*, *2*, and *3*, and an *Employee Seniority Code* might contain the values of *A*, *B*, and *C*. However, not all combinations of *Employee Type Code* and *Employee Seniority Code* are valid. A data domain is established to define the valid combinations, as shown in Figure 12.4. This table shows that all combinations are valid, except *1C* and *2A*.

Employee Type Code	Employee Seniority Code
1	A
1	B
2	B
2	C
3	A
3	B
3	C

Figure 12.4 Data domain for a relation between two-data attributes.

A data domain may have effective dates for which the values are allowed. If effective begin and end dates are required they are added as data attributes to the data entity representing the data domain the same as data attributes are added to any other data entity. Data attributes may also be added as necessary to further define or clarify values in the data domain. For example, the combination of values shown in Figure 12.4 were valid beginning in *1987*, but beginning in *1988* the combination of *3C* is no longer valid and new combinations of *4A* and *4C* become valid. The use of effective dates in the table would indicate when the combination of values was valid, as shown in Figure 12.5

Employee Type Code	Employee Seniority Code	Begin Date	End Date
1	A	1/1/87	
1	B	1/1/87	
2	B	1/1/87	
2	C	1/1/87	
3	A	1/1/87	
3	B	1/1/87	
3	C	1/1/87	12/31/87
4	A	1/1/88	
4	C	1/1/88	

Figure 12.5 Data domain for a relation between two-data attributes with effective dates.

The name for this data domain between *Employee Type Code* and *Employee Seniority Code* might be *Employee Type Seniority Integrity*. The standard word *Integrity* indicates the data entity represents a set of values used for data integrity. However, like summary data entities, the names for data entities representing the relations between data attributes can become quite long. The same convention used for summary data entities is used for integrity data entities by using the data entity name the data attributes characterize, the word *Integrity*, and a qualifier. For example, *Employee Type Seniority Integrity* might become *Employee Integrity 1* and the definition would indicate what data attributes belong to this relation.

Employee Marital Status	Employee Spouse Name
M	Optional
S	Prevented

Figure 12.6   Data domain for marital status and spouse name.

A data domain representing the relation between *Employee Marital Status* and *Employee Spouse Name* is shown in Figure 12.6. If marital status is *married* the spouse's name is *optional*. If marital status is *single* then the spouse's name is *prevented*. If a spouse's name is entered for a marital status of single, there is an error that must be corrected.

A data domain for a relation between data attributes can also contain values that indicate required, optional, or prevented constraints. For example, the *Employee Type Code* and *Employee Seniority Code* example in Figure 12.5 shows that data values *1A* and *1B* are valid. Since no other values are listed for an *Employee Type Code* of *1*, a seniority code is required. However, an entry for *Employee Type Code* of *1* and *Employee Seniority Code* of *blank* indicates that *Employee Seniority Code* is optional for *Employee Type Code* of *1*. One entry for *Employee Type Code* of *1* and *Employee Seniority Code* of *blank* indicates that *Employee Seniority Code* is prevented for *Employee Type Code* of *1*.

The data domain for a relation between data attributes can be shown as a rule using the logical operators listed in Figure 12.2. For example, the relation between *Vehicle Value* and *Vehicle Maintenance Cycle* might be expressed as shown in Figure 12.7. This rule means that if the vehicle value is greater than $5000 the vehicle must have maintenance performed every 30 days or less.

Vehicle Value	Vehicle Maintenance Cycle
LE 5000	GT 30
GT 5000	LE 30

Figure 12.7   A data domain rule using logical operators.

Data Structure Rules

The next category of data integrity rules includes the rules pertaining to the structure of the data resource. The term **referential integrity** is generally used to represent data integrity rules for the structure of the data. **Existence dependency** means essentially the same thing and refers to integrity rules that maintain the structure of data in the data resource.

Referential Integrity and cardinality. **Referential integrity** means that in a one-to-many data relation each subordinate data occurrence must have a parent data occurrence. If that parent data occurrence does not exist, the subordinate data occurrence can not be entered into the database. The reverse situation is also true. A parent data occurrence can not be removed from the database as long as there are subordinate data occurrences attached to that parent. A violation of either of these rules results in an **occurrence anomaly** that severely hinders navigation in the database. For example, an *Employee* has many *Pay Checks*. Each *Pay Check* must have a corresponding *Employee*. A *Pay Check* can not be entered into the database without a corresponding *Employee* and an *Employee* can not be removed while there are still *Pay Checks* referencing that *Employee*.

Referential integrity requires that each subordinate data occurrence has a corresponding parent data occurrence.

However, referential integrity shows only what data occurrences are required in the database, not what data occurrences are prevented or the quantity of data occurrences that may be required. These data integrity rules must be added to form a comprehensive set of data integrity rules for the structure of data in the data resource.

The **cardinality** of a data relation indicates the quantity of subordinate data occurrences allowed for each parent data occurrence. Generally, cardinalities are zero, one, or many represented by a *0*, a *1*, or an *M*. Numbers greater than one can be stated explicitly, such as *5*, to show that five subordinate occurrences are allowed. However, when a number larger than one is stated explicitly, that number must represent a valid data integrity rule, not a business rule.

Cardinality has been moved from the entity-relationship and entity-type hierarchy diagrams to data integrity rules because it represents the integrity of a data relation. The entity-relationship and entity-type hierarchy diagrams represent only the existence of data entities and the data relations between those data entities, not the integrity rules pertaining to data entities or data relations between those data entities.

Cardinality is defined as a data integrity rule and is not shown on entity-relationship or entity-type hierarchy diagrams.

Cardinality and referential integrity may be in conflict with each other. The conflict arises when cardinality must be one or many, meaning that a parent data occurrence must have at least one child data occurrence or that parent data occurrence can not exist in the database. Referential integrity says that a subordinate data occurrence can not exist unless there is a corresponding parent data occurrence. If this situation were taken literally, no data could be entered into the database because the parent can not be entered without the subordinate and the subordinate can not be entered without the parent. However, applied as an integrity constraint after a series of transactions representing the status of an entity, both cardinality and referential integrity rules can be met.

Relations and constraints. When the logical data resource model is complete only one-to-one and the one-to-many data relations are of concern. Many-to-many data relations have been resolved to one-to-many data relations. The one-to-one data relation can exist between two data occurrences within a recursive data entity as a closed recursive relation, or between data occurrences in two or more data categories. The one-to-many data relation can exist between data occurrences within a recursive data entity as an open recursive relation, or between data occurrences in two separate data entities. Data integrity rules must be defined for each of these situations.

Data integrity rules are defined for each one-to-one and one-to-many relation between data occurrences.

Structural data integrity rules pertain to data relations between occurrences. Each data relation must have a data integrity rule that assures consistency of that data relation. Since each data relation must have a data integrity rule, it is mandatory that each data relation in the data resource be properly identified. This is why it is important to explicitly show each data relation on the data resource model. It is also important to identify recursive data entities because there is a data relation between data occurrences within the recursive data entity. If each valid data relation is not explicit, a data integrity rule can not be developed for that relation and its consistency may not be properly maintained.

Three constraints can be applied to each data relation in the database. A **required constraint** means that one or more data occurrences are required for the relationship to be complete. An **optional constraint** means that one or more data occurrences are acceptable, but no data occurrences are required. A **prevented constraint** means that no data occurrences are allowed in the relationship. These constraints represent the cardinality and the referential integrity of a data relation and must be defined for each data relation.

The relationship between the types of data relations, the types of constraints, and the cardinality that is possible for each is shown in Figure 12.8. Valid data relations are shown at the top of the table and valid constraints are shown on the left side of the table. The body of the table shows valid cardinalities.

	1:1	1:M
Optional	0, 1	0,1,M
Required	1	1.<

Figure 12.8   Valid cardinality for data relations.

Each data relation has constraints for each direction along the data relation and these constraints may be different. In the *Pay Check* example above an *Employee* may optionally

Chapter Twelve

have a *Pay Check* but it is not required for an *Employee* to be entered into the database. When an employee is first hired and placed on the database there will be no *Pay Check* data to place on the database until that employee is paid. However, an *Employee* is required for each *Pay Check* before the *Pay Check* can be entered into the database. Both of these constraints must be defined to assure that the proper data relations are maintained.

When the employee is first hired they must be assigned to a job. Therefore, at least one *Job Assignment* must exist for each *Employee*. Each *Job Assignment* must also have a corresponding *Employee*. Both of these constraints must also be defined to assure the proper data relations are maintained.

A constraint is defined for each direction on a data relation.

Data structure rule format.   Structural data integrity rules can be shown on a diagram, as a matrix, or in table form. The **structural data integrity diagram** uses arrows between data entities with the constraints listed on the arrow, as shown in Figure 12.9. Each *Employee* requires a corresponding *Person* because *Employee* is a data category of *Person*, but an *Employee* is only optional for each *Person*. *Student* is prevented when there is a corresponding *Prospective Student* entity type and *Prospective Student* is prevented when there is a corresponding *Student* entity type. An *Employee* may optionally have *Pay Check*, but each *Pay Check* must have a corresponding *Employee*. Finally, an *Employee* may optionally be a *Student* and a *Student* may optionally be an *Employee* since they are both data categories of *Person*.

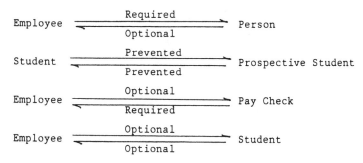

Figure 12.9 Structural data integrity diagram.

The **structural data integrity matrix** consists of a matrix with data entities listed across the top and down the left side, as shown in Figure 12.10. Data entities on the left side represent the source of the relation and the data entities on the top represent the destination of the relation. The contents of the matrix represent the constraints of optional, required, or prevented. The same structural rules defined in the diagram above are shown in the table.

Source Data Entity	Person	Employee	Pay Check	Prospective Student	Student
Person		Optional		Optional	Optional
Employee	Required		Optional	Optional	Optional
Pay Check		Required			
Prospective Student	Required	Optional			Prevented
Student	Required	Optional		Prevented	

Figure 12.10 Structural data integrity matrix

The **structural data integrity table** lists all constraints for each direction for each data relation, as shown in Figure 12.11. Each data entity in the database is listed twice in the table as the source of the data relation and as the destination of the data relation. For example, *Employee* is listed within *Person* to show the constraint on the data relation from *Person* to *Employee* is optional, and *Person* is listed within *Employee* to show the constraint on the data relation from *Employee* to *Person* is required. The data entities are usually listed in alphabetical order for easy reference.

```
Person
        Employee              Optional
        Student               Optional
        Perspective Student   Optional

Employee
        Person                Required
        Pay Check             Optional
        Student               Optional
        Perspective Student   Optional

Pay Check
        Employee              Required

Prospective Student
        Student               Prevented
        Person                Required
        Employee              Optional

Student
        Employee              Optional
        Prospective Student   Prevented
        Person                Required
```

Figure 12.11 Structural data integrity table.

All three forms are acceptable and it is up to the enterprise which form to use. The structural data integrity diagram is acceptable because of the instant meaning implied in the graphics, but when there are more diagrams, it is more difficult to locate all data relations for any particular data entity since they may appear on several diagrams. The structural data integrity matrix takes less space but becomes large when there are many data entities, unless a separate matrix is developed for each data segment. The structural data integrity table provides ready reference but it is sometimes difficult to find the corresponding constraint.

Conditional Data Structure Rules

The existence of a data occurrence may depend on a particular value in another data occurrence. For example, a *Student* can have many *Degrees* and the structural data integrity rules show that data relation is optional. *Student* contains a data attribute indicating whether the student in an undergraduate student data entity type or a graduate student data entity type. An undergraduate student will, by definition, not have received a degree and a graduate student will, by definition, have received one or more degrees. Therefore, the existence of degrees for a student depends on whether that student is an undergraduate student or a graduate student. If the student is an undergraduate student a degree is prevented, and if the student is a graduate student at least one degree is required. The optional relation of student and degree has become prevented for an undergraduate student and required for a graduate student.

Conditional situations can be shown in a **conditional structural data integrity table** similar to the table for structural data integrity rules. However, a new attribute is added to the table for the condition, as shown in Figure 12.12. If a student is an undergraduate as identified by a *Student Type Code* of *1*, a degree is prevented. If a student is a graduate student as identified by the *Student Type Code* of *2*, a degree is required. The notation *0* could be used instead of *Prevented* and the notation *1, M* could be used instead of *Required* to indicate that one or more degrees are allowed.

Conditional situations can also be shown as conditional structural data integrity rules. Using the example above, the conditional rules would be:

```
Student
        Undergraduate          Student Type Code 1
            Degree             Prevented
        Graduate               Student Type Code 2
            Degree             Required
```

Figure 12.12   Conditional structural data integrity table.

IF Student Type Code EQ 1 THEN Degree Prevented

IF Student Type Code EQ 2 THEN Degree Required

The exact format of these conditional integrity rules is not important. What is important is that all conditions are shown in a format that is readily interpretable and can be used for implementation of the data integrity rules. Any format that is confusing or results in a lack of understanding will not result in good data integrity rules and could result in incomplete or inaccurate data in the data resource.

During development of conditional rules a contradiction may be encountered. For example, a subordinate data entity has two parents and one of those parents requires the existence of a subordinate data occurrence based on values contained in the parent data occurrence. The other parent prevents the existence of a subordinate data occurrence based on values it contains. Obviously, a subordinate data occurrence can not be required and prevented at the same time. These situations must be identified and resolved before the data integrity rules are implemented.

Generally, development of a good data resource model based on single units of data, and verification of that model, will prevent these contradictions. However, contradictions do occur and must be resolved. Resolution is relatively easy when the units of data and the business rules for managing entities are thoroughly defined. A review of the data domains supporting data attributes and the relations between data attributes usually resolves any remaining problems. If the contradiction still exists there is a basic design flaw in the structure and definition of data entities and data relations. This flaw must be identified and corrected before the data resource model is completed.

Derived Data Rules

The third category of data integrity rules includes rules for maintenance of derived data and redundant data. The data values in derived data attributes are developed from the values in one or more contributing data attributes based on a derivation algorithm. The major problem with derived data attributes is that once the data values have been derived they are generally ignored. When the value of one or more of the contributing data attributes changes, the derived data attribute is not adjusted and the quality of the data resource deteriorates.

> Comprehensive integrity rules must be defined for derived data.

Derived data attributes represent **implied data redundancy**. The data value exists in a contributing data attribute and each derived data attribute that is based on those values is a redundant existence of those values. If derived data were not allowed and all calculations were made at execution time there would be no problem with derived data attributes. However, this is not the case and many databases contain derived data for operational efficiency.

Derived data attributes contain either actual data values or coded data vales. **Actual data values** are derived from contributing data attributes that contain actual values. For example, *Person Body Size Ratio* is an actual value that is calculated from *Person Height* and *Person Weight*. **Coded data values** can be derived from data attributes containing actual values or coded values or a combination of both. For example, *Candidates* have a *Date Contacted*, a *Date Applied*, a *Date Certified*, and a *Date Hired*. To avoid unnecessary processing a *Candidate Tracking Status Code* is defined with values of *1, 2, 3,* and *4* representing a status of *contacted, applied, certified,* and *hired*.

Active derived data attributes depend on the value of their contributing data attributes and present a major problem in a database. Their values must be recalculated each time the value of one or more of the contributing data attributes changes. If the derived data attribute value is not recalculated when the value of one or more contributing data attributes change then the database is not synchronized and provides false data. **Static derived data attributes** are never rederived and do not present a problem.

One of the major concerns with derived data attributes, whether active or static, is the timing of their derivation. *Quarter Vehicles Serviced* could be derived once each quarter at the end of the quarter, it could be derived once each quarter 15 days after the quarter, it could be derived each week during the quarter, and so on. It is equally important to know when derived data are rederived following a change to one or more of the contributing data attributes. The time frame, such as immediately, weekly, monthly at the end of the month, and so on, must be defined for each derived data attribute. This decision is based on the frequency of change for contributing data attributes, the frequency of use of derived data attributes, the need for accurate derived data, and the time involved in recalculating the derived value.

> Active derived data must be rederived when contributing data change based on the needs of the enterprise.

All derived data are based on a **data derivation algorithm**. That derivation algorithm can be in the form of a table, an equation, or some other form of process logic. For example, the conversion of *miles* to *kilometers* could easily be represented by an equation. The derivation of *Candidate Tracking Status Code* could be represented by process logic. The form of a derivation algorithm is not important as long as it accurately represents the derivation and can be easily interpreted. It must include all contributing data attributes and must refer to those data attributes with their primary name.

Derived data relations.   Depending on the relations between contributing data attributes and a derived data attribute a **data derivation diagram** can be created. When a change occurs to the value of one of the contributing data attributes, that change may ripple through several levels of derived data attributes. The relations between derived data attributes and their contributors and the ripple effect of a change must be documented. The timing of the initial and subsequent derivations must also be documented and must conform to the data attribute in the sequence that has the most critical need.

There are three **data derivation relations** between derived data attributes and contributing data attributes. A one-to-one relation means that a derived data attribute has one contributing data attribute and that contributing data attribute contributes only to the derivation of one data attribute. A one-to-many relation means that a derived data attribute has two or more contributing data attributes, but each of those contributing data attributes contributes to the derivation of only one data attribute. A many-to-many relation means that a derived data attribute has two or more contributing data attributes and those contributing data attributes contribute to two or more derived data attributes. The data attributes involved in the derivation may be in the same data occurrence, in different data occurrences in the same data entity, such as a recursive data entity, or in different data occurrences in different data entities.

A typical one-to-one derivation is the *miles* to *kilometer* conversion. A typical one-to-many derivation is the use of a persons *height* and *weight* to determine *body build* where *height* and *weight* do not contribute to any other derived data attribute. A typical many-to-many derivation is the use of *monthly salary* to determine both *calendar year salary* for federal reporting and *fiscal year salary* for budgeting.

> A data derivation diagram is used to define the sequence of derivation for derived data.

These data derivation relations are defined on a data derivation diagram, shown in Figure 12.13. The arrows point from the contributing data attributes to the derived data attribute and the lines are solid to indicate a use of data for calculation. Data attributes B and C contribute to data attribute A. Data attributes D and E contribute to data attribute B, and data attributes E and F contribute to data attribute C.

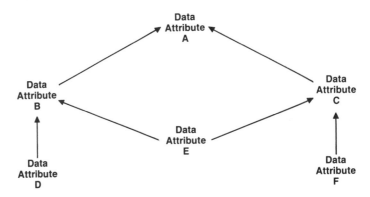

Figure 12.13 Data derivation diagram.

To properly define the creation and maintenance of derived data, the data attributes involved in the derivation, both the contributing data attributes and the derived data attributes, must be shown on a data derivation diagram. A data derivation algorithm must be defined for each derived data attribute and the frequency and timing of the initial and subsequent derivations must be defined. The definition of a derived data attribute must indicate whether that derived data attribute is active or static.

Redundant data rules. Although the objective of a well structured subject data resource is to have minimum redundant data, this objective is not always possible and redundant data do exist in the data resource. Also, conventional application files contain considerable redundant data. Those redundant data must be consistently updated whenever there is a change.

Redundant data can be either unnecessary redundant data, such as the redundant data that exists in conventional application files, or necessary redundant data that are allowed in a true subject database. Ideally, the redundant data in conventional application files will be eliminated as those files are converted to a subject database which eliminates the need to maintain those redundant data. However, redundant data must be maintained until the files can be converted.

Ideally, the first application that updates one existence of redundant data should have the responsibility for updating all existences of that redundant data. However, because of the structure of conventional applications it is not always possible for one application to update the files that belong to another application. When this situation occurs other alternatives must be selected. These alternatives belong to system architecture design and are beyond the scope of this book.

> Active redundant data must be maintained the same as active derived data.

To properly maintain each existence of redundant data, those existences must be identified and documented. If the sequence of updating is known, a **data redundancy diagram** can be prepared similar to the data derivation diagram. This diagram shows which existences of redundant data are updated first and the sequence for updating additional existences of the redundant data. If the updating sequence is not known, a **data redundancy table** showing all existences of redundant data can be prepared. All existences of redundant data attributes are listed in the table, as shown in Figure 12.14. If the primary data attribute has been designated, it is placed at the top of the list and is labeled *primary*. All other existences of that data are listed under the primary data attribute. The data attribute names usually include the repository name to uniquely identify each existence of redundant data. That table can then be used to plan the proper maintenance of redundant data and develop a data redundancy diagram.

```
Employee.Birth Date          Primary
        Vehicle Authorization.Birth Date
        Payroll:BD
        Training:Employee Birth
        Manager:Date Born
```

Figure 12.14 Data redundancy table.

To properly maintain all existences of redundant data, including time relational data, all existences must be identified and documented. Once they are identified, the sequence of maintenance, the method of maintenance, and the timing of maintenance can be determined.

Data Retention Rules

The last category of data integrity rules includes rules for the retention of data. A major area of concern with an enterprise's data is the loss of critical data through updating or destruction. The business rules must explicitly state what data are to be saved as historical data and what data may be destroyed without loss to the enterprise. Although this task sounds simple, it is difficult to define the retention of data because it is difficult to predict the future need for data.

> The future value of data must be determined before any data are destroyed.

Data go through a life cycle of entering the database, being updated, being retrieved, and ultimately being destroyed. Traditionally, a data item existed for the life of the data record. All data items began when the record was created and ended when the record was destroyed. Some data items may have been blank at some point in time but they still existed for the duration of the record. In a database management system the duration of a data item is independent of the duration of a data record. A data item could be created or destroyed at any time resulting in the creation of a data record when the first data item was created and destruction of a data record when the last data item was destroyed. This life cycle of data has a duration that depends on entity behavior and the enterprise's business rules.

The first consideration for data retention is identification of the criteria for retaining data in the data resource. In conventional application files it was relatively obvious when the usefulness of the data was over and data could be destroyed simply by deleting them from the file. However, with an enterprise-wide subject data resource it is more difficult to determine when data cease to be useful. In addition, the extensive use of ad hoc processing and expert systems to answer unanticipated requests or to perform historical trends and make future projections requires the use of data that may otherwise be considered useless and destroyed. Therefore, determining when data should be destroyed in a subject data resource is not always easy.

When the known usefulness of data is over, the unknown or hidden usefulness of the data must be evaluated. Unless the needs are anticipated, future critical data may be discarded as useless by today's standards. Therefore, the future value of data must be carefully evaluated.

> The hidden usefulness of data must be identified and defined before data are destroyed.

The second consideration in destroying data is definition of how to destroy the data. It is relatively easy to say delete the data as was done in conventional application files. But, all data integrity rules must be considered. If parent data are to be removed because their usefulness is over but subordinate data is retained then the parent data must remain, or at least enough of the parent data to support continued existence of the subordinate data. If subordinate data are to be removed because they are no longer useful to one parent, the usefulness to other parents must be considered. Subordinate data can only be removed when the they cease to be useful to all parents.

> The data integrity rules must be considered before data are destroyed.

The best method to manage the retention and destruction of data is to develop a complete data resource model for all the data in the enterprise's data resource including conventional application files and the subject data resource. The data integrity rules govern how data are removed from the data resource. The uses of each data unit can be identified on a data management matrix. Based on this information, an initial plan can be developed for the retention and destruction of data.

This approach assures that data needed today are not inadvertently destroyed. However, it does not assure that all future needs for data will be met. A good strategic plan for the enterprise's data resource will determine what future data may be needed. These plans can be defined on a data management matrix where future data needs are listed rather than existing processes. These data management matrices are used to determine what data should be retained for future use.

Data duration is the reverse of data retention. Data duration indicates how long data are stored in the database, such as when they are created and when they are destroyed. This information is used to plan the storage capacity and performance of the database. Data duration indicates when, according to business rules, the data are to be captured, updated, and destroyed.

MANAGING DATA INTEGRITY

Management of data integrity includes identifying the data integrity rules and enforcing those rules by applying them to the data and taking corrective action when the data violate the rules. If the data integrity rules are properly identified by the appropriate people, are placed in the appropriate repository, and are applied at the proper time with the proper corrective action for violations, the quality of the data resource will be maintained. When these tasks are combined with comprehensive data resource modeling and conversion to a subject data resource, the data will provide quality support to the business activities in the enterprise.

Identifying Data Integrity Rules

Identification of data integrity rules involves more than just identifying the individual data integrity rules. It includes the responsibility for identification and maintenance of those rules and proper documentation of those rules.

Data integrity responsibility. One of the primary objectives of a subject data resource is to encourage users to be responsible for management of their data. There is no *owner* of the data in an enterprise's data resource. Instead, there is a *shared responsibility* for management and control of the data resource. Anyone that is involved with the data is responsible for management of that data whether they are the president of the enterprise or a temporary clerk.

> Data are cooperatively managed by everyone using the data resource and are not owned by anyone in the enterprise.

This shared management responsibility extends to the identification and maintenance of data integrity rules. However, one of the problems with management of data integrity rules has been a lack of understanding of the extent and the importance of those rules. This lack of understanding, combined with conventional application files and strong control over data by the data processing departments has resulted in users having minimum, if any, involvement in the management of data integrity rules. Identification and explanation of the specific types of data integrity rules and conversion to a subject data resource, plus emphasis on direct user involvement in the management of their data, will resolve this problem and produce a higher quality data resource.

> Users that know the business must be involved in defining data integrity rules.

As a subject data resource is developed, more data integrity rules will be placed in the data resource and data entities will be defined for each set of data integrity rules. These metadata are no different than other metadata currently stored in the data resource. As metadata entities are defined, applications can be developed or acquired for the management of metadata and users can become directly involved in the management of their data through management of the metadata. As active data resource directories and expert systems become prominent, users will be able to use these metadata entities to enforce data integrity rules, which puts users directly in charge of the quality of their data.

This approach allows rapid changes to data integrity rules based on changes to the business environment and results in reduced maintenance for conventional data integrity routines. When users find that changes are necessary to data integrity rules, they can change those rules the same as they change other data. These changes are based on the users intimate knowledge of the business and their direct contact with behavioral entities. This intimate knowledge and direct involvement in maintaining data integrity rules is just as important as the direct involvement in other aspects of data resource management.

Identification process.   Management of data integrity rules begins with identification and documentation of the data integrity rules. All data integrity rules must be defined before the data resource model is considered complete.

The first step in defining data integrity rules is to define the structural constraints for each data relation in the data resource model. All data relations must be identified and shown explicitly on entity-relationship and entity-type hierarchy diagrams and the constraints must be shown for each direction on each data relation. In other words, each data relation requires two constraints. These constraints may be defined in a diagram, a matrix, or a table, but they must be defined.

The second step is to define all conditional structural constraints for each data relation on the data resource model. Each data relation, particularly optional data relations and data relations within a recursive data entity, is reviewed to determine if there is a conditional constraint for that data relation. If there is a conditional structural constraint, that constraint is defined in a table or as one or more rules. When the structural and conditional structural data integrity rules have been defined they should be reviewed to determine if there are any contradictions that will result in automatic failure. These contradictions must be resolved before the rules become final.

The third step is to define the data attributes required on each data occurrence. Each data entity is reviewed to determine which data attributes are required for every data occurrence in that data entity. Generally, primary keys and foreign keys are required, except for calculated foreign keys where the data attributes required to derive the foreign key are required. Additional required data attributes are identified as needed.

The fourth step is to define a data domain for each data attribute whether it contains actual data or coded data. These data domains contain an exhaustive set of data rules or data values. Each data attribute in the data resource model is reviewed to determine the data domain that supports that data attribute.

The fifth step is to define data domains that support each relation between data attributes. When these relations are defined, they are documented in a data domain containing either values or rules. The sets of values in these data domains must be exhaustive to assure that data are properly edited. When these data domains have been defined, they should be reviewed to determine if there are any contradictions that result in automatic violation of the data integrity rules. If any contradiction is found, it must be resolved.

The entries in any data domain, whether it supports one data attribute or a relation between data attributes, must be exhaustive. Every possible value or combination of data values must be considered and invalid data values must be eliminated. Too often a data domain is developed where only valid data values or combination of data values are considered without reviewing the full set of possible combinations. The data values that are entered are usually correct, but valid combinations are frequently missed causing unnecessary errors and correction. Therefore, all possible combinations of data values should be considered and then the valid data values may be placed in the data domain.

An entity type hierarchy is very useful for determining valid combinations of values for relations between data attributes. It is used to develop a data domain containing valid combinations of values for each branch in the hierarchy. Each branch on the entity type hierarchy represents a valid combination of values and becomes a separate entry in the data domain.

When there are many relations between data attributes, there is a chance for contradictory integrity rules. For example, one relation involving a data attribute may require the existence of a value for that data attribute. Another relation involving that same attribute may prevent the existence of a value for that data attribute. These situations must be identified and resolved before the data integrity rules become final. The formal definition of data integrity rules and the placement of those rules in one location helps to identify these contradictory situations.

The sixth step is to define the duration for each data attribute and how that data should be retained for future use when its current usefulness is completed. Each data attribute is reviewed and the rules for the duration of that data attribute are documented in the data resource directory.

The seventh step is to define the maintenance of derived data. A data derivation algorithm is defined for each derived data attribute and all data attributes that contribute to the derivation of that data attribute are documented on that data derivation diagram. Documentation for derived data attributes shows whether it is an active or a static derived data attribute and when initial and subsequent derivations are made.

The eighth step is to define the maintenance of redundant data. Every data attribute is reviewed to determine if it is part of a set of redundant data, either explicitly or implicitly.

If it is part of a set of redundant data attributes, it is documented on a data redundancy table or a data redundancy diagram.

One technique to start identifying data integrity rules is to review existing applications and determine what data editing is performed by those applications. As the existing data edit criteria are defined, they may be documented as described above. Usually retrodocumenting data edit criteria illustrates the inconsistence and incompleteness of conventional data edits. Once these conventional data edit criteria are documented they can be enhanced to provide a full set of data integrity rules that can be applied to the subject data resource or to the existing database.

Enforcing Data Integrity Rules

Enforcing data integrity rules includes applying those rules to data entering the database as well as to data already in the database and taking the proper action when data either pass or fail the rules. Enforcement of the data integrity rules assures that data are maintained in a state of high quality and are not allowed to deteriorate.

Data integrity rules must be defined before they can be enforced. It is a poor practice to acquire an active data resource directory or to develop applications to enforce data integrity and then randomly place data integrity rules into those routines. This procedure is little better than the current situation, except that the rules are in one place, and results in another set of confused data integrity rules that must be properly structured before they can be truly effective. The data integrity rules must be properly structured and defined and then placed into the appropriate repository for enforcement.

Applying data integrity rules. Data integrity rules are enforced by a data integrity application whether that application is an active data resource directory or a data integrity application. That application must not only enforce the data integrity rules but must take the appropriate action when the data pass and fail those rules. The corrective action may be to adjust the data or to return the transaction to the business application for correction.

> A data integrity application must take appropriate action when data fail the data integrity rules.

There are four basic actions that can be taken against a database. These four actions are to create new data in the database, to update data already in the database, to destroy data in the database, and to retrieve existing data from the database. Data integrity rules must be defined and enforced for the first three of these actions. There is no need to enforce data integrity rules for inquiry into the database to retrieve data because data are not being altered in any way.

These actions against the database are connected to the data views of the database. Each data view can add data to the database, update data in the database, destroy data in the database, or retrieve data from the database. Any data view that has the ability to alter data in the database in any way must pass all data in that data view through the data integrity rules. It is a poor practice to assume that if only one piece of data contained in a data view is altered only that piece of data need be passed through the data integrity rules. All data contained in a data view updating a database must be passed through the data integrity rules to assure that there are no inadvertent changes to the database that violate the data integrity rules.

All data in a data view updating the database must be passed through the data integrity rules.

Results of enforcing data integrity rules.   When actions are taken against the database there can be two results. The data can either pass the data integrity rules or they can fail. If data pass the data integrity rules, the appropriate change is made to the database. If data fail the data integrity rules, the database is not updated and some additional action needs to be taken. Generally, the transaction is returned to the business application for correction.

Allowing overrides to data integrity rules is a dangerous game. One of the problems with existing applications, in addition to incomplete and inconsistent data editing, is the random and uncontrolled use of overrides to the data integrity rules. These overrides allowed data to enter the database that do not meet the data integrity rules and result in a low quality data resource. The days of random overrides to data integrity rules by anyone in the enterprise must end and comprehensive data integrity rules must be enforced.

Overrides to data integrity rules should be carefully controlled, documented, and frequently reviewed.

Data integrity rule overrides may be allowed, but only in extreme cases and only by selected individuals with the authority to initiate an override. When a data integrity rule override is made it should be carefully documented, either by the person taking the override or by the application, and reviewed to determine if those overrides were proper. If the override was proper, an adjustment should be made to the data integrity rules to include that condition. If the override was improper, a correction should be made to the database to maintain the quality of the data.

In other words, data integrity rule overrides must be carefully controlled, documented, and reviewed to assure the quality of the data in the database. Good data integrity rules and direct user involvement in the management of their data will eliminate much of the need for overrides to data integrity rules.

Error messages.   Data integrity error messages, like data integrity rules, have been hard coded in applications and have added to the maintenance load for those applications. However, as data integrity rules are removed from applications and placed with the data, the data integrity error messages can also be removed from applications and placed with the data integrity rules. These error messages are placed in error message tables that become data entities in the subject data resource similar to code tables. These **error message tables** are accessed as necessary to obtain the proper error message depending on the result of actions against the database.

> Error messages are placed in tables similar to code tables.

Error messages should indicate what is wrong with the data, how the data might be corrected, and may even give examples of the types of corrections. Many of the error messages being developed today include lengthy explanations of the type of error and how it may be corrected. The comprehensive definition of errors and possible correction procedures leads to development of expert systems that manage errors. Correcting errors is a decision making process not unlike other decision making processes and can be performed by expert systems.

Error messages should be designed like any other data are designed. Each error message must be unique within the enterprise and must have a unique identifier. Each error message must be used for only one error condition to prevent any confusion between error messages, the conditions they represent, and the possible corrective actions for those conditions. The structured definition of conditions resulting from actions against the database, the error messages representing those conditions, and the actions to resolve the errors begins the definition of expert systems to process errors that occur during actions against the database.

The errors that do occur should be documented and reviewed periodically to determine what can be done to prevent the error rather than allowing it to occur and be resolved. This proactive approach to data resource management results in reduced maintenance, higher productivity, and higher quality data in the data resource.

> An enterprise should be proactive in identifying errors and preventing those errors rather than resolving them after the occur.

SUMMARY

A good set of data integrity rules improves the data resource model and assures the quality of data in the enterprise's data resource. A weak set of data integrity rules, or nonexistent data integrity rules, results in a deteriorating database and destroys the credibility of the enterprise's data resource.

The quality of the business activities performed by the enterprise is directly dependent on the quality of the data in the data resource. High-quality data result in high-quality business activities and low-quality data result in low-quality business activities. The quality of the data is dependent on the quality of the data integrity rules that control data entering the database and data in the database. Therefore, definition of a comprehensive set of data integrity rules directly impacts the quality of business activities.

Conventional data integrity rules are incomplete and inconsistent and have been spread throughout a variety of applications. Many of these data integrity rules have been mixed with the business rules used to manage behavioral entities. Many overrides to existing data integrity rules have been allowed because those rules are incomplete and inconsistent. The result has been low-quality data in the data resource. The only way this situation can be resolved is to develop a comprehensive set of data integrity rules that are separate from the business rules. Guidelines for developing comprehensive data integrity rules are summarized below.

The people who know the business and the data needed by the business must be involved in definition and enforcement of data integrity rules.

Data structure constraints are defined for each direction of a data relation between data entities.

Conditional data structure constraints are defined for each relation on the entity-type hierarchy diagram.

Required data attributes are identified for each data entity.

A data domain is defined for each data attribute.

A data domain is defined for each relation between data attributes.

Data retention rules are defined for each data attribute.

A data derivation diagram is prepared for all active and static derived data attributes.

A data redundancy table or diagram is prepared for all existences of redundant data attributes.

Data integrity rules are placed with the data, not with business applications.

Data integrity rules are applied to all data entering the database.

If failures and errors can not be resolved by data integrity routines they are returned to the business application for resolution.

Overrides to data integrity rules should be limited and carefully monitored.

Data integrity rules should be managed like any other data subject.

Error messages should be managed like any other data subject.

STUDY QUESTIONS

The following questions are provided as a review of data integrity and to stimulate thought about the current status of data integrity and how the quality of data can be improved in the enterprise's data resource.

1. What is data integrity?
2. Why is the quality of the data in a enterprise's data resource important?
3. Why does conventional data integrity not produce high-quality data?

4. How can conventional data integrity problems be resolved?
5. What is the difference between data rules and business rules?
6. Why is it necessary to define single units of data to have good data integrity rules?
7. What is a data domain and what does it contain?
8. Why should data domains support only single data attributes?
9. What is meant by data domain management?
10. What types of relations can exist between data attributes and why are they important?
11. How are the relations between data attributes defined in data integrity rules?
12. What are data structure rules and why are they important?
13. What are the types of constraints that can be applied to data structures?
14. How are data structure constraints documented?
15. How are conditional data structure constraints documented?
16. How are derived data integrity rules documented?
17. What is the difference between active and passive derived data?
18. Why is it important to document all the existences of redundant data?
19. How are redundant data documented?
20. Why is it important to document the retention of data?
21. Who should be responsible for defining data integrity rules?
22. What is the process for defining data integrity rules?
23. How are data integrity rules enforced?
24. What types of actions can be taken against the database?
25. What are the benefits of good data integrity rules?

Data Resource Documentation

Documentation of the entire data resource model is mandatory for an effective and efficient data resource.

The data resource model for an enterprise must be completely documented to fully define and support the enterprise's data resource and the documentation must be readily available to anyone in the enterprise interested in the status of the data resource. This documentation must be constantly and consistently maintained to reflect the current status and future plans of the enterprise's data resource. Any change to an existing data resource model and any new data resource model must be added to the documentation.

The terms *dictionary*, *directory*, and *encyclopedia* are frequently used to describe documentation and use of the data resource by the enterprise. None of these terms really covers the detail that needs to be captured about the data resource and its use by the enterprise. The term *data resource directory* is used in this book to include dictionary and directory information about the data resource and its use. That data resource directory can exist in any form and is best when integrated with graphics capability and database management systems.

This chapter begins by describing the abbreviation rules for data names that need to be made to meet software product restrictions, particularly data resource directories. Next, the techniques for documenting each component of the data resource model in a data resource directory is described. The chapter concludes with comments about management of a data resource directory to support an enterprise.

DATA NAME ABBREVIATION

Most source languages, database management systems, data resource directories, and other software products have restrictions on the length of data names. One way to stay within these length restrictions is to keep data names as short as possible without compromising the meaning. However, this may not always be possible and the fully spelled out real world name may be too long for a particular software product. When this happens, the data name needs to be abbreviated.

> Data name abbreviations must meet length restrictions and retain as much meaning as possible.

Data name abbreviation is part of the formal data naming taxonomy described in the Data Definition chapter. The objective is to meet the length restrictions of software products yet retain as much meaning as possible. To achieve this objective the heaviest abbreviation is done on the most general portion of the data name and the least abbreviation is done on the most specific portion of the data name. Since the data name progresses from the general to the specific, the heaviest abbreviation is on the left and the least abbreviation is on the right.

Some software products require that the words in a data name be concatenated with no embedded blanks and some do not allow certain special characters. When this syntax is necessary the colon, period, comma, and blanks may be replaced with dashes, underscores, or any other symbol that is required by the software product.

Data Repository Name Abbreviation

The data repository name is generally used during interface management, retrodocumentation, file conversion, and decentralization of data to designate the specific data repository. In most cases it is not subject to length restrictions imposed by software products. However, if the data repository name is subject to length restrictions it follows the same abbreviation rules as data subject names.

Data Subject Name Abbreviation

The data subject name can receive the heaviest abbreviation because it is the most general part of the data name. For example, when people access *Employee* they generally know they are getting employee data and, therefore, *Employee* can be heavily abbreviated. In the case of severe length restrictions the data entity name can be shortened to a few characters.

The first alternative for abbreviating a data subject name is to define standard abbreviations for each word in the name. Using these standard word abbreviations makes a reasonably short data subject name yet maintains a reasonable meaning. For example, *Customer* might be abbreviated *Cust*, *Account* might be abbreviated *Acct*, and *Activity* might be abbreviated *Acty*. The data entity named *Customer Account Activity* would then be abbreviated as *Cust Acct Acty* which shortens the name about 40%.

If this first alternative does not shorten the data subject name sufficiently, a second alternative can be used. This second alternative uses a two- to four-letter abbreviation for each word in the name and concatenates those abbreviations without spaces to form the shortened data subject name. For example, *Customer* would be abbreviated to *CST*, *Account* would be abbreviated to *ACT*, and *Activity* would be abbreviated to *ATY*. The data subject name *Customer Account Activity* would be shortened to *CSTACTATY*. This abbreviation shortens the full data subject name by 65% which gains more space but reduces the meaning of the name.

If the second alternative does not meet length restrictions, a third alternative may be used. This third alternative uses a three character data subject abbreviation that is unique within the enterprise. For example, *Customer Account Activity* would be abbreviated to *CAA*. With this alternative there are no standard abbreviations for each word in the name. A unique three character abbreviation is designated for each data entity that is encountered. Whenever possible these three characters should be as close as possible to representing the data subject name. This alternative provides an extremely short name, but much of the meaning is lost.

Any of these abbreviation techniques can be used. However, it is best to pick one technique and use it for all data entity names within the enterprise. Mixing unabbreviated data subject names, standard word abbreviations, shortened data subject names, and three character abbreviations leads to more confusion than is necessary. Even the three-character data entity name is better than interchanging the four alternatives for data subject names. For example, if a person had to deal with *Customer Account Activity*, *Cust Acct Acty*, *CSTACTATY*, and *CAA* there would be increased confusion. Multiply this confusion by several hundred or several thousand data entities in an enterprise and the confusion becomes unmanageable.

A list of the standard words and shortened abbreviations should be maintained in the enterprise data resource directory and used when abbreviating data subject names. For example, if *Acty* is the standard word abbreviation for *Activity*, it should be used whenever a data subject name containing the word *Activity* is abbreviated. Likewise, if *ACT* is the shortened word for *Account*, then it should be used whenever a data subject name containing the word *Account* is shortened. The three-character abbreviations are documented with their respective data entity, but a separate list may be maintained to assist in defining new data subject abbreviations.

Data Characteristic Name Abbreviation

When a data characteristic name is too long to meet length requirements it must also be abbreviated. However, the abbreviation process follows a precise set of rules that is different from the abbreviation of data subject names. This set of abbreviation rules is necessary to produce shorter meaningful names, to prevent synonyms and homonyms, and to provide easy lookup in a data dictionary. When data characteristic name abbreviation rules are not established, or established and not followed, meaningless data attribute names are created, redundancy increases, and data name reference becomes time consuming.

> Data characteristic names should be abbreviated to meet length restrictions yet maintain as much meaning as possible.

Data characteristic word abbreviation.
A data characteristic word abbreviation must substantially shorten the word, yet retain its meaning. For example, shortening *Distribution* to *Dstrbtn* is a substantial reduction while still retaining meaning. Shortening *Distribution* to *Distributn* retains the meaning but is not a substantial reduction and should not be used. Shortening *Distribution* to *Dbn* results in a substantial reduction but also a substantial loss of meaning and should not be used.

When possible, abbreviation of a data characteristic word should be an abbreviation that is commonly known, such as *Pg* for *Page*, *Ht* for *Height*, and *Lb* for *Pound*. Shortening these words to *Pge*, *Hght*, and *Pnd* results in a substantial shortening but does not supply the meaning that is provided with commonly known abbreviations.

> Common abbreviations should be used whenever possible.

A string of words in a data characteristic name should not be abbreviated to the first letter of each word in the string unless it is a well-known abbreviation. For example, abbreviating *Monthly Wage Total* to *MWT* would be meaningless to most people and should not be used. However, *OASI* is a common abbreviation for *Old Age Survivors Insurance* and would be a valid abbreviation.

Some words in a data characteristic name should be left unabbreviated. For example, trying to find meaningful abbreviations for *Meter* and *Motor* that provide substantial length reduction could prove difficult. Also, abbreviating two- and three-letter words, such as *set*, *age*, and *end* could also prove to be difficult. These words should always be left unabbreviated.

Any common and frequently used words should always be abbreviated. For example,

Indicator should always be abbreviated to *Ind*, *Number* should always be abbreviated to *Num*, and *Code* should always be abbreviated to *Cd*. These mandatory abbreviations improve the meaning of data characteristic names because there will not be both an abbreviated and an unabbreviated version of the word and space will be available for words that are not common to be left unabbreviated.

When defining abbreviations for a data characteristic word, the root word should be identified first and all manifestations of that root word should be abbreviated at the same time. This practice prevents use of the same abbreviation for another version of the root word. For example, if *distribution* is encountered first, there might be a tendency to abbreviate it as *distrb*. At a later date when *distribute* is encountered, another abbreviation would need to be used, such as *dstbr* because *distbr* has been used. This makes the meaning of abbreviations more difficult to understand.

It is better to take the root word, *distribute*, find all manifestations of that word, such as *distributed*, *distributing*, and *distribution*, and abbreviate all manifestations at the same time. The result would be *distrb*, *distrbd*, *distrbg*, and *distrbt*. The result is that all manifestations of the root word have similar abbreviations making them easier to understand. A common practice is to pick standard letters for suffixes to the abbreviation of the root word. For example, *d* for *ed*, *g* for *ing*, *t* for *tion*, *m* for *ment*, and *s* for all plurals. These letters are appended to the end of the root word abbreviation which adds to the structure and meaning of abbreviations.

> Abbreviations are formed for all manifestations of the root word.

The same abbreviation should not be used for all manifestations of the root word. Although this makes the abbreviation process easier and may save a character or two in the length it causes problems with interpretation of the data name. For example, using *Distbr* for all manifestations of *distribute* could result in interpretation errors. In addition, any automated expansion of abbreviated names would be extremely difficult if not impossible when one abbreviation is used for multiple words.

Sequence of abbreviation. It should be obvious that there are some data characteristic words that are always left unabbreviated or fixed, there are some words that receive a mandatory abbreviation in all cases, and there are some words that are abbreviated only when a length restriction is not met. The appropriate use of these three sets of words and their abbreviations assures most length restrictions can be met and the abbreviations can still retain meaning.

The sequence for abbreviating the words in a data characteristic name is very important. First, any word that is always abbreviated should be abbreviated regardless of where it appears in the data characteristic name. Second, any word that is fixed length should remain unabbreviated regardless of where it appears in the data characteristic name. Third, the remaining words that may be optionally abbreviated are abbreviated as necessary to achieve the length restriction.

> Mandatory abbreviations should be made first to retain as much meaning as possible.

The sequence of abbreviation for optional words progresses from the left to the right in order to preserve as much meaning as possible. When a length restriction cannot be met with the mandatory abbreviations, each word that can be optionally abbreviated is abbreviated beginning at the left of the data characteristic name. After each optional word is abbreviated the name length is checked to determine if the length restriction has been met. If it has not been met the next optional word is abbreviated and the length is again checked. When the length restriction is met, abbreviation stops and there is no further abbreviation of any words. In addition, no words already abbreviated are unabbreviated.

> The sequence of abbreviation is from left to right to retain as much meaning as possible.

If the length restriction can not be met after all the optional words have been abbreviated, then another data characteristic name should be selected that uniquely identifies the data characteristic yet meets the length restriction. If a large number of the data characteristics can not be abbreviated within the length restrictions, the name should be reviewed and shortened.

As data attribute names are being formed and abbreviated, a standard output heading should also be designated for each data characteristic. These standard headings should be stored in the data resource directory and used on all outputs to enhance the meaning of the reports. For example, if *Emp SSN* were the standard heading for *Employee SSN*, it should appear on all outputs, whether screens, reports, or microfiche. This standard output heading provides a commonalty that enhances the understanding and interpretability of all outputs. If possible, the same abbreviations used for data characteristic names should be used for report headings.

Data Value Name Abbreviation

Coded data value names can be abbreviated similar to the way data characteristic names are abbreviated. These abbreviations may be useful for listing data value names on outputs similar to the data attribute output heading abbreviations described above. For example, data value names for *New Student*, *Returning Student*, and *Continuing Student* may be abbreviated to *New Stdt*, *Retng Stdt*, and *Cntng Stdt* respectively.

> Data value names are abbreviated the same as data characteristic names.

Generally, when data value names are abbreviated each word in the name is abbreviated rather than following a sequence like the one used for data characteristic names. The abbreviations for words in data value names should be the same abbreviations used for the words in the data characteristic name. This standard provides a common base for people to use whether they are using data characteristic names or data value names. When the same abbreviations are used, the same abbreviation list can be used to form the abbreviations which reduces the effort of maintaining separate data name abbreviation lists.

Abstract Data Name Abbreviations

Once the abbreviation techniques for basic data units are understood, it is easy to extend those techniques to abstract data units. Generally, abstractions of data units above the data occurrence level follow the abbreviation rules for data subject names and abstractions of data units below the data occurrence level follow the abbreviation rules for data characteristic names. In an absolutely ideal situation, both sets of abbreviations would be the same and one set of abbreviations could be applied to all levels of the data hierarchy. However, this is usually not possible and two separate sets of abbreviation rules must be followed.

> Abstract data units above data occurrences are abbreviated like data subject names.

Data segment and database names usually do not encounter length restrictions and are not often abbreviated. However, if they need to be abbreviated for any reason the same abbreviations used for the data subject name words are used to abbreviate the data segment and database name words. Data categories and data entity types are abbreviated the same as other data subject names.

> Abstract data units below data occurrences are abbreviated like data characteristic names.

The only difference between a data occurrence group name and the data subject name is the qualifying word or words that prefix the data subject name. These words are abbreviated the same as other words in the data subject name. For example, the data subject name *Employee* is abbreviated as *Emp*. The data occurrence group of *Pilot Certified Employee* might be abbreviated *Plt Crtfd Emp*.

Data attribute group names are abbreviated the same as data characteristic names. The words used to form the data attribute group name are the same words used to form the data characteristic names, therefore the same abbreviations are used. The only difference is they have the word *Group* appended to the end of the name which is usually abbreviated as *Grp*. Since it is a common abbreviation, it is a mandatory abbreviation. For example, *Phone Number Group* would be abbreviated as *Phone Num Grp* since *Num* and *Grp* are mandatory abbreviations.

Multiple Abbreviations

A situation that many enterprises face today is multiple length restrictions that result from different length restrictions on individual software products. For example, some products allow 32-character names, some allow 18-character names, and some allow 10-character names. When all of these products are products of choice for an enterprise there can be an issue of how many abbreviations to allow and what those abbreviations should be.

Two problems arise when dealing with multiple data name abbreviations. First, programmers are faced with words that may be abbreviated in some data names and unabbreviated in other data names based on the length of the data name and the need for abbreviation. This situation causes confusion for the programmer and is a source of program error that must be corrected when it occurs. Second, analysts and users face a similar situation where data name abbreviations change depending on the stage of development and which software product is used. If they are involved in design, editing, and data definitions, they use the primary name. If they are using other products with length limitations, they have the same problems programmers experience with abbreviations.

The solution becomes a selection of the lesser of several inconveniences. Should there be several different abbreviations of the same data attribute name to meet the restrictions of several different software products? This alternative would retain as much meaning as possible for each software product at the risk of having several versions of the data attribute name. Or, should there be only one data attribute name that meets the shortest length restriction at the risk of losing meaning for all software products? If there is only one length restriction the choice is easy, but if there are several different restrictions the choice is more difficult, and the more restrictions there are the more difficult the choice. Each enterprise must answer this issue based on their particular environment. There is no standard solution.

> The decision on multiple abbreviations is up to each individual enterprise.

A related issue is the impact of changing existing standards once they are established. Any change to an existing abbreviation standard, once it is established and in use, could cause an impact greater than any benefits. These changes must be carefully evaluated and implemented only when the impacts and the benefits are known. In other words, there should not be change just for change sake.

Once naming standards are established and abbreviations are set, selection of future software products should consider the possible impacts of changing naming or abbreviation standards. If the change is severe, acquisition of the software product should be carefully evaluated.

Business Transaction Name Abbreviations

Business transaction names are abbreviated using the same word abbreviations as are used for abbreviating the words in a data characteristic name. The sequence of abbreviation is from the left to the right until a length restriction is met, following the same rules as for abbreviating data characteristic names. As an option, the entire name may be abbreviated using all mandatory and optional abbreviations.

DATA RESOURCE DIRECTORY

Metadata are data about the data and must be properly documented to effectively and efficiently support the data resource. A **data resource directory** provides a repository for metadata, directory capability between metadata members, and a directory to metadata that are stored outside the data resource directory. A true data resource directory is more than the conventional data dictionary. A data dictionary, like any other dictionary, provides definitions about data units and some references between those data units. Although data unit definitions are certainly important, there is much more information on a data resource model, such as diagrams, that can not be effectively stored in a data dictionary. A data resource directory provides the capability to both store metadata and to indicate where metadata are stored outside the data resource directory.

Entity-relationship diagrams, entity-type hierarchy diagrams, data control diagrams, and file-relationship diagrams are best documented with graphics software. The basic and abstract data units, data keys, data relations, data views, data integrity rules, and their physical counterparts data management and data responsibility matrices are best documented in a data resource directory.

Metadata are the data about the data resource and are stored in a data resource directory.

A data resource directory supports the value added concept of data resource development. It directly supports design and development of the data resource by providing an on-going repository and directory for data. As each development step is completed the appropriate metadata are stored in the data resource directory and are available to all subsequent steps for that development project and to all other development projects. They are also available to anyone else in the enterprise interested in the data resource.

A data resource directory could contain metadata about all the objects shown in Figure 13.1. Although all these objects are important, the objects of interest in this book are those contained in the data resource model.

Data Entities	Data Flows	Business Activities
Data Attributes	Data Accesses	Processes
Data Values	Data Occurrence Groups	Calculations
Data Files	Data Segments	Business Entities
Data Records	Databases	Business Units
Data Items	Data Relations	Data Integrity Rules
Data Views	Data Keys	Data Attribute
Groups		

Figure 13.1 Data subjects in a data resource directory.

Data Entitles

One member is defined for each single subject data entity and an additional member is defined for each nonsingle subject data entity. Each single subject data entity member contains a complete definition of that data entity, including similarities and differences with closely related data entities, and a cross reference to any associated nonsingle subject data entities. Each nonsingle subject data entity contains a definition unique to that data entity and a cross reference to all single subject data entities that it contains.

> A member is defined for each single subject and each nonsingle subject data entity.

For example, a multiple subject data entity for *Employee Pay* that contains *employee* information, *pay check* information, and *deduction* information would require definition of four members in the data resource directory, as shown in Figure 13.2. One member is defined for the multiple subject data entity *Employee Pay*, and three members are defined for the single subject data entities *Employee*, *Pay Check*, and *Deductions*. Cross references would be made between the employee member and the other three members.

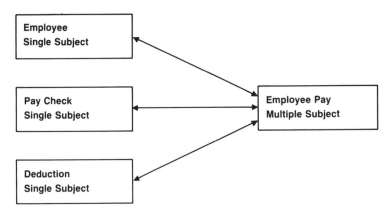

Figure 13.2   Multiple subject data entity.

A partial subject data entity requires definition of a member for the partial subject data entity and a member of the single subject data entity it represents. For example, a partial subject data entity for *Faculty* represents a subset of the *Employee* data entity, since faculty members are a data entity type of employee. A member is defined for *Faculty* with a definition pertaining to the use of faculty data and a member is defined for *Employee* with a definition pertaining to all employees, as shown in Figure 13.3. The faculty definition indicates it is a data entity type of employee and the employee definition would include a cross reference to faculty as a subtype of employee.

Figure13.3 Partial subject data entity.

A complex subject data entity requires definition of one member for the complex subject data entity and one member for each single subject represented in that complex subject data entity. Each of those members are defined and cross references are provided between the complex subject data entity and the single subject data entities.

Data categories are defined in the data resource directory the same as data entities. A separate member is defined for each data category and references are made to the parent data entity and other associated data categories. Each data entity type can also be identified as a separate member in the data resource directory the same as a data entity. A separate member is defined for each data entity type and references are made between supertypes and subtypes.

> A separate member is defined for each data category and each data entity type.

Data Relations

Relations between data entities can be easily defined with key words for each data entity. Generally the standard words *Peer, Parent, Child, Cyclic,* and *Recursive* are used to define these data relations. For example, *Person* contains the clause *Peer Employee* to indicate a peer relation with *Employee,* as shown in Figure 13.4. *Employee* also contains a clause *Peer Person* to show its relation to *Person. Vehicle* contains the clause *Child Vehicle Maintenance* to show there are many maintenances for each vehicle, and *Vehicle Maintenance* contains the clause *Parent Vehicle* to show its relation to *Vehicle.*

Figure 13.4 Data relations.

> Data relations are defined with each data entity involved in the relation.

The inclusion of data relations in data entity definitions supplement data entity-relationship and entity-type hierarchy diagrams. These diagrams show the overall architecture of data entities which is difficult to determine from reviewing the data resource directory. However, not all data relations may be shown on any one diagram. The definitions in the data resource directory indicate all the data relations for a particular data entity but do not provide the overall architecture of the database.

Data Attributes

Each data attribute must be documented in the data resource directory. In a well-structured subject data resource each data attribute represents a single data characteristic and is easily documented as one member in the data resource directory. That member contains the primary name of the data attribute as the name of the member and any supporting information, such as a definition, alias names, formats, integrity rules, source of the data, and so forth. These single characteristic data attribute members define the data attributes in the enterprise's subject data resource.

A separate member is defined for each single data characteristic data attribute.

Most data resource directories have the ability for one primary data attribute name with multiple aliases. The primary name should be the fully spelled-out, real-world data unit name. All other forms of the primary name, such as abbreviated name, source code name, database management system identifier, and so on, should be aliases of the primary name.

Many single characteristic data attributes have alias names. These alias names may be abbreviations of the primary name, or they may be alias names used in applications. These alias names can be documented in two different ways in a data resource directory. The first technique is to list the alias names in the member describing the single characteristic data attribute. For example, *Birth Date*, *Emp BD*, and *Employee Birth*, would be listed as aliases in the member defining *Employee Birth Date*, as shown in Figure 13.5. This technique is acceptable when the alias names are nothing more than an alias name.

```
Employee Birth Date
Alias   Birth Date
        Emp BD
        Employee Birth
Single Characteristic
```

Figure 13.5   Alias names listed in primary member.

However, there are situations when the alias names have a unique definition or a unique use in addition to the definition contained in the primary member. Although these unique definitions could be listed as an extension of the primary definition, it is better to create a separate member for the alias name and to place that unique definition in that member, as shown in Figure 13.6. That alias member definition must reference the primary member and the primary member must reference the alias member for proper navigation. This technique is also useful when a data resource directory can not provide access by alias names. Although there is slightly more initial effort to enter the additional members in the data resource directory, these additional members provide a clearer understanding of the data.

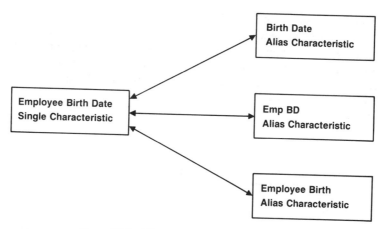

Figure 13.6 Alias names listed as separate members.

Aliases and variations of data characteristics are defined as separate members.

Separate members for alias names are also useful when retrodocumenting existing data files. A member is created for each data attribute in the data file or for each data attribute used by an application. A definition of that data attribute is provided based on information gained during retrodocumentation. Following retrodocumentation, the definitions of those members can be reviewed and merged as necessary. Single characteristic data attributes can be defined and cross referenced with any nonsingle characteristic data attributes. The result is a very formal approach to retrodocumenting existing data and defining single characteristic data attributes.

Variations of data characteristic names, such as those used in foreign keys, can be documented the same as alias names. For example, if *Equipment* contained foreign keys to *Vendor* for *Vendor Number Maintenance, Vendor Number Lease, Vendor Number Sales,* and *Vendor Number Installer,* then four members would be defined for these four data attributes. These members contain a brief definition of the specific use of these data attributes and a reference to the primary member for a further explanation.

Much of the data in the enterprise's database is in the form of multiple, variable, complex, and mutually exclusive data attributes. These situations must be properly documented so that both the existing information systems can be maintained and the enterprise's subject data resource can be constructed. Although the specific techniques vary from one data resource directory to another, general guidelines can be provided for defining members for nonsingle characteristic data attributes.

Documentation of multiple characteristic data attributes requires one member to be defined for the multiple characteristic data attribute and one member to be defined for each single characteristic in that multiple characteristic data attribute. For example, the multiple characteristic *Customer Type Code* that includes *Customer Hair Color, Ethnic Origin Code,* and *Gender Code* would result in four members being defined in the data resource

Data Resource Documentation

directory, as shown in Figure 13.7. One member is defined for the multiple characteristic *Customer Type Code* which contains a definition of that code indicating there are three data characteristics composing that code and a reference to those three single characteristic data attributes. Three members are defined for *Customer Hair Color*, *Ethnic Origin Code*, and *Gender Code* which contain definitions of those data characteristics and references to the multiple characteristic *Customer Type Code*.

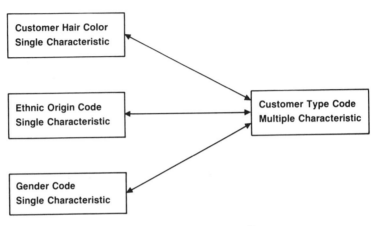

Figure 13.7 Multiple characteristic data attributes.

The two-way cross reference between the multiple characteristic data attribute member and the three members for the single characteristic data attributes allows navigation in either direction in the data resource directory. Providing a cross reference only one way, or no cross reference at all, limits the ability of people to find the relationships between multiple and single characteristic data attributes. Elimination of the member for the multiple characteristic data attributes further limits the ability of people to manage both conventional and subject data for the enterprise. Therefore, the multiple characteristic data attribute and all single characteristic data attributes must be completely documented as separate members in the data resource directory and the relationships between those members must be defined.

> A separate member is defined for each multiple characteristic of a data attribute and for each single characteristic data attribute it contains.

Variable characteristic data attributes are documented in much the same way as multiple characteristic data attributes. The only difference is that the definitions must include the conditions for determining the single characteristic data attributes. For example, the *Student Date* variable characteristic data attribute includes an initial contact date for prospective students, a date of first enrollment for undergraduate students, and a date of graduation for graduate students. Members are defined in the data resource directory for *Student Date*, *Student Date Initial Contact*, *Student Date First Enrolled*, and *Student Date Graduated* the same as they were defined for multiple characteristic data attributes, as shown in Figure 13.8. In addition, the definition for *Student Date* indicates the conditions for determining if the value for *Student Date* represented prospective students, undergraduate students, or graduate students. The definitions for the three single characteristic data attributes indicate the same conditions.

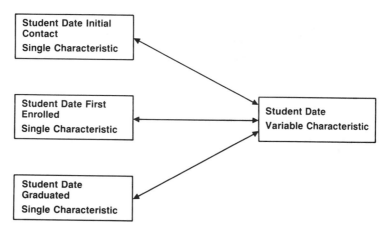

Figure 13.8 Variable characteristic data attributes.

Placing a description of the conditions for determining prospective student, undergraduate student, and graduate student in all four members provides ready identification of the nature of the variable characteristic and the references between members. Eliminating the conditions from any members limits this identification and leads to problems with interpreting data. If the conditions are extensive, they could be eliminated from the three single characteristic data attributes and a statement could be entered referring to the variable characteristic data attribute member for a description of the conditions.

> A separate member is defined for each variable characteristic of a data attribute and each single characteristic data attribute it contains.

Complex characteristic data attributes are also documented in a similar manner. A member is defined for the complex characteristic data attribute, and for each single characteristic data attribute that is contained in the complex characteristic data attribute. For example, the *Customer Code* that included the seven data attributes for new customers,

customers with good credit, and customers with bad credit would require eight members to be defined in the data resource directory, as shown in Figure 13.9. One member is defined for the complex characteristic *Customer Code*, and seven members are defined for *Customer Income*, *Customer Interests*, *Customer Buying Potential*, *Customer Credit Limit*, *Customer Payment Rate*, *Customer Credit Rating*, and *Customer Collection Probability*. The variable characteristic data attribute member references the single characteristic data attributes and contains a description of the conditions for determining those characteristics. The single characteristic data attribute members reference the complex characteristic data attribute member.

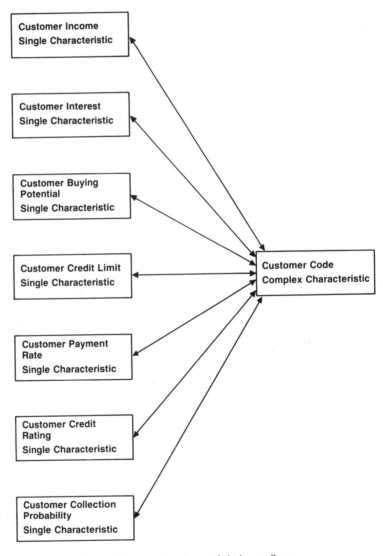

Figure 13.9 Complex characteristic data attributes.

> A separate member is defined for each complex characteristic of a data attribute and each single characteristic data attribute it contains.

Mutually exclusive data attributes are documented differently. One member is defined for the single characteristic data attribute that includes all the mutually exclusive data attributes, and one member is defined for each mutually exclusive data attribute. Each member is completely defined and cross references are made between the single characteristic data attribute member and the mutually exclusive data attribute members. For example, the *Shipment Code* single characteristic data attribute that was split into three mutually exclusive data attributes for *Air Shipment*, *Regular Shipment*, and *Parcel Shipment* requires four members to be defined in the data resource directory, as shown in Figure 13.10. The *Shipment Code* member contains a definition of the single characteristic for shipment with a cross reference to the three mutually exclusive data attributes. The *Air Shipment*, *Regular Shipment*, and *Parcel Shipment* members contain definitions of their respective uses and cross references to the *Shipment Code* member.

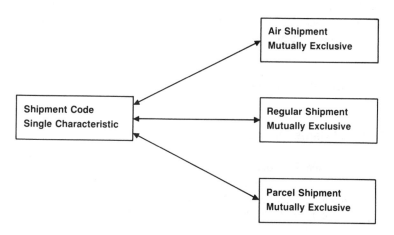

Figure 13.10   Mutually exclusive data attributes.

> A separate member is defined for each mutually exclusive characteristic of a data attribute and for the single characteristic data attribute they represent.

Data Values

Data values are generally not documented in the data resource directory. They are better documented in a data entity representing a data domain or a code table. That data entity can be accessed by applications or by users to determine the data values and their definitions. Documenting data values in both the data resource directory and a data entity is a poor practice because of the high maintenance required to maintain both sets of data and the probability that the two sets of data will not coincide. If it is necessary to document data values in both the data resource directory and a data entity, then these redundant data must be managed the same as any other redundant data.

> Data values are contained in a data entity and not documented in the data resource directory.

Abstract Data Units

Abstract data units are documented in the data resource directory the same as basic data units. Each data attribute group, data occurrence group, data segment, and database is defined as a separate member in the data resource directory. Each of those members have a complete definition explaining what the data unit represents including similarities and differences with other closely related data units. The definitions for data occurrence groups include the criteria for selecting the data occurrences in that group. Data occurrence groups that have variable selection criteria, as identified by the standard word *Selected*, are defined in the data resource directory with an explanation that the selection criteria are variable.

> A separate member is defined for each abstract data unit.

Data Unit Name Thesaurus

A data resource directory can be used to develop a thesaurus of data unit names. A **data unit name thesaurus** works like any typical thesaurus by providing a list of similar names that are not used in the formal data names. A data unit name thesaurus does not contain alias names since they are listed with each member in a data resource directory and the capabilities of that data resource directory can be used to search for aliases. The thesaurus lists only similar data names so people can quickly locate data units or determine that they do not exist. For example, the words *Town*, *Village*, *Municipality*, and *Burg* could all be entered into a thesaurus and point to *City* as an existing data subject.

> A data unit name thesaurus provides a reference between similar names and formal data unit names.

Generally, a data unit name thesaurus is developed for data entity and data attribute names. For example, a data entity has been formally named *Employee*. However, people involved with other development projects or people accessing the database may be interested in *Personnel*, *Worker*, or *Staff*, none of which are formal names in the database or are listed as aliases in the data resource directory. The data unit name thesaurus lists *Personnel*,

Worker, and *Staff* and indicates *Employee* is the formal data entity name, as shown in Figure 13.11.

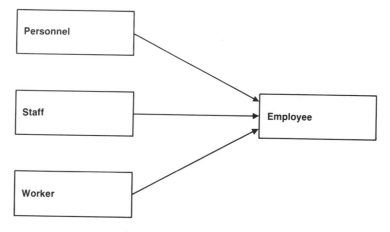

Figure 13.11 Data entity name thesaurus.

The standard data attribute words could be placed in a thesaurus and any similar words that were not standard words could be referenced to the standard words. For example, *Number* might be a standard word for an identifying number and *Value* might be a standard word for monetary value. A data attribute name thesaurus would reference *Integer*, *Numeral*, and *Digit* to *Number*, and *Charge*, *Cost*, *Price*, and *Expense* to *Value*, as shown in Figure 13.12. Anyone accessing the thesaurus with these words would be given a reference to the standard word for the enterprise.

A data unit name thesaurus could also be developed for data value names, for any of the abstract data units, and for standard words and abbreviations. Phrases can also be placed in a data name thesaurus. For example, if someone were interested in *Financial Detail* the thesaurus would indicate *Account Activity*, *Account Activity Detail*, and *Customer Billing* as data entities involving financial detail. As additional phrases are encountered they are entered into the thesaurus with references to the formal data names. The result is a mechanism that allows people to find the data they are interested in obtaining from the database or to find data units that have already been defined. Once the concept is understood it can be applied wherever it is needed.

Data Keys and Data Views

The primary key for each data entity is documented with that data entity. If there are alternate primary keys they are also documented with the data entity. In some cases primary keys are documented as separate members in the data resource directory with a reference to the data entities they identify. This approach is useful in large enterprises where data optimization is a major task or where a data resource directory can not provide access to members based on definition of the primary key. Accessing a data resource directory by

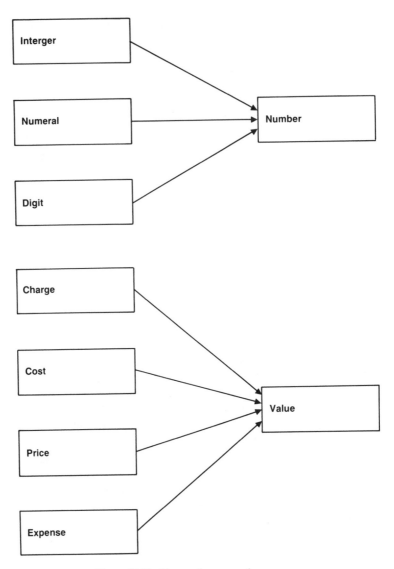

Figure 13.12 Data attribute name thesaurus.

primary key helps the data optimization process by readily locating primary keys and the data entities they identify.

Defining separate members for each primary key and referencing those members to data entity members is also useful for identifying multiple uses of the same primary key. For example, data entity types and data categories may have the same primary key. Defining a separate primary key member helps identify all the data subjects that use that primary key. A separate member could also be identified for each alternate primary key which would also assist the data optimization process.

Secondary keys are documented as separate members in a data resource directory with reference to the data entities they support. These secondary keys also reference the physical files and the data views they support. Data views are documented as separate members in a data resource directory with reference to the data entities they support. These data views also reference the physical files and the applications they support.

> A separate member is defined for each primary and secondary key and each data view.

Data Integrity Rules

Data integrity rules are documented in the data resource directory or other data repository such as the database for the enterprise. If the enterprise maintains its own data integrity rules in its database, applications are written to enforce those rules and are linked to business applications for maintaining data integrity. Every business application updating the database must access the appropriate data integrity application. Any changes to these data integrity applications will be effective with the next execution with minimum maintenance, if any, on the business application. This procedure assures that the data integrity rules are applied uniformly and consistently to all data entering the database.

Progressive enterprises encourage development of an enterprise subject data resource and the direct involvement of users in the maintenance of their data, including data integrity rules. With the availability of good data integrity identification techniques, with proper training of users in the use of these techniques, and with proper authorization for the maintenance of the data integrity rules, users can be actively involved in the improvement and maintenance of the quality of data in the data resource.

As business rules are separated from data integrity rules, the data integrity rules will be moved out of the business application and placed in an active database management system or an active data resource directory. The business rules will remain in business applications and those applications will be aligned with the business activities. This trend will ease the maintenance of both the data integrity rules and the business rules.

Physical Data

Each data file and data record are documented as separate members in the data resource directory. Data items are not documented separate from data attributes. If a data attribute becomes a data item, reference is made to the data record where it is contained. If there is no reference to a physical data record, that data attribute is not stored physically. Secondary keys and data views are treated the same way. If a secondary key becomes a physical key, reference is made to the appropriate data record. If a data view becomes a physical data view, reference is made to the appropriate data record.

Decentralized data are documented by defining references between data entities and data attributes and the data files where they are stored. A member is defined for each data file and the definition indicates the type and location of that file. Any references between a data file and a data attribute member, whether directly or indirectly, indicates the data attribute is stored in that data file. This approach is preferable to using the data file name as a prefix to the data entity or data attribute name and creating a member for each location of each data attribute. The latter approach causes excessive overhead and additional maintenance and should be used only in situations where there are specific definitions unique to a data repository.

Decentralized data are defined by references between data files and data attributes.

MANAGING A DATA RESOURCE DIRECTORY

The members described above should be documented in the data resource directory as soon as they are identified. This immediate documentation allows other people, whether users or developers, to build on information that has already been gained and is part of the value added concept data resource development. If information gained is not immediately documented, it can not be referenced and used by other people. The result is development of synonyms and homonyms that will ultimately need to be resolved, or redefinition of data that have already been defined and may be in use. Either situation is a loss of productivity.

A current, accurate data resource directory supports value added data resource development.

Several standard words should be established to indicate the accuracy or validity of a data unit. *Proposed* indicates the data unit has just been identified and definition of that data unit may be questionable. Proposed generally applies to strategic data modeling where there is minimal substantiation for existence of a data unit. *Tentative* indicates the data unit has been substantiated as existing and that the definition is firm. Tentative generally applies to retrofit modeling or retrodocumentation where there is some substantiation for the data, but that data may not represent valid data units. *Approved* indicates the data unit has been substantiated and that it represents a valid single unit of data in the subject data resource.

Approved data can be used for construction of information systems with minimal probability of changes.

Standard words help identify the status and validity of data units.

Limited indicates data units that are currently in use but that use should be limited to the current applications. Use of that data unit should not be propagated to new applications. Limited generally applies to data units that are not single units of data. *Obsolete* indicates data units that are no longer in use in any application or database. Obsolete data units should not be removed from the data resource directory because they provide some historical information. An old application or old documentation may surface with that name and the data resource directory indicates that it is obsolete and references the replacement data unit.

Data name changes sometimes occur when developing a subject data resource. Although the design method greatly reduces the need for data unit name changes, it does not eliminate that possibility. When a data name change occurs a new member is created for the new name. The member representing the old name is labeled *Obsolete* and reference is made to the new member. The definitions of each member should indicate the change and any reasons for the change. This procedure encourages use of new data names as soon as they are identified and prevents any further use of an old data name.

Data unit names and definitions should be entered into the data resource directory as soon as they are defined, and should be updated as soon as any changes are made. This procedure allows other members of the project team, and other project teams, to have access to the current status of data units and allows them to build on the information that has already been gained. If discrepancies or conflicts are found, the development teams can be proactive in resolving those problems before they become critical and impact project development.

Data definitions should be complete and comprehensive. They should explain everything about the data unit that a person totally unfamiliar with that data unit would want to know. Generally, one to three paragraphs is sufficient for a data unit definition. One sentence is insufficient and more than three paragraphs becomes excessive. However, some definitions involving nonsingle units of data or many closely related data units can have definitions that exceed three paragraphs. When a data definition is developed it should not become static. It should be constantly enhanced to provide a definition that is clear to anyone accessing the data resource directory. Anyone accessing a definition that considers it unclear should seek an enhanced definition through the unit responsible for maintenance of the data resource directory. These enhancements provide better definitions and are part of the value added and data sharing concepts of data resource management.

People must have ready access to a data resource directory. Sharing the data in an enterprise means sharing the metadata in an enterprise. Everyone in the enterprise must have the capability to inquire into the data resource directory to obtain metadata for their use. Limiting inquiry into the data resource directory limits the use of the metadata which has the same result as limiting access to any other data in the enterprise.

> The data resource directory must be readily accessible to anyone in the enterprise needing that data.

Most people have the perception that any metadata in a data resource directory are good data and they are very willing to accept that metadata, particularly if it is readily available. If the metadata are readily available but of low integrity, the result is widespread use of that metadata which could be disastrous. Therefore, a data resource directory must be properly designed, acquired or constructed, populated, and maintained to be useful. The entry of metadata into the data resource directory must be controlled the same as the entry of any other data into the enterprise's data resource. The metadata are part of the enterprises data resource and have data integrity rules the same as any other data in the data resource.

Development of a data resource directory is no different than development of any other information system. It should be modeled, designed, constructed, and implemented the same as any other information system. The logical model can be used to either acquire a data resource directory that is commercially available or to develop one in-house. It is a very poor practice to acquire a commercial data resource directory and begin dumping data into that directory without any prior planning or design, or any mechanism for keeping the data current. The result is the same as conventional documentation, or worse.

> A data resource directory is designed and developed the same as any other application and database.

A data resource directory can be passive in the sense that it is not linked or directly connected with the path to the data in a database management system. A **passive data resource directory** can not be used to directly support the data, such as enforcing data integrity. A passive data resource directory stores metadata about data in the enterprise's data resource, but it can not initiate action or take action on data in the database. It can take action on the metadata it contains, such as editing, formatting, and so on, but not on data in the database. It is passive in the sense that the metadata are stored in the directory and that directory can be queried for that metadata.

An **active data resource directory** is directly connected with the path to data in the database. It can be used to directly support data by enforcing data integrity rules, data names, data formats, and so forth. The power of active data resource directories increases with the capabilities they have for directly supporting data in a database management system. An active data resource directory can take action on data being entered into or stored in the database depending on the data integrity rules it contains. Most active database management systems have some form of an active data resource directory integrated with them. As active data resource directories and active database management systems become more prominent, more metadata will be placed in these systems.

A data resource directory is considered a CASE tool, or at least a tool that directly supports CASE tools. The use of any CASE tool without a good supporting data resource directory does not make full effective use of those tools. The metadata must be reentered into the data resource directory which reduces productivity and increases the chance for error or other discrepancy. Therefore, a good data resource directory must be integrated with any CASE tools that are used for developing the enterprise's data resource.

As commercial database management systems incorporate more powerful data resource directories, many of the data support functions, such as enforcing data integrity rules, can be placed in the database management system. As CASE tools evolve and become more powerful, and become integrated with data resource directories, the processes of design, construction, and operation will become more integrated. The result will be faster and more productive development of the data resource and information systems.

> Active data resource directories should be integrated with CASE tools and database management systems.

In a decentralized environment it is often desirable and necessary to have a decentralized data resource directory. Decentralizing a data resource directory is no different than decentralizing any other data, since a data resource directory is part of the data resource for an enterprise. The same principles and rules for decentralizing data apply to decentralizing a data resource directory. The metadata can be stored in different commercial data resource directories the same as data are stored in different database management systems.

> Data resource directories may be decentralized the same as any other part of the data resource.

A data resource directory can be used to store information about business activities and business entities in the enterprise. The structure of business activities and the organizational structure of business units in the enterprise are easily be stored in a data resource directory. The relationships between business units, business activities, data, and information systems are also easily stored. By storing information about the business use of the data, a data resource directory can directly support the four-schema architecture concept. This approach provides complete documentation about the infrastructure of an enterprise that pertains to the use of data to support that enterprise.

SUMMARY

The data resource model must be completely documented to provide support for the design, development, and use of that data resource to support the enterprise. Documenting the data resource requires establishment of a data resource directory which either contains the documentation or points to where the documentation is stored. Documentation contained in the data resource directory is stored as members that represent the data units defined on the data name abbreviations. The following check lists provide criteria for abbreviating data units names, for defining members in a data resource directory, and for managing the data resource directory.

The techniques for abbreviating data names are summarized in the guidelines listed below.

Data name abbreviations should result in substantial reductions yet retain as much meaning as possible.

One technique for abbreviating data subject names should be selected as standard for the enterprise.

Standard words should be defined for data subject names.

Common data name abbreviations should be used whenever possible.

All manifestations of a root word should be abbreviated when an abbreviation is required.

The same abbreviation should not be used for all manifestations of a root word.

Mandatory abbreviations should be defined for common words.

Fixed abbreviations should be defined for words that can not be readily abbreviated.

The sequence of optional abbreviations is from left to right until a length restriction is met.

If a length restriction can not be met a new name should be selected.

Data values names are abbreviated the same as data characteristic names.

Abstract data units above data occurrences are abbreviated the same as data subjects.

Abstract data units below data occurrences are abbreviated the same as data characteristics.

Multiple abbreviation decisions must be made by each enterprise.

The techniques for defining members in the data resource directory are summarized in the guidelines listed below.

Each single subject data entity is defined as a separate member.

Each multiple, complex, and partial subject data entity is defined as a separate member and referenced to the single subject member.

Each data relation is defined within each data entity involved in that relation.

Each single characteristic data attribute is defined as a separate member.

Each alias of a data attribute is defined as a separate member and referenced to the primary member.

Each variation of a data characteristic is defined as a separate member and referenced to the primary member.

Each characteristic of a multiple characteristic attribute is defined as a separate member and referenced to the primary member.

Each characteristic of a variable characteristic attribute is defined as a separate member and referenced to the primary member.

Each characteristic of a complex characteristic attribute is defined as a separate member and referenced to the primary member.

Each data attribute of a mutually exclusive characteristic is defined as a separate member and referenced to the primary member.

Data values are not generally defined in the data resource directory.

Each abstract data unit is defined as a separate member.

A data unit name thesaurus is defined for data subject references, data characteristic references, and standard words.

Primary keys may be documented with a data subject or as separate members.

Each secondary key is defined as a separate member.

Each data view is defined as a separate member.

Data integrity rules are placed where they can enforce the integrity of all data entering the database.

Each data file and data record is defined as a separate member.

Data items are indicated by a reference between data attributes and data records.

Data accesses are indicated by a reference between secondary keys and data records.

Physical data views are indicated by a reference to a data record.

Decentralized data are indicated by the data file containing the data.

The criteria for developing a useful data resource directory are summarized in the guidelines listed below.

Members should be defined as soon as they are identified.

Standard words are used to indicate the status and validity of the member.

Obsolete members are left in the data resource directory for reference.

Definitions of each member must be complete and comprehensive.

The data resource directory must be readily available to everyone in the enterprise.

A data resource directory is developed like any other information system.

Active data resource directories should be integrated with CASE tools and database management systems.

Data resource directories are decentralized the same as any other data.

STUDY QUESTIONS

The following questions are provided for a review of data name abbreviation and data resource documentation and to stimulate thought about documenting the enterprise's data resource.

1. Why are data names abbreviated?
2. What is the procedure for abbreviating data subject names?

3. What are the alternatives for abbreviating data subject names?
4. What is the procedure for abbreviating data characteristic names?
5. How do standard words help data name abbreviation?
6. Why are mandatory word abbreviations identified?
7. Why are all manifestations of a root word abbreviated?
8. How should an enterprise handle multiple data name length restrictions?
9. How are abstract data unit names abbreviated?
10. What can be done when a data characteristic name is still too long after abbreviation?
11. Why has good data resource documentation been a problem?
12. What is a data resource directory?
13. Why is a data resource directory necessary?
14. How can a data resource directory provide good documentation?
15. Why should members be defined in the directory as soon as they are identified?
16. What should be contained in a good data resource directory?
17. How are nonsingle subject data entities defined.
18. How are nonsingle characteristic data attributes defined.
19. How are decentralized data resource directories managed?
20. How are data relations defined in a data resource directory?
21. How are alias names defined in a data resource directory?
22. How are data keys defined in a data resource directory?
23. How are physical data units defined in a data resource directory?
24. What is the purpose of a data unit name thesaurus?
25. How are data integrity rules documented?

Data Availability

> The availability of data to support the business activities of an enterprise is the ultimate goal of the data resource.

Data availability is the primary objective of developing a good subject data resource. Data availability means getting the right data, to the right people, in the right place, at the right time, in the right form, at the right cost, so they can make the right decisions and take the right actions. If there was no need for data there would be no need for design of a data resource and development of databases to maintain data. However, most enterprises today have a critical need for high quality data and that data must be properly structured, complete and accurate, easily interpretable, and readily available for the enterprise to be responsive to the business environment.

However, there are several problems that prevent many enterprises from achieving this objective. Many people are not aware of data that exist in the database and can not use those data. Even when people are aware that data exist, it is difficult to interpret data and determine which data they need or where they are located. When they do determine what data are needed, it is often difficult to determine where data are stored and how to access data. This situation is further confused by unknown data integrity and many existences of redundant data.

Design of an enterprise's data resource includes designing for data availability. The data resource needs to be properly structured, described, and documented, and data need to have high integrity. These objectives are met with the data architecture design techniques explained in previous chapters and provide a foundation for data that are easily identified and interpreted. Data must then be readily available to those in the enterprise who need data to perform their business activities.

Data availability is the third tier of the data resource and contains components for data access, data privacy, data security, and data use. Data privacy includes safeguards for assuring the privacy and confidentiality of the data. Data security includes protection of data from unauthorized access, alteration, or destruction, and adequate backup and recovery procedures. Data use includes proper and ethical use of data. These three components are very important to the availability of data and must be properly managed by the enterprise. However, the techniques for managing these three components are beyond the scope of this book.

This chapter explains the techniques for assuring that data are readily accessible by those in the enterprise who need data to perform their business activities. Techniques for capturing data as early as possible and as near the source as possible are explained. Techniques for decentralizing data and maintaining the integrity of those decentralized data are also explained. Techniques for determining what data are needed and the best way to access those data are presented. These techniques allow the data resource to support the changing data needs of an enterprise in a decentralized business environment.

DEFINITIONS

Data access is often overlooked when a enterprise's data resource is designed. The rapid emergence of decentralized data and the terms surrounding management of decentralized data are often confusing. Techniques for capturing, storing, moving, and accessing data in both central and decentralized environments and maintaining the integrity of decentralized data are not well understood by many people. These situations result in poor and improper use of an otherwise well-designed data resource. A definition of standard terms for data access provides a base for describing access to the enterprise's data resource.

Redundant Data

Data redundancy is a term that is frequently used, often misused, and generally misunderstood. Statements like *redundant data are bad, the relational model eliminates all redundant data, all redundant data must be eliminated to have a good database*, and *redundant data are mandatory for operational efficiency* are often heard. To resolve this confusion and place data redundancy in the proper perspective the true meaning of data redundancy needs to be defined.

There are two categories of redundant data. The first category includes superfluous or needless repetition of data that exceeds what is normal or necessary and can be eliminated without loss. The second category includes duplicates or backups that are necessary to prevent failure or to recover from failure, and redundant data that are necessary because of location or efficiency. The first category is unnecessary redundant data that must be eliminated to have a well-structured data resource. The second category is necessary redundant data that must be properly documented and maintained to have a well-structured data resource.

> Unnecessary redundant data must be eliminated and necessary redundant data must be properly documented and maintained to have a well-structured data resource.

Data redundancy means identical data values for the same existence of a data entity for the same instance of time. For example, a customer's current phone number represents a data value for a data occurrence for an instance of time. If that phone number is stored with each order for that customer, redundant data values are created for the same customer for the same instance of time. These redundant data values are unnecessary and should be removed. However, backup of the customer file will create redundant values for the phone number in both the live file and the backup file. These redundant data values are necessary and should be properly maintained.

> Redundant data are the same data values for the same existence of a data entity for the same instance of time.

Data values and data attributes are often confused when data redundancy is defined. For example, *Employee Name* in *Employee* and *Employee Name* in *Employee History* are identical data attributes. However, they do not constitute redundant data because any single employee is either currently employed and appears in *Employee* or is no longer employed and appears in *Employee History*. The same data values for the same existence of a data entity do not appear in both *Employee* and *Employee History*. Therefore, identical data attribute names do not necessarily mean redundant data values.

Explicit redundant data are necessary redundant data that are obvious because they are shown explicitly in data attributes. For example, data needed for navigation are necessary redundant data that are shown explicitly. The data attributes in a foreign key contain data values identical to the data attributes in the primary key of a parent data entity. These identical values must be maintained to provide navigation between parent and subordinate data entities.

Backup data are explicit redundant data that must be maintained by each enterprise to provide recovery from disasters or other destruction or alteration of data. Generally, backups have been handled very well on mainframes and backbone production applications, but have been handled very poorly on minis and micros. Since data on minis and micros are part of the enterprise's data resource, more emphasis needs to be placed on backup of critical data on minis and micros to prevent loss of data and assure continued operation.

Time relational data may contain explicit redundant data. Time slices of data are maintained for proactive and retroactive updating, online audit trails, and navigation based on time. The most efficient way to manage time relational data, in the absence of time relational database management systems, is to store redundant data for each time slice.

Denormalization of partial key dependency data (second normal form) creates explicit redundant data. In extreme cases of operational efficiency this form of denormalization is allowed and represents necessary redundant data. However, the appropriate procedures must be implemented to maintain all existences of that redundant data when updates are made to the database.

Concatenated keys that are defined when a database management system can not handle the number of data attributes in a physical key represent explicit redundant data. When a concatenated key is formed the contributing data attributes are also maintained, which results in necessary redundant data. The values of these redundant data must be maintained to provide proper navigation.

Implicit redundant data are necessary redundant data that are not obvious because the redundancy is contained within other data attributes. For example, derived data represent implicit redundant data when their contributors are also stored on the database. The data values are contained in the contributing data attributes and those same values are contained implicitly in the derived data attributes. Derived data must be properly documented and properly maintained when their contributors change.

Necessary redundant data, whether explicit or implicit, may be active or static. **Active redundant data** are maintained to represent current accurate data. For example, the necessary redundant data in data keys and denormalization of second normal form data represent active redundant data because any change in value must be made to all existences of that redundant data. **Static redundant data** are not maintained in a current accurate state. For example, backup files are static redundant data because changes to their values are not made after they are created. Historical data are static and may be modified or altered for alternative analysis of business opportunities.

All existences of active redundant data must be known, documented, and maintained in a complete and accurate state.

Decentralized data for operational efficiency is becoming common and may represent necessary redundant data if the same data values for the same existence of a data entity for the same instance of time are stored in two or more data repositories. Decentralized data may be explicit or implicit and may be active or static.

Data Replication and Duplication

Data replication is the process of capturing, editing, and storing the same data values for the same existence of a data entity for the same instance of time two or more times. Data replication is time consuming and expensive and in most cases is totally unnecessary. In addition to being more expensive and time consuming, data replication can lead to conflicting versions of redundant data and different levels of data integrity.

Data duplication is the process of duplicating data that already exist in an enterprise's database. Once data have been captured, edited, and stored in the database they can be easily copied from one location to another. Since data pass through one set of data integrity rules, the duplicated versions have the same level of integrity. Data duplication is less expensive and more accurate and should be used when necessary redundant data are required.

> Redundant data should be duplicated from existing data not replicated through repeated capture, editing, and storage.

Database Transparency

Data independence represents the independence between the structure of the data resource and the structure of business activities using that data resource. Access to data by business applications is performed with data views. Each business application uses only the data it needs from the data resource and may not be aware of all data that are contained in the data resource. When a database management system is used to maintain the data resource, the business application may not even know where data are stored or how they are accessed. This independence allows the structure of either the business application or the data to change with minimum, if any, impact on the structure of the other.

However, there is another level of data independence emerging with decentralized data. Data may exist anywhere in a network and can be presented to a business application without that application knowing where data are stored. This **transparent database** concept allows the data in a network to be moved around the network for optimum efficiency without impacting business applications. The concept is not unlike data being moved around the files in a database management system for optimum efficiency without impacting applications.

> Database transparency allows data to be decentralized through a network and still remain readily available to applications.

Database transparency allows data to be obtained from more than one location to meet application needs. For example, data for employees in the eastern region are stored on one database and data for employees in the western region are stored on another database and these databases are connected with a communication network. An application needing data about eastern employees would obtain that data from the eastern database. An application needing data about all employees would obtain that data from both databases. The application need not know where data are located, but only what data are needed and that data are provided by the communications network through a file server or a database server.

Data Volatility

Data volatility represents how frequently data values change. If data values change frequently, they are highly volatile and must be captured and stored more frequently to be accurate. If data values do not change very frequently, they have low volatility and do not need to be captured and stored as frequently. For example, data used to monitor a patient during heart surgery is highly volatile and needs to be captured frequently to accurately represent the patient's status. A person's name is less volatile and needs to be captured less frequently. The volatility of each data attribute must be determined and documented in the data resource directory and proper updating procedures must be designed to maintain data integrity.

> Data volatility and the need for current data govern the update frequency for data.

Data volatility is related to the instance of data. The data instance pertains to the time frame for which the data are valid and data volatility pertains to the length of time the data are valid. In the example above, the patient's condition changes every few seconds. The volatility is high and the instance represents a few seconds. However, a person's name changes infrequently and often never changes. The volatility is low and the data instance is much longer.

Data volatility is also related to data redundancy. If there are many existences of active redundant data and the data are highly volatile, there is considerable maintenance to be performed to keep the data current and correct. If data are less volatile, there is less maintenance to be performed to keep the data current and correct. Therefore, data volatility must be considered when redundant data are created. Highly volatile data should have fewer existences of redundant data.

> Highly volatile data should not be considered for creating redundant data.

Data Repositories

A **data repository** is the specific location where data are stored and is designated by a unique data repository name. A **primary data repository** is the official enterprise repository for data and contains a full set of data. The primary data repository may, but does not always, contain the most recent data and is not necessarily located on the mainframe. A **secondary data repository** is any data storage other than the primary repository and may include subsets of data contained in the primary data repository. The common perception is that primary data must reside on the mainframe and secondary data must reside on departmental minicomputers or personal computers. This perception is not true and has caused considerable difficulty with determining where the official set of data is located.

> Primary and secondary data repositories pertain to whether they contain full sets or partial sets of data.

An **initial data repository** is a data repository where data are stored when they first enter the database. A **subsequent data repository** is any data repository where data are stored after their initial entry into the database. An initial data repository may be a primary or a secondary data repository and a subsequent data repository may be a primary or a secondary data repository. The initial entry of data into the database and subsequent duplication of redundant data in the database have no relation to primary or secondary data repositories.

> Initial and subsequent data repositories pertain to how data enter the database and are duplicated within the database.

An initial data repository contains data that are as close to reality as possible. Subsequent data repositories contain data that are farther from reality. The closeness to reality for initial data repositories depends on the frequency of data capture and the volatility of data. The closeness to reality for subsequent data repositories depends on the frequency for duplicating redundant data. If the update frequency is high and data volatility is low, data will be closer to reality than if the update frequency is low and data volatility is high. The frequency of data capture and redundant data duplication must be based on both the volatility of the data and the needs of the enterprise.

> The frequency of data capture and duplication is determined by the volatility of the data and the needs of the enterprise.

All data in the database should be maintained in the highest state of data integrity. Data that enter the initial data repository must pass through a comprehensive set of data integrity rules. Data that fail those rules may be placed on the database for correction, but must not be propagated through the database. Data that pass the data integrity rules may be duplicated as necessary to maintain redundant data.

A data control diagram can be used to identify major data flows and the use of initial and subsequent data repositories for duplicating redundant data. The initial capture and storage of data can be identified and the frequency of data capture and maintenance of redundant data can be defined based on the needs of the enterprise.

Loading Data Repositories

Downloaded data are data moved from a primary data repository to a secondary data repository. Entire data files, selected data occurrences, or selected data attributes may be downloaded. Downloaded data are not necessarily moved from the mainframe to a departmental computer or a personal computer. Data can be downloaded from a personal computer to the mainframe or from a departmental minicomputer to a mainframe.

Uploaded data are data moved from a secondary data repository to the primary data repository. Like downloaded data, entire data files, selected data occurrences, or selected data attributes may be uploaded. Although the data integrity for all data in an enterprise's database must be maintained in a consistent manner, errors can occur in the database. To prevent propagation of these errors any uploaded data must pass through the data integrity rules before entering the primary data repository. This procedure assures that all data in primary data repositories have the highest integrity possible.

> Uploaded data must pass through the data integrity rules to assure high quality data in primary data repositories.

Crossloaded data are data moved from one secondary data repository to another secondary data repository. Like downloaded data, entire data files, selected data occurrences, or selected data attributes may be crossloaded. Generally, crossloaded data are not passed through data integrity rules, although this may be done if there is uncertainty about integrity of the data.

DECENTRALIZED DATA

Decentralized means the dispersion or distribution of data processes and data storage from the central office. Processing can be performed in two or more locations and data can be stored in two or more locations. Although decentralized processes are important, only decentralized data will be discussed here.

Decentralized data refer to data that exist in two or more data repositories in different locations. Decentralized data are becoming common in many enterprises, particularly with the proliferation of smaller computers and communication networks. Conventional database design has not included design of decentralized data, particularly data stored on departmental and personal computers. However, with the distinction between mainframe computers, midframe computers, minicomputers, and personal computers becoming less evident and with the increase in quantity and capacity of personal computers, it is important to include all decentralized data in design of an enterprise's data resource.

Decentralized data offer an advantage by allowing quicker and less costly access to data for direct support to business activities. However, there is a disadvantage because decentralized data may not be properly designed or maintained and may not directly support business activities. Orphan databases could be developed, unnecessary redundant data could be stored, and data quality could be lowered. These problems can be resolved by including decentralized data in design of the enterprise's data resource.

> Decentralized data must be included in design of the enterprise's data resource.

Managed decentralization emphasizes proper management of decentralized data. It includes incorporating modeling and design procedures for decentralized data into design of the enterprise's data resource, identifying major data flows and the initial and subsequent data repositories, identifying primary and secondary data repositories, maintaining data integrity in all data repositories, defining the volatility and instance for each data attribute, defining the frequency of data capture and maintenance for each data attribute, and assuring readily available data to support business activities.

Data decentralization is an important issue in many enterprises. Data decentralization can not be stopped because there will be an impact on performance of business activities and productivity. However, rampant fragmentation of decentralized data can not be allowed because it leads to deterioration of the data resource. Decentralization of data must be properly managed to provide a structurally stable data resource that meets the business needs of the enterprise.

Decentralized data may be distributed or dispersed. **Distributed data** refers to data that are placed in two or more data repositories, at least one of which is a primary data repository containing a full set of data. Secondary data repositories could contain a subset of data entities, a subset of data occurrences in a data entity, a subset of data attributes for each data occurrence, or a subset of data attributes for a subset of data occurrences.

Distributed data have at least one primary data repository.

Dispersed data refers to data that are placed in two or more data repositories and none of those data repositories contains a full set of data. Each secondary data repository contains a subset of data and the full set can only be obtained by combining two or more subsets of data. Dispersed data exist in secondary data repositories and there is no primary data repository.

Dispersed data have no primary data repository.

Designing Decentralized Data

Decentralized data are designed and documented the same as centralized data using the techniques described earlier. Data resource models show the structure of the decentralized data and system architecture models show the method of maintaining decentralized data. The data resource directory shows all data in the enterprise, including decentralized data.

Modeling decentralized data. Decentralized data are modeled using the same tools and techniques used for modeling centralized data. A data resource model is developed for each location showing all data contained at that location. When data entities and data attributes appear on the data resource model, it means those data are available at that location. If the data entities and data attributes do not appear on the data resource model it means they are not available at that location.

> A data resource model is prepared for each decentralized data repository.

The only distinction made on decentralized data resource models is the existence of data occurrences in decentralized data repositories. This distinction is made by using the data occurrence group name in the data resource model rather than the data entity name. For example, the data resource model for a centralized database would include a data entity for *Employee*, indicating that all employee occurrences are available. A decentralized database may have two repositories, one for the eastern region employees and one for the western region employees. The data occurrence groups for the employees in these two regions would be *Eastern Employees* and *Western Employees* and these names would appear on the respective data resource models. These data occurrence groups must be properly defined in the data resource directory to avoid any confusion.

Combination of decentralized data resource models provides a total data resource model for the enterprise. If contributing data resource models have data occurrence group names, those names should be converted to data entity names to assure that all data attributes for each data entity are listed together. This combined model helps determine proper names and definitions for each data attribute in the enterprise.

> Models of existing distributed data are combined to form a total enterprise model.

The physical data resource models for decentralized data may be different if those data repositories are in different operating environments. The logical data resource model is universal for the enterprise and is independent of any operating environment. When the operating environment has been defined, the logical model is denormalized for each physical operating environment. It is desirable to keep the physical data resource models as close as possible, particularly when data are being transferred between data repositories. However, similarity of physical data resource models should not be the objective to the detriment of optimal processing in a particular operating environment. The balance between similarity of physical data resource models in a decentralized environment and optimum performance in any particular operating environment is up to the individual enterprise.

> Models for different physical environments are developed by different denormalizations of the same logical model.

Once the concept of developing data resource models for decentralized data is understood, those models can be used to define the enterprise's logical data resource and both logical and physical decentralized data. If an enterprise is planning to decentralize their data, the data resource models can be used to analyze various alternatives for data decentralization. If data are already decentralized, the data resource models can be used to identify those data and to develop an enterprise data resource model.

Maintaining decentralized data. Decentralized data can be maintained in a variety of ways depending on the particular environment. The first method is to update the initial data repository as the data are obtained by the enterprise and then update the subsequent data repository on a regular schedule, as shown in Figure 14.1. The primary update process edits the data and updates the initial data repository. The update process extracts data that have been added or changed in the initial repository since the last secondary update and updates the subsequent data repository accordingly. The timing of the two update processes is different and the data instances in the two data repositories could be different depending on update frequency and data volatility.

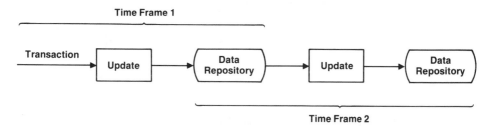

Figure 14.1 Simple update of initial and subsequent data repositories.

The example in Figure 14.1 requires indicators in the initial data repository to show which data were changed since the last secondary update. Those indicators are removed or reset when the secondary update is performed. An alternative approach is shown in Figure 14.2. The primary update process edits the data, updates the initial data repository, and places transaction data in a work data repository. The secondary update process takes the transactions off the work data repository and updates the subsequent data repository.

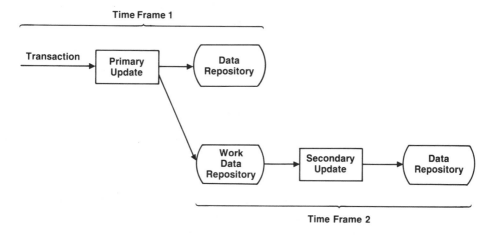

Figure 14.2 Simple update using a work data repository.

Both of these methods could result in data in the initial and the subsequent data repositories representing different instances if the data are highly volatile and the update frequency is low. The initial data repository is continually updated while the subsequent data repository remains static until the secondary update process is run. A third alternative that allows two data repositories to represent the same data instance is shown in Figure 14.3. A single update process edits the data and updates two data repositories at the same time. The only situation that must be processed properly is when one update is successful and the other update fails.

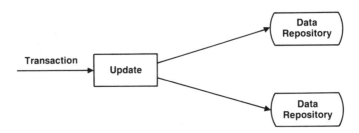

Figure 14.3   Concurrent updating of two data repositories.

There could be two primary update processes concurrently updating two initial data repositories. Two extract processes keep the two data repositories synchronized, as shown in Figure 14.4. Each update process updates their respective data repositories as the transactions are received, such as *Update 1* edits data and updates the *Data 1* repository. The extract processes are run as necessary to update the other data repository, such as *Extract 1* updating the *Data 2* repository. These extracts could be run at the same time or at different times depending on the operating environment, but they must include careful chronology control.

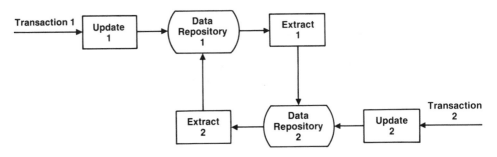

Figure 14.4   Concurrent updating of two initial data repositories.

Two concurrent primary update processes could update both initial and work data repositories. This process has the same problems described for the model shown in Figure 14.1. Indicators need to be placed in each data repository so the extract process can identify which data have changed since the last extract. This situation can be resolved with the update process shown in Figure 14.5. Each update process edits the data and updates its respective data repository and a work data repository. The extract processes are run at a later time to update the other data repository.

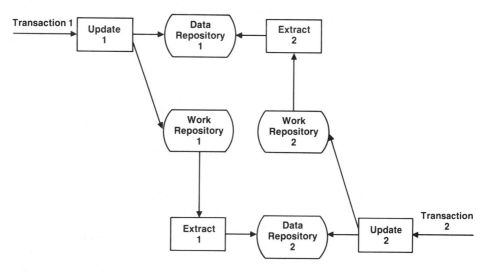

Figure 14.5 Concurrent updating of initial data repositories and work data repositories.

Two concurrent primary update processes could simultaneously update two initial data repositories, as shown in Figure 14.6. This simultaneous updating keeps both data repositories synchronized, but processing needs to be defined for a failure of the second update from any update process. Processing would also need to be defined when there are conflicting updates to the same data.

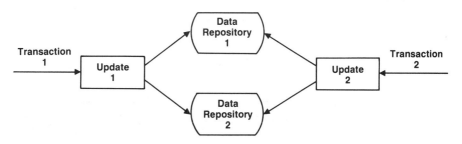

Figure 14.6 Concurrent updating of two initial data repositories.

The update process shown in Figure 14.7 is a variation of the process shown in Figure 14.4. Two additional work data repositories have been added and the extract processes place data in those work data repositories. The update processes edit the data and update the data repositories from both incoming transactions and transactions on the work repositories. This update process could be useful when there is extensive processing that needs to occur during the update process.

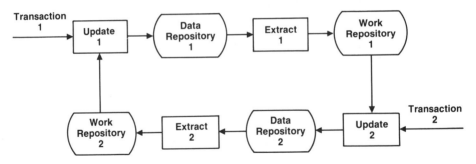

Figure 14.7   Updates to data repositories through one update process.

A variety of other update processes could be developed based on the basic processes described above. Each update process is unique to the operating environment where the update is occurring and the type of processing being performed. These update processes can also be expanded to include more than two initial data repositories and more than two subsequent data repositories. When these basic processes are understood they can be modified and expanded to define any update situation that may occur in an enterprise.

Upload and download data processes.   Uploaded data must pass through the data integrity rules before entering the primary data repository, as shown in Figure 14.8. It is a poor practice to allow a variety of processes to directly update the primary data repository even if those data have passed the data integrity rules. It is better for feeder processes to store transactions on work data repositories and allow the primary update process to take transactions from those work repositories and update the primary data repository.

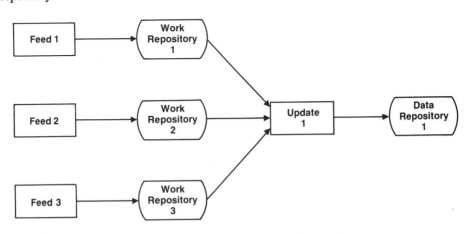

Figure 14.8   Multiple feeds to the primary data repository.

Chapter Fourteen

Data can be downloaded in two basic ways. The download process shown in Figure 14.9 moves data directly from the primary data repository to one or more secondary data repositories. This download process can be developed by the user or by the data processing staff. It is not a critical process, although it must be a correct process, because it does not alter the data in the primary data repository. It is a process to duplicate data to another data repository.

Figure 14.9 Simple data download process.

This download process is acceptable for simple extracts for a single secondary data repository. However, when the extract becomes very detailed, there are multiple secondary data repositories where that data will be placed, or there is a high probability of reextraction of the same data, another alternative should be considered. The download process shown in Figure 14.10 performs the extract and places the data on a work data repository. A variety of users could access this work data repository and extract data they needed for their particular secondary data repositories. This approach saves the extensive extract time that would occur when accessing the primary data repository.

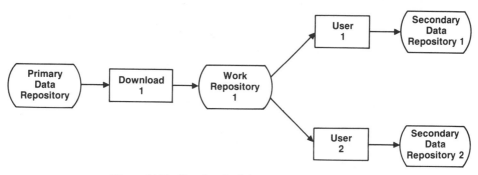

Figure 14.10 Data downloaded to a work data repository.

Download work data repositories can have a generic structure or a specific structure. The generic structure provides a fixed file format and data are placed in those fixed format fields. When this approach is used the names and formats of the data attributes that are placed in those data fields must be passed with the data or predefined to the receiving database or application. The specific data structure matches data that are being downloaded and the names and formats for data attributes do not need to be passed with the downloaded data.

Downloaded data may be either permanent or temporary in the secondary repository. Temporary data present less of an impact than permanent data if the data structure changes. However, users of temporary downloaded data could be impacted if there were structural changes to the primary data repository and they were not aware of the changes. Therefore, any downloaded data, whether permanent or temporary, must be documented in the data resource directory to identify all uses of the data and what download processes need to be changed if changes are made to the data structure.

> All downloaded and crossloaded data must be documented to prevent impacts from structural changes.

Data can be downloaded on a regular cycle to maintain a secondary repository, downloaded for a short period of time and then discarded, downloaded and never maintained, or downloaded and completely altered. Appropriate terms, such as *maintained*, *static*, *altered*, and *temporary* should be used to define these secondary data repositories. Data can be crossloaded similarly to the way data are downloaded. The same processing techniques that are used for downloading data apply to crossloading data. Crossloaded data must also be defined in the data resource directory the same as downloaded data.

Managing decentralized data. A major problem with decentralized data is fragmentation. It is relatively easy to obtain data from any data repository whenever they are needed and it often appears unnecessary to perform any data modeling or documentation. People begin using data and rely heavily on the data to support their business activities. When there is a change to the data structure, particularly when an enterprise is converting its conventional database to a subject data resource, data may not be readily available, which impacts business activities. Therefore, all data in the data resource, whether decentralized or not, must be properly structured, named, defined, and documented in the data resource directory.

> All data, whether decentralized or centralized, must be properly structured, named, defined, and documented.

Another major problem with decentralized data is a lack of consistent data integrity and unknown data integrity. When data are captured and stored indiscriminately without a comprehensive set of data integrity rules that are consistently applied, the level of data integrity is inconsistent and often unknown. In order to have consistently high-integrity data, all data entering the database must pass through comprehensive data integrity rules. If there is any chance for errors occurring within the database, any process moving data to another data repository must pass those data through the data integrity rules.

> All data must be passed through the data integrity rules when there is any doubt about the integrity of the data.

Most enterprises can not operate in isolation from other enterprises. They must interact with a variety of other enterprises in order to perform their business activities. This interaction frequently includes transmission or sharing of data. Since a subject data resource is developed from the enterprise's perspective of the business world and their analysis of behavioral entities, that data resource can be structured differently from one enterprise to another. These different structures frequently cause problems exchanging data between enterprises.

The best approach is to develop a subject data resource containing single units of data that are properly named and well defined. The movement of data between enterprises consists of identifying aliases for each single data unit and exchanging those data units. If an outside enterprise requires multiple unit data, the appropriate single units may be combined to meet the needs of that other enterprise. Frequently an enterprise is in the position where several outside enterprises want different combinations of multiple unit data. If an enterprise has a database of single data units, those units can be combined in whatever way is necessary to meet the requirements of the outside enterprise.

> Maintaining single units of well-described data allows an enterprise to exchange data with other enterprises with minimum problems.

This same approach can be followed for distributed databases within a large enterprise. Even though these distributed databases may be structured differently, if the structure consists of single units of properly named and well-defined data those data can be easily moved from one database to another. It is the different combinations of multiple units of data and the lack of proper names and comprehensive definitions that cause problems moving data from one database to another and from one enterprise to another.

DATA ACCESS

Data access is the process of entering the database, navigating between data entities in the database, and storing or retrieving data. Data access with conventional applications and application files was relatively easy. Data access in a centralized database using a database management system is easier than conventional applications because data views represent only data needed by an application and the database management system performs file maintenance tasks. However, the database must be properly designed and maintained to facilitate use of shared data. Data access in a decentralized environment can be easier than in a centralized environment, but the management and maintenance of decentralized data becomes more difficult than in a centralized environment.

> As data access becomes easier, the task of designing and maintaining a stable data resource becomes more difficult.

Data Interpretability

Data interpretability is important for proper use of the database. Many people in an enterprise are aware that data they need exist somewhere in the database but it is often difficult for them to find and interpret that data. In many cases they find the data they think they need, access that data and perform their processing, only to find out the data were not what they had originally thought.

Data interpretability can be enhanced by providing a good data resource directory of all data in the enterprise. Data interpretability can also be enhanced with a good overview of the data resource. An overview can be provided with entity-relationship diagrams and entity-type hierarchies that show the basic structure of the data resource. A definition of each data entity, a listing of data attributes in each data entity, and data keys that are available enhance the overview. The overview should provide a high-level view of the data resource, not replace a good data resource directory. People can refer to this overview and then use the data resource directory to obtain detail information about the portion of the data resource that interests them.

> An index to the enterprise's data resource increases interpretability and access to data.

A well-structured subject data resource containing single units of well-described data that have high integrity enhances data interpretability. Users have a deep understanding of their business activities and the data needed to support those activities. Involving users in the retrodocumentation of existing databases and design of a subject data resource is one of the best opportunities for enhancing data interpretability. Appropriate training about the concepts of a subject data resource, use of a data resource directory, and proper use of the data resource also increase data interpretability.

Data interpretability can be enhanced with proper use of accept and reject logic, particularly for ad hoc applications. When there are many data values that are selected and only a few of those values are not desired, there is a tendency to reject those data values. This process works as long as there are no new data values added to the database that should not be included. If new data values are added and they should be excluded from the selection, there will be an error. This situation is not obvious because rejection criteria are usually listed with the data which tells nothing about the data actually selected.

A better approach is to accept all data that are desired to assure that the data values specified are selected. Any change in the data values that are desired may result in a change of the selection criteria, but it is easy to identify changes that need to be made by reviewing the selection criteria. However, both accept and reject logic are acceptable and training on proper use of accept and reject logic will prevent data interpretation problems.

Data Access Analysis

When conventional applications were closely connected to their application data files, there was little concern over alternate routes to access data. Data needed by an application were stored in the applications data files and those data files were directly accessed by an application. However, with development of a subject data resource and use of database management systems there can be several alternative routes for accessing data. The route that should be used is the one that accesses the database with the least use of resources or the one that provides the quickest response.

When access is made to only one data entity there are no alternatives for making that access. However, when access is made to two or more data entities there could be several possible routes for accessing those data entities. A **data access route** is a series of access paths along data relations between data entities that are followed to access data. Generally, users have a good idea of the access paths to obtain data because they know their data. Database analysts know the database, the database management system, the operating environment, and how to calculate resources used for each alternative. A team consisting of database analysts and users can identify the alternative routes and select the best route.

> A team of database analysts and users can identify the best access route.

Data access diagram.   The alternative data access routes can be analyzed with a **data access diagram** to determine which access route is the best. A data access diagram is developed much like a Program Evaluation and Review Technique (PERT) chart where each task represents access to one data entity and a series of connected tasks represent a data access route. All alternative data access routes are placed on the diagram and the resources for each route are determined. The data access route that uses the least resources or provides the quickest response is the best alternative.

> Data access routes are used to analyze alternatives for accessing the database.

For example, students that are attending school can live in housing provided by the school or they can live in private housing. Housing provided by the school can be either private residences, apartments, or residence halls, all of which are considered facilities by the school. Students are assigned to school housing by a residence contract which specifies the type of housing. The structure of students, facilities, and residence contracts is shown in Figure 14.11. Students are identified by a *Student ID Number*, facilities are identified by a *Facility Number*, and residence contracts are identified by a *Student ID Number*, a *Facility Number*, and an *Effective Date*.

If the number of foreign students that are living in residence halls is desired, there are several data access routes that could be used. The first route is to access *Student* to determine the ID number of all foreign students, then access *Residence Contract* using the *Student ID Number* of foreign students to determine which of those foreign students have residence contracts, and then access *Facility* to determine which of those contracts are for residence halls. The second route is to access *Facility* to determine which facilities are

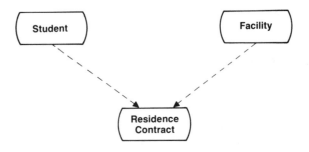

Figure 14.11 Structure of students, facilities, and residence contracts.

residence halls, then access *Residence Contract* to determine the students that have contracts for those residence halls, and then access *Student* to determine which of those students are foreign students. The third route is to determine the foreign students from *Student* and the residence halls from *Facility* and then access *Residence Contract* to determine the foreign students that live in residence halls. These three data access routes are shown in the data access diagram in Figure 14.12.

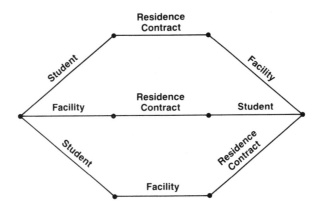

Figure 14.12 Data access diagram for determining foreign students in residence halls.

Once these three data access routes are identified, an analysis can be performed to determine which route is the best. The resources used for each access are placed on the data access diagram. The total resource used for a particular data access route is the total of the individual resources used for each task on that route. For example, if access to *Student* took 10 resource units to identify the foreign students, access to *Resident Contract* took 30 resource units, and access to *Facility* took 5 resource units, the total resources used for that data access route is 45 resource units. If the total resource units for the second data access route was 60 resource units and for the third data access route was 35 resource units then the third data access route would be the best.

> The best access route is usually the one that uses the least resources or provides the quickest response.

Calculation of resource units depends on the particular database management system, how that database management system is used, the particular operating environment, and any billing algorithm. The resource units themselves could be database I/O's, records read, records selected, CPU time, elapsed time, cost, or any of a number of other resources. Generally, the resource units are oriented toward either cost or elapsed time which are the two critical resources in most enterprises.

In many cases several resources are analyzed and the best data access route is selected by evaluating all of the resources. For example, one data access route is faster but more expensive and a second data access route is slower but less expensive. The objective of the enterprise may be to provide fast response to customer inquiries as long as the cost is not excessive. Under these conditions the first data access route would be selected.

Access down the data structure generally produces more data records, although it could produce the same number of records or less depending on the number of subordinate data occurrences. For example, a *Vehicle* has many maintenance records and access to those maintenance records would produce more data records. However, if there were only one maintenance or no maintenance performed on a vehicle there would be fewer records obtained. Access up the data structure generally produces the same number of records or fewer. For example, if an *Employee* had only one *Pay Check* then access up the data structure would produce one record. If an *Employee* had several *Pay Checks* access up the data structure would still produce only one record.

The selection criteria can be either expanded or restricted at each step in a data access route. In the foreign student example all residence contracts were accepted if they pertained to a foreign student. However, the selection could be reduced by specifying that only residence contracts for one year or longer should be considered. Each residence contract for a foreign student would be selected only if the term of the contract was for a year or more. The selection could also be expanded by specifying that both past and present contracts would be included rather than just the current contracts. If the resources for each of these alternatives were desired the data access diagram would be expanded to show these data access routes and the appropriate resources would be determined and analyzed.

This example is relatively simple compared to some data access route alternatives that could be identified. For example, students take courses which are taught by teachers. Since students and courses, and courses and teachers, are both in a many-to-many data relation two resolution data entities are required, as shown in Figure 14.13. Determination of the best data access route to identify students that took specific classes taught by a certain teacher could involve the analysis of several alternative data access routes.

Data access analysis procedure. The procedure to follow for selecting the best data access route is to identify data that are needed from the database. Then the data entities and data relations that are involved in obtaining the result can be identified on an data entity-relationship diagram. Next, the alternative data access routes are identified by reviewing the data entity-relationship diagram. When these data access routes have been

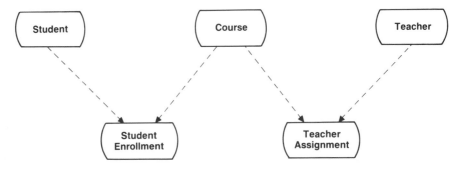

Figure 14.13 Structure of students, courses, and teachers.

identified they can be placed on the data access diagram similar to the one shown in Figure 14.12.

When a data access diagram is prepared and database access is completed the actual statistics should be collected and documented for others to review. This data access documentation helps people identify the best data access routes and bad data access routes that should be avoided. The result is a set of acceptable data access routes and the resources required for each route.

Data access diagrams can also be prepared for data in a decentralized environment. The only difference is the inclusion of the data repository name and more alternative data access routes. The resources that are identified may include the resources to move data through a network to the proper destination. Once this concept is understood, the data access diagrams can be used to determine the best location of data repositories based on resources utilized for known accesses. As statistics of actual use are collected they can be used to adjust the decentralization of data. If transparent databases are available then distributed data can be adjusted with minimal, if any, impact on the user.

SUMMARY

Data availability is the primary objective of a good subject data resource because most enterprises have a critical need for high quality data that is easily interpreted and readily available. Developing a good enterprise data resource, documenting the data in that data resource, decentralizing data when necessary, and providing ready access to data helps make data readily available to anyone in the enterprise. Providing readily available data is what the whole data resource design process is about.

The enterprise's data must be properly designed and documented. The people in the enterprise must be involved in that design, they must be trained on how to properly use the data, and they must be encouraged to actively use the data to support their business activities.

Data access is the key to data availability. Guidelines for assuring that data are readily accessible by people in the enterprise are listed below.

Unnecessary redundant data must be eliminated from the data resource.

All existences of necessary redundant data must be identified and documented.

Necessary redundant data must be properly maintained.

Redundant data should be maintained by data duplication not by replicated data capture, editing, and storage.

Highly volatile data should not be considered for creating redundant data.

Decentralized data should be considered when it offers advantages over centralized data.

Primary and secondary data repositories should be identified and documented.

Initial and subsequent data repositories should be identified by defining major data flows into and through the database.

Frequency of maintenance for redundant data should be determined based on data volatility and the needs of the enterprise.

Data should be passed through data integrity rules anytime there is concern over the integrity of the data.

Decentralized data can be modeled and combined to develop an enterprise data resource model.

Centralized data can be modeled to analyze alternatives for decentralizing data.

All data in the data resource, including decentralized data, must be structured, named, defined, and documented.

Maintaining a subject data resource of single units of data allow ready use of data within an enterprise and ready exchange of data with other enterprises.

Data interpretability is enhanced with a good data resource directory, a good overview of the data resource, user involvement in design of the data resource, and proper training.

A data access diagram of possible access routes is used to select the best alternative for accessing the database.

A team of database analysts and users should determine the best access routes.

STUDY QUESTIONS

The following questions are provided as a review of data availability and to stimulate thought about the purpose of an enterprise data resource and access to that resource.

1. What is data availability and what does it include?
2. What problems are faced by many enterprises in achieving full data availability?
3. What is the difference between data duplication and data replication?
4. How is data redundancy related to data duplication?
5. How is database transparency related to data independence?
6. How is the instance of data related to data volatility?

7. What are the differences between primary and secondary data repositories?
8. What are the differences between initial and subsequent data repositories?
9. What does managed decentralization mean?
10. How do distributed and dispersed data differ?
11. What is the best approach for managing data that are shared between enterprises?
12. How are decentralized data modeled?
13. How does decentralized data modeling differ from centralized data modeling?
14. How is the maintenance of decentralized data modeled?
15. Why is uploading of data of more concern than either downloading or crossloading of data?
16. Why is data interpretability important?
17. How can data interpretability be enhanced?
18. How can data access routes be effectively analyzed to determine the best route for accessing a database?
19. How can data availability in an enterprise be enhanced?
20. Why should users be involved in design of the data resource?

Database Transition

An enterprise must convert to a subject data resource and adjust applications to use subject data without impacting business operations.

A well-designed, fully operational subject data resource designed to support the business activities of an enterprise is an ideal many enterprises would like to achieve. However, there are two problems that must be overcome. The first problem is that most enterprises have a variety of data files structured by the applications they support and those applications expect a certain data structure from those conventional files. To achieve a well-structured subject data resource an enterprise must convert those conventional data files to a subject data resource. However, when conventional files are converted the applications will no longer be able to access the data structures they expect. The second problem is development of new applications that expect subject data, but the data actually exist in conventional files. These new applications should be structured to access subject data, but the conventional data files can not be immediately converted to support these new applications.

To resolve these problems there must be an adjustment to applications to reflect the data structures they expect to have, regardless of the data structure available. Conventional applications must be adjusted to access subject data and new applications must be adjusted to access conventional data. If these adjustments are not made the applications will not be able to process data properly and there could be a large impact on business operations.

The process of converting from a conventional database to a subject data resource has proven difficult for many enterprises. The task of identifying conventional data, determining what those data should be in a subject data resource, designing a subject data resource, and converting data without impacting business operations seems almost insurmountable. Most enterprises can not afford to stop their business operations for an extended time to reorganize their data, nor can they afford to continue with conventional databases. This contradiction leaves most enterprises in a quandary. The need to change to a subject data resource is clear. However, most enterprises are extremely concerned about how to make the change, how to manage their data while the change is being made, and how to keep the business operating during the change.

This chapter presents techniques for converting from a conventional database to a subject data resource with minimal, if any, impact on business operations. It describes techniques for designing a subject data resource, defining data interfaces between the subject data resource and conventional data files, installing data converters on that interface to minimize impact on applications, converting conventional files and applications, and removing the data converters. These techniques are based on the same techniques for developing a subject data resource, but have been enhanced to include the situations encountered when converting a conventional database to a subject data resource. They result in a successful conversion with minimum impact on business operations.

RETRODOCUMENTING CONVENTIONAL DATABASES

To convert a conventional database to a subject data resource the data in the conventional database must be identified, described, and documented. This retrodocumention process produces single units of data that are used to design or enhance the subject data resource. That subject data resource becomes the repository for conventional data as they are converted.

There are many nonsingle data units in most conventional data files and many alias data names for those data units. The retrodocumentation process identifies each data unit in the conventional database and then identifies each single data unit included in those conventional data units. All the techniques presented in earlier chapters are used to retro-document the conventional database and identify single data units for the enterprise's subject data resource.

Data Names

The full data naming taxonomy is used during retrodocumentation. Conventional data files contain many synonymous data units with many alias names. Use of the repository and variation names uniquely identify each data attribute. For example, an employee's birth date is stored in *Training* as *Birth Date* in the format *MMDDYY* and in *Payroll* as *Date Born* in the format *YYYYMMDD*. The repository and variation names makes these data attributes unique. Birth date in *Training* becomes *Training:Employee.Birth Date* and birth date in *Payroll* becomes *Payroll:Employee.Birth Date*.

> The full data naming taxonomy is used to name conventional data.

There are two approaches to naming conventional data. The first approach is to identify the formal data name and use that name with the repository name. This approach provides names like *Payroll:Employee.Name* and *Training:Employee.Name* which have an implied meaning. However, these data names do not represent data names used by applications which causes confusion when referencing conventional applications. The second approach is to keep the existing data name and prefix it with the data repository name. This approach provides names like *Payroll:Name* and *Training:Name Empl* which have less implied meaning but are the actual data names used by conventional applications.

Data names are not used consistently in most conventional applications. The problem described above becomes even more confusing when several applications access *Training* and refer to aliases of employee name as *Employee, Name, Name Empl, Employee Name, Identification, Person*, etc. The best approach is to use the application data name on any data structure pertaining to the application and the formal data name on any data structure of the data file. This procedure allows ready identification of data both for application maintenance and data conversion.

There are many existences of redundant data in conventional data files. Using the example above, the formal data name for an employee's name might be *Employee.Name* and since the data repository is *Employee* the full data name is *Employee:Employee.Name*. The redundant data attributes would be listed with the primary data attribute to assist in maintaining all the redundant data in a consistent manner.

Employe:Employee.Name   Primary
Payroll:Employee.Name
Training:Employee.Name

If redundant data attributes have different formats, these formats are identified with a variation name. For example, if *Employee Name* in *Payroll* were 30 characters, and *Employee Name* in *Training* were 60 characters, the variation names would be listed after the data attributes.

Employe:Employee.Name   Primary
Payroll:Employee.Name,30
Training:Employee.Name,60

This information is used to determine which data attribute will be used to populate *Employee.Name* or whether there should be two data attributes for *Employee.Name Complete* and *Employee.Name Abbreviated*.

Each nonsingle characteristic data characteristic must be identified, formally named, and defined. Multiple characteristic data attributes are shown as a separate set on the data structure. The conventional name becomes the set label and the data characteristic names become the contents of the set. For example, if a data attribute representing the existing type code in *Customer* consists of data characteristics for the customers hair color, ethnic origin, and gender, they would be placed on a data structure as shown in Figure 15.1.

```
               --
                |   Customer.Hair Color
Customer:Type Code <<  Ethnic Origin.Code
                |   Gender.Code
               --
```

Figure 15.1 Multiple characteristic data attribute identification.

Variable characteristic data attributes are shown in a similar manner. However, the conditions are placed on the data structure to indicate when each data characteristic is used. For example, a data attribute represents the date originally contacted for prospective students, the date enrolled for undergraduate students, and the date of undergraduate graduation for graduate students, as shown in Figure 15.2. The condition is placed above the data characteristic name in the set.

```
                  --
                   |   Prospective Student
                   |      Student.Date Initial Contact
                   |
                   |   Undergraduate Student
Student:Date   <<        Student.Date First Enrolled
                   |
                   |   Graduate Student
                   |      Student.Date Graduated
                  --
```

Figure 15.2 Variable characteristic data attribute identification.

Complex characteristic data attributes are shown in a similar manner. The conditions are listed and the individual data characteristics for each condition are listed under that condition. For example, *Customer Code* would be documented as shown in Figure 15.3.

```
                  --
                   |   New Customer
                   |      Customer.Income
                   |      Customer.Interests
                   |      Customer.Buying Potential
                   |
Customer:Code  <<    Customer with Good Credit
                   |      Customer.Credit Limit
                   |      Customer.Payment Rate
                   |
                   |   Customer with Bad Credit
                   |      Customer.Credit Rating
                   |      Customer.Collection Probability
                  --
```

Figure 15.3 Complex characteristic data attribute identification.

Mutually exclusive data attributes are also shown on a data structure using a separate set. However, since many data attributes representing individual data values are combined into one data characteristic, the set label represents the mutually exclusive data attributes and the contents represent the data characteristic. For example, if the values for type of shipment were each defined as data attributes, such as air mail, regular mail, and parcel post, these three mutually exclusive data attributes become the set label and the set contents is the data characteristic for shipment code, as shown in Figure 15.4.

```
Mail:Air Shipment        |
Mail:Regular Shipment <<    Shipment.Code
Mail:Parcel Shipment     |
                          --
```

Figure 15.4 Mutually exclusive data attribute identification.

A temporary data attribute group can be defined for multiple characteristic data attributes. The name of that data attribute group contains the standard words *TMP GRP* to indicate it is a temporary data attribute group and its use should not be propagated. For example, a conventional application uses a *Vehicle Type Code* that represents the vehicle model and engine fuel type. All new applications access the two data characteristics separately. However, conventional applications need to access the multiple characteristic data attribute. Therefore, a data attribute group is defined for *Vehicle Type.Code Tmp Grp* for conventional applications and the data attributes *Vehicle Model.Code* and *Engine Fuel.Code* are defined for new applications.

A temporary data attribute group is difficult to define for an intertwined multiple characteristic data attribute. In this situation both the multiple characteristic data attribute and the corresponding single characteristic data attributes are maintained. The multiple characteristic data attribute name contains the standard word *TMP* indicating that it is a temporary data attribute and its use should not be propagated. For example, *Customer:Type Code* would become *Customer:Type Code Tmp*.

All of these situations must be documented in the data resource directory, as described in the Data Documentation chapter. When any situation changes that change should also be noted in the data resource directory. The data resource directory can be consulted by anyone in the enterprise for the current status of any data attribute, how that data attribute should or should not be used, and identification of corresponding data attributes for the subject data resource.

Data Subjects

Identifying data subjects is the most difficult task of retrodocumentation. Conventional file structures, naming conventions, and use do not readily indicate true data subjects. However, several techniques can be used to identify true data subjects in conventional data files.

> Identifying true data subjects is the most difficult task of retrofit data modeling.

Repeating groups can be identified by conventional data names and definitions. For example, if data items exist for *First Month Enrollment*, *Second Month Enrollment*, and so on, up to *Twelfth Month Enrollment*, there is a strong indication that a repeating group for *Month* exists and a data subject should be defined. A tumbling of data is another good indication of a repeating group. Tumbled data can be identified from applications, from data names, and from data file structures. For example, there are four data items named *Data1*, *Data2*, *Data3*, and *Data4*. At some point the value from *Data1* is discarded and the value from *Data2* is placed in *Data1*, the value from *Data3* is placed in *Data2*, the value from *Data4* is placed in *Data3*, and *Data4* is cleared for use. This tumbling of data indicates a separate data subject that should be defined. Multiple record types can also indicate data subjects.

Data Characteristics

Each conventional data item is reviewed to identify single data characteristics. An awareness of multiple characteristic, variable characteristic, complex characteristic, and mutually exclusive data attributes will help identify single data characteristics. The identification of mutually exclusive data attributes takes extensive knowledge of the data and very perceptive data analysts. Generally, multiple, variable, and compound characteristic data attributes are not difficult to identify with a good description of each data item.

> An awareness of the types of data attributes helps identify data characteristics.

Mutually exclusive data attributes are more difficult because their names mask their commonalty. The best approach to identify mutually exclusive data attributes is to completely define each data item and review those definitions for single characteristics of data. Another indication of mutually exclusive data attributes is a data item with only one possible value. This situation indicates there may be other data items that form a common data characteristic. Mutually exclusive data attributes can also be identified through an applications use of data.

Data Values

Each data attribute that contains coded data values is reviewed to identify, name, and define each data property. An awareness of multiple property data values helps identify these situations. The complete definition of each data property helps identify single property data values and uniquely name those properties. Identifying and defining each data property also helps identify multiple characteristic data attributes. For example, definition of the values for *Customer Type Code* indicate that a value of *1* means a *female*, *Caucasian*, with *blond hair*. It should be immediately obvious that there are three data characteristics.

> An awareness of the types of data values helps identify data properties.

The data domain for each data item is determined by reviewing conventional data to identify all data values that currently exist. Any additional documentation showing what the data domain should contain can also be reviewed.

Data attributes in conventional applications that contain coded data values often contain multiple property data values, and often contain redundant existences of the same data values. The best way to document multiple property data values is to define a table for each data characteristic that contains coded values and document all variations of those data values in that table. The single data properties are listed on the left and the data attributes representing those properties are listed across the top. The body of the table contains the values used by each application.

For example, the fuel-type code for vehicles is shown in Figure 15.5. The single properties of fuel type are *Electric*, *Gasoline*, *Diesel*, and *Propane*. The official data attribute is *Fuel Type.Code* containing the single property values *1* through *4*. Two sources of fuel type code were found in conventional application files. The first contains coded values *A*, *B*, and *C*, with *B* as a multiple property data value representing both *Gasoline* and *Diesel* powered vehicles. The second data attribute contains the values *10*, *26*, and *14* which are single property values, but a value for electric powered vehicles is missing.

Data property	Data attributes		
	Fuel type code	Vehicle: Motor Type	Supply: Engine Fuel Type
Electric		1	A
Gasoline	2	B	10
Diesel	3	B	26
Propane	4	C	14

Figure 15.5   Extended data domain for Fuel -Type Code.

The first two columns represent the data domain for *Fuel-Type Code*. Adding two additional columns for data values in the other data attributes that represent fuel-type code extends the data domain to include all values for fuel-type code. This **extended data domain** can be used to edit conventional data and to convert conventional data to the subject data resource. If additional fuel-type codes are identified, such as steam powered, they can be added to the extended data domain so that it represents all values for all properties of fuel-type code. When all data are converted to a subject data resource and there is no further use for the extended data domain, it can be reduced to a normal data domain for *Fuel-Type Code*.

Data Integrity

Conventional data integrity rules can be identified through conventional applications since most conventional applications perform some type of data edits. If data integrity rules are enforced by active database management systems, those rules should also be reviewed so a total set of existing data integrity rules can be defined.

Most conventional data edits check only for valid data values. A few applications check for valid value relationships between data items. Very little checking is done for structural integrity, maintenance of derived and redundant data, or retention and destruction of data. Data edits in existing applications are very incomplete and inconsistent and are spread throughout many applications. As these separate edit criteria are defined they form the beginning of a comprehensive set of data integrity rules for each data subject.

DATABASE TRANSITION CONCEPTS

Database transition is the process of converting from a conventional database to a subject database without impacting business operations. The term **migration** could have been used, but it indicates a periodic movement from one place to another place and implies a possible return to the original place. Although a database could move from one place to another, it generally stays in the same place and only changes from one form to another form. In addition, the database generally does not change periodically and, hopefully, does not return to the original form. It is converted from an old form to a new form and stays in that new form.

> Database transition is the process of converting conventional data to subject data.

The primary objective of database transition is to achieve a subject database at the earliest date with the least effort and the least impact on data integrity and business operations. This objective can be achieved by defining a subject data resource, documenting data in the conventional database, identifying interfaces between conventional data structures and subject data structures, installing data converters on the interface to convert one data structure to another, adjusting applications to use data converters, converting the conventional database to a subject data resource, and adjusting conventional applications to use subject data. It is a process that can be performed by any enterprise with careful planning and use of the techniques described earlier.

> The objective of database transition is to achieve a subject database without impacting data integrity or business operations.

The real problem with database transition is not with conversion of a conventional database to a subject data resource. That conversion process is a workload that must be carefully planned and scheduled like any other critical project and it is very detailed and time consuming. But it is not a real problem. The real problem is identifying the different data structures in the conventional database, identifying the data interfaces between those different data structures and subject data structures, and converting data between those structures until the database and applications can be converted. The quality of this conversion depends on proper documentation of data structures and data conversions that need to be made between those data structures.

> The real problem with database transition is conversion between conventional data structures and subject data structures while databases and applications are being converted.

The subject data resource is relatively easy to define using the techniques described earlier. The difficulty is defining conventional data. A major retrodocumentation effort must be made to document conventional data and all the applications that use conventional data. It is a very difficult and time consuming process because conventional data are not well-structured or documented and the applications using conventional data are not readily apparent. Once the conventional data structures are documented and all applications using conventional data are identified the data interfaces can be identified.

Understanding database transition begins with the definition of new terms and concepts. Data entities that contain a single data subject are referred to as **subject data entities**. Data entities that do not contain a complete single subject of data are referred to as **conventional data entities**. Applications that expect subject data are referred to as **subject applications** and applications that expect conventional data are referred to as **conventional applications**. Data that are structured by data subject, whether in a data entity or in an application, are referred to as **subject data** or as having a **subject data structure**. Data that are not structured by data subject, whether in a data entity or in an application, are referred to as **conventional data** or as having a **conventional data structure**.

A **data interface** is the boundary between subject data and conventional data. A data interface is designated with a dashed line that crosses data flows between subject data and conventional data on a data flow diagram, as shown in Figure 15.6. In other words, it passes between conventional applications and subject data entities or between subject applications and conventional data entities. It does not pass between conventional applications and conventional data entities or between subject applications and subject data entities because there are no structural differences in the data. A data interface only crosses internal data flows between applications and data entities. It does not cross data flows into or out of an information system.

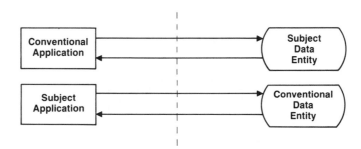

Figure 15.6   Generic data interface designation.

A data interface must connect with itself or run off the edge of the data flow diagram. It can not begin or end within the data flow diagram because it becomes uncertain what interface is being defined. Data interfaces can become very detailed when there are many separate sets of subject and conventional data on the same data flow diagram. However, there is only one data interface between subject data and conventional data. That interface may appear in several locations on the data flow diagram. The distinction between subject and conventional data can also be shown with background patterns or colors on the data flow diagram if dashed lines are not explicit enough.

Both conventional and subject data entities may reside within a database management system or outside a database management system. If they reside within a database management system, the data flow may represent the full record of data or a data view. If they reside outside a database management system the data flow represents a full record of data. If the data flow represents a full record of data then the name is not placed on the data flow. However, if the data flow represents a data view the name of that data view is placed on the data flow.

When a data flow crosses a data interface the data structure needs to be changed, either from subject data to conventional data or from conventional data to subject data. This change is made by a data converter. Its sole purpose is to change one data structure to another data structure so that subject applications can access conventional data and conventional applications can access subject data.

> A data converter converts data structures across a data interface.

When a data converter is placed between a subject application and a conventional data entity one data flow is shown between the data entity and the data converter and one data flow is shown for each data subject between the data converter and the subject application. For example, a conventional *Student* data entity contains data about a student and many addresses for that student. If a subject application needs both *Student* and *Address* data it needs two data flows, one for *Student* and one for *Address*. A data converter is placed between the conventional data entity and the subject application, as shown in Figure 15.7. The data converter takes one data flow from *Student* and provides the application with data flows for *Student* and *Address*.

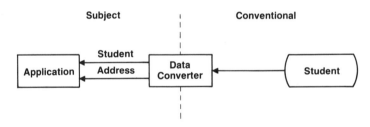

Figure 15.7   Data conversion from a conventional data to a subject application.

If a subject application requires data about one data subject that is contained in two conventional data entities, the data converter accesses both data entities to obtain that data and would provide that data in one data flow to the application. For example, if student data were contained in both *Student* and *Grade* conventional data entities a data converter accesses each of those data entities for *Student* data and provides one set of *Student* data to the application as shown in Figure 15.8. The data flows are labeled *Student* to indicate that student data are being converted.

If a subject application requires *Student* data from both *Grade* and *Student*, and *Address* data from *Student*, the data converter obtains student data from both *Grade* and *Student* and provides one set of student data to the application, as shown in Figure 15.9. It also obtains address data from *Student* and provides it to the application.

The reverse situation is also true. If the subject application needed to store *Student*

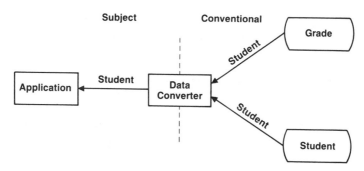

Figure 15.8 Data conversion of one subject from two conventional data entities.

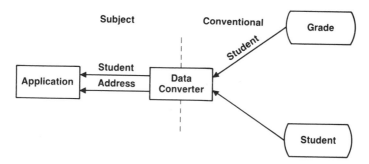

Figure 15.9 Data conversion of two subjects from two conventional data entities.

and *Address* data in the conventional *Grade* and *Student* data entities, there are two data flows from the application to the data converter and one data flow from the data converter to each conventional data entity, as shown in Figure 15.10.

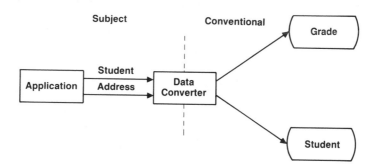

Figure 15.10 Data conversion from a subject application to conventional data entities.

Data converters convert data in only one direction across a data interface. If both of the conditions described in Figures 15.9 and 15.10 existed there would need to be two data converters. One data converter converts the data from data entities to the application and one data converter converts data from the application to data entities.

A data converter can convert data only one direction across a data interface.

The same technique is used to show data flows between conventional applications and subject data entities. For example, if a conventional application expects to have *Student* and *Address* data together, but the data are stored in two subject data entities the data converter accesses those two data entities and provides one set of data to the application, as shown in Figure 15.11.

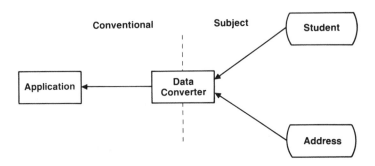

Figure 15.11   Data conversion from subject data entities to a conventional application.

A data interface also exists between conventional data entities and subject data entities. When a conventional database is converted to a subject data resource, data are moved across this interface the same as they are moved across a data interface between data entities and applications. A **database converter** converts the data structures when databases are converted. For example, conventional Student data are converted to two subject data entities for *Student* and *Address*, as shown in Figure 15.12.

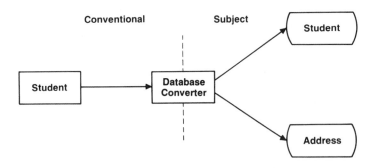

Figure 15.12   Database conversion from a conventional data to subject data.

These techniques are used to define the flow of data either way between conventional or subject applications and conventional or subject data entities. The presence of a data interface and the location of a data converter on that interface indicates that data structures are changed across that interface. The presence of both application and data entity on the same side of a data interface without a data converter indicates the data structures are identical and do not need to be changed.

DATA CONVERTER

A **data converter** is a process located on the data interface that converts data from one data structure to another. It contains instructions to convert a data structure on one side of the data interface to a data structure on the other side of the data interface. A data converter may stand alone as a process, it may be included as a module within the application, or it may be included with the I/O routines for the database management system.

A data converter reduces maintenance on an application during database transition. It provides a buffer between the application and the data and creates a level of stability during database transition that prevents any major impacts to business operations or data integrity. An application is adjusted to access a data converter rather than the database and when transition is complete the application is adjusted back to accessing the database. Any maintenance impact during database transition is made to the data converter, not to the application.

A data converter contains two types of tables that define instructions for conversion of data across a data interface. The **Data Attribute Conversion Table** defines structural conversions between data attributes, including moving data attributes between data entities, converting between single and nonsingle characteristic data attributes, and creating or resolving data redundancy. The Data Attribute Conversion Table is mandatory for each data converter. An optional **Data Value Conversion Table** defines conversions between data values and appears only when there is a conversion of data values.

Data Attribute Conversion Table

The Data Attribute Conversion Table shows how data attributes are converted as they move across the data interface. It has a specific format and specific notations to define the conversion, as shown in Figure 15.13. The data names include the repository name to assure that each data unit is explicitly defined. Source data attributes are shown on the left and target data attributes are shown on the right. The conversion occurs from source data attributes to target data attributes. The conversion shown in this table is from the intertwined

Data attribute conversion table

Source data attribute	Type	Target data attribute	Type	Value	Redundancy
Building:Building Type	I	Facility:Building.Floor Area Code	N	Yes	No
+		Facility:Building UseCode	N		
+		Facility:Building.Material Code	N		

Figure 15.13   Typical data attribute conversion table.

multiple characteristic data attribute *Building Type Code* in the *Building* conventional data entity to three single characteristic data attributes in the *Facility* subject data entity.

A data attribute table shows how data attributes are converted from one data structure to another.

The type of data attribute is shown in the *TYPE* columns for both the source and the target data attributes. The meaning of each data attribute-type code is listed in Figure 15.14. Indication of data value conversion is shown in the *VALUE* column. A *Yes* indicates data value conversion is necessary and a Data Value Conversion Table must be defined. A *No* indicates no data value conversion is necessary and data values are the same on both sides of the data interface. The existence of data redundancy is indicated in the *REDUNDANCY* column. A *No* indicates there is no data redundancy, *Create* indicates redundant data attributes must be created, and *Resolve* indicates data redundancy exists and must be resolved.

```
N    Normal Single Characteristic Attribute
S    Sequential Multiple Characteristic Attribute
I    Intertwined Multiple Characteristic Attribute
V    Variable Characteristic Attribute
C    Complex Characteristic Attribute
E    Mutually Exclusive Attribute
```

Figure 15.14 Data attribute type codes.

The Data Attribute Conversion Table is developed by entering individual sets of data showing the conversion for one data characteristic. A data characteristic is represented by a single data attribute in either the source or the target data attribute column. The corresponding column may have either single or multiple data attributes depending on the type of conversion that is performed. In the example in Figure 15.13 the intertwined multiple characteristic data attribute for *Building Type*, indicated by an *I*, is converted to three normal single characteristic data attributes, indicated by an *N*.

The plus sign (+) indicates the same data attribute is used in the conversion. In the example in Figure 15.15 the plus signs under *Building Type* indicate *Building Type* is used

Data attribute conversion table

Source data attribute	Type	Target data attribute	Type	Value	Redundancy
Building:Building.Type	I	Facility:Building Floor Area Code	N	Yes	No
+		Facility:Building Use Code	N		
+		Facility:Building Material Code	N		
Employee:Ethnic Origin.Code	N	Staff:Type Code	I	Yes	No
Employee:Sex.Code	N	+			
Employee:Employee.Hair Color	N	+			

Figure 15.15 Example of multiple data attribute conversion.

for conversion to the three single characteristic data attributes. The plus signs could be eliminated, but that elimination causes some confusion as to whether the blank represents the same data attribute or a missing data attribute name. Since the data conversion process is extremely detailed and often confusing, the use of a plus sign explicitly indicates the same data attribute is used in the conversion. The plus signs under *Staff Type Code* indicate the three single characteristic data attributes in the source data attribute are combined into the intertwined multiple characteristic attribute *Staff Type Code*.

A minus sign (-) indicates the corresponding data attribute is not converted. Frequently, there are data attributes in the data structure that have no corresponding use on the other side of the data interface. Rather than ignoring these data attributes and creating confusion as to whether they are not used in conversion or whether they were inadvertently omitted from the table, the data attribute is entered into the table and the minus sign is used to explicitly indicate that data attribute is not converted. For example, *Employee Type Code* shown in Figure 15.16 is available to the data converter but is not converted and does not appear on the output.

DATA ATTRIBUTE CONVERSION TABLE

Source data attribute	Type	Target data attribute	Type	Value	Redundancy
Employee:Employee Type.Code	N	-			
		File039:Facility Capacity	N	No	No

Figure 15.16 Example of data attributes not converted.

The minus sign can also be used to indicate that a data attribute is not obtained from this conversion. Although this is not a common practice and leads to some confusion as to where that data attribute is obtained, it is a legitimate notation explicitly showing the data attribute was not obtained from this conversion. *Facility Capacity* shown in Figure 15.16 appears on the output data structure but is not involved in any conversion by this data converter.

Conversion from one single characteristic data attribute to another single characteristic data attribute is shown in Figure 15.17. This conversion indicates the same data values are retained and there is no data redundancy to be created or destroyed. The conversion is simply a change of names and data entities.

DATA ATTRIBUTE CONVERSION TABLE

Source data attribute	Type	Target data attribute	Type	Value	Redundancy
Personnel:Birth Data	N	Employee:Birth Data	N	No	No

Figure 15.17 One-to-one conversion of data attributes.

Conversion from a single characteristic data attribute to a sequential multiple characteristic data attribute is shown in Figure 15.18. The format is the same as the conversion for the intertwined multiple characteristic data attribute in Figure 15.16 with the exception that an *S* in the *TYPE* column for the target data attribute indicates a sequential multiple characteristic data attribute.

DATA ATTRIBUTE CONVERSION TABLE

Source data attribute	Type	Target Data Attribute	Type	Value	Redundancy
Employee:Employee.Hire Date Year	N	Staff:Date Hired	S	Yes	No
Employee:Employee.Hire Date Month	N	+			
Employee:Employee.Hire Date Day	N	+			

Figure 15.18   Converting a sequential multiple characteristic attribute.

Conversion of variable and complex characteristic data attributes are defined in the same format, except that the data attribute type is a *V* for variable characteristic data attribute or *C* for complex characteristic data attribute. During actual conversion of the data, the current status of the data occurrence must be known so the proper single characteristic data attribute could be developed. Each of those statuses must be included in the process logic of the data converter.

Conversion of a mutually exclusive data attribute is shown in Figure 15.19. The type one, two, and three mutually exclusive data attributes for equipment type, indicated by an *E*, are combined into a single characteristic data attribute *Equipment Type Code*, indicated by an *N*.

DATA ATTRIBUTE CONVERSION TABLE

Source data attribute	Type	Target Data Attribute	Type	Value	Redundancy
Equipment:Type-1	E	Equipment:Equipment.Type Code	N	No	No
Equipment:Type-2	E	+			
Equipment:Type-3	E	+			

Figure 15.19   Conversion of mutually exclusive data attributes.

When a data redundancy situation is indicated in the *REDUNDANCY* column the data redundancy must be managed as indicated. Data redundancy usually exists in conventional data entities and resolution of data redundancy occurs when data are converted from conventional data entities to subject data entities. For example, if the conversion were from *Training:Employee.Name* to *Employee.Name* and *Resolve* was indicated then the employees name would be taken from one data occurrence in *Training* and placed in *Employee*. The only problem that could occur is if the employee's name were different between records for the same employee in *Training*. The process logic for this situation should be placed in the data converter.

> Data redundancy must be identified and properly managed during conversion of data across a data interface.

Chapter Fifteen

Creation of data redundancy occurs when data are converted from subject data entities to conventional data entities. For example, if conversion were from *Employee.Name* to *Training:Employee.Name* and *Create* was indicated, the employee's name would be propagated to all training records for that employee. This situation does not present a problem because the same value for the employee's name is placed in all training records for that employee.

The only difference between data redundancy indicated in a data converter and data redundancy identified in the data integrity rules is that data integrity rules show all existences of redundant data in the database and the data converter indicates only redundant data unique to that data conversion. In addition, the data converter indicates only data redundancy involved in converting data across a data interface, not the necessary data redundancy that is maintained within the subject data resource.

Data attributes that are involved in more than one conversion are shown multiple times on the Data Attribute Conversion Table. For example, if *Ethnic Origin Code* is used to form two different multiple characteristic data attributes, then it appears in each of those sets. This situation occurs frequently with the implied redundant data that exists in conventional data entities.

The sets in a Data Attribute Conversion Table must be exhaustive. They must show all the data attributes on the data structures associated with the data converter. If data attributes are not used or are not converted a minus sign is used to explicitly indicate that situation. If a data attribute is used in multiple conversions, it is shown once for each of those conversions where it participates. This procedure assures that the Data Attribute Conversion Table explicitly shows the use of each data attribute for each conversion and avoids any confusion.

> The data attribute conversion table must contain entries for all data attributes on the data structures being converted.

Data Value Conversion Table

The Data Value Conversion Table shows how data values are changed as data are converted across the data interface. The table has a specific format that is very similar to an extended data domain. The only difference between this table and the extended data domain is that the extended data domain represents all possible conversions for one data attribute and the Data Value Conversion Table represents only the conversions needed by the data converter. In addition, the Data Value Conversion Table shows conversions between single and multiple characteristic data attributes which are not shown on the extended data domain.

> The data value conversion table shows how data values are converted from one data structure to another.

The format of the Data Value Conversion Table is shown in Figure 15.20. *Gender Code* is the source data attribute and its data values are converted to *Staff Sex Code*. Specifically, the values for *Male*, *Female*, and *Unknown* are converted to a *1*, *2*, and *3* respectively.

DATA VALUE CONVERSION TABLE

Source dat attributes	Target data attributes
Employee:Gender.Code	Staff:Staff Sex Code
M	1
F	2
U	3

Figure 15.20 Conversion of data values.

Conversion of data values from a multiple characteristic data attribute to single characteristic data attributes is shown in Figure 15.21. A *Personnel Type Code* of *1* is converted to a *Gender Code* of *M* and an *Ethnic Origin Code* of *CAU*. The reverse situation could be shown on another Data Value Conversion Table where a *Gender Code* of *M* and an *Ethnic Origin Code* of *CAU* were converted to a *Personnel Type Code* of *1*.

DATA VALUE CONVERSION TABLE

Source data attributes	Target data attributes	
Personnel: Type Code	Gender.Code	Ethnic Origin.Code
1	M	CAU
2	F	CAU
3	M	ORI
4	F	ORI
etc		

Figure 15.21 Conversion from single to multiple characteristic data attributes.

When defining a Data Value Conversion Table, there could be a situation of converting data values in one direction across the data interface, but not being able to convert them back the other direction. This situation occurs when two or more data values on one side of the data interface are equated to one data value on the other side. Once that conversion is made those data values can not be converted back. For example, if a pair of data values *X* and *R* were converted to a data value of *9* and another pair of data values *A* and *K* were also converted to a data value of *9*, it would be impossible to convert the *9* back to the original pair of data values.

> Any situations where data values can be converted one way but not the other way must be identified and properly managed.

This no-return situation must be identified before it becomes a problem. Each time a Data Value Conversion Table is developed the values in that table should be reviewed, no-return situations identified, and a decision made about managing that situation during data conversion.

DATABASE TRANSITION PROCESS

Database transition is the process of defining the subject data resource for an enterprise, documenting data in the conventional database, identifying data interfaces between conventional and subject data, defining data structures on either side of the data interface, installing data converters on the data interface, adjusting applications to use those data converters, and converting the database. Data conversion is the process of converting data between applications and data entities. Database conversion is the process of converting data from a conventional database to a subject database. Application conversion is the process of converting applications from using conventional data to using subject data.

Data Conversion

Data conversion is the process of converting data between applications and data entities. The first step in data conversion is to prepare a data flow diagram showing the information system architecture and the location of any data interfaces. Data flows are modified as necessary to represent single subjects of data to and from subject data entities and subject applications. Single subject data flows may be defined for conventional data entities if they represent subsets of data from a database management system. Data converters are indicated as processes on data flows that cross the data interface.

> Data conversion is the process of converting data between applications and databases.

A decision needs to be made about how many data converters will be defined and which data flows those data converters will process. Generally, there should be many data converters and each data converter should convert only a few data flows flowing in one direction. When large data converters are developed to convert many data flows there is increased maintenance on that data converter and there is increased chance for errors.

> A data converter converts data flowing one direction across an interface and should convert only a few closely related data flows.

The second step is to identify data structures for each data flow into or out of the data converter. These data structures represent data the data converter must process and are used to define the contents of a data converter. Conventional data files must be retrodocumented and the data must be documented in the data resource directory.

The third step is to define each set of conversions in the data converter. Each data attribute on each incoming data flow is listed as a source data attribute in the Data Attribute Conversion Table. The appropriate entries are made for the type of source data attribute, the target data attribute, the type of target data attribute, the need for data value conversion, and the need for creating or resolving data redundancy. When an entry has been made for each data attribute on the incoming data structures the outgoing data structures are reviewed to determine if every data attribute on those data structures has been identified as a target data attribute. If not, an entry needs to be made for that data attribute in the target data attribute column and the appropriate entries made for a source data attribute.

> Every data attribute on the incoming and outgoing data must be accounted for in the data converter.

Structural changes that can occur during conversion across a data interface are movement of data attributes between data occurrences within the same data entity or between data entities, a combination or separation of data characteristics within data attributes, a change in the data values of a data attribute, and the creation or resolution of redundant data. Conversion of any data structure frequently includes a combination of these changes. With the wide variability in the types of data structures that appear in conventional application data entities there is a high probability of many changes that need to be made during conversion.

A movement of data attributes between data occurrences generally occurs when the data attribute is not in the proper data entity. When data are converted from conventional data to subject data each data attribute must be placed in its proper subject data entity. When data are converted from subject data to application data the data attribute must be placed where the applications expects to find that data attribute.

Data characteristics in a multiple characteristic data attribute are separated into single characteristic data attributes during conversion from conventional data to subject data. Single data characteristics are combined into multiple characteristic data attributes during conversion from subject to conventional data.

The reverse situation occurs for mutually exclusive data attributes. Mutually exclusive data attributes are combined into one single characteristic data attribute during conversion from conventional data to subject data. Mutually exclusive data attributes are separated into partial characteristic data attributes during conversion from subject data structures to conventional data structures.

Redundant data are resolved when data are converted from conventional data to subject data by moving one value from the conventional data to the corresponding data attribute in the subject data. Redundant data are created when data are converted from subject data to conventional data by propagating a data value to all existences of that redundant data attribute. For example, if a subject application maintained the employee's name in the conventional *Training* data entity, it would maintain that employee's name redundantly in each training record. If, however, a conventional application maintained the employee's name in *Employee*, it would maintain the employee's name only once for each employee.

Data values may need to be changed when data are converted across a data interface.

For example, if a conventional application expected *Vehicle Motor Type Code* with one set of allowable values but the data are stored in a subject data entity as *Fuel Type Code* with another set of allowable values, those values need to be converted. If a subject application expected *Fuel Type Code* but the data are stored in a conventional data entity as *Vehicle Motor Type Code*, those values also need to be converted.

The fourth step is to review the Data Attribute Conversion Table for any data value conversions that need to be made. When a data value conversion is indicated, a Data Value Conversion Table is created for that data attribute. Every data value, or set of data values, for the incoming data attribute is listed on that table as a source data attribute. Corresponding entries are made for the target data attribute. When these entries have been made the table should be reviewed to identify any no-return situations where data may be converted in one direction and not the other direction. Identification of these situations may require review of companion Data Value Conversion Tables representing conversion of data both directions across the data interface. If a no-return situation is found a decision must be made about how to manage that situation.

The fifth step is to review the resolution of data redundancy to determine if there are several sources of conflicting data. This determination often requires a review of the actual data values in the data files to determine if there are conflicting data values. If conflicting data values are found a decision must be made about which data values to use. Identification of conflicting redundant data often leads to a correction to the data in conventional data files and an adjustment to conventional applications to prevent that situation from occurring again.

The final step is to develop, test, and implement the data converter. The data converter is used as long as the data interface exists. When the data interface is eliminated the need for the data converter ceases and it can be removed. The appropriate changes are made to the applications so that they can process subject data directly from the database.

When an enterprise begins to convert its data to a subject data resource, many small data interfaces are created. If there are many conversions in progress at any one time, there will be many data interfaces created and each of those data interfaces must be properly managed. Therefore, it is best to pick a group of related applications and data entities for conversion and complete that conversion before another conversion is started. This approach reduces the number of data interfaces that must be managed. Ideally, when the conversion process is completed, all data will be converted and there will be no need for data interface management. However, this ideal is not always possible, such as with acquired applications that have a data structure different from the enterprise's subject data resource, and some data interface management must always be performed.

Database Conversion

Database conversion is the process of converting a conventional database to a subject data resource. The process is similar to the conversion of data between applications and data files described above. The only differences are that the conversion is done only once, it is done between data files, and data are edited according to data integrity rules. **Database converters** are defined and developed to convert the database just like data converters were defined and developed for converting data between applications and data entities.

> Database conversion is the process of converting data from a conventional database to a subject database.

When conventional data files are properly documented, the subject data resource has been defined, data interfaces have been identified, and data converters are available, the process of converting a conventional database to a subject data resource can begin. This conversion process requires a thorough and detailed plan to assure that data are properly converted, data integrity is maintained, and business operations are not severely impacted. If the database conversion plan is prepared properly and data are converted successfully, an enterprise can enjoy the benefits of a subject database.

> A database converter is used to convert data between a conventional database and a subject database.

A database conversion plan contains several components. The subject data resource must be defined with a complete logical and a physical data resource model. If the strategic and retrofit data modeling processes were done properly the data resource model will include all data that will be converted from conventional database to the subject data resource. The conventional database must also be defined with a physical data resource model showing the data files that will be converted. These models of the conventional database and the subject data resource provide the base for developing a database conversion plan.

The next step is to pick a portion of the database for conversion. Generally, the entire database can not be converted at one time. Therefore, a small segment of the database is selected for conversion and when that conversion is complete another segment is selected for conversion. A segment may include one or more data files and could include part of a data file, particularly where there are several subjects in one application data file. This approach makes conversion easier and minimizes the impacts. It also allows a review of each conversion to identify any problems that were encountered and identification of steps to prevent those problems in subsequent conversions.

> Small segments of the database should be converted to maintain control of the conversion process.

The third step is to develop one-time **database converters** for moving data from a conventional database to a subject data resource. Data resource models of the segment to be converted are reviewed to determine where these database converters will be placed. Once that decision is made, database converters are defined the same way data converters are defined. Data flows into a database converter represent conventional data and data flows out of a database converter represent subject data. The contents of the database converter define how the incoming data structures are converted to the outgoing data structures.

All applications accessing data files to be converted must be identified. The data management matrix described in the Data Resource Model chapter is developed to identify all applications that use each data file. Each of these applications must have a data converter defined prior to database conversion. The impact on ad hoc applications using conventional data files should also be reviewed. Generally, ad hoc processing can be suspended during database conversion, but the people using those ad hoc applications must be aware of the conversion effort.

> All applications accessing files in the database that is being converted must be identified to avoid any impact on business operations.

The fourth step is to determine the method of enforcing data integrity. Data can either be edited during conversion or prior to conversion. If data are edited during conversion and substantial errors are found the conversion effort may need to be abandoned. In this situation it would be better to edit the data in conventional data files and correct that data before conversion. The disadvantage of editing data in conventional data files is that any structural or relationship edits that need to be performed with data already in the subject database can not be performed. The best approach is a two-stage data editing process to make the appropriate changes to data in conventional data files prior to conversion and to make a final data edit during conversion. This final data edit process includes all the data integrity rules for each data subject.

> Comprehensive data integrity rules must be enforced for all data entering a subject database.

The fifth step is to develop and thoroughly test database converters and data edits to assure they will convert the data and enforce the data integrity rules. This development and testing process follows the normal procedures for developing and testing any application. When testing is completed successfully, the database converters are ready.

The sixth step is to schedule the database conversion. This step requires careful analysis and planning. Timing of the conversion must be planned according to the use of data by production applications, availability of computer resources, sequence of data changes, and so forth. It includes a complete schedule of events by time and appropriate checkpoints to determine whether to continue or to abandon the conversion effort. It also includes fallback and recovery procedures in case insurmountable errors are encountered.

> Adequate fallback and recovery procedures must be planned in case problems are encountered during database conversion.

The seventh step is to perform the conversion. Data files are converted according to the conversion plan and data are evaluated at each check point to determine if conversion should continue or should be abandoned. If database conversion should be abandoned, the appropriate fallback procedures are implemented, the database conversion plan is adjusted, and another schedule is established.

The last step is to review the subject database to determine if conversion was successful. If conversion was successful, data converters can be removed from the subject applications and they can begin accessing the subject database. Data converters for converting subject data for conventional applications are implemented and maintained until those applications can be adjusted to access the subject database directly.

Database conversion planning is not a difficult process but it requires careful planning and scheduling and includes considerable detail. Each plan is unique to an enterprise and to the data being converted. The people involved in database conversion must work closely together to include all details and recovery procedures. If this planning effort is performed successfully, database conversion will be successful and the enterprise can begin to obtain the benefits of a subject data resource.

The best method to control database conversion is to develop a data flow diagram showing the applications, data entities, data converters, and database converters. For example, the conversion of a conventional data entity for *Student* to subject data entities for *Student* and *Address* is shown in Figure 15.22. A data converter converts conventional Student data into *Student* data and *Address* data for a subject application. A database converter converts conventional *Student* data into *Student* and *Address* subject data entities. Before the database is converted the application accesses the data converter to obtain the proper data. When the database has been converted the application will access the data entities directly.

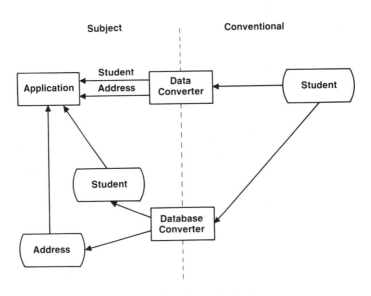

Figure 15.22 Total data flow diagram for database conversion.

The same technique is used for all applications and all data entities in the segment of the database being converted. When database conversion has been completed a new data flow diagram is developed showing the architecture of the information system in a subject data resource environment.

Application Conversion

Applications can be severely impacted by database transition. Changes to the structure of data directly impact the way applications access the database to store and retrieve data. Any impact on applications results in an impact to the business operations of the enterprise. This is the main reason why most enterprises avoid conversion to a subject data resource. Therefore, the impact of database transition on applications must be minimized or eliminated to allow an enterprise to convert to a subject data resource.

The best technique for minimizing the impact of database transition on applications is by the use of data converters between applications and the database. These data converters relieve the maintenance on applications during the conversion process and allow them to continue near normal operation until the database is converted. Changes to the database are balanced by changes in the data converters which continue to provide data to applications in a near normal manner.

> Data converters relieve the maintenance load on applications and assure minimum impact on business operations during database conversion.

Application conversion is the process of converting conventional applications from using conventional data to using subject data. The total process of application conversion is beyond the scope of this book. However, the method of adjusting applications to access data converters will be explained.

Adjustments to an application pertain only to access to the database. Database accesses are changed to data converter accesses. The specific changes are different for each application but involve bypassing a code that accesses the database and inserting a code that calls a data converter. In most cases both sets of codes are kept in the application and selection of the code to be used is indicated by a parameter entered at execution time. This technique allows flexibility during database transition without extensive application maintenance.

> Adjustments are made to applications to access data converters rather than to access the database directly.

Both conventional and subject applications need to be changed to access a data converter. Conventional applications need to access data converters as soon as their conventional data entities are converted to subject data entities. Data converters remain in operation until the application is changed to access subject data entities. When the conversion to a subject data resource has been completed, conventional applications can be scheduled for upgrade, the application is adjusted to access subject data entities, and the data converter is removed. Subject applications need to access data converters as long as they are using conventional data. As soon as conventional files are converted to subject data entities, the data converters can be removed and the application can access the database directly.

In extreme situations it is difficult to make a complete transition to a subject data resource and eliminate all conventional files because of some peculiarity. In these extreme situations both subject and conventional data are maintained redundantly until the peculiarity is resolved. Processing needs to be implemented to maintain the redundant data until the situation can be resolved.

SUMMARY

Database transition is the process of converting conventional data structures in application files to a subject data resource. This conversion must be done with minimal impact on business operations and without impacting data integrity. Data interfaces are defined between conventional and subject data structures and conventional data must be analyzed and documented. Data converters convert data between applications and the database during database transition and database converters convert the database. Conventional applications are adjusted to access subject data. The result is a subject data resource that supports all applications in the enterprise.

The guidelines listed below summarize the steps to convert data across a data interface during database transition.

Design a subject data resource by using the strategic, retrofit, and project data modeling processes.

Prepare a data flow diagram and identify data interfaces between subject data and conventional data.

Identify data converters for closely related data flows across a data interface.

Assure that all data flows across a data interface are accounted for by a data converter.

Define the data structure for each incoming and outgoing data flow for a data converter.

Define the changes made by each data converter to convert one data structure to another.

Create a Data Attribute Conversion Table to convert incoming data structures to outgoing data structures.

Create a Data Value Conversion Table for any data values that need to be converted.

Identify any instances of data redundancy that need to be resolved or created.

Review data redundancy resolution to determine if there are multiple sources of conflicting data that need to be resolved.

Test each data converter to verify proper data conversion.

Adjust applications to access data converters rather than the database.

Implement access to data converters as necessary during database conversion.

Operate the data converters until conventional applications are changed to access subject data or conventional files are converted to a subject database.

Remove data converters when they are no longer required.

The guidelines listed below summarize the steps to convert a conventional database to a subject database.

Develop a physical data resource model for the conventional database.

Retrodocument all data in the conventional database.

Develop a logical and physical data resource model for the subject database.

Select a reasonable segment of the database for conversion.

Identify all applications and data files in that segment of the database.

Define database converters for the applications in the segment, including data integrity rules.

Develop and test the database converters.

Define data converters for conventional applications that will be impacted by the conversion.

Develop and test the data converters.

Plan and schedule database conversion, including backup and recovery procedures.

Perform the database conversion, including evaluation at each check point.

Review the new subject database to determine if conversion was successful.

Remove data converters from subject applications and implement data converters for conventional applications.

The guidelines listed below summarize the steps to adjust an application to access a data converter.

Identify accesses to the database in each application.

Add access to data converters for each database access.

Add selection capability for execution time selection of database or data converter access.

Use those options as necessary during database conversion.

Remove access to data converters when the database and applications have been converted.

The following questions are provided as a review of database transition and to stimulate thought about the process and problems of converting a conventional database to a subject data resource.

1. Why is it necessary for an enterprise to convert to a subject data resource?
2. Why is it difficult for an enterprise to convert to a subject data resource?
3. What could happen if an enterprise chose not to convert to a subject data resource?
4. What is the primary objective for converting to a subject data resource?
5. What does database transition include?
6. What is a data interface and what does it represent?
7. How is a data interface identified and documented?
8. How are the data structures on either side of a data interface identified and documented?
9. What are the major functions of data converters?
10. What types of changes can occur when data are moved across a data interface?
11. What is a data converter and what does it represent?
12. What are the components of a data converter?
13. What does each component of a data converter do?
14. How is a data converter defined and developed?
15. What problems can be encountered when converting to a subject data resource?
16. What should be included in a database transition plan?
17. What precautions should be taken when converting to a subject data resource?
18. How are applications adjusted during database conversion?
19. Who should be involved in planning conversion of the database?
20. What are the benefits of converting to a subject data resource?

Data Resource Design

An enterprise's data resource is designed by pulling all the techniques together into a formal procedure.

The benefits of an enterprise-wide subject data resource should be obvious by now. The need to design data and the basic data design concepts within the context of the information technology discipline have been presented. The components of business design and data resource models have been explained. The components of an enterprise data resource, particularly the data resource architecture components, have been presented and techniques were explained for developing those components. Techniques for converting conventional databases to a subject data resource have also been presented.

The only remaining question is *how to get started*. With all the concepts, techniques, and processes to use, and bad practices to avoid, how does one get started designing a subject data resource for an enterprise. This chapter pulls all the techniques together into a sequence of events that define how to get started developing an enterprise-wide subject data resource. It describes where to start designing the data resource and who should be involved in that process. The sequence explained here is part of the total Business Driven System Development method presented in the Appendix. A small example is used to illustrate the process of developing an enterprise's data resource.

DATA RESOURCE MODELS

When an enterprise starts organizing its data resource there is a certain sequence to follow to develop a structurally stable data resource with a minimum of effort. This sequence begins with development of a strategic data resource model that establishes the basic structure of the data resource. Retrofit data resource models of existing data are developed to add detail to that basic structure. Project data resource models provide all the detail necessary to develop physical data files for production applications and ad hoc data resource models add the detail necessary to support an efficient ad hoc environment. The enterprise data resource model shows the current status of the entire data resource for an enterprise.

Strategic Data Resource Model

A strategic data resource model defines the initial structure of the data resource. It shows the major data subjects in the enterprise and the relations between those data subjects. It provides a broad view of the data resource structure for an enterprise but has minimum detail about data in that structure and includes both present and future information about the enterprise's data resource. The strategic model includes an entity-relationship diagram, an entity-type hierarchy, a description, primary keys, and major data characteristics for each data subject. Generally, secondary keys, foreign keys, data integrity rules, data views, and data properties are not defined. However, if that information is readily available it should be documented.

> A strategic data resource model defines the initial structure of an enterprise's data resource.

Developing a strategic data resource model is a top-down process driven by the business environment. The behavioral entities managed by the enterprise define the initial data subjects. For example, *Employees*, *Vehicles*, and *Customers* are behavioral entities managed by the enterprise. These behavioral entities define the *Employee*, *Vehicle*, and *Customer* data subjects. As each data subject is defined the data relations between those subjects, the primary keys, and the major data characteristics that describe each data subject are identified and described.

When data subjects representing behavioral entities have been identified and defined, data subjects supporting those behavioral entities can be identified and defined. For example, supporting data subjects for *Employee*, *Vehicle*, and *Customer* might be *Pay Check*, *Vehicle Maintenance*, and *Customer Order*. These data subjects lead to other supporting data subjects that can be readily identified. Generally, any repeating groups and code tables that support behavioral entities are defined. Partial key and interattribute dependencies are usually not identified.

An attempt should not be made to identify all data subjects and data relations in an enterprise with a strategic data resource model. The result is identification of false data subjects and data relations. False data subjects represent business events, or business processes that may not be true data subjects. These false data subjects are identified because people developing the strategic model have an intimate knowledge of the business environment and tend to identify data subjects based on happenings that occur in that environment rather than by data subjects. For example, training is an event in the business environment and *Training* might be identified as a data subject. However, training really represents data subjects for *Student, Instructor, Course, Class, Location,* and so on, and is not a data subject.

Attempting to identify all data subjects and data relations also produces false many-to-many data relations. Resolution of these many-to-many data relations creates additional data subjects and sometimes additional many-to-many data relations that must be resolved. Many of these data relations are not of interest to the enterprise and their identification and resolution creates data entities that will never be used by the enterprise.

For example, an employee can have many addresses, such as residence, mailing, emergency contact, and so on, and the enterprise is interested in tracking these addresses for an employee. However, more than one employee can use the same address, such as the same residence, forming a many-to-many relation between *Employee* and *Address.* If this data relation were identified it would be resolved with *Address Assignment.* However, if the enterprise were not interested in tracking employees by address, then as far as the enterprise is concerned there is only a one-to-many relation between employees and addresses and *Address Assignment* would not be needed.

These two problems can be prevented by limiting strategic data modeling to identification of data subjects that represent behavioral entities and data subjects that are directly related to those behavioral entities. Data relations are identified between those data subjects and any many-to-many data relations are resolved, either with a resolution data entity or a business rule. Additional data subjects and data relations are defined on other data resource models where more detailed information is available.

Development of strategic models is limited to data subjects directly supporting behavioral entities.

The strategic data resource model is developed by people in the enterprise that have a knowledge of the business environment and the behavioral entities in that environment. Training these people in data resource modeling concepts and techniques will provide a firm base for developing a correct strategic data resource model. Development of good entity life cycle and business information models helps identify behavioral entities.

The strategic model may be developed as one project or as several projects representing major areas of the enterprise, but it is a finite process. Once the basic structure of the enterprise's data resource has been defined there is little additional strategic modeling to be done. The only need for additional strategic modeling would be expansion into a totally new business area not previously included in the strategic data resource model.

To illustrate the strategic data modeling process a small example of a veterinary clinic will be used. The area of particular interest in this clinic is patient treatment and processes directly related to patient treatment. Other processes in the clinic, such as employee recruitment and training, are not included in this model.

Data Resource Design

Behavioral entities for the veterinary clinic are animals (patients), clients, and employees. Data subjects are defined for each of these entities. A *Patient* is identified by a *Patient Number*, a *Client* is identified by a *Client Account Number*, and an *Employee* is identified by an *Employee SSN*. The initial structure of the data resource is shown in Figure 16.1. A client can have many patients, but a patient has only one client responsible for that patient. A patient is seen by many employees and an employee sees many patients.

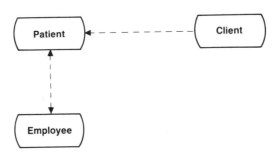

Figure 16.1 Behavioral entities for a veterinary clinic.

Supporting data for these behavioral entities are visits by patients, medical treatments, medical supplies, vendors, and jobs held by employees. Data subjects are defined for *Patient Visit*, *Medical Treatment*, *Medical Supply Item*, *Vendor*, and *Job*, as shown in Figure 16.2. A patient can have many visits, but a visit represents only one patient. Only one employee is responsible for each visit. A patient can receive many medical treatments and the same medical treatment can be given to many patients. Similarly, a medical treatment can use many medical supply items and a supply item can be used for many treatments. The same relation exists between medical supplies and vendors and between employees and jobs.

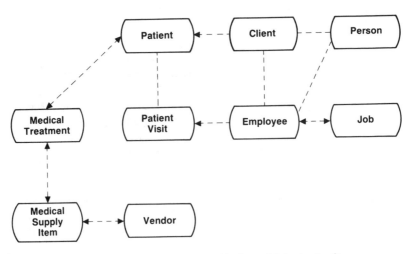

Figure 16.2 Supporting data entities for each behavioral entity.

Patient visit is identified by *Patient Number* and *Patient Visit Date*. Vendors are identified by a *Vendor Number*, medical supplies are identified by a *Medical Supply Product Number*, medical treatments are identified by a *Medical Treatment Number*, and jobs are identified by a *Job Number*. Additional data attributes are defined as they are identified.

Clients and *Employees* are data categories of *Person* and an employee of the clinic may also be a client of the clinic. *Medical Supply Item* is an entity type of *Supply Item*, as shown in Figure 16.3.

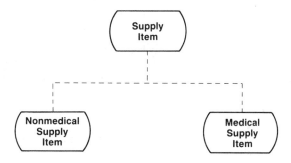

Figure 16.3   Entity type hierarchy for supplies.

Retrofit Data Resource Model

A retrofit data resource model enhances the strategic data resource model based on existing data files. It includes an entity-relationship diagram, an entity type hierarchy, data attributes, data descriptions, data values, primary, secondary, and foreign keys, data views, and data integrity rules. It has a narrower scope than the strategic model, but contains more detail than the strategic model.

> A retrofit model enhances the strategic model by adding data that already exist in the enterprise's data files.

Retrofit data modeling is a major task if there are many existing data files. It is a major untangling process to sort through conventional data file structures, data names and aliases, data file definitions, people's memories, applications, and other documentation to determine the basic data. However, it is a finite process because each existing data file is modeled only once. When all conventional data files have been modeled there is no further need for retrofit data modeling.

The retrofit data modeling process shows how bad conventional data really are and how poorly they have been managed. It is usually a time of great frustration and discouragement when people involved with data resource management begin to realize that data have not been properly structured or managed. It is a time when many enterprises give up trying to change the existing data structure because it appears to be an impossible task that could never be accomplished without a severe impact on the business. It is the point of lowest enthusiasm for developing a well-structured, stable data resource.

However, the retrofit data modeling process can be the most rewarding and productive time for developing a good enterprise data resource. As people become more involved in retrofit data modeling they become more enthused by discovering data that already exist in the enterprise and the value that can be gained from those data. A good strategic model increases this enthusiasm by providing the initial data resource structure that allows people to see where conventional data fit into that structure.

Retrofit data modeling defies precise definition. However, the general approach is to review each existing data file, document data in that file, and define true data subjects, data characteristics, and data properties. It is a two-step process of retrodocumenting the existing data files and redesigning the data into a subject data resource. It is a process of discovery that requires deep analysis, extensive searching for the truth, intuition, a little bit of luck, and tremendous patience. It is a time consuming and thought provoking process that is very rewarding.

> Retrofit data modeling is a process of retrodocumenting existing data files and redesigning the data by subject.

The first step is to select a major functional area in the enterprise, such as personnel or real property, and identify all existing data files supporting that functional area. A system architecture model is developed for this functional area to assist identification of applications and data files. Next, a physical data resource model is developed for those data files. Then, a logical data resource model is prepared for the data contained in the physical model. This is the difficult redesign process that converts conventional data structure into subject data.

Applications are usually not reviewed during initial retrofit data modeling because it detracts from the task of defining and restructuring the data. In many cases people become unhappy with the application and are so concerned about changes to the application that they lose track of retrofit data modeling. However, considerable information can be gained from reviewing applications, such as primary keys, data accesses, and data integrity rules. If applications are reviewed during retrofit data modeling they must be reviewed only for information that will enhance the data modeling process.

When applications are reviewed there are several things that can be identified. Substringing data items indicates a multiple characteristic data attribute. Search and selection criteria indicate secondary keys. Data actually used by the application, not the data it has available, provide the application data view. Data edits provide initial data integrity rules and possible primary keys.

Application data views are defined with data structures using the same data names used for defining application data entities. However, to assist with data conversion it is necessary to know exactly what data are actually used or modified by each application, which in many cases is a subset of data available to the application. If it is not possible, or is too time consuming, to determine exactly what data are actually used by an application, all data that are available to the application should be considered used by that application.

Generally, no future data are identified during retrofit data modeling. Only existing data are documented and redesigned. However, since retrofit data modeling enhances the strategic data resource model, which includes both existing data and future data, any future data needs that are identified should be documented. This procedure captures the knowledge and intuition of the people doing the retrofit data modeling.

Anyone with an intimate knowledge of existing data should be involved in retrofit data modeling. These people may be users, system analysts, or data base analysts. Generally, people that have been with the enterprise and have had direct involvement with managing or using data are the best people to perform retrofit data modeling.

The veterinary clinic data resource model can be enhanced by modeling the data existing in their conventional data files. The retrofit data modeling process identified data for species of animals, medical diagnoses, medical treatment types, medical supply item types, prescriptions for medicine, job assignments for employees, client bills, and client payments. Based on these data, data entities are identified for *Animal Species*, *Medical Diagnosis*, *Prescriptions*, *Job Assignment*, and *Client Account Activity*, as shown in Figure 16.4

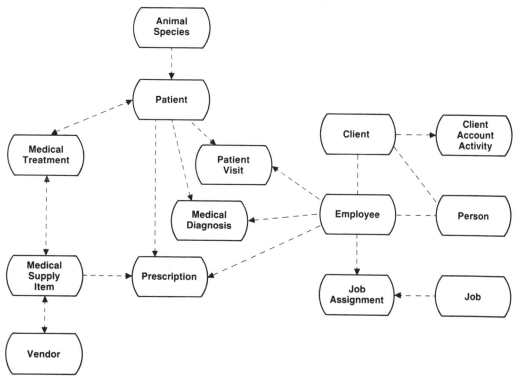

Figure 16.4 Enhanced veterinary clinic model from retrofit data modeling.

Data Resource Design

Each *Patient* is one *Animal Species*, such as dog or cow, a *Client* has many *Client Account Activities*, an *Employee* provides the *Medical Diagnosis* for a *Patient*, and an *Employee* writes a *Prescription* for a *Medical Supply Item* for a *Patient*. *Job Assignment* relates an *Employee* to a *Job*.

Data entity types are identified for medical supply items and for medical treatments, as shown on the entity-type hierarchy diagrams in Figure 16.5. Medical supply items can be either controlled substances, medications, or nonmedications. Medical treatments can be surgical, nonsurgical, or consultation.

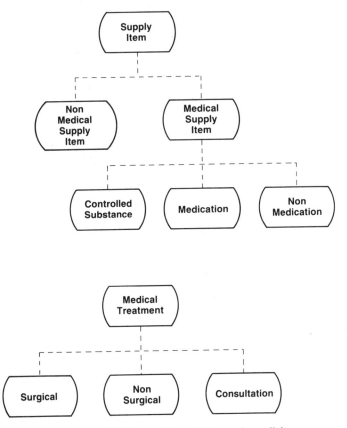

Figure 16.5 Entity-type hierarchy for veterinary clinic.

The appropriate definitions, primary keys, secondary keys, foreign keys, and data integrity rules are defined for each of these data subjects. Each data attribute and data value is also defined and all data units are documented in the data resource directory.

Project Data Resource Model

The project data resource model enhances the retrofit data resource model by adding all the detail necessary to construct a physical database to support an information system. A project model is developed for each individual information system and includes all the components of a logical data resource model. All the techniques explained in earlier chapters are used to develop the project model. It has a narrower scope than the retrofit model, but it contains extensive detail about the data.

> A project data resource model adds all the detail necessary for developing a database to support an information system

The project data resource model can not be used to develop an enterprise-wide data structure. There is too much detail for too narrow a scope to gain the full perspective of the enterprise's data resource. Trying to develop a complete data resource structure produces false data entities that represent conventional application files. In fact, this is the way conventional application files were originally developed.

Defining an enterprise data resource with a project data resource model is the counterpart of trying to define too much detail with the strategic model. When a strategic model includes too much detail, data entities representing business events and business processes rather than data subjects are identified. When the project model is used to develop the enterprise data structure application, data entities are identified rather than data subjects. To properly develop an enterprise-wide data resource each data modeling technique must be used at the proper time and within the proper scope.

As information systems are defined for the veterinary clinic additional data subjects are identified and included in the data resource model, as shown in Figure 16.6. Supplies are ordered from vendors with *Vendor Order* that contains many *Vendor Order Items*. This relation removes the direct relation between *Vendor* and *Medical Supply Item*. *Medical Supply* becomes a parent of *Medical Supply Item*. An *Employee* orders a *Medical Treatment* through a *Prescription* which resolves the relation between *Medical Treatment* and *Patient*. A *Prescription* is also used to order a *Medical Supply Item* which resolves the relation between *Medical Supply Item* and *Medical Treatment*.

Different types of employees were also identified, as shown in Figure 16.7. *Employees* can be *Medical* or *Nonmedical* and medical employees can be *Doctors* or *Paramedical*. These data entity types are added to the data resource model. All other components of the data resource model are defined during project data modeling and are documented in the data resource directory.

This veterinary clinic example is relatively simple, but it shows the process for developing a subject data resource for an enterprise. It is used to develop subject data files for new information systems and for identifying the conversion of conventional data files to a subject data resource. It is also used as a base for enhancement from definitions provided by other information system projects. For example, vendor payments and returns to vendors could be added. Employee pay, training, and recruitment could be added. Laboratory tests, the results of those tests, and their meaning for different animal species could be added. An inventory of supplies, both in a central location and in distributed locations throughout the clinic, could be defined, and thresholds could be defined for triggering orders to vendors.

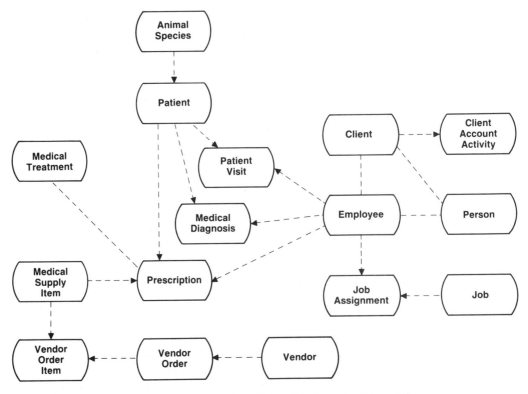

Figure 16.6   Veterinary clinic model after project data modeling.

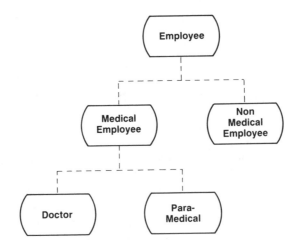

Figure 16.7   Employee data entity types.

The possibilities are limitless. Once a well-structured data resource model is developed that model can be easily enhanced to meet the needs of the enterprise.

Ad Hoc Data Resource Model

Project models provide all the detail necessary to support production applications. However, a project model may not include the detail necessary to support ad hoc processing. Ad hoc applications may need additional data attributes, data keys, and data views. Ad hoc data resource models are developed to identify data attributes, data keys, and data views needed to support ad hoc processing. This ad hoc model is developed just like the project model except that more projections are made about use of data in an ad hoc environment. These additions are not random additions, but are planned based on what may be reasonably required for ad hoc processing.

> Ad hoc data resource models provide additional detail to support ad hoc processing.

Once these additions are identified they can be implemented, but the process does not stop there. The use of those new data attributes, data keys, and data views must be constantly reviewed to determine if their continued maintenance is warranted. If their maintenance is not substantiated they should be destroyed. In addition, if there is processing that is being performed by ad hoc applications without data keys where the definition of a data key would improve processing, a data key should be defined. This analysis is the responsibility of database administration to assure optimum efficiency of the database and still meet the needs of the enterprise.

Ad hoc processing is becoming prominent, particularly in a decentralized environment. Ad hoc access to data is access to data *at this time for this purpose*. It is access to data on a temporary basis for a specific use and is not intended to be a production application. It represents access to data by users based on immediate and often unpredictable needs. However, this term can represent more than a one-time access into the database for a specific purpose. Realistically, ad hoc processing can be either permanent or temporary.

Ad hoc data access must be documented in the data resource directory. Ad hoc documentation does not need to be as detailed as production documentation, but it does need to indicate the use of data by ad hoc applications. For example, if an ad hoc application is developed and maintained as a permanent form of processing that application must be documented in the data resource directory.

Ad hoc processing takes a workload off the data processing departments. However, the user bears responsibility for maintenance of ad hoc applications. The use of data by ad hoc applications must be considered when database changes are made and the degree of importance of that consideration is up to the particular enterprise. The users must be made aware that they bear responsibility for documenting their applications and maintaining those applications, particularly when database changes are pending.

Substantial training needs to be provided to ad hoc users so that they can effectively and efficiently access the database. They need to be trained on the particular ad hoc application, the methods of accessing the database, the time involved to obtain their answer, the approach to obtaining their answer, how to check if alternate access paths are available, and how to interface with data administration and database administration personnel.

One of the major issues with ad hoc processing is access to conventional data files. Access to conventional files can not be prevented because people legitimately need access to data to perform their business activities. However, ad hoc processing can not be allowed to become dependent on these conventional data files if they are being converted. Users should be trained to use data converters to convert data, particularly if the ad hoc applications are to become permanent. If the ad hoc application is really temporary then access can be made to the existing application data files without any conversion.

Enterprise Data Resource Model

The enterprise data resource model represents the current and future status of the enterprise's data resource. It includes application and subject data, and logical and physical data models. It is the master data resource model for the enterprise.

> The enterprise data resource includes all information about the enterprise's data resource, including current status and future plans.

Development of an enterprise data resource is an evolutionary process. The strategic data resource model provides the basic data structure of the data resource. It is a top-down process that defines the basic data needed to support major functions of the enterprise. It has a broad scope but contains a minimum amount of detail. Retrofit data resource models add detail to that basic data structure based on data contained in existing data files. Project data resource models have a limited scope and contain considerable detail. Project data modeling is a bottom-up process that provides all the detail necessary to construct physical data files. Finally, ad hoc data resource models are developed within the scope of project data models. They have all the detail necessary to support extensive ad hoc processing.

> Developing an enterprise-wide subject data resource is an evolutionary process.

Strategic and retrofit data modeling eventually ceases because the data resource structure has been set for the enterprise and conventional data files have been reviewed. Occasional strategic data modeling may be done when new business functions are acquired or automated.

Project data modeling continues for each information system project but evolves from defining the detail needed to construct the database to determining if data already exist in the database and how they can be accessed. Data modeling still needs to be performed to identify data required by applications, but rather than developing a complete data resource model to construct the database, data resource models are reviewed to determine if data already exist. If data do exist then the database can be accessed for that data. If data do not exist, then it is a relatively minor task to add data to the database.

Ad hoc data modeling continues on an ongoing basis as long as there is ad hoc access to the database. Ultimately, the data modeling process becomes a process of identifying the data needed by an application and checking the database to determine if the data exist. In most cases the data exist and an enterprise can begin to reap the benefits of a subject data resource.

DATA RESOURCE MODEL VERIFICATION

When a data resource model has been developed it should be verified to assure that it is correct and adequately represents the data needed by the enterprise. If all of the rules and techniques were followed the model should be complete and correct. However, it is a good practice to verify the logical model before continuing development of the physical model. Any errors or discrepancies can be corrected rather than propagating those errors through the physical model into the physical database. The criteria for a good data resource model were presented in the Data Resource Model chapter. The verification process for assuring the data resource model is valid is presented below.

> Each data resource model must be carefully reviewed to assure it is a valid model of the data resource.

Data Structure Verification

Structural verification includes everything related to the structure of the data resource defined by the logical data resource model. The data structure is the most important part of the data resource model because it establishes the architecture of the data entities, defines the navigational routes between those data entities, and assures unique identification of data occurrences. If this structure is incomplete or in error, access into and navigation within the database to store and retrieve data can not be properly performed.

> Data structure verification assures the structure of the data resource is properly defined and that structural integrity will be maintained.

Verification of the data structure begins with a review of data entities and data relations between those data entities. Each data entity must represent a single subject of data, must have a primary key that uniquely identifies each data occurrence, must have a formal name that is meaningful and unique within the enterprise, and must have a comprehensive definition. These features assure that a subject data resource will be developed and that there are no synonymous or homonymous data entities in that database.

Each coded value data attribute must be represented by a separate code table data entity which also serves as the data domain for definition of data integrity rules. Data entities must be shown to verify the existence of data attributes in the primary key. Key-only data entities that have been identified should remain in the model as long as they are valid data entities, such as phantom data entities, data entities for verification and authorization, or future data entities.

Each valid data relation must be explicitly shown on the entity-relationship diagram. Each data relation is reviewed to determine if it is a valid data relation and each data entity is reviewed to determine if there are implied data relations that should be explicitly stated. These features assure that all valid navigational paths between data entities have been identified and defined. Any data relations that are not valid must be removed from the model.

Each data relation must be either a one-to-one data relation or a one-to-many data relation. All many-to-many data relations must be resolved with a resolution data entity or a business rule and the many-to-many data relation must be removed. The relations between data occurrences within each data entity must be reviewed to assure that cyclic data entities, recursive data entities, and data categories have been properly identified.

There must not be any around-the-corner data relations. For example, data entity *A* has a one-to-many data relation to data entity *B*, which has a one-to-many data relation to data entity *C*, which has a one-to-many data relation with data entity *A*. One of these data relations is not valid and must be corrected before the logical data resource model is correct.

All data entity types must be identified on an entity type hierarchy diagram. A data attribute must be identified for each branch on that hierarchy to uniquely identify each different data entity type.

Each data attribute in the primary key is reviewed to assure that its presence is necessary for unique identification of each data occurrence. If a data attribute in the primary key is a foreign data attribute there must be a parent data entity that substantiates the existence of that data attribute. This feature assures that there is a complete data resource structure and that no synonymous or homonymous data entities exist.

Each data entity that has a parent data entity must have a foreign key to that parent data entity. That foreign key must contain all the data attributes contained in the primary key of parent data entity in the same sequence as they are defined in the parent data entity. Those data attributes may be calculated or qualified with a variation name, but each data attribute in the primary key of a parent data entity must be represented in the foreign key of the subordinate data entity. If a data entity has more than one parent data entity, there must be a foreign key defined for each of those parent data entities.

Data Access Verification

Data access verification includes everything that is related to access into data entities in the database. Access into the data is the second most important part of the logical data resource model because if access can not be made to the data, data can not be obtained from or stored in the database. Once the structure of the data resource is established, navigational routes are defined, and secondary keys are established for entry into the database and into each data entity.

> Data access verification assures secondary keys are valid and their conversion
> to physical data keys will not impact performance of the database.

Verification of data access begins with verification of secondary keys. Each secondary key is reviewed to assure that its existence is reasonable. If any secondary key is not reasonable it should be removed from the model. Next, the frequency and periodicity of each secondary key is reviewed to determine if they are reasonable. If there are many secondary keys and their maintenance could be a problem, alternate secondary keys should be identified, such as the use of another secondary key that contains the same data attributes.

Any secondary keys that contain too many data attributes for a database management system need to be reduced by either identifying alternate secondary keys, eliminating those secondary keys, or creating one or more multiple characteristic data attributes as the secondary key. Any calculated data attribute in a secondary key must be reviewed to assure that the data attributes necessary for calculation are available. Each data attribute defined in the secondary key must be available in the data entity for creation of that secondary key.

Each secondary key is reviewed to determine if that data access will be maintained by the database management system, created at execution time, or be processed by the application. If the data access will be maintained by the database management system, the appropriate data key will be defined and maintained. If the data access will be created at execution time, it need not be maintained by the database management system. If the data access will be handled by the application program, then a data key does not need to be defined.

Data Content Verification

Data content verification includes anything related to the data attributes that characterize each data entity and the data values contained in each data attribute. The content of the data entities is the third most important part of the logical model. When the data structure has been reviewed and data accesses have been verified, entry may be made into the database. Once entry to the database has been made the appropriate data attributes must be defined for storage and retrieval of data and the values allowed for each data attribute must be defined.

> Data content verification assures data attributes and data values are properly
> identified and defined.

Each data attribute must represent a single characteristic of data. Each data attribute must be properly named according to the naming taxonomy and must be completely defined. Each data attribute name must be unique within the enterprise and that name must indicate the data entity the data attribute characterizes, which many not necessarily be the data entity where it resides. These features assure that there are no synonymous or homonymous data attributes in the database.

Each data attribute must have a corresponding data domain indicating the values allowed for that data attribute. Each coded data value must represent a single property of a data characteristic, must be uniquely named within the enterprise, and must be comprehensively defined. These features assure that there are no synonymous or homonymous data values in the database and that data values in each data attribute are valid.

Data View Verification

An application data view is a set of data attributes from a data entity that is used only by one application. Application data views are the data views used to develop the logical data resource. A full data view contains all the data attributes in a data entity. During data resource design the full data view represents the conceptual schema. A physical full data view represents all the data items in a data file and is generally used for data files with few data items and for data files that are of a utility nature, such as code tables. It is also used when the physical combined data views have a high frequency of overlap and it would be more efficient to create one physical full data view.

> Data view verification assures application data views are documented and are properly merged to provide physical data views.

Data views represent sets of data that are stored in or retrieved from the database. With the two-stage data view capability of some current database management systems it is important to identify both the data view available from the database and the data view used by each application. Both data views must be defined and documented to assure that data views are properly maintained and that all applications are adjusted when there is a change to the data.

Physical data views are defined during the logical to physical conversion process. However, this identification is based on application data views. Each data view in the logical model is reviewed to assure that it contains the data needed by the application. Each data view must be uniquely named and completely defined to assure that each application is using the correct data view.

Data Integrity Verification

Data integrity rules assure that the structure and content of the data resource are maintained at all times under all conditions. If data integrity is not maintained, the data resource will deteriorate and will not support the enterprise. Each data integrity rule is reviewed to assure that it is complete and correct. Data integrity rules are also reviewed for their completeness. Any part of the data resource that is not covered by a data integrity rule must have a rule defined. This comprehensive set of data integrity rules assures that the data in the data resource remain in a state of high quality.

> Data integrity rules are reviewed to assure they are complete and correct and will maintain high quality data.

Data Documentation

The entire logical resource model must be documented. Any changes to that model during the verification process must also be documented. Any major decisions about adjustments to the logical data resource model should be documented so when the same situation is encountered, or there are questions about the data resource model, those decisions can be reviewed. When changes are made to the logical data resource model the data structures contributing to that model should also be changed. If the data structures are not changed there could be a severe impact on application programs and the correct data may not be available or may not be maintained.

> The entire data resource model must be documented and that documentation must be readily available.

All abstractions of the basic data units must be formally named, completely defined, and placed in the data resource directory. Each database, data segment, data occurrence group, and data attribute group must be reviewed to assure that it has been properly named and defined. When the logical data resource model has been reviewed and verified as being correct the physical data resource model can be developed and the database can be developed.

MANAGING KEYS

Primary, foreign, and secondary keys are very important in a subject data resource. They are used to uniquely identify each data occurrence and to access data in the database. If these keys are not properly identified, defined, or maintained the database can not be effectively or efficiently used. Proper management of these keys includes proper identification of a primary key, changing a primary key when a discrepancy is found in either the value or structure of that key, and reducing the number of data attributes in a secondary key when a database management system has limitations on the number of data attributes in a data key.

Changing a Primary Key

Generally good data resource modeling techniques eliminate the need to change a primary key. However, errors are made during design and conditions in the business world do change, resulting in the need to change a primary key. In addition, the conversion of application files to a subject data resource often creates a need to change the primary key.

Data Resource Design

The changes to a primary key fall into two categories: changes to the data attributes that compose the primary key and changes to the values of the existing primary key.

Structural changes to the primary key. Data attributes that compose a primary key may need to be changed for a variety of reasons. First, a primary key that has been used is no longer a valid primary key. This situation may result from a primary key in an application file that was redesigned during retrofit data modeling, from a primary key that was initially proven to be valid but was later proven to be invalid, or from identification of another primary key that would be more efficient.

Second, redundancy may have been found in a primary key and the redundant data attributes need to be removed. This situation may result form a data attribute that is in the primary key but is not needed for unique identification or from identification of a multiple characteristic data attribute which contains characteristics that are not required for unique identification of each data occurrence.

Third, data attributes in a primary key may not uniquely identify each data occurrence and one or more additional data attributes need to be added or changed to obtain unique identification of each data occurrence. This situation could arise from an error in the original identification of the primary key, from an expanded scope for the data entity, or from addition of the time relational concept to a data entity.

When a primary key needs to be changed the determination is made whether the data entity is the same data entity that requires a different primary key or whether it is a new data entity. The situations that could occur are the same data entity with a new primary key, a new data entity where the old data entity ceases to exist, or a new data entity where the existing data entity is still valid. This determination can be made by reviewing the definition of each data entity.

Whatever the reason for changing a primary key, it must be changed with care. When a primary key is changed, the foreign key in all subordinate data entities must also be changed so proper reference can be made to the parent data entity. If foreign keys are not changed, reference to the parent data entity is lost and navigation in the database will be severely crippled. All applications must also be changed which may be the most difficult task, particularly if there are many applications accessing the data or the number of applications accessing the data are unknown. The physical keys in the database must also be changed. All of these changes must be coordinated to assure that data can be accessed when needed to support business operations.

Primary keys must be changed with care to assure structural integrity of the data resource.

One approach to changing a primary key is to add the new primary key and foreign keys to the database and keep the old keys, at least temporarily. The new primary key is used to identify each data occurrence in the parent data entity and the new foreign key is added to each data occurrence in subordinate data entities. When the addition process is complete and verified, and all applications have been changed, the old primary and foreign keys can be removed.

Changes to a primary key should begin with identification of a need to change the key and identification of an appropriate primary key. Then, the logical and physical models are adjusted to show the new primary key and the associated data entities that need to be changed. Next, all applications accessing those data entities must be identified and a determination made of the frequency and periodicity of access to the data. Once this information is obtained a schedule can be prepared for changing the database and the applications so there is no impact on the business operations. Data converters may be used to ease the impact of changing a primary key, but they do not always provide a benefit worth the development effort.

Good documentation of the database and applications using that database is important to making primary key changes without impacting business operations. However, it is important to plan adequate fall back and recovery procedures in case errors are encountered during conversion of a primary key. Failure to have adequate backup and recovery procedures could severely impact the business operations if an unexpected error were encountered.

Value changes to a primary key. Data values in an existing primary key may need to be changed even though the data attributes in the primary key are valid. This situation could arise from discovery of duplicate values on two or more data occurrences or from changing the data domain for one or more data attributes in the primary key. This latter situation is often encountered when converting application files to a subject data resource.

Changing existing primary key values is usually less serious and easier to perform than changing the data attributes that compose a primary key. Usually the data values in individual records on the database are changed. No changes need to be made to applications unless the values that are changed are hard coded in the application. Each application is reviewed to determine if any primary key values are hard coded in the application. If hard coded primary key values are identified, the appropriate adjustment needs to be made or a data converter needs to be developed.

When the value of a primary key is changed, the values in the foreign keys of subordinate data occurrences must also be changed. If the foreign key values are not changed at the same time the primary key value is changed, identification of the parent data occurrence is lost.

Changes to an existing primary key value begins with identification of the values that need to be changed. Generally, the logical and physical data resource models do not need to be changed. However, those models can be consulted to identify data entities that are related to the data entity being changed to assure that all the foreign keys are identified and changed when the primary key is changed. When this information has been obtained, a schedule can be prepared for changing the database without impacting business operations. An adequate recovery procedure should be planned in case an unknown situation is encountered.

Reducing a Large Secondary Key

Some database management systems have a limit on the number of data attributes that can be used in a physical data key. When the number of data attributes identified for a data key exceed the limit for a particular database management system an alternate data key or a concatenated data key must be considered. In many cases it is difficult to identify an alternate data key, particularly if the data key represents the primary key for a data entity. The usual approach is to identify a concatenated data key to meet the restrictions of the database management system. If the data key represents a primary key an alternate primary key could be selected or a primary key could be manually assigned or computer generated.

> A concatenated data key is developed when the number of data attributes in the key exceed the capability of a database management system.

A concatenated data key is formed by creating a sequential multiple characteristic data attribute containing two or more of the data attributes composing the data key. Several sequential multiple characteristic data attributes could be defined for the concatenated key depending on the use of the data attributes composing the data key. For example, if the data key represented the composite primary key of a data entity and there were several parent data entities for that data entity, multiple characteristic data attributes need to be created for the data attributes composing the foreign key to each of the parent data entities.

When a concatenated data key is identified, the individual data attributes used to form the sequential multiple characteristic data attribute are still maintained as individual single characteristic data attributes to allow easy access to the database. Even though maintenance of both the multiple characteristic data attribute and the individual data attributes that compose it constitutes redundant data, it is necessary redundant data that allows easy access to data in the database. It also allows those single characteristic data attributes to be used in the definition of other data keys.

PHYSICAL DATA RESOURCE MODEL

The physical data resource model represents design of the physical database. It must be developed to meet the needs of the business as defined in the logical data resource model, but it must also produce a physical database that is efficient in a particular operating environment. In other words, the logical model is adjusted to operate efficiently in a particular operating environment without compromising the integrity of that logical model.

Any considerations of operational efficiency must include both production application access and ad hoc access to the database as well as short term and long term use of the database. The physical database should not be designed to have peak efficiency for one type of access to the detriment of other types of access, nor can it have peak efficiency to the detriment of the integrity of the logical model. However, the logical data resource model can not be implemented exactly as defined without considerations for the physical operating environment. There must be a balance between integrity of the logical data resource model, the physical operating environment, and the types of applications using the data.

The operating environment consists of physical features, such as hardware, system software, database management system, and so on, and the organization's standards for use of the physical features. Since there is a wide range of features and standards, each operating environment is different. Therefore, the conversion from a logical data resource model that is independent of any operating environment to a physical data resource model that includes unique features and standards requires a unique set of conversion criteria. This conversion is very detailed in many environments and requires the skills of competent database analysts and good interaction with data analysts and application analysts.

> Development of a good physical database requires a good logical model, the skills of database analysts, and interaction with data analysts.

The initial physical data resource model is a first cut physical model. Performance statistics should be collected during operation and analyzed. Based on the results, the physical data resource model may be adjusted to be more efficient while still maintaining the integrity of the logical data resource model. This task requires the expert skills of database analysts who are thoroughly familiar with the physical operating environment and the database management system.

> The physical database must be adjusted based on performance statistics, particularly when the data resource is evolving.

If the operating environment changes or the physical data resource model is found to be incomplete or in error, a new physical data resource model is developed from the existing logical data resource model. If the operating environment is substantially changed the conversion criteria may need to be changed to reflect that new operating environment. Each enterprise must decide whether a new physical data resource model must be developed, and if the conversion criteria need to be changed.

SUMMARY

Getting started with development of an enterprise-wide subject data resource requires commitment from the entire enterprise. That commitment includes a commitment to managing data as a resource of the enterprise, eliminating ownership issues, and accepting shared management of the data resource. It means a commitment to using resources to train people on the concepts and principles of data resource management, to design the subject data resource, and to convert existing data to that new structure. It requires a commitment to carefully plan those conversions with minimum impact on business operations.

When the commitment to managing data as a resource has been made, definition of the resource can begin. A major functional area of the enterprise is identified for development of the data resource. The area should be an area critical to the success of the enterprise and should be directly involved with management of behavioral entities. Behavioral entities are identified and a strategic data resource model is developed for the data required to manage those entities. When the data resource structure has been established with the strategic model, retrofit data resource models can be developed for existing data. These processes can continue through the enterprise until the basic structure of the data resource has been established.

After the basic data resource structure has been established, project and ad hoc data resource models can be developed for selected information systems. Entity life cycle models and business information models are developed to define the business environment. System architecture and data resource models are developed to identify all data needed to support the business activities of the enterprise. Once the process is started it evolves rapidly and in many cases must be slowed to assure the modeling is performed completely and correctly. The problem is getting started with the first strategic data resource model, not keeping the process going after it has started.

An alternate approach to initiating development of a subject data resource is to start with smaller areas that have less impact on critical operations of the enterprise. Isolated areas can be selected for definition of the data resource and development of applications. This approach allows people to train and learn on smaller projects with less impact and produces quicker results. However, there is a risk involved in developing a data resource without a strategic data resource model. As the data resource evolves data may need to be changed which impacts applications using those data.

The best approach is to develop strategic and retrofit data resource models for a major area of the enterprise. Development of these models does not impact any business operations of the enterprise and provides the structure for developing project data resource models. Once the basic data resource structure is set, an isolated area within that structure can be selected for development of data resource. As people learn and become skilled with the techniques, the data resource can evolve into other areas of the enterprise where larger benefits can be realized.

As the enterprise's data resource evolves, the benefits of that resource can be achieved. Data becomes readily available and can be easily shared by any application that needs the data. The data resource can evolve to meet needs of additional applications without impacting existing applications. Application needs can change without impacting the structure of the data resource. The quality of data used by applications is high and credibility of the data resource increases. The result is improved decisions, proper actions, and increased productivity.

The change to a subject data resource is as much a cultural change as it is a technological change. People must begin thinking about data as a resource and asset of the enterprise, not as pieces of information belonging to applications. They must begin to learn how to cooperatively manage the data resource for achievement of the enterprise's goals rather than create islands of structurally different data for personal reasons. They must learn to share the data through shared management of the data resource. They must learn to manage the data resource with the same management principles used to manage other resources of the enterprise.

Data can be designed and managed as a resource of the enterprise. Techniques are available for designing and managing data as a resource and automated tools are becoming available to assist design and management of data as a resource. An enterprise just needs to make the commitment to accepting a cultural change, developing an enterprise-wide data resource, and reaping the benefits of that resource.

The following questions are provided as a review of the data modeling process and to stimulate thought about developing a data resource for an enterprise.

1. What is the basic premise for development of a subject data resource?
2. What happens when this basic premise is violated?
3. What are the major types of data resource models?
4. What drives development of a strategic data resource model?
5. What happens when too much detail is placed on the strategic data resource model?
6. How does a retrofit data resource model differ from a strategic data resource model?
7. What drives development of a retrofit data resource model?
8. What problems might be encountered with development of a retrofit data resource model?
9. How does a project data resource model differ from a retrofit data resource model?
10. What drives development of a project data resource model?
11. What does an ad hoc data resource model provide that a project data resource model does not provide?
12. What is an enterprise data resource model?
13. How does the development of a enterprise data resource evolve?
14. What factors must be considered when managing primary keys?
15. Why does a data resource model need to be verified?
16. What are the criteria for verifying a logical data resource model?
17. Why do primary keys need to be changed?
18. How is a primary key changed without impact?
19. What factors must be overcome to develop a data resource model?
20. How does an enterprise start developing an enterprise-wide data resource?

Postscript

The human element is not fully realized in today's high technology environment. The socio-technical environment that should exist in an enterprise, and in the business world at large, is far more technical than social. This unequal emphasis between the social and technical elements of the environment results in a loss far greater than any gains made by improved technology.

We are in a socio-technical environment, not a techno-social environment. The human element must be emphasized equal to the technical element because it drives the technical element. People must be encouraged to be innovative, creative, and imaginative. They must be encouraged to understand, comprehend, visualize, and conceptualize their environment. They must be encouraged to conceive, create, and invent new technology to make that environment better.

The people in an enterprise have a largely untapped creative and innovative ability. This ability must be tapped to drive advancements in technology that will improve the environment. Current technology must be utilized to tap the creative ability of people so they can further improve technology. Emphasis must be placed on developing skills to quickly learn and apply current technology to improve the environment and to further improve technology. An infrastructure to maximize the abilities of people must be developed.

The abilities of the human mind must not be limited by technology, particularly computer technology. The human mind must not be used to maximize use of the computer. The computer must be used to maximize the capability of the human mind. Mind cycles are far more important than computer cycles and mindware is far more important than hardware or software. Computer cycles must be used to maximize mind cycles.

The benefits are not in the artificial intelligence of computers, but in the real intelligence of people. Maximizing the real intelligence of people allows them to become true knowledge workers and shifts the emphasis to the human element. It is this real intelligence that must be tapped, nurtured, enhanced, and expanded to provide the real long term competitive advantage most enterprises are seeking.

Business Driven System Development

The data resource design techniques presented in this book are part of the Business Driven System Development method. The method is a total information system development method that includes strategic, tactical, and operational steps to identify, define, design, and construct information systems for an enterprise. It is based on the goals of the enterprise and their information needs in a dynamic business environment. This appendix explains the structure of that development method, but does not include all the details of each phase and step in the method.

The term **business driven** is used because the method is driven by the business needs of the enterprise. These business needs define both the processes that need to be performed and the data needed to support those processes. The processes and the data are structured separately and data views connect the two structures. The process structure does not drive the data structure, nor does the data structure drive the process structure. Both structures are driven by the business needs of the enterprise to achieve its goals.

Initially, information system development methods placed emphasis on processes within the system and treated data as a secondary issue. As information system development methods became more formal emphasis was placed on data that were processed by the system and how those data were processed to meet the needs of the enterprise. This approach led to the concept that the structure of the information system should match the structure of the data being processed by that system.

As the concept of an enterprise-wide data resource structured by data subjects emerges, more emphasis is placed on the analysis of behavioral entities and their management by the enterprise to identify the basic data subjects. Business activities are defined to manage behavioral entities to meet the enterprise's goals. This business driven concept produces the structure of data and the structure of business activities that are used to define and develop information systems.

A good system development method must integrate the data and the business activities into a set of components that operate in unison to support the enterprise. That method must start with the business needs of the enterprise and progress through a series of steps for analysis, design, construction, and implementation of an information system that meets those needs. The progression supports the valued added concept of information system development.

The concept of an information system development method is not dead. Some individual information system development methods have ceased to be useful and effective because they have ceased to evolve with changing technology. In many cases the current technology of information processing has far outdistanced the ability development methods to include that technology. A useful development method must evolve with the evolution of information technology.

Some people believe that no formal development method is required with the technology that exists today. They attack various pieces of integrated development methods, and even change those pieces, without understanding the full impact of changes on an integrated development method. They believe that current development tools can be selected and used to produce systems faster than ever before. Systems can be developed faster than before, and the result is worse than before. Some of the development tools available today can produce spaghetti code and conventional application files faster than they were ever produced before if they are used without the benefits of a good development method.

Some development methods are little more than project management methods. Other development methods address one small portion of the total development process, such as data modeling, or code generation, or testing, and refine that portion to a high degree with no means to integrate it into a total development method. Few development methods are fully integrated to form a continuum from initial problem identification to final resolution of the problem. Few development methods fully integrate both the business and the data in an enterprise. Few development methods include the strategic, tactical, and operational aspects of information systems development.

The Business Driven System Development method solves many of these problems. It provides a consistent, disciplined approach to developing information systems with formal reviews and feedback cycles to identify and correct mistakes and prevent failure. It allows flexibility during analysis and design and requires more rigid constraints during construction. It provides one method for the enterprise to develop information systems that support the enterprise.

The method is self-documenting through an ongoing documentation process where all documentation is a natural product of the development process. Formal documentation is produced at each step in the method and is available to all subsequent steps. No documentation is required that is not a natural product of the development process.

The method provides a framework to manage the complexity of today's information systems that support an enterprise in a dynamic business environment. It provides a precise analysis and specification of requirements that set the scope of the project, and a progressive transition of those specifications into the processes and databases that compose an information system. It provides a proof of correctness for quality control at the end of each step and each phase.

The method is strongly oriented toward analysis and design rather than limited design with extensive debugging and correction. Design is heavily dependent on modeling techniques that are based on semiotic and mathematical theory. It provides formal conversion of logical models into physical processes and data files. It provides a framework of analysis, design, and construction that allows people to work smarter as well as faster to design and construct effective and efficient information systems.

The method is complete from identification of initial problems to the final solution to those problems. It integrates business modeling, system architecture modeling, application modeling, and data modeling to produce a complete model of the business, the data, and the information system. It integrates development of processes and the data with the business information modeling process to produce a system that meets the needs of the enterprise. It provides a formal set of rules to follow and proof of correctness criteria that can be applied at each step to assure development as error free as possible.

The method is applicable for real world practical design. It hides the mathematical details in a method that is easy to apply to the everyday task of developing information systems. It is rigid enough to be consistent and reproducible yet flexible enough to be adjusted to the peculiarities of any enterprise. It is user oriented and encourages direct user involvement in a majority of the development steps. The success of any information system depends on the knowledge and skills of both the user community and information processing professionals.

The method is equally applicable both to design of new systems and to retrofitting of old systems. It is applicable to large and small systems, although larger benefits will be realized from its use on large systems. It is applicable to mainline systems, end user systems, and ad hoc applications. It is applicable to centralized and decentralized information systems and to manual as well as automated information systems.

The method is compatible with prototyping, and prototyping is frequently used with various design steps of the method. Many portions of the method can be automated to remove the routine mechanics from the people involved in the development effort and allow them to concentrate on the thought, analysis, evaluation, and decisions involved in developing information systems. It is useful for system acquisition where the basic processes and databases are designed and that design is used to evaluate prospective systems. It is also compatible with project management by providing finite tasks that can be assigned to individual team members.

The method is not a panacea. It cannot replace all the problems, analysis, evaluation, or decisions that are involved in developing information systems. It cannot replace the frustration and anxiety of the design process. It is not a cookbook that can be blindly followed from beginning to end to produce a perfect system. It provides a formal method for identifying, designing, and constructing information systems to support enterprise goals.

The method can be adjusted into a development cycle that fits the particular needs of an enterprise and allows the enterprise to use the method more effectively. This adjustment takes the basic procedures, techniques, and rules of the method and molds them into the particular way an enterprise does business. The enterprise surrounds the basic development method with its own unique requirements for using the method. It adds the specific forms, method of receiving and prioritizing requests, approval procedure, team assignments, responsibility and accountability, location and type of documentation storage, file names, and so on, to the basic development method.

STRUCTURE OF THE METHOD

The Business Driven System Development method consists of a strategic segment and four development segments. The strategic segment is used to model the business environment and the enterprise and to identify and define the organizational structure, business activities, and data needed to support the enterprise. The remaining four segments are used to define and construct information systems. The top level of the method is shown in Figure A.1

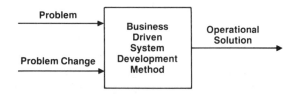

Figure A.1   Business Driven System Development.

The Business Driven System Development method consists of a hierarchy of segments, phases, and steps, as shown in Figure A.2. The method is subdivided into five major segments for strategic planning, setting the project scope, analyzing and designing the information system based on that scope, constructing the system according to that design, and implementing the system after construction. Each segment is subdivided into one or more phases that contain a set of procedures to be accomplished and reviewed before moving to the next phase. Each phase is subdivided into individual steps that contain a series of tasks to be performed. Each of these steps requires one or more inputs and produces one or more outputs that contribute to the final information system.

The architecture of the method is shown in Figure A.3. Each segment has a specific input and a specific output. Each segment also has a feedback loop to the previous segment to allow changes to the previous segment when errors or changes are detected. These feedback loops provide an on-going correction and enhancement cycle that keeps development synchronized and documentation current.

Enterprise goals and information about the business environment are input to the *Strategic Segment*. It produces a set of business models that define the business environment and drive the design process. Initial problem and problem changes are input to the *Project Segment*. A project definition is produced that controls the project through the entire development method. The *Design Segment* produces a physical database model of the data files needed by the information system and an application model of the processes contained in the information system. Any changes to the project scope are cycled back

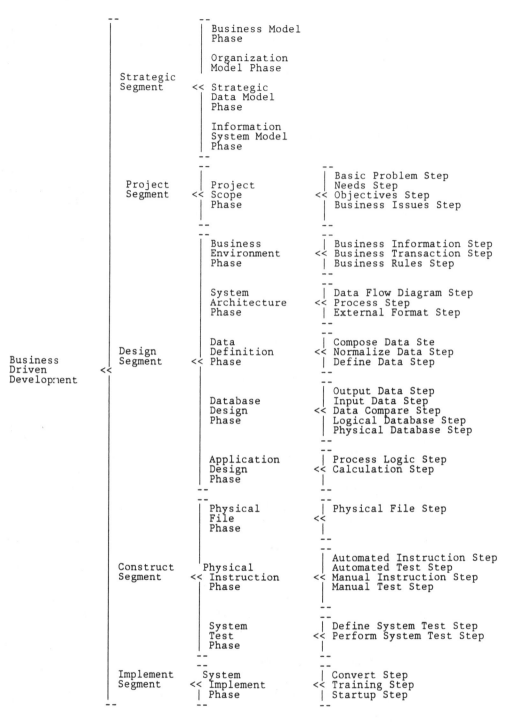

```
          --                  --
          |                   | Business Model
          |                   | Phase
          |                   |
          |                   | Organization
          |                   | Model Phase
          | Strategic         |
          | Segment      << Strategic
          |                   | Data Model
          |                   | Phase
          |                   |
          |                   | Information
          |                   | System Model
          |                   | Phase
          |                  --                  --
          |                  --                  | Basic Problem Step
          | Project          | Project          | Needs Step
          | Segment      << Scope         << Objectives Step
          |                  | Phase            | Business Issues Step
          |                  |                  |
          |                 --                 --
          |                 --                 --
          |                  | Business         | Business Information Step
          |                  | Environment  << Business Transaction Step
          |                  | Phase            | Business Rules Step
          |                 --                 --
          |                  | System           | Data Flow Diagram Step
          |                  | Architecture << Process Step
          |                  | Phase            | External Format Step
          |                                    --
          |                  | Data             | Compose Data Ste
          | Design           | Definition   << Normalize Data Step
          | Segment      << Phase            | Define Data Step
Business  |                  |                 --
Driven << |                  |                  | Output Data Step
Development|                 | Database         | Input Data Step
          |                  | Design       << Data Compare Step
          |                  | Phase            | Logical Database Step
          |                  |                  | Physical Database Step
          |                  |                 --
          |                  |                 --
          |                  | Application      | Process Logic Step
          |                  | Design       << Calculation Step
          |                  | Phase            |
          |                 --                 --
          |                 --                 --
          |                  | Physical         | Physical File Step
          |                  | File         <<
          |                  | Phase            |
          |                 --                 --
          |                 --                 --
          |                  |                  | Automated Instruction Step
          | Construct        | Physical         | Automated Test Step
          | Segment      << Instruction   << Manual Instruction Step
          |                  | Phase            | Manual Test Step
          |                  |                  |
          |                  |                 --
          |                  | System           | Define System Test Step
          |                  | Test         << Perform System Test Step
          |                  | Phase            |
          |                 --                 --
          |                 --                 --
          | Implement        | System           | Convert Step
          | Segment      << Implement     << Training Step
          |                  | Phase            | Startup Step
          --                 --                 --
```

Figure A.2 Hierarchy of the Business Driven System Development Method.

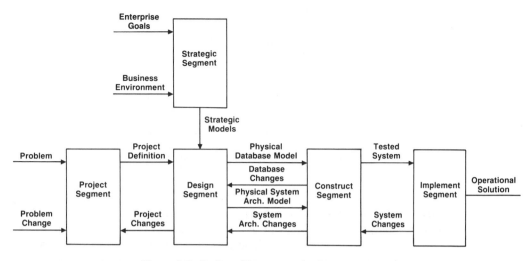

Figure A.3   Business driven system development architecture.

through the project segment for a revision to the project definition. The *Construct Segment* uses the database model and the application model to develop a tested information system. Any changes to the database model or the application model are cycled back to the design segment. The *Implement Segment* places the tested information system into operation. Any changes identified during implementation are cycled back to the construct segment.

Documentation is an integral part of each step in the method and must be maintained to assure a successful system. The documentation produced from any step is available at every other step, as shown in Figure A.4. Storage and retrieval of documentation is not shown for each step in the method. However, it is implied that documentation is produced from each step, stored, and is available to every other step.

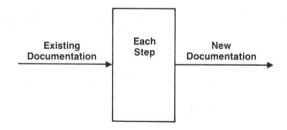

Figure A.4   Documentation storage and availability for each step.

The knowledge and skills of both users and data processors are also implied at each step in the method, as shown in Figure A.5. They are not shown at each step for the same reason that documentation is not shown at each step. However, knowledge and skills are part of every step in the development process to ensure a successful system. If either the knowledge or skills are constrained in any way or eliminated, the resulting system will not be fully successful.

Business Driven System Development

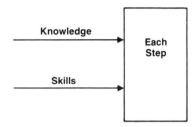

Figure A.5 Knowledge and skill requirements for each step.

A review and approval step is implied at the end of each phase, as shown in Figure A.6. The review can be a walk-through, a presentation, distributed documents, or whatever method the enterprise establishes, and should be performed prior to final approval of the phase. The proof of correctness criteria is applied and verified during this review step. Final approval must be granted before the next phase can begin to avoid propagation of errors. With the emphasis on direct user involvement, reviews are generally shorter and more productive and result in fewer changes.

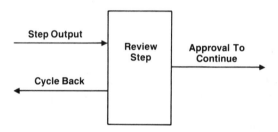

Figure A.6 Review and approval step.

The method should be followed for all projects. If a project does not require a particular step, or does not alter the documentation produced by a particular step, that step may be bypassed. However, for a step to be bypassed it must first be reviewed to verify that it is not necessary for the project in question. Many projects are faced with critical deadlines that include penalties or other impacts if the deadline is not met. Deferred and mandatory steps may be identified for projects that have critical deadlines. The mandatory steps are performed to meet the deadline and deferred steps are performed after the deadline has been met.

STRATEGIC PLANNING

The *Strategic Segment* establishes the overall plan for developing information systems. There are four phases in the *Strategic Segment*, as shown in Figure A.7. The *Business Model Phase* produces the business activity model for the enterprise. The business activities must be identified, modeled, and defined before the information system is constructed to assure the proper business activities are used in the proper information systems.

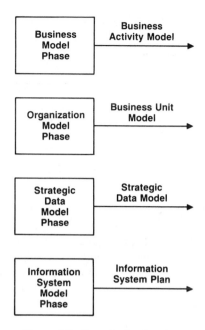

Figure A.7 Strategic planning phases.

The *Organization Model Phase* produces the business unit model of the enterprise and identifies business entities outside the enterprise that the enterprise interacts with during performance of its business activities. These internal and external business entities are used to develop the business information model.

The *Strategic Data Model Phase* produces the strategic and retrofit data resource models of the enterprise. The strategic data modeling process reviews the behavioral entities to determine the data subjects that need to be identified. The retrofit data modeling process reviews existing data files to determine the data subjects that already exist within the enterprise.

The *Information System Model Phase* identifies the major information systems that are critical to the enterprise and produces a plan for development of those systems. The business activities are reviewed and those activities that are critical to the enterprise are prime candidates for automation. These critical business activities, along with the data supporting those activities, form the base for defining major information systems for the enterprise.

PROJECT SEGMENT

The *Project Segment* consists of one phase that takes the initial problems and problem changes and produces a project definition that sets the scope and bounds for the remainder of the project, as shown in Figure A.8. This project definition is not a requirements definition in the traditional sense, but a formal, well structured set of basic problems, needs to resolve those problems, objectives to accomplish the needs, and business issues that need to be resolved. It is a tactical approach to identification and resolution of those problems with the implementation of an information system.

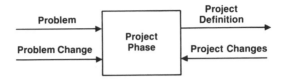

Figure A.8 Project Segment.

The development team is designated at the beginning of the project and is composed of representatives from the user community since the problems that are being resolved are largely business problems. The objective is to involve people in the analysis and resolution of their problems to produce better solutions to the problems and have better acceptance of those solutions. The development team must represent the entire user community, not just a portion of the user community. When part of the user community is excluded, there is a high probability that the resulting information system will not meet the needs of the total user community.

The problems, needs, objectives, and business issues are established through group sessions. Generally, individual interviews are not used, except in situations of personal problems or conflict. The group sessions create a synergy that produces more than individual interviews could ever produce and result in a more complete statement than could be produced by the person performing individual interviews. The size and mix of the groups must be considered in order to create an interactive environment that is productive. A good group facilitator is necessary to keep the interest and involvement up and the group productive.

Project Phase

The *Project Phase* is the first and only phase of the *Project Segment* and consists of four steps, as shown in Figure A.9. The objective of the project phase is to provide a formal definition of the basic problems, the needs to resolve those problems, the objectives to accomplish the needs, and any open business issues to be resolved. This project definition sets the scope and bounds for the remainder of the project. Resolution of the business issues provides a base for defining business policy and procedures.

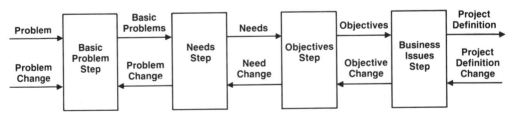

Figure A.9 Project Phase.

Project phase steps. The *Project Phase* consists of four steps for identifying the basic problems, the needs to resolve those problems, the objectives to meet the needs, and the open business issues.

Basic Problem Step. The *Basic Problem Step* identifies basic problems to be resolved. A good statement of basic problems is the best start to a good resolution of those problems. Correctness and completeness of the information system is based on a complete and correct statement of the problems. This step begins with an analysis of each symptomatic problem to determine the cause of that problem which leads to more specific symptomatic problems and ultimately to the basic problem. When the basic problem is determined, it is documented and the next symptomatic problem is analyzed. When the last symptomatic problem has been analyzed, then the current list of basic problems is complete.

Each problem is stated in a complete simple sentence and no problems are discarded. Formally documenting each problem allows people on the team to get to the next problem without concern for previous problems. When problems are discarded or modified beyond what was stated, the group synergy is destroyed. Generally, symptomatic problems are listed first and are later resolved into basic problems and, generally, the most current problems are listed first. As the process evolves, all of the basic problems are listed.

New problems and problem changes that occur during the development process enter through this *Basic Problem Step*. These new problems revise the set of basic problems so there is only one set of basic problems for the project. The new problems must be within the scope of the project to assure that the project does not keep expanding indefinitely.

Needs Step. The *Needs Step* identifies needs that will resolve the basic problems. The statement of needs begins the requirements definition that will be enhanced throughout development until the system is implemented. One or more specific needs are listed for each basic problem that will, when implemented, resolve that basic problem. It is not a statement of how that need is to be met, but a statement of the need. If the discussion drifts into how the need is to be met, the process becomes one of design and analysis of alternative rather than a statement of the needs.

One need could resolve several problems and one problem could be resolved by several needs. Therefore, as each problem is reviewed to identify what is needed to resolve that problem, all the existing needs should be reviewed. If one or more of the existing needs completely resolve the problem, then there is no reason to state additional needs. However, if the existing needs do not completely resolve the problem, then additional needs must be stated.

Needs are stated as complete simple sentences just like the problems and each need should be referenced to a problem. This cross reference assures that each problem is resolved and that each need resolves a problem. The format of the problems and needs is up to the individuals on the team and the enterprise standards.

The basic problems may be unclear or new problems may be identified during definition of the needs. When this situation occurs, changes need to be made to the basic problems which could result in an adjustment to the needs. The problem change feedback loop assures that the problem set is kept current and that the needs answer all of the problems.

Objectives Step.   The *Objectives Step* identifies objectives to meet the needs. Objectives are specific items to be performed or accomplished in order to meet the needs. One or more specific objectives are listed for each need that will, when implemented, accomplish the needs. Definition of objectives to meet the needs begins the analysis to determine how the needs are met. The analysis continues during design of the system architecture model. It is these objectives that are assigned to individuals and become the initial tasks that are monitored through project management.

The needs may be incomplete, inaccurate, or unclear, and new needs may be identified. When this happens, adjustments are made to the needs, and if necessary, to the basic problems through the feedback loops. The set of needs is then adjusted and the objectives are restated. This adjustment cycle keeps the problems, needs, and objectives synchronized with each other.

Business Issues Step.   The *Business Issues Step* identifies open business issues that arise during identification of the basic problems, needs, and objectives. These open business issues are questions about the business that must be answered. Outstanding business questions and issues can cause an otherwise well-designed information system to fail. When these outstanding questions are answered, they are stated as business rules which eventually become the business policies and procedures for the enterprise.

One of the major problems an enterprise faces today is lack of formal business rules. If business rules are not formally stated and documented they can not be supported by information systems. If the information systems do not support business rules, they are virtually useless. Therefore, business rules must be formally stated and documented.

There is a chance that the objectives are unclear when business issues are identified and defined. When the objectives are unclear they must be adjusted, which may result in an adjustment to the needs or the basic problems through the feedback loops. When these adjustments are made, the business issues will coincide with the statement of the problems, needs, and objectives.

Project definition.   The project definition is complete and can be reviewed when the problems, needs, objectives, and business issues have been identified and accurately stated. However, the project definition can be modified during the *Business Environment Phase*. Any project definition changes from the *Business Environment Phase* are cycled back to the *Project Phase* to assure that the project definition coincides with the business environment phase. The project definition is stored in whatever repository is identified by the enterprise.

DESIGN SEGMENT

The *Design Segment* consists of five phases, as shown in Figure A.10. The objective of the design segment is to model the business environment, the architecture of the information system, the data resource to support the information system, and the processes in the information system. The physical database model and the application model are produced by the design segment.

The *Design Segment* is the largest segment of the method. Since emphasis is on the

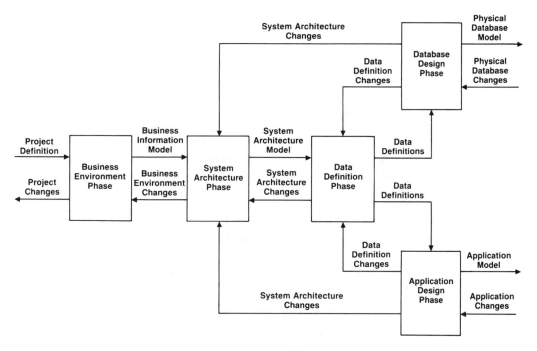

Figure A.10 Design segment.

analysis and design of information systems, not on coding and debugging, the major portion of development is oriented toward the design and analysis process. The analysis and design process is based on the modeling techniques.

Business Environment Phase

The *Business Environment Phase* consists of three steps, as shown in Figure A.11. The project definition and the users knowledge of the business environment are used to define a business information model for the portion of the business environment that the information system supports.

The only way an information system can be truly effective is to thoroughly under-

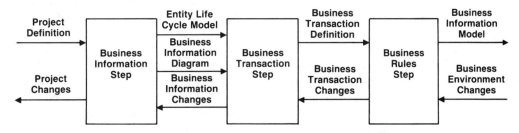

Figure A.11 Business environment phase.

Business Driven System Development

stand the business environment that information system supports. Many past failures of otherwise excellent information systems have been because of their failure to support the business activities of an enterprise. This phase assures the business environment is properly defined and provides the detail for developing an information system that will support that environment.

The business information model identifies the flow of data in the enterprise. It identifies business transactions that are needed and business transactions that can be adjusted or eliminated. It identifies data needed by the enterprise and in many cases the format of those data. The format of the business transactions is not required until the end of the *System Architecture Phase*, but identification of that format during this phase helps identify business transactions.

Business environment phase steps. The *Business Environment Phase* consists of three steps for developing a business information diagram, defining the business transactions on that diagram, and defining the business rules.

Business Information Step. The *Business Information Step* develops business information diagrams. Business entities and business transactions on those diagrams must be within the scope of the project. It is very easy to allow identification of business entities and business transactions to extend beyond the project scope. The information gained is not wrong, but it is not within the scope of the project and actually delays progress. Therefore, development of business information diagrams must be constrained by the project scope.

It may be helpful to prepare a written or oral description of the business environment. This description helps start development of business information diagrams. Needs and objectives from the project definition also help start development of business information models. Another help is to start with existing business entities and the transactions between those entities. Once the business information diagrams are started it is relatively easy to continue until they are completed.

Entity life cycle models can be helpful for developing business information models. An entity life cycle model identifies various states a behavioral entity moves through during its contact with the enterprise and the transitions between those states. These transitions frequently require or depend on some type of transaction between the enterprise and that entity which become transactions on the business information diagram. In addition, the data required to make the transition is frequently contained in the business transaction and identification of those data helps identify details of the business transaction.

Project changes identified during this step are cycled back to the *Project Phase*. A revised project definition is returned to the *Business Environment Phase*. This process assures the business information model is within the scope of the project definition and completely models the business within the scope of the project definition.

Business Transaction Step. The *Business Transaction Step* defines each business transaction on business information diagrams. These business transactions become external data flows on the system architecture model and must be thoroughly defined before the system architecture model is complete. Definition of the format and content of these business transactions begin in the business transaction step. The volume, frequency, and periodicity of business transactions can also be defined and used to determine peak periods for processing. Changes to the business information diagrams may be identified as business transactions are defined. These changes are cycled back to the *Business Information Step*.

Business Rules Step. The *Business Rules Step* defines business rules. These business rules are developed from the statement of objectives and from resolution of business issues listed in the project definition. Each objective is reviewed and one or more business rules are developed for each objective if appropriate. Each business issue is also reviewed and one or more business rules are developed for each issue. Definition of these business rules often requires assistance from outside the project team and often from outside the enterprise.

Changes to business transactions, business information diagrams, or the project definition may be identified as the business rules are being defined. These changes are cycled back to the *Business Transaction Step* for revisions to the business transaction definitions.

Business Information model. Entity life cycle models and the business information models are the final outputs of the *Business Environment Phase* and must be reviewed and approved before development continues. These models drive development of the system architecture model. Failure of these models to be complete and accurate results in an incomplete and inaccurate system architecture.

Any changes from the *System Architecture Phase* are cycled back to the *Business Environment Phase*. These changes may apply to the business rules, the business transactions, or the business information diagram. When these changes are made, new models are available to the *System Architecture Phase*.

Business information diagrams and entity life cycle models can be developed and maintained by hand or by a suitable graphics package. They are stored in the appropriate repository identified by the enterprise. Business transactions and business rules are also stored in the appropriate repository.

System Architecture Phase

The *System Architecture Phase* consists of three steps, as shown in Figure A.12. It follows the *Business Environment Phase* and uses business information models to develop the system architecture model. That model is used for development of the data resource and application models, and as a plan for actual construction of the information system.

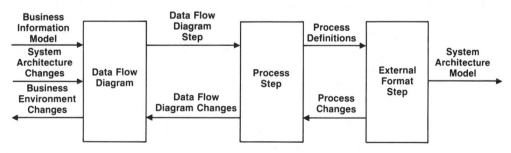

Figure A.12 System architecture phase.

Before any information system is constructed, a blueprint or floor plan showing the architecture of that system is needed. This blueprint is used to construct the system just like a blueprint is used to construct a house or a major building. The resulting information system will only be as good as the architecture represented in the blueprint. Therefore, every effort should be made to assure the system architecture model is complete and accurate.

System architecture phase steps. The *System Architecture Phase* consists of three steps for developing data flow diagrams, defining processes on those diagrams, and defining the formats for external data flows.

Data Flow Diagram Step. The *Data Flow Diagram Step* produces one or more data flow diagrams for the system. Development of data flow diagrams is driven by business transactions from the business information model. Business transactions become external data flows on the system architecture model. Ideally, there is a one-to-one relation between business transactions and external data flows. However, with some business information models there could be a one-to-many or a many-to-one relation between business transactions and external data flows and these situations should be considered when defining external data flows on the system architecture model.

Once external data flows are placed on the system architecture model, the processes, data entities, and internal data flows can be defined. This is the analysis and design part of system development where alternatives are identified and evaluated to determine the architecture of the information system. External data flows set the constraints because they represent data needed by the enterprise to operate in the business environment. The internal part of the information system must meet those needs.

Changes to the business environment may be identified as data flow diagrams are developed. These changes are cycled back to the *Business Environment Phase* to update the business information model. When the business information model is updated it is available to the *System Architecture Phase*. System architecture changes from the *Construct Segment* or the *Data Definition Phase* of the *Design Segment* are used to modify the data flow diagrams.

Process Step. The *Process Step* defines each process on the data flow diagram. This process definition is a narrative about the function and scope of the process, not a definition of the detail tasks that are performed by the process or the logic of performing those tasks. The detail tasks and logic are defined in the *Application Design Phase*. The purpose of process definitions is to assure that all processing that needs to be performed by the information system is performed, that no processing is performed redundantly, and that no processing is forgotten. The best way to make this assurance is to define the function and scope of each process shown on the data flow diagram and to review those definitions for completeness and consistency.

Business processes are the processes shown on the business activity model and internal processes are processing resulting from design of the information system. Internal processes do not show on the business activity model. Both business and internal processes need to be defined, although the definition of business processes may already have been defined on the business activity model. If these processes have been defined, that definition is reviewed to assure it is synchronized with the process being developed for the information system.

It may be necessary to make changes to the data flow diagrams as processes are defined. These changes are cycled back to the *Data Flow Diagram Step* and the processes are redefined until all functions of the information system are included in the design.

External Format Step. The *External Format Step* defines the formats of external data flows. The format of external data flows, which represents business transactions, may have been started during the *Business Environment Phase* and may have been enhanced during development of data flow diagrams. It is not important when they are defined as long as they are completely defined before this step is completed. As the external data flow formats are defined, changes to processes may be identified, which in turn may result in changes to data flow diagrams. These changes are cycled back as necessary to keep the data flow diagrams, the process definitions, and the external data flow formats synchronized.

System architecture model. The output of the *System Architecture Phase* is the system architecture model. The system architecture model is the final architecture of the information system and is used to construct the processes and database that comprise that system. It must be reviewed and approved before the *Data Definition Phase* can begin. Any errors in the information system architecture will result in errors in the final information system.

Data flow diagrams can be developed and maintained by hand or by a suitable software package. They are stored in the appropriate repository identified by the enterprise. The process definitions and the formats of the external data flows are also stored in the appropriate repository.

Data Definition Phase

The *Data Definition Phase* consists of three steps, as shown in Figure A.13. The system architecture model is used to develop data definitions. The objective of this phase is to identify, structure, and describe all data needed by the information system.

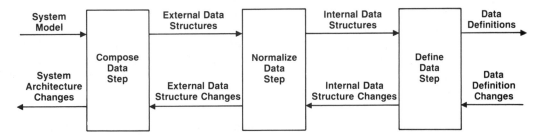

Figure A.13 Data definition phase.

The only way an information system can work properly is to correctly identify, structure, and describe all data processed by that information system. Any failure to completely identify, name, structure, or define all data used by an information system results in a failure of the information system to meet the needs of the enterprise.

Data definition phase steps.   The *Data Definition Phase* consists of three steps to compose data structures for all external data flows, to normalize those data structures into internal data flows, and to define each data unit.

Compose Data Step.   The *Compose Data Step* produces data structures for the external data flows defined on the system architecture model. An output data structure is composed for each external data flow moving out of the information system and an input data structure is composed for each data flow moving into the information system using the formats defined in the system architecture model. As the data structures are composed, changes to the system architecture model may be identified. These changes are cycled back to the *System Architecture Phase* through for correction. When the system architecture model has been updated, it is available to the *Data Definition Phase*.

Normalize Data Step.   The *Normalize Data Step* produces normalized internal data flows. Each output data structure is normalized into a required data structure, and each input data structure is normalized into a necessary data structure. As the required and necessary data structures are developed, changes may be identified to the input and output data structures. These changes are cycled back to the *Compose Data Step*.

Define Data Step.   The *Define Data Step* defines all data on the data structures. Each data entity, data occurrence group, data attribute, data attribute group, primary key, foreign key, and secondary access, must be defined. Definition of data integrity rules may begin in this step and must be completed by the end of the *Database Design Phase*. The data resource directory should be consulted to determine if the data are already defined and if the definitions are appropriate. If they are not defined or the definition is not complete or appropriate an adjustment needs to be made either to the data resource directory or to the data structure.

Data on all data structures must be defined, not just the internal data structures. The assumption is often made that only data on internal data structures need to be defined since it is the internal data structures that are used to define the database. However, data on external data structures are used by the enterprise and must be defined the same as data stored in the database.

Entity type hierarchy diagrams may be used to assist in defining data. One or more diagrams may be developed for each data entity being defined. Once the diagrams are developed the appropriate data attributes can be defined to represent the branches on the entity type hierarchy.

Data definitions.   Final output of the *Data Definition Phase* is data definitions. These data definitions consist of external and internal data structures and data definitions for all data on those data structures. These definitions are the beginning of the data resource modeling process that results in a physical database model that supports the information system. It is also the beginning of the application modeling process that results in physical instructions for each process on the system architecture model. Data definitions must be reviewed and approved before the *Database Design Phase* can begin. If one or more entity-type hierarchy models are developed they become part of the output for this phase.

Any changes to the data definitions from either the *Database Design Phase* or the *Application Design Phase* are cycled back to the *Data Definition Phase*. When these changes are made, new data definitions are available for database design and application design.

Data structures and entity-type hierarchies are stored in the appropriate repository identified by the enterprise. Each data definition is stored in the data resource directory. It is a good practice, particularly on large projects, to interact frequently with the data resource directory through the development of data structures. This interaction allows adjustment of the data names and their definitions if there is a discrepancy. In other words, short cycles of data structure development and data resource directory verification are better than one big cycle that could result in numerous changes.

Database Design Phase

The *Database Design Phase* consists of five steps, as shown in Figure A.14. It follows the *Data Definition Phase* and uses data definitions to develop the physical data resource model. This phase can proceed in parallel with the *Application Design Phase*. The objective of the *Database Design Phase* is to define a physical data resource model that contains all data needed by the information system.

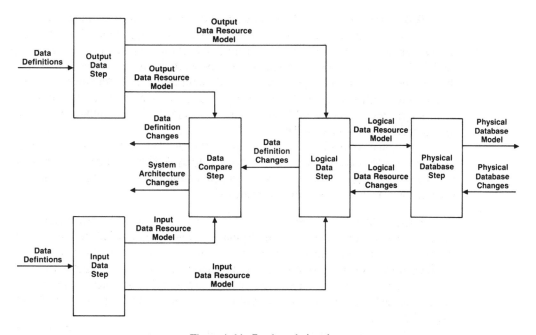

Figure A.14 Database design phase.

Data modeling is a critical step in the system development process. To assure correct development of a physical database, data must be carefully evaluated and modeled. This modeling process includes modeling output data and input data separately, comparing and adjusting those models, and forming a total logical data resource model from these two models. The logical data resource model is used to develop a physical data resource model, based on a formal set of denormalization criteria, that is used for development of the physical files.

Database design phase steps. The *Database Design Phase* consists of five steps for defining output and input data resource models, comparing those models with the system architecture, and defining a logical data resource model and a physical data resource model.

Output Data Step. The *Output Data Step* produces an output data resource model showing data needed from the database to support the outputs of the information system. All required data structures defined in the normalize data step are optimized by data subject to form the output data resource model.

Input Data Step. The *Input Data Step* produces an input data resource model showing the data necessary to maintain the database for the information system. All necessary data structures defined in the normalize data step are optimized by data subject to form the input data resource model. This step can be performed concurrently with development of the output data resource model.

Data Compare Step. The *Data Compare Step* compares the output data resource model, the input data resource model, and the system architecture model. All data entities are verified as existing both on the system architecture model and in the data resource models. If there is not a direct correspondence between the system architecture model and data resource models, an adjustment is made to either the data structures or the system architecture. Each data entity on the data structures must be represented on the system architecture model, and each data entity on the system architecture model must be represented in the data resource model.

During the comparison process, changes may be identified to either the data definitions or the system architecture. These changes are cycled back to those phases and result in enhanced system architecture model and data definitions. These corrected data definitions are then available for further comparison.

Logical Data Step. The *Logical Data Step* produces a logical data resource model. When the output and input data resource models are synchronized with each other and with the system architecture model, the two models are optimized to produce the logical data resource model. When the logical data resource model is defined, the structural and validity rules for maintaining data integrity are defined. These rules are carried into the physical design step and become integrity constraints that are implemented to maintain data integrity in the database.

Changes may be identified to the data definitions when defining the logical data resource. These changes are cycled back to the *Database Compare Step* for correction. If necessary, they are cycled back to the *Data Definition Phase* or to the *System Architecture*

Phase for correction. This process continues until the system architecture model and the logical data resource models are synchronized with each other.

Physical Database Step. The *Physical Database Step* produces the physical database model from the logical data resource model. The physical database model must be developed based on the denormalization process for the particular operating environment of the enterprise. The physical files defined on the physical database model are used to create the physical files in the construct segment.

When the physical database model is completed, it is reviewed to determine if it meets the needs of the information system and the operating environment. If it does not meet the needs of the information system, changes are made to the physical database model, the logical data resource model, or the system architecture model using the feedback loops until the model is correct. No arbitrary changes are allowed to the physical database model.

Physical database model. Final output of the *Database Design Phase* is a physical database model. This model is used to create physical files for the information system. Any changes to the database design from the physical file phase are cycled back to the *Database Design Phase*. When these changes are made, the new physical database model is available to the *Physical File Phase*. When the physical database model is completed, it is ready for review and approval. The model must be reviewed and approved before construction of the information system can begin.

The output and input data resource models are working documents that do not need to be maintained after database design phase is completed. The logical and physical models become permanent documentation. The entity-relationship and file-relationship diagrams can be developed and maintained by hand or by a suitable software package. They are stored in the appropriate repository identified by the enterprise. The remainder of the logical data resource model and the physical database model need to be documented in the data resource directory.

Application Design Phase

The *Application Design Phase* consists of two steps, as shown in Figure A.15. It follows the *Data Definition Phase* and can proceed in parallel with the *Database Design Phase*. It uses data definitions and business rules to develop an application model. The objective of the *Application Design Phase* is to define the process logic for each process on the system architecture model, whether that process is automated or manual and whether it is a large or a small process.

Application modeling is also a critical step in the system development process. Process logic must be carefully evaluated and modeled to assure correct development of processes. This modeling process includes developing the process logic structure based on the structure of the data processed and the business rules, verifying the process logic, and defining all the calculation rules used in each process.

Application design phase steps. The *Application Design Phase* consists of two steps to define the process logic for each process and to define the calculation rules used in those processes.

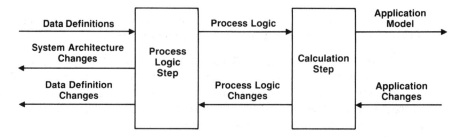

Figure A.15   Application design phase.

Process Logic Step.   The *Process Logic Step* defines the process logic for each process on the system architecture model. The structure of the data manipulated by the process sets the initial structure of the process logic. That initial process logic structure is then expanded to include all the details of processing based on the business rules.

During process logic definition, changes to data definitions or the system architecture model may be identified. These changes are cycled back to the *Data Definition Phase* or the *System Architecture Phase.* When the data definitions or the system architecture model have been enhanced, they are available for application design. Any adjustment in the data definitions or the system architecture model may also result in changes to the database.

Calculation Step.   The *Calculation Step* defines all the calculation rules for both manual and automated processes. Frequently the calculation rules are not documented or are buried in program source code without documentation. Any change in these algorithms is not made consistently for all uses of those rules. Therefore, calculation rules must be formally defined and documented. Any changes to process logic that are identified during definition of the calculation rules are cycled back to the *Process Logic Step* for correction.

Application model.   Final output of the *Application Design Phase* is the application model. When the application model is completed it is ready for review and must be approved before the information system can be constructed. Any application changes from the *System Test Phase* are cycled back to the *Application Design Phase.* When the application model is corrected, it is available for the *System Test Phase.*

Process logic charts can be maintained by hand or by a suitable software product and are stored in the appropriate repository identified by the enterprise. Calculation rules are documented in the data resource directory.

CONSTRUCT SEGMENT

The *Construct Segment* consists of three phases, as shown in Figure A.16. It follows the *Design Segment* and uses the physical data resource model and application model to construct and test the information system. The tested information system is produced by the *Construct Segment* and is ready for implementation.

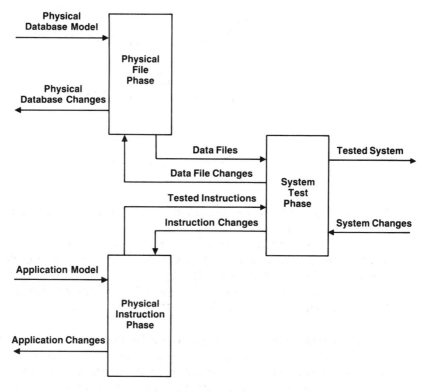

Figure A.16 Construct segment.

The *Construct Segment* builds the information system processes and databases as designed. If the design was done properly the construction should be routine and the resulting information system should operate with minimum difficulty. The emphasis on extensive design before construction results in a sound design that has minimum, if any, bugs to be removed. Only when the design is incomplete or faulty will the resulting system be faulty.

Physical File Phase

The *Physical File Phase* consists of one step, as shown in Figure A.17. It follows the *Database Design Phase* and can proceed in parallel with the *Physical Instruction Phase*. The objective of the *Physical File Phase* is to create physical data files as they were defined in the physical database model.

Physical File Step.   The *Physical File Step* creates physical data files. When the physical data files have been created, they are populated and used for testing and production operation of the information system. Unit testing of physical data files is performed

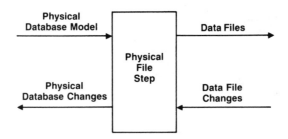

Figure A.17 Physical file phase.

during this step, not during the system test. Any problems with creation of the data files is corrected in this step.

Any changes identified with the physical database model are cycled back to the *Database Design Phase*. When the changes are made, an enhanced physical database model is available for redefinition of the physical data files. Any data file changes from the *System Test Phase* are cycled back to the *Physical File Phase*. When the changes are made, the enhanced data files are available for further system testing.

Data files. Final output of the physical file phase is physical data files. These data files are populated and used during testing and production operation of the information system. The data files must be reviewed and approved before they are placed into production. The physical data files and physical records are documented in the data resource directory.

Physical Instruction Phase

The *Physical Instruction Phase* consists of four steps, as shown in Figure A.18 It follows the *Application Design Phase* and can proceed in parallel with the *Physical File Phase*. The objective of the *Physical Instruction Phase* is to use the application model to develop physical instructions for each process on the system architecture model.

Physical instructions make the system operate. They may be either manual, in the form of user instructions, or automated in the form of source code. Physical instructions must be developed for each process on the system architecture model whether that process is large or small, simple or complex, manual or automated. The manual and automated instruction processes are shown separately to emphasize that instructions need to be developed for both manual and automated processes.

Physical instruction phase steps. The *Physical Instruction Phase* consists of four steps that develop and test the automated and the manual instructions.

Automated Instruction Step. The *Automated Instruction Step* produces instructions for all automated processes in the information system. The process logic charts and

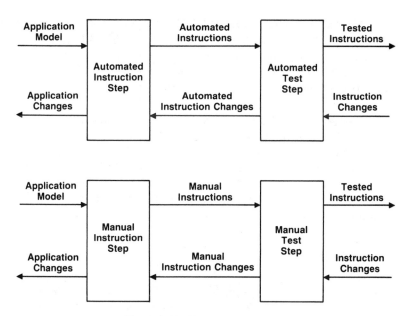

Figure A.18 Physical instruction phase.

system architecture model are used to develop source code for each automated process. The data integrity constraints are automated and placed in the appropriate location, whether in a data application, an active database management system, or a data resource directory. Any changes identified during development of the automated instructions are cycled back to the *Application Design Phase*. When those changes are made, a new application model is available for further development of automated instructions.

Automated Test Step. The *Automated Test Step* produces compiled and tested automated instructions. If changes are necessary, those changes are made and the instructions are recompiled and tested again. This process continues until the instructions are complete and correct. Any changes identified during testing are either corrected in the *Automated Instruction Step* or cycled back to the *Application Design Phase* for correction. The new application model is then available for coding and testing. This process keeps the process logic charts synchronized with the automated instructions. It is a poor practice to adjust automated instructions without adjusting the process logic charts accordingly.

Manual Instruction Step. The *Manual Instruction Step* produces instructions for all manual processes in the system. These instructions may consist of either the process logic charts or narrative instructions or both. In the case of online systems these instructions should be available online for immediate inquiry. Any changes are cycled back to the *Application Design Phase*. When the corrections are made, a new application model is available for continued development of manual instructions.

Manual Test Step. The *Manual Test Step* verifies and unit tests the manual instructions. This testing is usually done by the people that will be performing the manual procedures. If changes are necessary, they are made either in the *Manual Instruction Step* or to the application model through the feedback cycles and the test is performed again. This process continues until the instructions are correct.

Tested Instructions. Tested manual and automated instructions are the final output of the *Physical Instruction Phase*. Any instruction changes resulting from system testing are cycled back to the *Physical Instruction Phase* for correction. When the corrections have been made, the tested instructions are available for system test. The final instructions must be reviewed and approved prior to implementation of the information system. Physical instructions are stored in the appropriate repository identified by the enterprise.

System Test Phase

The *System Test Phase* consists of two steps, as shown in Figure A.19 It follows the *Physical Instruction Phase* and the *Physical File Phase* and uses physical instructions and data files for system testing and produces a tested system that is ready for implementation. Once the individual pieces of a system have been developed and tested, the entire system needs to be tested before implementation. This phase tests the operation of all the pieces as a system and assures the system is ready for implementation.

Various techniques, such as stress testing, destructive testing, volume testing, and so on, are used to test the entire system. All the features and components of the system must be tested, such as flow through the system, the correct processing of each incoming transaction, and the correct preparation of every outgoing transaction. System testing can also include prerelease testing by the users. Ideally, testing is done by an independent party which can maintain objectivity. Typically, the people that develop an information system have difficulty seeing the errors in that system. System testing must be well planned and adequate time must be allowed for thorough testing of the system before implementation.

System test phase steps. The *System Test Phase* consists of two steps for defining the system test criteria and performing the system test according to those criteria.

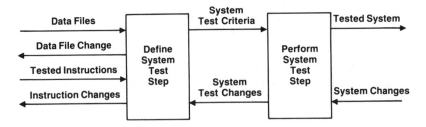

Figure A.19 System test phase.

Define System Test Step. The *Define System Test Step* defines the system test criteria since the detailed test criteria for system testing will vary with each project. The first step is to develop a test plan with the user based on the requirements of the system from the objectives of the information system. Its purpose is to track all transactions through the system and determine if they are processed correctly and the proper results are produced. The details of the test plan depend on the types of transactions that are being processed by the system.

Traditionally, test criteria were developed with the initial requirements definition. As the design of the system changed, the test criteria were not changed accordingly. When the system test was performed it was often performed on an incomplete or inaccurate set of test criteria resulting in incomplete and inaccurate testing. The resulting information system did not meet the needs of the enterprise.

In the current development method the definition of test criteria is done after construction to assure that all the features and all the components of the system are included. The expected results are listed along with each test criteria to determine if the processing was successful. These criteria and expected results are saved for future testing of any enhancements to the information system.

Changes to the data files and physical instructions may be identified during the definition of test criteria. These changes are cycled back to the *Physical File Phase* or the *Physical Instruction Phase* for correction. When the changes are made, the new data files and tested instructions are available to the *System Test Phase*.

Perform System Test Step. The *Perform System Test Step* carries out the system test plan. If the test fails, changes are routed back to the *Define System Test Step*. If the test criteria are defined correctly, then changes are routed back to the *Physical Instruction Phase* or to the *Physical File Phase* for correction. Any changes deferred for future enhancements are documented for the next project phase rather than ignored. No errors are left uncorrected or undocumented.

One of the problems with system testing is that errors are ignored and the assumption is made that they will be corrected in a future enhancement to the information system. However, those errors are not documented as problems and when the time for future enhancement arrives many of the errors are not remembered and are not corrected. Therefore, any errors that are left for future enhancements to the information system must be documented as problems for that project.

Tested system. Final output of the *System Test Phase* is the tested system which is ready for implementation. If any changes are found during implementation, they are cycled back to the *System Test Phase* for correction or documented for future projects. The final system must be reviewed and approved before implementation. A physical system architecture model can be developed if it is required by the enterprise. It is derived from the logical system architecture model and the physical database model and includes any modifications made during the logical to physical conversion process.

During system test there may be many minor changes that need to be made to the system. Usually these changes are made on a short time schedule without going through the entire development process. Therefore, documentation for the *System Test Phase* includes listing changes that were made so they can be documented after-the-fact. Documentation of these minor changes should not be ignored because they may be useful for future enhancements to the information system. If the changes are major, such as structural changes, then the project needs to be cycled back through the development cycle to ensure all aspects of the system are still synchronized. The extent of the feedback loop depends on the extent of the structural changes.

System test criteria are documented in the appropriate repository identified by the enterprise. These test criteria are used for future enhancements to the information system. It is better to save and enhance these test criteria than to develop a new set of test criteria for each enhancement to the information system.

IMPLEMENT SEGMENT

The *Implement Segment* consists of one phase, as shown in Figure A.20. It follows the *Construct Segment* and places the tested information system into production operation to resolve the initial problems as defined. Implementation of an information system is relatively simple if the design and construction of that system followed the prescribed steps and the appropriate people were included in those steps. Only when the steps are not followed and the proper people are not included will there be problems with implementation of an information system.

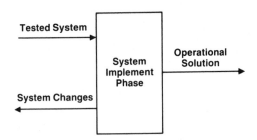

Figure A.20   Implement segment.

System Implement Phase

The *System Implement Phase* consists of three steps, as shown in Figure A.21. The objective is to take the tested information system, make any conversions from present operations that are necessary, train personnel, and place the information system into production operation. If all the steps of the method were followed correctly, the information system will be fully operational when implemented. If the steps were not followed, then the

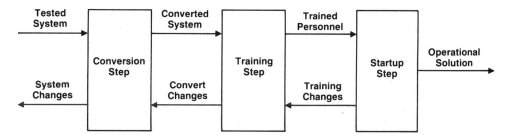

Figure A.21 System implement phase.

system may well fail in the sense that it will not meet the objectives as stated and will not resolve the problem.

System test phase steps. The *System Test Phase* consists of three steps to convert existing data and populate production files, provide training, and start production operation of the new system.

Conversion Step. The *Conversion Step* converts data from existing data files into the new data files or populates new data files with the appropriate data. The conversion and population of production files may have been done during system testing or at some other time prior to the *System Implement Phase*. Regardless of when the conversion and population was done, this step assures that data files are populated with the production data necessary for production operation. This step may proceed in parallel with the *Training Step*.

Any changes are cycled back to the *System Test Phase* for correction, or deferred for future enhancements to the information system during another project. Any deferred corrections must be documented as problems for the next enhancement project.

Training Step. The *Training Step* trains both users and operations personnel in the use and operation of the information system. A training plan is developed for all people that will use or operate the system. Frequently this step is shortened or eliminated because of time or budget constraints which only result in inefficient and ineffective use of the information system. Any problems identified during training are either cycled back for correction or deferred to the next project.

Startup Step. The *Startup Step* puts the information system into operation and allows users to operate the system on a production basis. Any changes identified during startup are usually documented for the next project. Adequate fall back and recovery procedures should be put into place before final startup of the new information system. In some situations, parallel systems are maintained until the new system is proven to be fully operational.

Operational solution. Final output of the *System Implementation Phase* is the operational solution to the initial problem. Documentation consists of any changes made to the system made during the *System Implement Phase* and documentation of any changes to be made during future enhancements to the information system. When system implementation is completed, all changes must be documented as they would have been if done during the development process.

A postimplementation review should be conducted to determine how well the information system met the needs and resolved the problems as defined. Any discrepancies should be used to revise and modify the development cycle to prevent such discrepancies from occurring again. It is only through this constant revision process that the development cycle for any particular enterprise can be constantly revised to produce quality information systems. As people learn to use the development cycle and become proficient with the techniques, better information systems will be developed faster and will provide the best level of support to the enterprise.

Glossary

Abstract data unit A data unit, such as a database, a data segment, a data occurrence group, and a data attribute group, that is created from basic data units.

Accept / reject logic The type of logic used to either accept data from the database into an application or reject data from an application.

Access See Data access.

Access down data structure Data access from the parent data entity to the subordinate data entity.

Access for verification Entry into a data entity to verify if a record exists, but not to store or retrieve any data.

Access up data structure Data access from the subordinate data entity to the parent data entity.

Acquired data attribute A characteristic that is assigned to an entity for a special purpose and is not inherent to that entity. See Inherent data attribute.

Action See Business action.

Active database management system A database management system that can initiate action on the data in the database based on the values of data in that database.

Active data resource directory A data resource directory that can take action on data entering the database or in the database, such as enforcement of data integrity rules.

Active derived data Data attributes that are derived and the contributing data attributes still exist in the database and can be modified. Must be rederived when the contributing data attribute values change.

Active redundant data Redundant data attributes that can be modified when their contributing data attribute changes value.

Actual data value A data value that represents a true measurement or description of an entity and is not coded in any manner.

Ad hoc Inquiry into the database and processing against that data at this time for this purpose. Ad hoc means a one-time temporary process, but its general meaning can include permanent decentralized applications and database inquiry.

Ad hoc data resource model A data resource model used to identify data accesses and data views that are needed for ad hoc processing but were not identified on project data resource models.

Affinity analysis A process used to identify data segments by determining the frequency of data relations between closely related data entities.

Alias data name Any data name other than the primary data name by which a data unit is known. Not considered to be a structural anomaly but an *also known as* name.

Alternate primary key A set of one or more data attributes that identifies a unique data occurrence in a data entity, but is not the official primary key. May lose its uniqueness over time. See Official primary key.

Ampersand A data attribute symbol used to represent a calculated foreign key.

Anomaly A deviation from the general rule or standard method. See Data anomaly.

Application The portion of an information system that contains the process logic for both automated and manual processes. See Business application and Data application.

Application conversion The conversion of conventional applications to access subject data.

Application database A conventional database consisting of a set of application data files that are structured by data subject and do not always contain single units of data.

Application data entity A single, multiple, partial, or compound subject data entity that has been defined to support a set of applications. Also referred to as an Application data file.

Application data file A conventional data file, usually of partial, multiple, or compound subject data entities used to support a set of applications. Also referred to as an Application data entity.

Application data view A data view that supports an individual application. Contains only the data needed by that application.

Application model A model of the applications in an information system consisting of a definition of each process, a process logic chart for each application, and the definition of each calculation algorithm.

Application object A single business activity that has the processing completely defined. Application objects can be linked through tables, commands, or icons to form information systems under the object oriented concept.

Application ownership controversy The controversy that has resulted over the ownership of applications that are used by a variety of users in a shared environment. Similar to the Data ownership controversy.

Application process The processes in an information system consisting of business processes, internal processes, and data processes.

Artificial intelligence The second wave of the information age that includes expert systems, robotics and locomotion, natural language processing, image analysis, and the ability to think and learn as well as people can.

Associative data entity A relation between entities on an entity-relationship diagram that contains data and usually resolves a many-to-many relation between entities. This relation becomes a data entity known as an associative data entity.

Asterisk A symbol used to indicate a comment on process logic charts.

At sign A data attribute symbol used to represent a calculated data attribute.

Attribute See Data attribute.

Availability See Data availability.

Back slash A data attribute symbol used to represent a descending sort sequence.

Basic data unit A fundamental unit of data that is used to define the enterprise's data resource. Basic data units are data entities, data occurrences, data attributes, and data values.

Behavioral entity Entities in the business world that behave and respond to the business rules of an enterprise. The objects of behavior modeling.

Behavior modeling The process of modeling the behavior of entities managed by the enterprise and determining the changes in that behavior based on changes in the business rules.

Bidirectional access Data access that enters one data entity and progresses both to parent data entities and subordinate data entities.

Borderless integration The integration of information systems such that the boundary between those systems is not apparent to the user. Also known as Seamless integration.

Box with bulging sides A symbol that represents a data entity on data entity-relationship diagrams and data flow diagrams.

Box with rounded corners A symbol that represents a data file on data file-relationship diagrams.

Business action The specific operations taken within a set of process logic. The actions are listed below the conditions in a set of process logic.

Business activity An individual activity performed by an enterprise. Business activities are structured into a hierarchy known as a business activity model.

Business activity diagram One part of the business activity model showing the business activities performed by an enterprise and the hierarchy of those activities.

Business activity independence The independence of the structure of business activities from the organizational structure of the enterprise and the structure of the data resource.

Business activity model A model showing the business activities performed by an enterprise consisting of a business activity diagram and definitions of each business activity.

Business application An application containing only business conditions and business actions. Does not include any data integrity or file management processing.

Business condition The criteria used to identify a business situation.

Business data resource model A model of the data contained on the business schema. Compared to a logical data resource model and a physical data resource model.

Business driven A term referring to the business needs driving development of an information system.

Business driven system development method A development method that is business driven. It integrates the people, data, and business into the development of an information system.

Business entity A person or group of people within or without the enterprise that can take action on business transactions. Represented by a hexagon on the models.

Business entity transaction matrix A matrix showing which business entities initiate or receive business transactions.

Business environment A term referring to the environment where the enterprise is conducting business. Definition of this environment is necessary to begin development of information systems.

Business environment models A set of models representing the business environment, including entity life cycle models, business activity models, and business information models.

Business event The arrival of a business transaction, the demand for a business transaction, the passage of time, or a point in time. Creates a situation that must be resolved by a set of business actions.

Business function A set of related business activities on the business activity diagram.

Business independence Independence of the structure of business activities from the organizational structure of the enterprise and the structure of the data resource.

Business information diagram A part of the business information model showing the business entities and the business transactions between those entities.

Business information model A model consisting of the business information diagram, the definitions of each business transaction, and the business rules.

Business issue An issue that has arisen and is unresolved with respect to how the enterprise will conduct its business affairs. These issues must be documented and resolved before the information system can be developed.

Business modeling The process of developing business models, such as business activity model, business entity model, and entity life cycle model.

Business oriented actions The actions in a business activity that carry out the business rules of an enterprise.

Business process Processes that are oriented toward business rules and do not include data integrity processes or file management processes. See Business application.

Business process responsibility matrix A matrix showing which business processes are performed by each business unit in the enterprise.

Business rule A rule supporting the actions that are defined for business activities. Business issues are resolved and become business rules. Will be the only remaining tasks in applications after the file rules and data rules are removed.

Business schema The structure of data in business transactions. Referred to as the fourth schema. Used to develop external schema by the data normalization process.

Business situation A situation created by the current state of a behavioral entity and its actions.

Business transaction A transaction of information between two business entities by manual or electronic form. Represented by a solid line with an arrow on business design models.

Business transaction name The name of the business transaction moving between two business entities. Usually the name of the document or report. Same as the name of the external data flow representing that business transaction.

Business unit A person or group of people within the enterprise that can take action on business transactions.

Business unit diagram A part of the business entity model showing the business entities within an enterprise. Commonly referred to as the organization chart.

Business unit model A model of business entities in an enterprise consisting of a Business Unit Diagram and definitions of each business entity.

Calculated data attribute See Derived data attribute.

Calculated foreign key A foreign key that is calculated at execution time and is not maintained on the database.

Calculation algorithm The algorithm used to calculate the value of derived data attributes.

Calculation rule See Calculation algorithm.

Can also be A term used to represent data categories. An entity can exist in one or more data categories in a *can also be* situation. A mutually inclusive situation.

Can only be A term used to represent the data in an entity type hierarchy. An entity *can only be* one branch in an entity-type hierarchy. A mutually exclusive situation.

Candidate primary key A primary key that has been identified as a possible primary key but has not been verified as a valid primary key.

Cardinality The number of elements in a mathematical set. With respect to data modeling it pertains to the number of data occurrences that are allowed or required in a data relation.

Centralized database A database that exists in one location and contains primary data repositories.

Characteristic See Data characteristic.

Child A term referring to the subordinate data entity in a one-to-many data relation.

Childless data entity A data entity that has no subordinate data entities.

Chronology stamp A time stamp placed in the data that defines the time to the detail needed by the enterprise.

Circle A symbol used to indicate an entity state on the entity life cycle model.

Class name See Data class name.

Clean Data A slang term referring to data that have a high degree of data integrity.

Closed recursive data entity A recursive data entity where the data occurrences are in a one-to-one relationship and refer to each other.

Code table A table consisting of coded data values and the descriptions or range of measurements of each coded value.

Coded data values A data value that is coded and does not represent the actual measurement or description of the characteristic of the entity.

Colon A data attribute symbol used to represent data that is not entered into the system but is calculated or derived and placed on the database.

Column A column of data in a relation (table) of the relational model.

Combined data flow An internal data flow between two processes that represents an output of one process and an input to another process.

Combined data view A data view that contains less than the full set of data attributes from a data entity but more than are required from a specific application. Used to support multiple applications.

Complex characteristic data attribute A data attribute that has a combination of multiple characteristics and variable characteristics.

Complex subject data entity A data entity that consists of multiple data subjects that may be full or partial data subjects.

Composite primary key A primary key consisting of two or more data attributes from two or more data entities.

Compound primary key A primary key consisting of two or more data attributes from the same data entity.

Concatenated key A physical data key that is formed from the concatenation of two or more data items due to the physical limitations of a database management system. The individual data items are also maintained in the database.

Conceptual data resource model A data resource model of the conceptual schema. See Logical data resource model.

Conceptual schema The common denominator between the internal and external schema in the three- and four-schema concept. The conceptual schema are defined during logical data modeling. Referred to as the Third Schema.

Conditional data structure constraints Data integrity rules pertaining to the structure of data occurrences in the database that are based on data values.

Conditional data structure rule A data integrity rule defining the conditional existence of a data relation.

Conditional data value rule A data integrity rule defining the conditional existence of a data value.

Conditional structural data integrity table A table containing conditional data structure rules.

Confidentiality See Data confidentiality.

Contributing data attribute A data attribute that contributes to the derivation of another data attribute. It may be a primitive data attribute or a derived data attribute.

Conventional application An application that is structured to use data from application files or an application database.

Conventional data See Conventional database.

Conventional database A database containing data that are structured by the applications use of data and not by data subjects. See Application database.

Conventional data files See Conventional database.

Conversation A sequence of individual tasks that are linked by commands, tables, or icons to form an information system. See Object oriented; Reusable code.

Crossloaded data The movement of data from one secondary data repository to another secondary data repository. Usually does not involve the enforcement of any data integrity rules.

CRUD matrix See Data management matrix and Data responsibility matrix.

Cyclic data entities Two data entities that are in a one-to-many data relation that resulted from resolution of a single data entity where the data occurrences were in a many-to-many data relation.

Dashed line A line representing a relation between objects, not a flow between objects.

Data The individual facts and figures that are retrieved, manipulated, and stored in a database.

Data access A set of data attributes used to access the database. Data accesses are defined with secondary keys on the logical data resource model and become data keys on the physical data resource model.

Data access analysis The analysis of a set of data access route to determine which one would use the least resources as defined by the enterprise.

Data access conversion The conversion of secondary keys on the logical data resource model to data keys on the physical data resource model.

Data access diagram A diagram similar to a PERT chart that shows all data access routes. Used to determine the route that uses the least resources.

Data access route A specific route taken between two or more data entities to obtain the data needed. Consists of a series of tasks representing an access into a data entity.

Data access task The entry into one data entity. A set of tasks form a data access route.

Data access verification Verification of each data access on the logical data resource model to assure that they are valid, properly defined with foreign keys, and explicitly shown on the data resource model.

Data actions The actions related to enforcement of data integrity rules.

Data administration The unit in an enterprise responsible for developing plans and administering policies and procedures relating to effective and efficient use of the enterprise's data resource.

Data ambiguity The meaning of the data units as currently defined is uncertain or doubtful. The opposite of data interpretability.

Data analyst A person that defines the data needed by an application and designs the logical database. Develops the business, external, and conceptual schema and assists with development of the internal schema.

Data anomaly A deviation from the general rule which for a subject data resource is single units of well defined and formally named data that are properly structured by data subject.

Data application An application that contains only data integrity rules and no business processing or file management tasks.

Data architecture The second tier of the data resource component in the information technology discipline.

Data attribute A basic data unit representing one or more characteristics of a data entity. Has a definition, but may not have any physical parameters.

Data attribute constraints The data integrity rules applied to data attributes. Constraints on the relations between data attributes, such as Required, Prevented, and Optional.

Data attribute conversion Conversion of data attributes on the logical data resource model to data items on the physical data resource model.

Data attribute conversion table A table in the data converter that identifies the conversions that are made between data attributes during their movement across a data interface.

Data attribute group An abstract data unit consisting of a set of single characteristic data attributes that are commonly used as a set, but need to be defined separately according to the rules of data normalization and a single data unit subject database.

Data attribute group name The name of a data attribute group that consists of two or more data attributes. Usually contains the standard word Group.

Data attribute name The combination of the data entity name, data characteristic name, and variation name that uniquely identifies a data attribute.

Data attribute name thesaurus A data name thesaurus for data attribute names.

Data attribute number A unique, arbitrary number assigned to each data attribute for identification and use of that data attribute. The use of a data attribute number as a primary reference is not recommended.

Data attribute relation The relationship between data attributes consisting of one-to-one, one-to-many, and many-to-many relations. Used for defining data integrity rules.

Data attribute symbol The symbol used to prefix data attributes on data structure charts indicating their use as primary keys, foreign keys, secondary keys, physical keys, derivation, etc.

Data availability The degree that data exhibit the state or quality of being readily accessible and usable. The objective of a subject data resource is to have easily interpretable data readily available to anyone in the enterprise that needs that data to perform their business activities. The third tier of the data resource component of the information technology discipline.

Data backup and recovery The task of making appropriate copies of the database to be used to restore the database when it becomes altered or destroyed.

Data block A set of data attributes that are not fully normalized because of loss of understandability or loss of production efficiency, such as addresses.

Data category A data subentity that represents a *can also be* situation. Data categories are treated similar to data entities when designing a data resource.

Data characteristic The smallest piece of information that still retains meaning. Used to describe a data entity. Also referred to as a Data element.

Data characteristic name The portion of the data attribute name that identifies the data characteristic. Consists of one or more words.

Data characteristic variation Any variation of a single data characteristic, such as a format difference.

Data characteristic variation name The portion of the data characteristic name that qualifies the variation of that data characteristic.

Data class name The use of a standard word, such as Date, at the end of a data name to indicate the class of that data attribute. See Standard word.

Data confidentiality The task of withholding data that should not be disclosed, or providing data only to authorized sources.

Data content verification Verification of the data attributes and data values on the logical data resource model to assure they are single units, properly named, and completely defined.

Data controlled A term meaning that the data control the design of the information system. The Business Driven System Development method is business driven not data driven or data controlled.

Data conversion The conversion of data structures across a data interface.

Data converter A routine that converts or translates data from one data structure to another data structure across a data interface.

Data definition The comprehensive definition developed for each basic or abstract data unit in the enterprise.

Data denormalization The process of converting the conceptual schema to the internal schema for a specific operating environment.

Data derivation algorithm An algorithm that shows the process for deriving the values of derived data attributes.

Data derivation diagram A diagram of the relations between data attributes showing which data attributes contribute to the derivation.

Data derivation relation The relations between contributing and derived data attributes. Can be one-to-one, one-to-many, and many-to-many.

Data description A term referring to the combination of a formal data name and a comprehensive data definition.

Data dictionary An automated or manual method to maintain definitions about data. Generally a subset of the processing contained in a full data resource directory.

Data disclosure The task of disclosing data that legitimately need to be disclosed by law or enterprise policy.

Data domain A set of values allowed for a particular data attribute. May be a list of values, ranges of values, or a rule. Treated as a data entity in the subject data resource.

Data domain management The task of managing data domains and using data domains to define data integrity rules.

Data driven A term referring to the fact that the data drive development of an information system. The Business Driven System Development method is business driven not data driven.

Data duplication The process of duplicating data that have been edited and stored in the database rather than replicating the capture and editing of data. See Data Replication.

Data duration The length of time data are retained in the database. The counterpart of Data retention.

Data element The smallest piece of information that still retains meaning. Also referred to as a Data characteristic or a Data item.

Data entity A set of data attributes that are stored together for a particular purpose. A data entity may represent single, multiple, or compound subjects of data.

Data entity conversion Conversion of data entities on logical data resource models to data files on physical data resource models.

Data entity keys A collective term representing primary, secondary, and foreign keys.

Data entity name The portion of the data name consisting of one or more words that identifies the data entity.

Data entity name thesaurus A data name thesaurus for data entity names.

Data entity number A unique, arbitrary number assigned to each data entity for identification and use of that data entity. The use of a data entity number as a primary reference is not recommended.

Data existence The presence of a data entity in the form of a data occurrence, such as single employee.

Data field See Data item.

Data file A set of data records organized in a particular manner. The physical counterpart of a data entity.

Data flow The movement of data into an information system, out of an information system, or within an information system. Each data flow has a corresponding data structure.

Data flow diagram One part of the system architecture model consisting of a graphic representation of the architecture of a system consisting of data storages, processes, and the flow of data.

Data independence The separation of the structure of data from the structure of business activities and the structure of organizational units.

Data inheritance The use of the definition and features of parent data units to further qualify a particular data unit. Each data unit inherits the definitions and features of all of its parent data units.

Data instance The time frame or point in time that a data value represents. The time frame for which a data value is valid.

Data integrity The degree that data exhibit the state or quality of being complete, accurate, and unimpaired. The degree that data are complete and correct at all times under all conditions.

Data integrity constraint The physical counterpart of the data integrity rules that are placed in applications or an active data resource directory for enforcement. Result of the logical to physical conversion of the data integrity rules.

Data integrity rule A rule defining the data integrity that is to be performed on each data unit. Data integrity rules consist of value, structural, retention, derivation, and redundancy rules.

Data integrity rule conversion Conversion of data integrity rules on the logical data resource model to data integrity constraints on the physical data resource model.

Data integrity rule enforcement The consistent application of a comprehensive set of data integrity rules against data entering the database and data already in the database.

Data integrity verification Verification of the data integrity rules on the logical data resource model to assure that they completely define the rules necessary for maintaining data integrity.

Data interface A boundary between dissimilar data structures. Generally used to refer to the boundary between subject data and conventional data.

Data interface management The task of managing data across a data interface until the data can be converted to a subject database and applications can be converted to use that subject database.

Data interpretability The ability to interpret data in a database including locating the data and interpreting the meaning of those data. The objective is an enterprise data resource with data that are easily interpretable and readily accessible.

Data item A data element with definition and physical parameters. An individual field in a data record. A data item is used to define physical files and physical records. The physical counterpart of a data attribute.

Data key A physical key defined to the database that allows access to a data file to store or retrieve specific data. Defined from secondary keys during definition of the physical data resource model.

Data life cycle The life cycle that data follow during their existence in the database. Data are created, retrieved, updated, and ultimately destroyed.

Data model The construct of a database management system, such as network, hierarchical, relational, and inverted.

Data name The name applied to a basic or abstract unit of data for unique identification of that data unit.

Data name abbreviation The abbreviation of the primary data name resulting from length restrictions of software products.

Data name thesaurus A thesaurus containing references between words that are not used and data names and the corresponding word or words that are used in data names. It does not include alias data names.

Data naming taxonomy The taxonomy used to name basic and abstract data units and to abbreviate those names when length restrictions are encountered. The complete data name consists of the data repository name, data subject name, data characteristic name, and data characteristic variation name.

Data navigation The movement between data entities in a database along explicit data relations. Navigation can be performed in either direction along an explicit data relation.

Data normalization The process of converting the data on unnormalized business transactions to data structured by data subject. Conversion of business schema to external schema.

Data object A set of data that are stored in or retrieved from the database. Used in conjunction with application objects to develop object oriented processes.

Data occurrence A specific existence of a data entity that is uniquely identified by a primary key.

Data occurrence anomaly See Referential integrity.

Data occurrence group An abstract data unit consisting of a set of data occurrences from a data entity that represent a logical grouping based on some selection criteria, such as all employees certified as pilots.

Data occurrence group name The name of a data occurrence group. Named like data entities but must be unique with all data entity and data occurrence group names in the enterprise.

Data occurrence relations See Data relations.

Data optimization The process of assuring that identical data entities are combined into one data entity to prevent synonymous data entities. Conversion of external schema to conceptual schema.

Data ownership controversy The controversy created over the ownership of the data as a result of moving data to a subject data resource and sharing that data. See Shared data.

Data property A quality or trait of a data characteristic. The ideal is single property data values for each data characteristic.

Data purification The process of assuring that the data have high integrity by passing a set of comprehensive data integrity rules.

Data quality The state of the data including structure, integrity, availability, and interpretability. High quality data are well structured, have high integrity, are readily available, and are easily interpretable.

Data record A physical grouping of data items that are stored or retrieved from a data file. The counterpart of a data occurrence.

Data redundancy The storage of the same data value for the same data occurrence for the same data instance in two or more locations in the database.

Data redundancy diagram A diagram showing the sequence of maintaining data redundancy in a database.

Data redundancy table A table showing all existences of redundant data. If the primary data attribute is known, all existences of redundant data are listed under the primary data attribute.

Data relation A relationship between two data entities designating how occurrences in one data entity are related to occurrences in the other data entity. See One-to-one, One-to-many; Many-to-many data relations.

Data replication The process of capturing and editing redundant data two or more times. Redundant data should be duplicated rather than replicated.

Data repository A unique location where data are stored. There may be one or more data files in a data repository.

Data repository name The portion of the data name that identifies the location where the data are stored.

Data resource The entire data resource of an enterprise.

Data resource directory An application or information system used to maintain data about the enterprise's data resource. Contains dictionary and directory capability and may be either active or passive.

Data resource model A model of the logical or physical data resource. See Logical data resource model and Physical data resource model. Not the same as a Data model.

Data resource modeling A process of developing data resource models, either logical or physical.

Data retention The length of time that data are retained on the database. The counterpart of Data duration.

Data retention rules The data integrity rules that govern the retention and/or destruction of data in the database.

Data retrodocumentation The process of documenting data in conventional data files.

Data retrofit The process of documenting conventional data and converting those data to a subject data resource.

Data rule domain A data domain containing rules governing the allowable data values that can exist in a data attribute.

Data rules The rules pertaining to the integrity of the data. Traditionally placed in applications, but will be placed with the data resource.

Data security The tasks associated with preventing unauthorized access, alteration, or destruction of data in the database.

Data segment An abstract data unit referring to a set of data entities that are closely related by a high frequency of data relations between those data entities. Different data segments are loosely related by a low frequency of data relations between those data segments.

Data segment name The name of the data segment. Usually contains the standard word Segment.

Data structure A hierarchy of one or more levels of data with each level containing one or more sets of data. A data structure is a modified form of set theory for use with data analysis and design. Logically, a data structure represents a hierarchy of data entities with their respective data attributes.

Data structure composition The process of composing data structures for the business transactions. Composition of the business schema.

Data structure constraints The data integrity rules applied to the structure of data in the data resource.

Data structure normalization The process of normalizing business schema to external schema.

Data structure optimization The process of optimizing external schema into conceptual schema.

Data structure rule A data integrity rule defining the relations between data entities, such as Required, Optional, or Prevented.

Data structure verification Verification of the logical data resource model to assure that true data entities and valid data relations have been defined.

Data subentity See Data category; Data occurrence group.

Data subject A set of data containing one or more data characteristics about a particular subject as defined by the enterprises view of the business world and verified by data normalization.

Data unit A unit of data in the hierarchy from the enterprise data resource to data values. Data units can be either basic data units or abstract data units.

Data validity An older term used for editing the values of data attributes to assure their correctness. See Conditional data value rule; Data value rule.

Data value A basic data unit representing the contents of a data attribute.

Data value conversion table A table in a data converter that is used to convert the values of data attributes as they are moved across a data interface.

Data value description The description of a coded data value. Usually differs from the data value name.

Data value domain A data domain consisting of the values that are allowed in a data attribute.

Data value name The name of the coded data value. Usually differs from the data value description.

Data value relation The relation between the values in two or more data attributes.

Data value rule A data integrity rule defining the allowable values for a data attribute.

Data view A set of data attributes that are stored in or retrieved from the database. Can be application data views, combined data views, or full data views.

Data view conversion Conversion of the application data views on the logical data resource model to application, combined, or full data views on the physical data resource model.

Data view verification Verification of the data views on the logical data resource model to assure that they provide the data needed by the application.

Data volatility An indication of the frequency with which a particular data attribute changes its value. Data that change frequently are considered highly volatile data.

Database An abstract data unit referring to a set of data entities that are used for a particular purpose.

Database administration The unit or function in an enterprise responsible for managing the database environment. Generally different from Data administration.

Database analyst A person that develops the internal schema and optimizes the database based on performance statistics.

Database conversion The conversion of a traditional database to the enterprise data resource. Compared to Data conversion.

Database converter A routine that converts data from one data file to another data file across a data interface.

Database evolution The evolution of a subject data resource through the birth, growth, and maturity stages.

Database management system An automated system for the maintenance, storage, and retrieval of data where the processes of maintenance, storage, and retrieval are done by the system not by the requesting application.

Database name The name of the database, which is an abstract data unit, depending on the data entities comprising that database. Usually contains the standards word Database.

Database transition The conversion of a conventional database to a subject data resource.

Database transition plan The plan that is developed for the transition of a database to a subject database environment.

Database transparency The concept that a storage of data in a decentralized environment is transparent or unknown to the user of that data.

DBMS Abbreviation for Database Management System.

Decentralized data Data that are contained in a variety of primary and secondary data repositories in two or more locations in an enterprise.

Decentralized time relational The concept of a time relational database in a decentralized environment.

Deletion anomaly The situation where a data attribute is stored redundantly in subordinate data occurrences and not in the parent data occurrence and is lost when the subordinate data occurrences are deleted.

Denormalization See Data denormalization.

Denormalized data Data in the internal schema that have been through the data denormalization process. Not the same as unnormalized data.

Department level information system An information system developed for support of a department within an enterprise.

Derivation algorithm The algorithm used to derive the values of a derived data attribute.

Derived data Data that are derived from other data and not obtained by direct measurement of an entity.

Derived data attribute A data attribute that is derived from one or more other data attributes, which may be primitive or derived, by a derivation algorithm.

Derived data relation The relation between data attributes that contribute to the derivation of derived data. Can be one-to-one, one-to-many, or many-to-many.

Derived data rules Data integrity rules pertaining to the derivation and the maintenance of derived data attributes under all conditions.

Design As a verb means to conceive, create, plan, and construct something. As a noun means the plan or underlying scheme that governs the functioning of something.

Development cycle The implementation of a development method into an enterprise and adapted to meet the specific needs of that enterprise.

Development method A generic method consisting of integrated concepts, principles, and techniques for the development of information systems.

Development phase A grouping of development steps within the Business Driven System Development method. A subdivision of development segments.

Development segment A major grouping in the Business Driven System Development method that consists of development phases and steps.

Development step An individual step that is accomplished within a development phase in the Business Driven System Development method.

Dirty data A slang term referring to data that are poor quality because of poor data integrity rules.

Disclosure See Data disclosure.

Dispersed data Decentralized data that do not have a primary data repository and the full set of data can only be obtained by a union of secondary data repositories.

Dissimilar data structures Data structures that do not represent the same database structure, such as application data and subject data.

Distributed data Decentralized data that have a primary data repository representing the full set of data.

Documentation The material that is produced to explain the design, operation, and use of an information system. Includes text and graphics and should be produced with each step in the development method.

Dollar sign A data attribute symbol that indicates a data attribute that was added to the physical data resource model to provide a unique primary key because of the combination of data entities onto one data file.

Downloaded data Data that are moved from the primary data repository to a secondary data repository.

Dual change The situation where both the user needs for information and the technology of managing information are both changing at an increasing rate.

Equal sign A data attribute symbol used to represent data that are obtained from the database to support an output but do not appear on that output.

Enterprise A term referring to any person, company, corporation, enterprise, endeavor, government agency, or other entity doing business.

Enterprise data resource A term referring to all electronic or machine readable data in an enterprise regardless whether the data are in a database management system or whether they are decentralized.

Enterprise data resource model A complete model of the enterprise's data resource that is compiled from the strategic, retrofit, project, and ad hoc data resource models.

Entity A person, place, thing, event, or concept that is being tracked and managed during its encounter with the enterprise. Also the mathematical term for a Data occurrence group. See Business entity; Data entity.

Entity behavior The behavior that entities exhibit when the management rules of that enterprise are applied to those entities.

Entity existence The presence of an entity, such as an employee.

Entity life cycle diagram A part of the entity life cycle model showing the states that an entity can occupy and the transitions possible between those states.

Entity life cycle model A model showing the entities being managed by the enterprise consisting of an entity life cycle diagram and definitions of each entity state and entity transition.

Entity management The management of entities during their encounter with the enterprise according to a formal set of business rules established by the enterprise.

Entity-relationship diagram A diagram showing data entities and data relations between those data entities. Part of the data resource model.

Entity set The mathematical term referring to what is commonly called a Data entity.

Entity state A particular state that a behavioral entity during its encounter with the enterprise.

Entity state transition The transition or movement of an entity between entity states. The transition results from an action triggered by a set of conditions.

Entity subtype A subtype of a data entity in a *can only be* situation. Shown on an entity-type hierarchy diagram.

Entity supertype A supertype of a data entity in a *can only be* situation. Shown on an entity-type hierarchy diagram.

Entity transition diagram A diagram showing the states that an entity can occupy and the transitions between those states.

Entity type The individual members in a *can only be* situation. Shown on an entity-type hierarchy diagram.

Entity-type hierarchy A hierarchy of data within a data entity that indicates *can only be* situations between data attributes. Used to identify data integrity rules.

Entity type hierarchy diagram A diagram containing an entity type hierarchy.

Error message table A table of error messages. Managed as a separated data entity in the enterprise's subject data resource.

Evolution Change characterized by gradual progress that is nonviolent.

Exclamation mark A data attribute symbol used to represent the addition of a data item to the physical data resource model that is not on the logical data resource model.

Existence See Data existence.

Existence dependency See Referential dependency.

Explicit redundant data Redundant data that appear explicitly in the database.

Expert system A system that performs its functions at least as good as human experts perform those same functions. An automated system that deals with analyzing problems and determining probable causes and/or solutions based on data contained in a knowledge base.

Explicit data relation A data relation that is shown explicitly on a data entity-relationship diagram.

Extended data domain A data domain that has been extended to include all synonymous data values for each data property of a data characteristic. Used to edit and convert those data values.

External data flow A data flow representing data moving into or out of an information system. External data flows represent business transactions and are considered as business schema. External data flows can be represented by either input or output data structures.

External format The format of an external data flow or business transaction.

External schema The data views of the database used by an application to store data in or retrieve data from the database. Represented by internal data flows on a data flow diagram.

False data attribute Any data attribute that is not a single characteristic data attribute, i.e., containing more than, or less than, a single characteristic.

False data entity Any data entity that is not a single subject data entity. May be an application data entity or a data entity representing a business event, a business transaction, or some other grouping of data.

False data value Any data value that is not a single property data value, i.e., containing more than a single data property of data.

Feedback cycle The mechanism within the Business Driven System Development method that allows errors to be cycled back to the previous step for correction before development is continued. A key mechanism for using the method in a prototyping environment.

Fifth normal form A form of data normalization referring to the identification of derived data attributes.

File oriented actions The actions taken to maintain the data on a data file. Traditionally performed by the application, but now performed by database management systems.

File-relationship diagram A diagram in the physical data resource model representing the data files that were defined during data denormalization and the relations between those files.

File rules The general set of rules pertaining to the maintenance of data files. Traditionally placed in applications, but moved to database management systems.

Final state The state an entity occupies when it is no longer managed by the enterprise.

First normal form A form of data normalization referring to identification and removal of repeating groups.

First order derived data Data that are derived from primitive data. All contributors are primitive data.

Fixed sequential multiple characteristic data attribute A sequential multiple characteristic data attribute that has fixed positions for each characteristic.

Fixed value The single value placed in a secondary key for access to the database. Defined with a minus sign.

Fixed word A word used in a data name that is not to be abbreviated during the abbreviation of that name.

Foreign data See Foreign data attribute.

Foreign data attribute Any data attribute that exists in a data entity other than its home data entity, including foreign keys and data attributes in a composite key. Compared to a home data attribute.

Foreign data entity A data entity that is foreign to a data attribute.

Foreign key Any data attribute that is contained in one data entity and is used for identification of the parent data occurrence in a parent data entity. Represents the primary key of a parent data entity. One form of a foreign data attribute.

Forward slash A data attribute symbol that is used to indicate an ascending sort sequence.

Four-schema concept A new concept that includes the business transactions as business schema that are normalized to produce the external schema of the three-schema concept.

Fourth normal form A form of data normalization referring to identification and separation of interentity dependencies.

Fourth schema The business schema in the four-schema concept.

Full data view A data view that represents all the data attributes in a data entity.

Graph theory The mathematical theory dealing with development and analysis of graphs. Used as a foundation for the models.

Hexagon A symbol representing a business entity on business entity diagrams and business information diagrams.

High-quality data Data that have passed a comprehensive set of data integrity rules and are complete and correct at all times under all conditions.

Home data attribute A data attribute that is located in the data entity that it characterizes. Compared to a Foreign data attribute.

Home data entity The data entity that a data attribute characterizes.

Homonymous data attributes A structural anomaly where two or more distinctly different data attributes (data characteristics) have the same name.

Homonymous data entities A structural anomaly where two or more distinctly different data entities (data subjects) have the same name.

Homonymous data values A structural anomaly where two or more distinctly different data values (data properties) have the same name.

IMAP A term used with data structures to indicate a peer relation.

Implicit data relation A data relation that exists between two data entities as identified by the existence of valid foreign keys but is not shown on the data entity-relation diagram.

Implicit redundant data Redundant data that are embedded in derived data attributes.

Implied data entity name A period prefixing a data attribute name on a data structure implies that the name of the set containing the data attribute is the data entity name.

Impure data Any data attributes that are not single characteristic data attributes. See False data attribute.

Information Multiple data attributes at a point in time or data attributes over a period of time that provide a more complete description than the individual data attributes.

Information age The age following the industrial age characterized by large scale information processing. Consists of the transaction wave and the artificial intelligence wave.

Information base A base of information. Comparable to a database for data. Generally difficult to separate a database and an information base.

Information processing The processing of data to produce information and the processing of information. Generally difficult to separate the processing of data and information.

Information system A system for processing data that consists of applications that contain process logic and databases that contain the data.

Information system development method A formal method used to develop information systems including the design, construction, implementation, control, and management of the system.

Information technology discipline The discipline for managing information technology in the information age.

Inherent data attribute A data attribute that belongs to an entity regardless of how that data attribute is used, such as a person's birth date.

Initial data repository The data repository where data are placed when they first enter the enterprise's data resource.

Initial state The state an entity occupies when it first encounters the enterprise.

Input data flow An external data flow representing a business transaction flowing into an information system.

Input data resource model A data resource model of the inputs to an information system that is used to substantiate and enhance the Output data resource model.

Input data structure A data structure representing an input data flow. It may also represent an internal data flow from one process to another process. Abbreviated IDS.

Input verification The process used during database design that verifies and adjusts the initial data resource model developed from the outputs to include the inputs.

Insertion anomaly The situation where data are stored redundantly in subordinate data occurrences and not in the parent data occurrence and can not be added when the parent data occurrence is entered without the existence of any child data occurrences.

Instance See Data instance.

Instructions A statement of the logic operations that are taken in an information system. May be manual instructions or automated instructions.

Intelligent database A database that contains shared logic as well as data and automatically initiates the appropriate logic when database is accessed. See Active databases; Object oriented processing.

Interattribute dependencies A dependency between two or more data attributes in the same data entity that must be resolved by removing the independent attribute to another data entity. This process is done during the third normal form of data normalization.

Interentity dependency A dependency between two data entities that results in those data entities being combined into one data entity. Also referred to as fourth normal form. Generally not encountered with good data entity definitions and a good third normal form.

Internal data flow A data flow between processes or between processes and data storages in an information system. Not an input or output data flow.

Internal process A process in an information system that does not represent a business activity.

Internal schema The structure of data in the data files. Developed from a denormalization of the conceptual schema.

Interpretability See Data interpretability.

Intersecting data entities Two data entities that are intersecting such that they both contain one or more common data attributes.

Intersection data attribute Any data attribute that is involved in the intersection of two or more data entities.

Intertwined multiple characteristic data attribute A multiple characteristic data attribute that has the characteristics mixed in such a way that they can not be separated by substringing.

Invalid data relation A data relation between two data entities that is not valid and is not substantiated by a primary and foreign key.

Invalid foreign key A data attribute that is identified as a foreign key but does not represent the primary key of a parent data entity.

Invalid foreign data attribute A data attribute that is in a foreign data entity but is not a foreign key and has not been placed in that data entity during denormalization of the second normal form.

Invalid primary key A candidate primary key that has been proven to be invalid.

Inversion The process of using a data attribute to create an index of data occurrences for each data value of that data attribute.

Inverted data relation A data relation where the value of a data attribute is used to create a list of data occurrences that have that same value.

Key An unqualified generally referring to a primary key. See Foreign key; Primary key; Secondary Key.

Key-only data entity A data entity that contains only data attributes that are identified as primary keys. No other nonprimary key data attributes have been defined for the data entity.

Knowledge Retained information.

Knowledge base A database that contains facts and figures, hueristics, rules, and historical trends that is used to support expert systems.

Knowledge worker A person that uses data, information, and knowledge to maximize their innovative and creative abilities, to make better decisions, and to increase their productivity.

Left caret A data attribute symbol used to represent data that exist on a document but are not entered into an information system.

Logical data resource model A data resource model consisting of an entity-relationship diagram, an entity-type hierarchy diagram, data attributes, primary and foreign keys, data accesses, data integrity rules, data views, and data descriptions. A data resource model of the conceptual schema.

Logical data modeling The process of developing the conceptual schema through the process of normalizing the business schema to create the external schema and optimizing those external schema to identify the logical data resource.

Logical data resource A database representing the conceptual schema. See Logical data resource model.

Logical data view See Data view.

Logical system architecture model A system architecture model representing the logical design of a system.

Logical view See Data view.

Low quality data Data that have not passed a comprehensive set of data integrity rules and are not complete and correct at all times under all conditions.

Managed decentralization The proper management of data in a decentralized environment without excessive control or rampant fragmentation.

Mandatory abbreviation A word in a data name that is always abbreviated when a data name is abbreviated.

Many-to-many data relation A data relation where a data occurrence in one data entity is related to many data occurrences in a second data entity, and each of those data occurrences in the second data entity is related to many data occurrences in the first data entity.

Metadata The data about the data that are contained in a data resource directory or a data dictionary.

Metainformation Metadata at a point in time or over a period of time that provide a more complete description than the individual metadata.

Method A systematic plan or procedure and set of techniques and rules for achieving something.

Mevolution An unofficial term representing change that is rapid and often complete, but is not accomplished by forceful or radical means and does not involve changes in governments.

Minus sign A data attribute symbol used to indicate a secondary key with a fixed value. Also used to indicate no conversion of a data attribute on the Data attribute conversion table.

Model A representation of the arrangement and relationship of elements in a system and descriptions of those elements. Based on Semiotic theory and Graph theory.

Multidirectional access A term referring to entry into a data structure and subsequent access to both parent and subordinate data entities.

Multiple characteristic data attribute A data attribute that has multiple characteristics imbedded in one data attribute rather than being defined in separate data attributes. See Intertwined multiple characteristic data attributes; Sequential multiple characteristic data attributes.

Multiple property data value A data value that has multiple properties imbedded in one data value rather than being defined as separate data values.

Multiple record types The placement of two or more data entities on the same physical file results in multiple record types. Each record type represents one data entity which is indicated by an additional data item that is inserted during physical data modeling.

Multiple subject data entity A data entity that has multiple subjects imbedded in one data entity rather than being defined as separate data entities.

Multivalued data attribute A special form of a repeating group where a data attribute in a data entity can have many values.

Mutually exclusive data attribute The situation where several data attributes are defined for each value of a true data attribute, only one of which will exist at any one time in any one occurrence. This results from raising a data value to the level of a data attribute.

Mutually exclusive parents A situation where a data entity has two or more parent data entities, only one of which is valid for any single data occurrence in the data entity.

Mutually exclusive subordinates A situation where subordinate data subjects are peers but are mutually exclusive. Shown on an entity-type hierarchy diagram.

Naming taxonomy See Data naming taxonomy.

Navigation See Data navigation.

Necessary data redundancy The creation and maintenance of duplicate data that are necessary for navigation or operational efficiency.

Necessary data structure A data structure representing the data that is used to maintain a data storage. Abbreviated NDS.

Need A complete statement of a solution to a problem.

Nonprocedural language A language where the coder defines what will be done but the language determines where and how it will be done. Compared to Procedural language.

Nonsingle data unit A data unit that is not a single unit, such as a multiple subject data entity, multiple characteristic data attribute, or multiple property data value.

Normal data entity A data entity that is defined to represent the characteristics of an entity. Not a resolution, summary, cyclic, or recursive data entity.

Normalization The process to bring something to a normal form. See Data normalization.

Normalized data Data that have been through the data normalization process. External schema are considered normalized data. Conceptual schema are also considered normalized data.

Object oriented processing The concept of defining application objects and data objects and connecting application objects to form information systems that process data objects.

Object management The basic principle of treating data, business activities, organizational units, and behavioral entities as objects and managing those objects to meet the enterprise's goals.

Objective A complete statement of a task to be performed to meet a stated need. Also used to begin project management for development of an information system.

Occurrence See Data occurrence.

Occurrence anomaly The situation that occurs when referential integrity is not maintained between a parent and subordinate data occurrences.

Official primary key A valid primary key that is selected to officially designate unique data occurrences in a data entity. Other valid primary keys become Alternate primary keys.

OF language A procedure for naming data attributes from the most detailed to the most general separating each word with the word OF. Not used in the formal data naming taxonomy.

One-to-many data relation A data relation where a data occurrence in the parent data entity has one or more related data occurrences in a subordinate data entity, and each data occurrence in the subordinate data entity is related to only one data occurrence in the parent data entity.

One-to-one data relation A data relation where a data occurrence in one data entity is related to only one data occurrence in the second data entity, and one data occurrence in the second data entity is related to only one data occurrence in the first data entity.

Open recursive data entity A recursive data entity where the data occurrences are in a one-to-many relationship.

Operating environment The physical operating environment consisting of hardware, software, database management system, and enterprise standards.

Operational solution The final output of the system development method consisting of a fully operational information system.

Optimized data Data that have been through the data normalization and data optimization processes. Data in the conceptual schema.

Optimization See Data optimization.

Optional abbreviation A word in a data name that may either be abbreviated or unabbreviated during data name abbreviation depending on the need to meet a length restriction.

Organization chart A chart of the arrangement and relationships of business units in an enterprise. See Organization structure.

Organization independence The independence between the organizational structure of the enterprise and the structure of business activities performed by the enterprise and the structure of the data.

Organization structure The structure of business units in an enterprise and the reporting relations between those business units.

Output data flow An external data flow representing a business transaction flowing out of an information system.

Output data resource model The initial data resource model developed by aggregating the required data structures.

Output data structure A data structure representing an output from the system, or an output from an internal process that does not have a user format. Abbreviated ODS.

Output driven The process during database design that defines the initial logical database based on the outputs of the information system. This output data resource model will be verified based on the inputs to the information system.

Oval A symbol that represents data files on the physical system architecture model and the data file-relationship diagram.

Parent A term meaning the parent data entity in a one-to-many data relation.

Partial key dependency The situation where data attributes in a data entity are dependent on only part of the primary key. These data attributes are removed and placed in another data entity. This process is the second normal form of data normalization.

Partial subject data entity A data entity that contains only part of a data subject. The remainder of the data subject is contained in one or more other data entity.

Passive database management system A database management system that can not take action based on the values of data contained in the database.

Passive data resource directory A data resource directory that can not take action on the data entering the database or data in the database.

Peer data entity A term meaning a one-to-one data relation between two data entities.

Percent sign A data attribute symbol used to indicate a secondary data access consisting of a range of values.

Period A data attribute symbol used to indicate an implied data subject name.

Permanent data attribute group A data attribute group that is permanently defined for existing and future application, and consists of two or more single characteristic data attributes.

Personal level information system An information system developed for support of a business unit or a person.

Phantom data entity A data entity that exists only to substantiate one or more data attributes in the primary key of a subordinate data entity but does not have any additional data attributes.

Physical data modeling The process of defining the physical data files for a particular operating environment by denormalizing the conceptual schema.

Physical data resource model A data resource model consisting of a data file-relationship diagram, data items, data keys, data integrity constraints, and data views.

Physical data view The physical set of data obtained from the physical database. See Application data view; Combined data view; Full data view.

Physical database A database representing the internal schema. The end result of database design.

Physical file A physical data repository for data either in a database management system or using a file management technique other than a database management system. See Data file.

Physical key See Data key.

Physical operating environment See Operating environment.

Physical record A distinct record type on a physical file. See Data record.

Physical system architecture model A system architecture model representing the physical construction of an information system as it is used in the operating environment. It may or may not necessarily be the same as the logical system architecture model.

Physical view A physical data view of the physical database. See Application data view; Combined data view; Full data view.

Plus sign A data attribute symbol used to represent a foreign key. Also used to represent a continuation on the Data attribute conversion table.

Pound sign A data attribute symbol used to represent a primary key.

Pragmatics That portion of semiotic theory dealing with practicality or practical use. With respect to models it pertains to the practical use of the model.

Preliminary data edit The data editing performed at the time the data are captured to assure that the data are as accurate as possible when they are captured.

Primitive data attribute A data attribute that is recorded directly from the entity being managed and is not derived from other data attributes. May be an actual value or a coded value.

Primary data edit The comprehensive set of data integrity rules that assures data have the highest integrity possible before entering the database.

Primary data name The official name of a data unit which is the fully spelled-out real-world name of the data unit. All other data names are considered alias data names.

Primary data repository A data repository that contains the full set of data that has passed a comprehensive set of data integrity rules and is considered the official version of the data for an enterprise.

Primary key A set of one or more data attributes designated to make each data occurrence in a data entity unique. Not used for access into a data entity. Can be single, compound, or composite primary keys. Primary keys can be candidates, official, or alternate.

Proactive updating A term representing entry of data into the database where the data will be effective at some later date. Used with time relational data.

Problem A complete statement of a problem that exists in the business environment or with an information system.

Procedural language A language where the coder determines what will be done and when and how it will be done. Compared to Nonprocedural language.

Procedure A series of steps that are followed in an orderly fashion to accomplish something.

Process A manual or automated process that is performed by an enterprise. Represented as a rectangle on a data flow diagram or a business activity model.

Processing algorithm A set of process logic contained in an application that represents the actions performed by that application.

Process logic The logic that is performed inside a process as represented on a process logic chart. Represented by one or more process logic operations in the form of a process logic chart.

Process logic chart A chart similar to a data structure chart that contains the process logic for a process or an application.

Project data resource model A data resource model built for a specific project using the full Business Driven System Development method. Builds on the strategic and retrofit data resource models and defines all the details necessary to construct the physical data files.

Project definition Output of the Project phase of the development method consisting of the problems, needs, objectives, and business issues.

Properly structured data Data that are structured according to the enterprises subject data resource.

Property See Data property.

Prototype The first of its kind that is used as a model to make many additional copies. Generally misused for developing information systems but applies to the repetitive enhancement of an application or database until it meets the needs as defined.

Question mark A data attribute symbol used to represent a questionable data attribute.

Quote mark A data attribute symbol used to represent a literal that appears on an output but is contained in the application producing that output.

Random data relation A data relation that is unfounded. See Invalid data relation.

Range of values The use of a value range for access into a data entity. Designated with a pound sign.

Rectangle A symbol that represents business activities on the business activity diagrams and processes on data flow diagrams.

Recursive data entity A data entity containing data occurrences that are in a one-to-one or a one-to-many relationship with other data occurrences in the same data entity.

Redundancy See Data redundancy.

Redundant code Redundantly coding the same business activity in two or more applications or information systems. Object oriented applications eliminate the redundantly coded activities.

Redundant data See Data redundancy.

Redundant data attribute A data attribute containing redundant data. See Data redundancy; Redundant data value.

Redundant data attribute table A table showing the existences of redundant data attributes in the database that need to be maintained.

Redundant data rules The data integrity rules pertaining to the maintenance of redundant data.

Redundant data value The existence of the same data value for the same occurrence of an entity for the same instance of time in two or more places in the database.

Referential integrity One of the data integrity rules pertaining to the existence of a parent data occurrence when there are subordinate data occurrences.

Relation A two-dimensional array (table) in the relational model consisting of columns and tuples (rows).

Relational database A database developed according to the rules of relational theory, consisting structural, integrity, and manipulative components. During logical design, it commonly includes only the structural and integrity parts.

Relational model A data model consisting of structural, integrity, and manipulative features. The structural and integrity features are important during database design.

Repeating group Sets of data attributes that repeat within a set of parent data attributes. The first normal form of normalization deals with the separation of repeating groups.

Repetitive set A set of process logic that is performed multiple times.

Required data structure A data structure representing the data required from the database to support a process. Abbreviated RDS.

Resolution data entity A data entity that resolves a many-to-many data relation between two other data entities by forming a one-to-many relation with each of those data entities. See Associative data entity.

Retroactive updating A term used to indicate entry of data into the database that will be effective at some previous time. Used with time relational data.

Retrodocument The process of documenting something that already exists but has not been documented or been completely documented. In the current context refers to retrodocumenting existing data files.

Retrofit data resource model A data resource model developed from existing physical files by defining how those files would be structured if they were to be normalized. Builds on the strategic data resource model.

Reusable code The use of the same coded business activity in two or more functions or business activities without redundantly coding that activity. See Object oriented.

Revolution Changes that are usually quick, complete, often radical and forceful, and usually involve changes in governments.

Right caret A data attribute symbol used to represent data that are entered into an information system but are not stored on the database.

Row A single line of data across a relational table representing a logical record. See Tuple.

Schema A diagrammatic representation of the structure of something, in this case data.

Second normal form A form of data normalization referring to identification and removal of data attributes that are not dependent on the full primary key and only the primary key.

Second order derived data Derived data whose contributors consist of one or more derived data attributes.

Secondary data repository A data repository that does not have a full set of data.

Secondary key A set of one or more data attributes that are used to access a data entity. May consist of primary key data attributes, nonprimary key data attributes, part of the primary key data attributes, or a mixture of primary and nonprimary key data attributes.

Seamless integration The integration of information systems such that their boundaries are not visible to the user. See Borderless integration.

Security See Data security.

Semantics That part of semiotic theory that deals with the meaning, including both denotative and connotative meaning.

Semiotic modeling A term applied to the full use of semiotic theory for developing models that are syntactically correct, meaningful, and have practical use.

Semiotic theory The philosophical theory that encompasses semantics, syntax, and pragmatics. Used as a foundation for developing integrated models.

Sequential multiple characteristic data attribute A multiple characteristic data attribute where the characteristics are placed sequentially and are readily obtained by substringing. May be fixed or variable format.

Set of entities The mathematical term referring to what is commonly called a Data occurrence group.

Set theory The branch of mathematics or symbolic logic dealing with the nature and relations of sets.

Shared applications Individual applications or information systems that are shared by a variety of business units in the enterprise.

Shared data The concept that data in the enterprise's data resource are shared with respect to their use and their management through a process of cooperative management.

Shared management The concept that people using data or applications cooperatively managing those data or applications for their mutual benefit. Compared to ownership of applications and data.

Single characteristic data attribute A data attribute that contains only one data characteristic. The desired form for a subject data resource.

Single data unit A data unit that represents a single unit of data, such as a single subject data entity, single characteristic data attribute, or single property data value.

Single primary key A primary key consisting of only one data attribute.

Single property data value A data value that represents a single data property. The desired form for a subject database.

Single subject data entity A data entity containing one complete data subject. The desired form for a subject data resource.

Situation The label on a set of process logic that identifies the real world situation represented by the set.

Solid line A line used on models to represent the flow or movement of something. Compared to a dashed line that represents a relation.

Source data attribute A data attribute that is on the contributing side of a data converter.

Standard verb A generic verb that is used to designate the type of action performed by a single process statement of process logic independent of any language.

Standard word The term used to represent standard words that are defined by an enterprise to be used in data names. Differs from Data Class Name in that a standard word can appear anywhere in the data name, not just at the end of the name. See Data class name.

Static derived data Derived data that do not need to be maintained because the contributing data attributes either no longer exist in the database or exist as static data attributes.

Static redundant data Necessary redundant data that do not need to be maintained, such as backup data.

Storage anomaly The situation where data are added or removed from the database causing an anomaly in the structure of the data. Storage anomalies include update anomalies, insertion anomalies, and deletion anomalies.

Strategic data resource model A data resource model developed for the behavioral entities managed by an enterprise from the knowledge of individuals in that enterprise.

Structural data integrity diagram A diagram of structural data integrity rules. Part of the logical data resource model.

Structural data integrity matrix A matrix of structural data integrity rules. Part of the logical data resource model.

Structural data integrity rule A data integrity rule for enforcing the structural integrity of the subject data resource.

Structural data integrity table A table of structural data integrity rules. Part of the logical data resource model.

Subentity See data category; Data occurrence group; Data subentity.

Subject application An application structured to store data in and receive data from a subject database.

Subject data Data entities that are structured by data subjects as defined by the enterprise's view of the business world and the behavioral entities it manages.

Subject data entity A data entity that represents a complete single subject of data.

Subject data resource A data resource for an enterprise structured by data subjects and relations between those data subjects. All data units represent single units of data that are well described, properly documented, and have high integrity.

Subject database A physical database structured by data subjects where each data entity represents a single data subject. All the data units in a subject database are single data units that are well described, properly documented, and have high integrity.

Subject oriented actions See Data oriented actions.

Subsequent data repository Any data repository where data go after their initial entry into the database.

Subtype A subordinate level on an entity type hierarchy. A data subject subordinate to another data subject and mutually exclusive with peer data subjects.

Summary data entity A data entity representing summary data values and identified by a composite primary key consisting of the primary keys of the parent data entities. Managed the same as any other data entity.

Supertype A parent level on an entity type hierarchy. A data subject that is a parent to two or more mutually exclusive data subjects.

Synonymous data attributes A structural anomaly where the same data attribute is represented as two or more separate data attributes with different names.

Synonymous data entities A structural anomaly where the same data entity is represented as two or more separate data entities with different names.

Synonymous data values A structural anomaly where the same data value is represented as two or more separate data values with different names.

Syntax That part of semiotic theory that deals with structure and rules. With respect to models it pertains to the rules for developing the models.

System A collection of component parts that operate in unison and result in a whole that is greater than the sum of its parts. See Information system.

System architecture model A model of the architecture of an information system consisting of data flow diagrams, process definitions, and the formats of the external data flows. See both logical and physical system architecture models.

Table A two-dimensional array (relation) in the relational model consisting of columns and rows (tuples).

Technique A set of technical procedures for doing something.

Technology infrastructure The second level of the information technology discipline representing the processing platform for information technology.

Technology of change A technology to manage social and technical change and their impacts on the business environment and the enterprise.

Temporary data attribute A data attribute that is temporary and its use should not be propagated. Identified by the standard word *Limited* in the data resource directory and the standard word *TMP* in the data attribute name.

Temporary data attribute group A data attribute group that is defined temporarily until all old applications are converted to true data attributes, or are abandoned. Usually defined for sequential multiple characteristic data attributes. Identified by the standard word *Limited* in the data resource directory and the standard words *TMP GRP* in the data attribute name.

Tested instructions Output of the instruction phase consisting of instructions that have been unit tested.

Tested system Output of the construction phase consisting of an information system that has been completely tested and is ready for implementation.

Third normal form A form of data normalization referring to identification and removal of data attributes that are dependent on other data attributes in the same data entity.

Third schema See Conceptual schema.

Three schema concept The concept that resulted from addition of the conceptual schema to the two schema concept. Consists of external, conceptual, and internal schema.

Time independence The concept of the independence of time from the structure of subject data entities. See Time occurrence.

Time occurrence A data occurrence that represents a time slice of a data occurrence in time relational data. Represents the time dimension of a data entity, not another data entity.

Time relational The concept where a data occurrence is not changed. Any new data creates a new data occurrence with a chronology stamp indicating the data instance.

Time relational database management system A database management system that processes time relational data.

Target data attribute A data attribute that is on the receiving side of a data converter.

True data attribute A data attribute that represents a single data characteristic and has no synonyms or homonyms.

True data entity A data entity that represents a single subject and has no synonyms or homonyms.

True data value A data value that represents a single property and has no synonyms or homonyms.

Tuple A single row in a relational table representing a logical record. See Row.

Two-schema concept The traditional concept consisting of only an internal and an external schema.

Type five database change A change to the database involving data integrity rules.

Type four database change A change to the database involving splitting data items or data files that already exist or moving data items between data files.

Type one database change A change to the database involving new logical views or new access paths to data already in the database.

Type three database change A change to the database involving creation of new data files.

Type two database change A change to the database involving addition of new data items in an existing data file or rearrangement of data items already in the data file.

Unnecessary data redundancy Duplicate data that are not necessary and can be eliminated without loss of data integrity. Unnecessary data redundancy generally occurs with application data entities.

Unnormalized data Data that have not yet been normalized. Business transactions (business schema) are considered unnormalized. Not the same as denormalized data.

Update anomaly The situation where redundant data are stored in the database and updates to those redundant data are made inconsistently resulting in different versions of the truth.

Uploaded data Data that are transmitted from a secondary data repository to a primary data repository. Uploaded data must pass through a primary data edit prior to entering the primary data repository.

User A term referring to the end user of information systems. Commonly used to identify nonprofessional and paraprofessional data processors.

User view See Data view.

Valid data relation A data relation between two data entities that is valid and is substantiated by valid primary and foreign keys.

Valid foreign data attribute A data attribute that is in a foreign data entity as a foreign key or as a result of denormalization of the second normal form.

Valid foreign key A foreign key that identifies the primary key of a parent data entity.

Valid multiple characteristic data attribute A multiple characteristic data attribute that is valid according to the rules for a subject database.

Valid primary key A primary key that has been verified as uniquely identifying each data occurrence in a data entity. Can be an official primary key or an alternate primary key.

Value See Data value.

Variable characteristic data attribute A data attribute that contains a different characteristic of data depending on the status or type of data occurrence.

Variable sequential multiple characteristic data attribute A sequential multiple characteristic data attribute where the format of the characteristics is variable from one data occurrence to the next.

Volatility See Data volatility.

Window of opportunity The time frame that an enterprise has to perform a task before that opportunity is lost.

Z-word A meaningless word beginning with a Z used to name data entities when there are preconceptions or misconceptions about the data entity name or definition.

Bibliography

ANON, Knowledge-Based Systems and Their Applications: Artificial Intelligence Satellite Symposium. Dallas, Tx.: Texas Instruments, 1985.

BEDELL, E.F., *The Computer Solution: Strategies for Success in the Information Age*. Homewood, Ill.: Dow Jones-Irwin, 1985.

BRACKETT, M.H., *Developing Data Structured Information Systems*. Topeka, Ka.: Ken Orr & Associates, Inc., 1983.

BRACKETT, M.H., *Developing Data Structured Databases*. Englewood Cliffs, N.J.: Prentice-Hall, 1987.

BUCHANAN, B.G., and SHORTLIFFE, E.H., *Rule-Based Expert Systems*. Reading, Ma.: Addison-Wesley, 1985.

BURK, C.F., and HORTON, F.W., *InfoMap: A Complete Guild to Discovering Corporate Information Resources*. Englewood Cliffs, N.J.: Prentice-Hall, 1988.

CHEN, P.P., *The Entity-Relationship Model: Toward a Unified View of Data*. ACM Trans Database Systems 1, 1976.

CLEVELAND, H., *The Knowledge Executive: Leadership in an Information Society*. New York: E.P. Dutton, 1985.

CODD, E.F., "A Relational Model of Data for Large Shared Data Banks," *Commun. ACM*, Vol. 13, No. 6, June 1970.

COX, B.J., *Object Oriented Programming: An Evolutionary Approach*. Reading, Ma.: Addison-Wesley, 1987.

CURTICE, R.M., and JONES, P.E., *Logical Database Design*. New York: Van Nostrand Reinhold, 1982.

DATE, C.J., *An Introduction to Data Base Systems*, Vols. I and II. Reading, Ma.: Addison-Wesley, 1982.

DATE, C.J., *Relational Database: Further Misconceptions #1*. InfoDB, Spring, 1986.

DAVIS, G.B., *Management Information Systems: Conceptual Foundations, Structure, and Development*. New York: McGraw-Hill, 1974.

DEMARCO, T., *Structured Analysis and Systems Specification*. New York: Yourdon Press, 1978.

DICKSON, G.W., and WETHERBE, J.C., *Management of Information Systems*. New York: McGraw-Hill, 1984.

DURELL, W.R., *Data Administration: A Practical Guide to Successful Data Management*. New York: McGraw-Hill, 1984.

FEIGNEBAUM, E.A., and MCCORDUCK, P., *The Fifth Generation*. Reading, Ma.: Addison-Wesley, 1983.

FLAVIN, M., *Fundamental Concepts of Information Modeling*. New York: Yourdon Press, 1981.

GANE, C.P., and SARSON, T., *Structured System Analysis: Tools and Techniques*. New York: Improved System Technologies, Inc., 1977.

GRONIN, B., Ed., *Information Management: From Strategies to Action*. London: Aslib, 1985.

HAYES-ROTH, F., WATTERMAN, D.A., and LENAT, D.B., *Building Expert Systems*. Reading, Ma.: Addison-Wesley, 1983.

HOLT, D.H., *Management Principles and Practices*. Englewood Cliffs, N.J.: Prentice-Hall, 1987.

HOROWITZ, E., and SAHNI, S., *Fundamentals of Data Structures*. Rockville, Md.: Computer Science Press, 1976.

INMON, W.H., *Information Systems Architecture: A System Developer's Primer*. Englewood Cliffs, N.J.: Prentice-Hall, 1986.

JACKSON, M.A., *Principles of Program Design*. New York: Academic Press, 1975.

JACKSON, M.A., *System Development*. Englewood Cliffs, N.J.: Prentice-Hall, 1983.

KLAHR, P., and Watterman, D.A., *Expert Systems: Technologies, Tools, and Applications*. Reading, Ma.: Addison-Wesley, 1986.

MARTIN, J., *Principles of Data Base Management*. Englewood Cliffs, N.J.: Prentice-Hall, 1976.

MARTIN, J., *Computer Data Base Organization*, 2nd ed. Englewood Cliffs, N.J.: Prentice-Hall, 1977.

MARTIN, J., *Computer Networks and Distributed Processing: Software, Techniques, and Architecture*. Englewood Cliffs, N.J.: Prentice-Hall, 1981.

MARTIN, J., *Design and Strategy for Distributed Data Processing*. Englewood Cliffs, N.J.: Prentice-Hall, 1981.

MARTIN, J., *The Telematic Society: A Challenge for Tomorrow*. Englewood Cliffs, N.J.: Prentice-Hall, 1981.

MARTIN, J., *Application Development Without Programmers*. Englewood Cliffs, N.J.: Prentice-Hall, 1982.

MARTIN, J., *Strategic Data Planning Methodologies*. Englewood Cliffs, N.J.: Prentice-Hall, 1982.

MARTIN, J., *Managing the Database Environment*. Englewood Cliffs, N.J.: Prentice-Hall, 1983.

MARTIN, J., *An Information Systems Manifesto*. Englewood Cliffs, N.J.: Prentice-Hall, 1984.

MARTIN, J., and McClure, C., *Diagramming Techniques for Analysts and Programmers*. Englewood Cliffs, N.J.: Prentice-Hall, 1985.

McCRACKEN, D.D., "Software in the 80's: Perils and Promises," *Computerworld Extra,* September, 1980.

MISHKOFF, H.C., *Understanding Artificial Intelligence.* Dallas, Texas: Texas Instruments, 1985.

NAISBITT, J., *Megatrends.* New York: Warner Books, 1982.

NOLAN, R.L., "Managing the Crises in Data Processing," *Harvard Business Review,* March-April, 1979.

ORR, K.T., *Structured Systems Development,* New York: Yourdon Press, 1977.

ORR, K.T., *Structured Requirements Definition.* Topeka, Ka.: Ken Orr & Associates, Inc., 1981.

PETERS, L.J., *Software Design: Methods and Techniques.* New York: Yourdon Press, 1981.

ROBINSON, S.L., "Database: The Next Five Years and Beyond." *Computerworld Extra.* September, 1980.

ROCHART, J.F., and Delong, D.W., *Executive Support Systems.* Homewood, Ill.: Dow Jones-Irwin, 1988.

ROCKART, J.F., "Chief Executives Define Their Own Data Needs," *Harvard Business Review*, Vol. 57, No. 2, 1979.

ROSS, R.G., "Data Dictionaries and Data Administration: Concepts and Practices for Data Resource Management," *AMACOM,* 1981.

ROSS, R.G., *Entity Modeling: Techniques and Applications,* Database Research Group, Inc., 1987.

RUSTIN, R., Ed., *Data Base Systems.* Englewood Cliffs, N.J.: Prentice-Hall, 1972.

SHNEIDERMAN, B., *Designing the User Interface: Strategies for Effective Human-Computer Interaction.* Reading, Ma.: Addison-Wesley, 1986.

TOEREY, T.J., and FRY, J.P., *Design of Database Structures.* Englewood Cliffs, N.J.: Prentice-Hall, 1982.

TOFFLER, A., *The Third Wave.* New York: Bantam Books, 1980.

TSICHRITZIS, D.C., and Lochovsky, F.H., *Data Models.* Englewood Cliffs, N.J.: Prentice-Hall, 1982.

ULLMAN, J.D., *Principles of Database Systems.* Rockville, Md.: Computer Science Press, 1982.

WARNIER, J.D., Current Developments in Logical Systems Methodology. Proceedings of the Structured Systems Design User's Conference/5. Ken Orr and Associates, Topeka, Ka., 1979.

WARNIER, J.D., *Logical Construction of Programs.* New York: Van Nostrand Reinhold, 1976.

WARNIER, J.D., *Logical Construction of Systems.* New York: Van Nostrand Reinhold, 1979.

WEIDERHOLD, G., *Database Design.* New York: McGraw-Hill, 1983.

WEINBERG, G., *An Introduction to General Systems Thinking.* New York: John Wiley & Sons, 1975.

WEINBERG, V., *Structured Analysis.* New York: Yourdon Press, 1978.

YAO, S.B., Ed., *Principles of Database Design: Volume 1 Logical Organizations.* Englewood Cliffs, N.J.: Prentice-Hall, 1985.

YOURDON, E., and CONSTANTINE, L.L., *Structured Design.* Englewood Cliffs, N.J.: Prentice-Hall, 1979.

YOURDON, E., *Techniques of Program Structure and Design.* Englewood Cliffs, N.J.: Prentice-Hall, 1975.

VETTER, M., *Strategy for Data Modelling.* New York: John Wiley & Sons, 1987.

Index

Conditional structural data integrity
rules, 241
Conditional structural data integrity
table, 241
Conventional application, 307, 312,
315, 318, 331
Conventional data, 315-16, 326
entity, 315, 318, 323
file, 307-9, 325, 328-29, 332
item, 312
structure, 315
Conventional database, 298, 308, 314,
325, 327-28
Conventional organization chart, 43
Conversation, 217
Conversion from logical to physical,
71, 73
Create data, 250
Critical success factors, 3
Crossloaded data, 290, 298
CRUD matrix, 73, 75
Cultural change, 29, 356
Cyclic data entity, 170-72

Data access, 109, 119, 225-26, 284,
287, 289, 304
analysis, 300, 303
component, 15
conversion, 159
diagram, 301, 304
down data structure, 130
multidirectional, 133
multiple parents, 134
mutually exclusive parents, 137
mutually exclusive subordinates, 135
route, 301, 303
single parent, 134
up data structure, 131-32
verification, 137, 349
Data anomalies, 141-42
Data applications, 20
Data architecture tier, 58
Data attribute, 60-62, 65, 66, 68, 105,
185-86
acquired, 189
active derived, 188, 242
complex characteristic, 196, 269

conversion table, 319-20, 323,
326-27
denormalization, 158
description, 212
false, 186
foreign, 105, 189
group, 64
group, temporary, 311
group name, 95
homonymous, 191-92
identification, 197
inherent, 188
multiple characteristic, 309, 311-12,
324, 326, 354
multivalued, 146-47
mutually exclusive, 196-97, 271, 310,
322, 326
name, 90, 93
name thesaurus, 273
primitive, 186, 188
redundant, 107, 141-42
relation, 128, 234
sequence specific, 107, 114
single characteristic, 187, 192, 231,
266-67, 312
static derived, 188, 242
submodel, 70
symbols, 208, 212
synonymous, 190-91
true, 186, 190
variable characteristic, 310, 322
Data availability, 6, 283-84, 304
Data availability tier, 58
Data block, 195
Data category, 60-61, 166, 180, 265
documentation, 274
names, 89
Data characteristic, 59, 61
name, 90-92
name abbreviation, 258
single, 108, 212
variation name, 93-94
Data content verification, 349
Data control diagram, 68-70, 289
Data conversion, 325
Data converter, 316-19, 323, 325,
327-28, 330-32
Data definition, 5, 6, 70, 84, 97
documentation, 277
Data denormalization, 155-56

Data derivation:
  algorithm, 243
  diagram, 243–45
  relations, 243
Data description, 59, 83, 98–100, 162
  component, 15
  guidelines, 100
  submodel, 70
Data dictionary, 263
  active, 20, 73
  passive, 20
Data documentation, 59, 351
  component, 15
Data domain, 71, 177, 232–33, 235–36,
    249, 312, 350
  management, 233
  name, 90
Data duplication, 287
Data duration, 22, 247
Data edits, 4, 19–20
Data element, 61
Data entity, 60–61, 66, 165–66, 185,
    211–12
  application, 166, 178
  associative, 167, 172
  complex subject, 179, 265
  conventional, 315, 318, 323
  cyclic, 170–72
  denormalization, 156
  false, 153, 166
  false key-only, 176
  foreign, 105
  home, 105, 189
  homonymous, 178
  key-only, 176
  keys, 70
  keys submodel, 70
  multiple subject, 178, 182
  parent, 60
  partial subject, 178, 264
  peer, 121
  phantom, 175–76
  recursive, 168–69, 243
  resolution, 172
  single occurrence, 212
  single subject, 181, 183, 231, 264
  subject, 166, 227
  subtype, 61
  summary, 173–74
  supertype, 61

  synonymous, 153–54, 178
  true, 166
  true key-only, 176
  type, 61, 67, 167, 181
  type documentation, 274
  type hierarchy, 67
  valid, 153
Data existence, 21, 23
Data field, 61
Data file, 54–55, 64, 72–73, 156–59,
    161
  conventional, 307–9, 325, 328–29,
    332
  data flow, 51–53, 74, 328
  diagram, 40, 51–53, 69, 325, 330
  name, 157–58
Data flow, 51–53, 74
  external, 51–52, 205–6, 211, 215
  internal, 51–53, 143, 205
Data independence, 3, 12, 287
Data inheritance, 97
Data instance, 22, 61, 288, 291
Data integrity, 4, 6–7, 48, 59, 150, 152,
    161, 233, 283, 289, 291, 298,
    329
  component, 15
  constraint, 71
  error message, 251
  process, 73
  responsibility, 247
  routines, 69
  rule conversion, 161
  rule documentation, 275
  rule override, 251
  rules, 20, 66, 68, 71, 128, 161, 196,
    230–31, 233, 236, 238, 241, 242,
    246–50, 252, 275, 296, 313, 323,
    350
  submodel, 66, 71
  table, 241
  verification, 350
Data interface, 4, 314–19, 323, 325–27,
    332
  management, 327
Data interpretability, 300
Data item, 65, 71–72, 158–59, 246
  conventional, 312
  documentation, 275
  submodel, 72–73
Data key, 73, 103, 160, 354
  concatenated, 354

Many-to-many data attribute relation, 128, 234

Many-to-many data relation, 122, 126

Matrix:
    business responsibility, 49, 54, 75
    CRUD, 73, 75
    data management, 73–74
    data responsibility, 75

Menu, 217

Metadata, 248, 263, 278

Mevolution, 2

Model, 25
    ad hoc data resource, 76, 336, 345–46, 356
    business activity, 32, 47, 49, 53–54, 74
    business environment, 34, 42, 45, 55
    business information, 31, 34, 37, 39, 41–43, 49, 53, 54, 356
    business process, 32, 44–45, 55, 66
    business unit, 31, 42, 49, 75
    conceptual data resource, 155
    data, 65
    data resource, 58, 65–66, 73, 75, 79–81, 231, 246, 252, 255, 291
    decentralized data, 292
    design, 25, 28–29
    enrichment, 26
    enterprise data resource, 77, 225–27, 336, 345
    entity life cycle, 31, 34–37, 42, 66, 356
    first-cut physical, 355
    input data resource, 225–26
    logical data resource, 58, 65, 71, 143, 205, 227, 238, 292, 340, 351, 354–55
    logical system architecture, 51, 53–54, 74
    output data resource, 225–26
    physical data resource, 58, 65, 71, 143, 205, 292, 340, 354–55
    physical system architecture, 51, 54–55, 72
    project data resource, 76, 336, 342–43, 345–46, 356
    relational, 21–23, 26, 29
    retrofit data resource, 76, 336, 339, 342, 346, 356
    strategic data resource, 75–76, 336–37, 339–40, 343, 346, 356

system architecture, 32, 50–51, 55, 225–26, 291, 340, 356
    time relational, 23–24

Multidirectional access, 133

Multiple access to single parent, 134

Multiple characteristic data attribute, 192–93, 267–68, 309–12, 324, 326, 354

Multiple data name abbreviations, 262

Multiple data subject names, 87

Multiple data subjects, 96

Multiple property data value, 200, 312

Multiple subject data entity, 178, 182

Multivalued data attribute, 146–47

Mutually exclusive data attribute, 196–97, 271, 310, 322, 326

Mutually exclusive data relation, 127

Mutually exclusive parent, 128, 181

Necessary data structure, 205, 207, 222, 225

Necessary redundant data, 244, 285–86

Nonsingle data unit, 308

Normalization, Data structure, 218

Object, 28
    business, 21
    data, 21
    management concept, 20–21, 29, 55, 80

Occurrence anomaly, 237

Official primary key, 104

OF language, 98

One-to-many data attribute relation, 128, 234

One-to-many data relation, 121, 125

One-to-one data attribute relation, 128, 234

One-to-one data relation, 120, 125

Open data relation, 126, 169

Open set of values, 232

Operating environment, 354–55

Optimization, data structure, 225

Optional constraint, 234, 238

Revolutionary change, 2
Row, 21

Schema, 17, 26
    business, 18, 140, 143–44, 205
    conceptual, 17–18, 59, 140, 143–44,
        156, 205, 350
    external, 17–18, 64, 140, 143, 205
    internal, 17–18, 140, 143–44, 155
Second normal form, 147, 149, 158
Second order derived data attribute,
    188
Secondary data repository, 288–91, 297
Secondary key, 70, 103, 110–11, 114,
        138, 160, 349
    fixed value, 113
    pure, 112
    range of values, 113–14
    reduction, 353
Secondary update process, 293, 297
Semantic modeling, 28
Semantics, 27, 29
Semiotic modeling, 28, 34
Semiotic theory, 27, 29
Semiotics, 27
Sequence specific data attributes, 107,
    114
Sequential multiple characteristic data
    attribute, 193, 321–22, 354
Set theory, 26–27
Shared management, 355–56
    responsibility, 247
Single characteristic data attribute,
    187, 192, 231, 266–67, 321, 324,
    326
Single data characteristic, 108, 212, 312
Single data subject, 212
Single occurrence data entity, 212
Single primary key, 105
Single property data value, 200, 231
Single subject data entity, 181, 183,
    231, 264
Special characters in data names, 93
Standard words, 87, 92–96, 150, 257,
    273, 276, 311
State, 33
States, 28

State transition, 28, 42
    diagram, 28–29
Static derived data attribute, 188, 242
Static redundant data, 286
Strategic data resource, 355
    model, 75–76, 336–37, 339–40, 343,
    346, 356
Structural anomalies, 79
Structural data integrity:
    diagram, 239–40
    matrix, 239–40
    rules, 231, 238, 240–41
Subject application, 315–16, 331–32
Subject data, 7, 8, 26, 315
    entity, 166, 227, 315, 318, 323
    resource, 21–22, 29, 77–79, 206, 225,
    244, 248, 266, 277, 298–99, 300,
    304, 307–8, 325, 327–28, 332,
    335, 355
    structure, 315
Subordinate data entity type, 61
Subsequent data repository, 289,
    293–94
Summary data entity, 173–74
Summary data subject name, 90
Surrogate key, 109
Synonymous data:
    attributes, 190–91
    entity, 153–54, 178
    subject names, 88
    value, 200, 350
Syntactics, 27
Syntax, 29
System, 25
System architecture, 54
System architecture model, 32, 50–51,
    55, 225–26, 291, 340, 356
    logical, 51, 53–54, 74
    physical, 51, 54–55, 72

Technological change, 29, 356
Technology infrastructure, 12
Temporary data attribute group, 311
Thesaurus, 87
Third normal form, 148–49, 156
Third schema, 17
Three-schema concept, 18–20